THE LANDSCAPE GARDEN
IN SCOTLAND

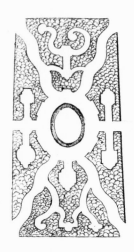

1735–1835

.

A. A. TAIT

THE LANDSCAPE GARDEN IN SCOTLAND
1735–1835

EDINBURGH
UNIVERSITY
PRESS

© A. A. Tait 1980
Edinburgh University Press
22 George Square, Edinburgh

ISBN 0 85224 372 3

Printed in Great Britain
by The Scolar Press Ltd, Ilkley, Yorks

The Publishers acknowledge the
financial assistance of the
Scottish Arts Council

PREFACE

The landscape is perhaps one of the more fragile and ephemeral pieces of western art. More so than a picture or a building, for it inhabits the border country between ornament and utility where a lawn can so easily become a hayfield, a shrubbery a jungle, and a tree a piece of firewood. It can only survive where there is a temperate zone of vigilance, judgement and imagination and where a keen sense of tradition prevails. It would be reassuring to assume that such a climate prevails in the gardens discussed here – heartening but false. For several of them the writing must now be on the wall, more will follow and others will simply fade away, unrecorded, perhaps unlamented, and largely unknown. Should this book have any practical purpose, it is to stay this tide.

I have received much kindness from the owners of the gardens described here, who also freely allowed me to consult papers and plans in their care. They include: Keith Adam, the Earl of Ancaster, Mrs Robert Anstruther, the Duke of Argyll, the Duke of Atholl, the Earl of Balfour, the Duke of Buccleuch (Miss MacEchern), the Marquess of Bute (Miss Armet), Colonel R. Campbell-Preston, Sir John Clerk, Captain N. Dalrymple Hamilton, Sir Robert Dundas, Sir Charles Fergusson, General Sir George Gordon Lennox, Major F. G. S. Graham, the late Duke of Hamilton, Lord Home of the Hirsel (Mr R. M. Hamilton), Mrs J. Home Robertson, James Hunter Blair, Marquess of Linlithgow (Mr Basil Skinner), the Earl of Mansfield, Mrs Murray-Usher, Captain Alexander Ramsay of Mar, Mrs Paul Mellon, the Earl of Strathmore, Captain David Wemyss.

I am also in the debt of all those who so generously helped me to find and directed me to read, and who were always prepared to discuss and advise. To David Walker I am especially grateful for reading this book in draft; to Howard Colvin for seeing it in proof, and to Miss Catherine Cruft and Richard Emerson of the National Monuments Record; James Holloway, National Gallery of Scotland; Eric Robson, National Trust for Scotland; John Bates, Miss Margaret Young, Miss Doreen Hunter and Mrs Joan Auld, National Register of Archives,

Scotland; John Dunbar, Royal Commission on Ancient & Historical Monuments, and to Dr Helen Brock, Mrs Mavis Batey, Dr J. M. Crook, David Green, John Harris, Professor Elisabeth MacDougall, Colin McLaren, Edward Malins, Miss Priscilla Mingay, Iain Mowat, Harry Gordon Slade, Miss Dorothy Stroud, Sir John Summerson, and to those in Glasgow University Library, particularly Jack Baldwin and Miss Hester Black. Miss Margaret Miller and her typewriter dealt speedily with my revisions and skilfully with my handwriting. I owe a special and now sadly unredeemable debt to the late Professor Andrew McLaren Young, who kindled my interest in the picturesque and who encouraged in his own inimitable way as enthusiasm dipped.

I wish to acknowledge the most generous grant this book has received from Sir George Taylor and his fellow Trustees of the Stanley Smith Horticultural Trust. The British Academy awarded me an Overseas Fellowship, which permitted me to write and think amid the splendours of Dumbarton Oaks, Harvard University, where I was a visiting fellow in 1975.

A.A.T.
University of Glasgow, March, 1979

CONTENTS

ABBREVIATIONS

DNB	*Dictionary of National Biography*
NGS	National Galleries of Scotland
NLS	National Library of Scotland
NMR	National Monuments Record
NRA	National Register of Archives, of Scotland
RCAHMS	Royal Commission on the Ancient and Historical Monuments, of Scotland (now includes NMR)
SRO	Scottish Record Office, Register House (all RHP and GD references are SRO)

NOTE

The county names used in this volume
are those that were in operation
before the May 1975
reorganisation

LIST OF ILLUSTRATIONS

COLOUR ILLUSTRATIONS
Aerial Views 1979

INTRODUCTION

The landscape garden in Scotland has been inevitably accepted as the poor relation of that of England. While there is nothing wrong with this view of poverty, which stunted so much of Scottish art, it should not deny the Scottish garden a character out of hand. The vitality and inventiveness of a Scottish gardening tradition in the late sixteenth and seventeenth centuries, and again in the nineteenth, has already been dealt with in Cox's *A History of Gardening in Scotland*, which appeared in 1935 and covered in a more orderly and scholarly manner what Sir Herbert Maxwell had offered pictorially in his *Scottish Gardens* of 1908.[1] Lacking, however, in both books was an attempt to come to terms with the landscape movement. In their own ways, both Maxwell and Cox viewed it suspiciously and as only an ambiguous part of the Scottish tradition. Its close English roots and its apparent radical break with the formal tradition made such a standpoint obvious. As a child of the Edinburgh Enlightenment, the landscape garden was indeed very much part of the wider culture of North Britain. It only became part of the more nationalistic Scotticism – the other side of the same coin – when the developing taste for the picturesque encouraged a pride in the countryside and its history. From there, it was but a short step to Fittler's generous characterisation of the Scots given in the preface to *Scotia Depicta*. He wrote in 1804, that 'No people have been more remarkable for their attachment to their natal soil, than those who first drew their breath amidst the sublime and picturesque beauties of North Britain'.

It is important that a distinction should be clearly made between the landscape garden in Scotland and the Scottish landscape garden. The first deals with this movement as it happened in Scotland: the second with a style of gardening that was particularly Scottish. While there can be little doubt that the former happened, that it followed any distinctly Scottish course is arguable. Certainly the early informal gardens in Scotland were decisively shaped by English tastes and men, and these were accepted in Scotland much as they were in the rest of Europe as the English garden – *der Englische Garten, il giardino inglese*.

1. To these two books should be added the important article by Robert Lorimer on 'Scottish Gardens' in the *Architectural Review* (Nov. 1899), which almost exclusively but imaginatively deals with the formal. There are also several essays on Scottish themes in Margaret Waterfield *Flower Grouping in English, Scotch, and Irish Gardens* (London 1907), and there is Elizabeth Haldane's *Scots Gardens in Old Times* (Glasgow 1934).

The careers of both Robert Robinson and James Robertson were based
on their advantage as Englishmen, working in Scotland in the seven-
teen sixties, and claiming some sort of association with Capability
Brown. The same was also more or less true of the Thomas Whites,
father and son, whose annual excursions to Scotland began around
1770 and ended approximately in 1820, and thus spanned the rise and
fall of the picturesque garden. But within this period, there can be little
doubt that there was a distinct feeling for the Scottish landscape and its
historical traditions, and that some designs from the very start
exploited such associations. This was perhaps best seen in the vision of
the picturesque conjured up by Robert Adam and John Clerk of Eldin,
although it was cast in artistic rather than strictly practical terms. Such
sensitivity was more aggressively and most nationalistically apparent
in the gardens and writings of John Claudius Loudon, who attacked
both Repton's garden at Valleyfield in Fife, and White senior's work at
Scone Palace, Perth, on the novel grounds that they applied English
solutions to Scottish problems. The dying fall of the landscape movement was paralleled by the full-blooded romanticism of Scott, whose
very adoration of the Scottish past helped to replace the informal with
the terraces and parterres of the formal.

Loudon, in his book *Treatise on Forming, Improving and Managing
Country Residences* of 1806, quoted from James Grahame's *The Birds of
Scotland*, which had been published in the same year. He did so
principally to give a national feeling to his landscape. Grahame's book
contained several apposite descriptions that tellingly reflected 'opinions which I have shortly and perhaps crudely advanced, [and] are
copiously and feelingly discussed in a book which every landholder
ought to pursue – I mean, Price's "Essay on the Picturesque"'. In
revealing this bias he was not alone: the *Essay* was alleged to have been
the Duchess of Gordon's bible at Kinrara, and at Duns Castle a little
later it was the yardstick against which all improvements were measured. Few other writers on the subject can be shown to have exerted so
strong an influence. While Price's *Essay On the Picturesque* of 1794 made
no particular reference to Scotland until the interpolations of the editor
of the 1842 edition, the more Scottish and philosophic works like
Francis Hutcheson's *Inquiry into the Original of Our Ideas of Beauty and
Virtue* of 1725, or David Hume's essay 'Of the Standard of Taste' of
1757, Henry Kames's *Elements of Criticism* of 1762, or Archibald Alison's
Essays on the Nature and Principles of Taste of 1790, seem to have had little
appeal in this quarter. Nor do its English companions, Richard Payne
Knight's *The Landscape* of 1794, or his *Analytical Inquiry into the Principles*

of Taste of 1805, appear to have attracted any more attention, and remained like the editions of Walpole, Whately and Mason, on the improver's bookshelf rather than in his coat pocket. But amidst all of these, the most distinctly Scottish voice was that of Hugh Blair's *Critical Dissertation on the Poems of Ossian*, which appeared in 1763, and was appendixed to the 1784 edition of Macpherson's *Ossian* itself. It was Blair who noted that in Ossian, 'we meet with no Grecian or Italian scenery; but with the mists and clouds, and storms of a northern mountainous region'. It was such a mood of highly coloured naturalism that inspired at least one landscape gardener, the Londoner Robert Robinson, to dress in tartan and eagles' feathers and go camping in the Cairngorms as a swallow of the Celtic Revival, seeking the 'rude scenes of nature, amidst rocks and torrents and whirlwinds and beauties'.

Such a yearning for a past Caledonia and its landscape, excelling in the sublime and grand rather than the beautiful, was not to be found in Price whose past was of Homer rather than Ossian. This awareness of a portentous Scottish past was apparent in most of the tour books and guides that followed in the wake of Ossian, of which Thomas Pennant's *Tour in Scotland, 1772* was perhaps the most distinguished. It undoubtedly inspired works like Adam de Cardonell's *Picturesque Antiquities* of 1788 and Francis Grose's *Antiquities of Scotland* of 1789, which were almost exclusively concerned with the Scottish castles and abbeys of the medieval period, and encouraged the Earl of Buchan to found the Society of Antiquaries of Scotland in 1780. Lord Buchan's own sentiments were formed early and clearly, for in 1761 he wrote in his diary that he 'roamed about the Glens of the West Highland, climbed the steepest mountains and penetrated into the deepest recesses for the curiosities of Nature. I studied the language and manners of the Gael examined the remains of their rude antiquities and with the Speech of Galcacus in my hand adored the Spirit of my Ancestors on the footsteps of their Glory; and in the country the rolling clouds below my feet meditated on the revolutions of Ages of Revolutions in the Womb of Futurity.'[2] After all this, his activity at Dryburgh Abbey, with its monument to William Wallace and its classical temple to the poet Thomson, was disappointing. Perhaps more pertinent, especially in its fusion of landscape and architecture, was Charles Cordiner's *Remarkable Ruins, and Romantic Prospects of North Britain* of 1788. His appreciation of the peculiar merits of such landscapes was made clear in his introductory address: 'The grandeur and beauty of many scenes, where with we are presented amid the *Caledonian* wilds; and the rude magnificence of the cliffs in her bold and rocky shores', he wrote,

2. Glasgow University Library, Murray Ms.502/61.

3. Cordiner, op. cit., vol.I, introduction.

4. ibid., vol.I, unpaginated.

'promised a series of romantic *Landscape*, deserving of notice and description: and the *Ruins* of ancient Buildings, which appear among them in forlorn decay, suggested variety of interesting reflection to the attentive Traveller.'[3] This essay was followed by a series of plates illustrating such views, including the Duke of Gordon's hunting lodge at Glenfiddich, whose associative powers Cordiner felt in Ossianic terms: 'There is a native wildness and beauty in the characteristic appellations which distinguish these remote districts, which interests travellers of taste in their derivation . . . The *Son of Fingal*, who has immortalized the picturesque grandeur of the *Caledonian* wilds in his son, shews how well he knew the emphasis and value of these characters: they realize while they animate description, and make the effect of paintings of fancy find its way to the heart.'[4] But there was little of this in the early informal gardens. There, the mood of the beautiful, as defined by Addison and practised by Kent and Brown, was both ascendant and appropriate to the undulating landscape of the Lothians in which these gardens were largely set. Edinburgh seems to have been its spiritual home and the adjoining counties its dominion. It was in this area, too, that most of the important nursery gardens were to be found, such as that of the Boutchers at Comely Bank and the Bowies probably near Musselburgh. Just outside Edinburgh, John Adam remodelled his father's garden at North Merchiston in the style of – though he did not imitate – Shenstone's The Leasowes, and nearby at Duddingston and similar country houses the first landscape gardens were laid out by James Robertson in the 1760s. It was here, too, that James Bowie probably began his career of making gardens 'in the natural way', before branching out into England and reversing the more familiar pattern. Robert Robinson lived in and practised from Edinburgh, although his landscape commissions ranged from Cullen in Banffshire to Paxton on the Berwick border, and the one Scottish garden associated with Pope's amanuensis and friend Joseph Spence was Prestonfield at Edinburgh. The style all of them attempted to master was well described in the third and fourth categories of Dalrymple's *Essay on Landscape Gardening*, written about 1750, and was rightly identified with the gardens of William Kent.

Conspicuously lacking in Dalrymple's essay was any attempt to associate the landscape garden with political feeling. Nor does there seem to have been in Scotland any identification of the formal garden with the dictatorial or, conversely, the informal with the liberal, as has been suggested was a significant element in English gardening. The enlightened and enriched supporters of the Union of 1707 were just as ready and likely to spend their money on avenues as upon clumps and belts, which made the Duke of Queensberry's baroque gardens at Drumlanrig no exception. There was probably no Scottish parallel with Stowe and its moral and political garden buildings, such as the Temple of Ancient Virtue. And while most of the mid-eighteenth-century landscapes like Mar and Dunkeld contained similar sorts of monuments, only Taymouth and Blair Atholl came close to matching Stowe's plethora of garden architecture. Yet at both of them the emphasis was exclusively visual rather than political. Although Lord Breadalbane was a notable Whig, his politics had little bearing on the style of his garden at Taymouth, nor did those of the second Duke of Atholl taint the landscapes at Blair and Dunkeld. In this way, the Temple of Fame at Blair was without the political rancour that characterised its Stoic precursor. But at Taymouth at least one temple, the circular Fairy Temple of before 1754, may have had a deeper significance than the rest of the grottoes and pavilions that dotted the huge park. Standing on a knoll near the castle, both its site and name, later disguised as Apollo's Temple, suggested as much a precocious and romantic monument to Celtic Caledonia as a shadow of Greek liberty.

The most vivid reaction both to the picturesque and to a Scottish way of seeing things, can be found in the eclectic and topographical drawings of Robert Adam and his brother-in-law John Clerk of Eldin. In theory there was a careful balance between history, architecture, and the picturesque in these watercolours, which made them often unmistakably Scottish. While neither practised as landscape gardeners, Adam at Culzean and Dalquharran came close to it and in his drawings for these commissions showed his buildings as an extension rather than an addition to the existing setting. His method of work was probably accurately described in the account given of the technique of his draughtsman Antonio Zucchi by a contemporary. Zucchi was praised as a 'great castle-maker' whose 'mode of composing them, was to draw first a bold varied outline of the rock, mountain, or eminence upon which his castle was to stand. He then, with according lines, added his castle; and you would be surprised to find how the imagination is assisted by this practice, and what towers, battlements, and projections are suggested by it.'[5] Such an empirical way of designing, strongly suggestive of Cozens's *A New Method*, was also followed towards the end of the century by Alexander Nasmyth in his drawings for Dunglass and Taymouth Castles. Although Clerk of Eldin showed considerably more antiquarian zeal than imagination, his drawings

5. *Sir Uvedale Price on the Picturesque*, ed. T. Dick Lauder (Edinburgh 1842) p.583.

were still irrevocably rooted in their landscape setting and this bond was increased by his persuasive use of mellow colour. Both Adam's and Clerk's watercolours reflected a typical picturesque love for dull tones, and fondness for the bleak browns and grey-blues that were the characteristic colours of the Scottish landscape.

A more practical and militant exponent of the picturesque landscape was Loudon. With more of a personal axe to grind than Adam, his *Country Residences* was an attempt to discredit publicly the beautiful, and disgrace its proponents. In this he was reasonably successful, and continued the campaign in his *Encyclopaedia of Gardening* of 1822, and anonymously in the *Edinburgh Encyclopaedia* of 1830, with the opposition making a rear-guard stand in Sir Henry Steuart's *The Planter's Guide* of 1828. In private, Loudon was even more critical and indulged in the most unprofessional of conduct, viciously attacking Thomas White, the elder, in his report of 1804 on White's earlier improvements at Scone. Although Loudon was endlessly critical of the Whites as exponents of a spiritless brand of the beautiful and of English ideas, his solution was only a more extreme form of the picturesque, which he called the natural. It emphasised the importance of deep consultation with the genius of the place, not only from the stylistic point of view, but also from the practical. To stress this, he perhaps rather ostentatiously quoted from *The Birds of Scotland*, and selected at least some of his plants from Lightfoot's *Flora Scotica*, and in the account he gave of his designs for Barnbarroch and Mabie in south-west Scotland he was scrupulously careful only to adapt and heighten the existing landscape. Later, in writing his account of Scottish gardening for the *Encyclopaedia of Gardening* in 1822, he still found the excellence of the landscape unmatched by the taste of the day: 'The country residences of Scotland', he wrote, 'in general excel these of England in the prominence of their natural features, being generally backed by hills or mountains; encompassed by a river or stream; or situated on a lake, or the seashore. But they are inferior to these of the south in magnificence, and even in taste, both as architecture and landscape gardening.'[6]

While a work like *Flora Scotica* catalogued the native plants of Scotland, it also made clear the limitations of gardening in Scotland, as did Patrick Neill in his *On Scottish Gardens and Orchards* of 1813. Many types of tree could be successfully planted in the country, but those that grew best and should be planted most widely, were a much smaller group. The Scots pine, the larch, especially the Dunkeld hybrid, the sycamore, the wych-elm and the gean, were historically

6. J.C. Loudon *Encyclopaedia of Gardening* (London 1822) p.1249.

Scottish trees, the successors to the oak forests of Caledonia, and were to be found in the great highland estates like Inveraray, Blair Atholl, Taymouth, and Mar. Their cause was eloquently pleaded in Sir Thomas Dick Lauder's emendations to his edition of Gilpin's *Forest Scenery*. But while such places lent themselves naturally to the picturesque in their unique combinations of mountain and loch and the vastness of their prospects, the climate and the soil was against their full exploitation as picturesque landscapes. Contrarily, in the more favoured lowland areas, where so much more could be grown, the elemental landscape was often lacking. It was only with the nineteenth-century discoveries of plants and conifers, and especially with Hooker's introduction of the Himalayan and Chinese rhododendron in the 1840s, that highland gardens like Brodick or Inverewe could be made to match their setting. Until then the botanical skill and ingenious husbandry of the archetypal Scottish gardener like Walter Nicol or John Hay were confined to the artificiality of the kitchen garden. If nothing else, this maintained a formal tradition in Scottish gardening strongly capable of revival, as Drummond Castle and the middle decades of the nineteenth century were to show.

But without doubt the publication in 1832 of William Sawrey Gilpin's *Practical Hints upon Landscape Gardening*, marked the death of the landscape garden, surely as much in Scotland as in England. Loudon's review of the book in his *Gardener's Magazine* made clear the critical attitude of a modern mind to both Gilpin's shortcomings and those of the picturesque. Although Gilpin had made concessions to the new spirit of formality and science, they were too little and too late. The pendulum had swung suddenly and swiftly, leaving him and others behind. Richard Morris, writing his *Essays on Landscape Gardening* of 1825, was sure of the superiority of the 'modern art of Gardening' where 'a natural irregularity has superseded the stiff geometrical system'. He was out of date before the ink dried on the paper. His conviction that 'the barrier being broken through, the citadel has surrendered, and the rapid progress this art has made is as triumphant as it is delightful' was even more thoroughly wrong. So much so, that eight years later in 1835, the destruction of the landscape park for the new-fangled parterres, terraces and flower gardens was already a cause for concern. Jonas Dennis wrote in his *Landscape Gardener* that 'through the termination of the revolutionary war, English principles have been injured, and English taste impaired, by adaptation to French style'. In Scotland, the romantic formalism that Scott preached but did not always practise, had inherited the earth.

THE INFORMAL

The first deliberate steps towards a landscape garden in Scotland were taken by William Adam. Towards the end of his career as an architect and garden designer, he wrote sensitively and revealingly to a prospective client about garden design. Adam laid down there the axiom that 'the risings and fallings of ground are to be humoured and generally make the greatest beautys in Gardens'. The extent to which he lived up to his statement, virtually a demand to consult Pope's genius of the place, is not altogether clear, for Adam had to cope with a patronage as conservative in garden matters as others. Certainly there was an informal spirit present in his serpentine riverside walk at Taymouth of around 1720, which wrought havoc with the orthodox geometry of the design, and this ambivalence was revealed again in his design for Chatelherault of 1735, where formality was put beside the utmost romanticism of a wild gorge. But in the other gardens he designed, Arniston, Castle Kennedy, Newliston, and so on up and down Scotland, he often hinted at but only sometimes displayed his taste for the natural. His advice at Niddrie Marshall, Edinburgh, to exploit a view of a millwheel slowly revolving in its lade was more typical of his feelings than his practice. While he may have contracted his *furor hortensis* from his long standing and pedagogic patron Sir John Clerk, his notion of the millwheel and the concept of the undulating landscape were beyond Clerk's factual comprehension, and were without doubt Adam's own. By his death in 1748, a feeling, respectful and sympathetic, for the landscape around the garden was born and the landscape movement begun.

Adam's life as a garden designer began in the baroque. It was only towards the middle of his career, in the 1730s, that he effectively struggled to free himself of its conservatism and convention. His stylistic parents were the succeeding masters of the formal garden in Scotland, Sir William Bruce and Alexander Edward. Both were versatile men, whose experience had been enlarged by travel abroad, Bruce in exile in the 1650s, Edward notably in France in 1701, and whose foreign exposure spanned the rise and fall of the *grand siècle*.[1]

1. For an account of the career of Sir William Bruce see the introduction by John Dunbar in *Exhibition Catalogue: Sir William Bruce 1630–1710* (1970); and for Alexander Edward, the article on Brechin Castle in *Country Life* (1971) pp.378–81. See also the entry in H.M. Colvin, *Biographical Dictionary of British Architects, 1600–1840* (London 1978) p. 283.

They were acquainted with one another, having both worked at Melville and Kinross, and together with the architects James Gibbs (who borrowed Edward's drawings of Marly), James Smith and Alexander MacGill, who built Mount Stuart in Bute and planned its gardens in 1716, they personified the baroque period in Scotland.[2] Their gardens accurately mirrored this formal and architectural approach to design with a passionate commitment to axial planning. At both Bruce's surviving, but radically restored gardens of Kinross and Balcaskie, as well as in Edward's designs for Kinnaird Castle and Hamilton Palace, a series of repetitive enclosures were centred upon a broad axial vista that was blocked by some feature either real or artificial.[3] It was in essence much the same formal style to be met with in William Adam's early work. It was an obvious choice too throughout the career of Adam's rival William Boutcher, and continued well into the eighteenth century in the practice of the Highland gardeners Thomas Winter and William Taylor. But in their designs the baroque had lost much of its vigour and all its self-assurance, and had degenerated into an unimaginative formality better suited to the walled kitchen and flower gardens. It remained there during its eclipse by the informal style, unfashionable and untamed, but still the first manner in which the practical gardener was trained. The day of reckoning, however, was to come with its revival in the nineteenth century when the botanist and plantsmen achieved undisputed sway.

For the early informal garden in Scotland, no designer of the stature of William Kent appeared. While Scottish patronage may have attracted Stephen Switzer to the country, he was probably exceptional and the field belonged to the various gardeners at the larger nurseries who were prepared to supply shrubs and trees, plant them and, if the occasion demanded, make a design for their layout.[4] Of such men, Boutcher and his son, operating from their nursery at Comely Bank in Edinburgh, were perhaps the most distinguished.[5] Although neither

---

2. See *Catalogue: Sir William Bruce*, p.15. In a letter to the second Earl of Bute in 1716, MacGill was mentioned as giving 'ane plane of your house and lykwayse of the grounds for gardens and other pollicies' (Mount Stuart Muniments: Letters of Ronald Campbell, W.S.). In the mason's contract the following year building walls round the whole gardens was specifically agreed upon (ibid., Building Agreement, 1717). For MacGill's architectural career see John Dunbar *The Historic Architecture of Scotland* (London 1966) p.104. There is a very full account of the laying out of the gardens between 1717 and 1736 in the 3rd Earl of Bute's 'A Journall of the Planting Executed att Mounstewart from the first laying out of the Gardens by my Father, May 1st. 1737' (Mount Stuart Muniments). These gardens were still reasonably intact in Leslie's survey of 1766.

3. The gardens at Kinross were rebuilt and restored by Dr Ross in 1902, when the house was reoccupied after having remained empty for eighty years. However, Bruce's and Edward's combined ideas for it may be seen in the garden design of c.1685 in the Edinburgh College of Art (*Catalogue: Sir William Bruce*, p.15). For Balcaskie see ibid., p.11, and for its restoration pp.228–9. Edward's design for Kinnaird is at Kinnaird Castle, Perthshire, Album 18v and 19K; for his design for Hamilton, of 1708, see photograph in NMR of plan formerly in the Hamilton Estate Office.

4. For Switzer's tentative career in Scotland, see William Brogden 'Stephen Switzer and garden design in Britain in the early eighteenth century', unpublished thesis (Edinburgh 1973) pp.339–87. In this account, he followed Loudon's statement that 'Switzer appears to have resided a considerable time in Edinburgh, as he there published, in 1717, a tract on draining, and other useful and agricultural improvements' J.C. Loudon *Encyclopaedia of Gardening* (London 1822) p.78. Loudon also remarked that 'New Liston, Dalkeith House, Hopeton House and various other places near Edinburgh, are also in Switzer's style' (ibid). These were, of course, stylistic rather than documentary attributions. In Robert Maxwell's *Transactions of the Honourable Society of Improvers . . . Scotland* (Edinburgh 1743) Switzer appeared as 'of London'.

5. A good account of the Boutcher family is given in Blanche Henrey *British Botanical and Horticultural Literature before 1800*, 3 vols. (London 1975) vol.II, pp.403–6. It seems likely that Boutcher, Bourchier and Boutchard were the same family, and a sufficiently distinguished one to appear as Edinburgh burgesses in 1726 and 1727; see C.B. Watson, 'Roll of Edinburgh Burgesses and Guild Brethren 1701–17' *Scottish Record Society* (1930) p.19; see also Priscilla Minay 'James Justice 1689–1763' *Garden History* IV (1976) pp.57–8.

6. William Boutcher *A Treatise on Forest Trees* (Edinburgh 1775) p.225; see also Henrey, op. cit., III, p.14, II, pp.403–5. The younger Boutcher had a certain posthumous reputation for Sir Henry Steuart referred to him in *The Planter's Guide* as the 'honestest and most judicious' gardener who was 'undervalued by the ignorance of his age. He was suffered to languish unsupported for years at Comely Garden, and died at last, in obscurity and indigence' (Steuart *The Planter's Guide* (London 1828) p.399). Steuart also claimed that he published his *Forest Trees* 'by subscription, to relieve his wants' (ibid.).

7. NLS Saltoun Mss. SC214.

8. NLS Ms.3554 f.194. Amongst the Dicksons' regular patrons in the late 1740s and 50s were the Earls of March, Hyndford and Marchmont, all with local estates, and minor lairds like Pringle of The Haining, and Scott of Gala. The last in 1746 was buying ash, limes, elms, etc., regularly until 1751, see ff.76, 188. This nursery firm later became one of the most notable in Scotland with branches in Edinburgh and Perth as well as the original ground at Hassendeanburn. According to the *Statistical Account*, 1793, VIII, p.540, it employed 50 people at Hawick, and a further 40 or so at Perth; ibid. 1796, XVII, p.546. For an account of it see Henrey, op. cit., II, pp.398–400; and in 'A Register of Monumental Inscription in St. Mary's Churchyard, Hawick' *Transactions of the Hawick Archaeological Society* (1935) pp.55–7. Archibald Dickson was a subscriber to Boutcher's *A Treatise on Forest Trees*.

9. Three plans for the gardens exist at Inveraray: two are unsigned and one dated March 1721, Edinburgh, is autographed Boutch(er)? (Estate Office, Inveraray Castle). Boutcher is mentioned as providing a garden plan for Castle Kennedy in 1722, SRO GD 135/139 vol.1. For Taymouth, see GD 112/21/77–9. At Alloa, Boutcher served as nurseryman to the Earl of Mar's design, see NLS

was a major force in the creation of the Scottish landscape movement, their collective careers spanned the rise and fruition of the style – so much so, that in 1775 the younger Boutcher remarked in his *Treatise on Forest Trees*: 'From the late and now universal taste in all new and expensive designs in the garden way, of throwing a large extent of ground about the house into lawns of grass, many fruit trees which in former times generally grew in the kitchen garden, and these gardens adjoining to the house, are now destroyed.'[6] For Boutcher himself this had meant poverty and a decay in the status of his profession whose more conservative members became casualties of the landscape movement. In 1761, the younger Boutcher attempted to try his hand as an improver at Portobello, near Edinburgh, and in the following year had decided to give it all up if a place could be found for him in the administration of the Annexed Estates.[7] He was not successful, and whatever boom there had been in nursery gardening was over by the 1760s, leaving Boutcher, unlike his father, as one of several firms struggling to make a living. Unfortunately, he was neither lucky nor had the business acumen of a concern like the Dicksons of Hassendeanburn at Hawick, who successfully survived well into the nineteenth century, and with whom the Boutchers had had an informal trading relationship.[8] Nor does the younger Boutcher appear to have followed in his father's footsteps as a garden designer, who was just as ready to sell seeds as lay out an avenue of hornbeams. It was this characteristic mix that took the elder Boutcher to Inveraray about 1721, where he supplied the Duke of Argyll with both, and he was consulted in this dual capacity at Castle Kennedy, Alloa, and Taymouth, all about 1722, and possibly at Blair Atholl before 1737.[9] His designs were strictly formal with a ruthless application of the ruler and set-square which made his proposed area of 'Naturall Wood' at the bottom of the park at Kilkerran, Ayrshire, of 1721 quite exceptional and unexpected in a scheme where so informal a moment as the small burn beside the house had been rigorously excluded (Plate 1).[10] Yet he did not lack patrons, even though his designs were often old-fashioned by wider standards and his sense of grandeur occasionally blinded him to the dull realities of a situation. This was certainly true of the scheme he proposed for Thomas Cochran at The Grange, later and quixotically called Lamancha, between 1728 and 1733 (Plate 2).[11] His design was a speculative affair, more a proposition than a plan, with a parterre, canal, and an impressively long avenue, together forming a piece of baroque art to be carved out of a bleak and boggy landscape. It was so obviously impractical that Cochran refused to settle the bill and instead

Ms.5158 f.48; and comparatively Lord Mar's album of plans SRO RHP 13257 and 13258. It was distinguished enough in 1742 for it to be recommended as worth a visit (SRO GD 10/1421/f.202). Though modernised around 1793, it was still sufficiently visible in 1803 and until the house was rebuilt in 1834, see James Hall

Travels in Scotland, 2 vols. (London 1807) vol.I, p.29. There is an unsigned and undated plan at Blair which may be Boutcher's titled 'A General Plan of Blair in Atholl'. It has been redrawn in parts and is in poor condition, but is stylistically acceptable (Blair Castle, Charter Room, B.5/3). Certainly 'Mr. Butchard' was supplying plants and trees to the Duke of Atholl about 1737, see Charter Room, Box 70 D.7. There is at Craigie Hall, Edinburgh, an undated plan, 'sketch by Mr Boutcher'.

10. His plan for Kilkerran of 1721 was signed 'Wm. Boutchart', though it is similar in style and date to the signed Inveraray drawing. The only note on the Kilkerran plan, apart from its title etc. is the 'Naturall Wood'. Though little of this planting at Kilkerran has remained, what is shown on later survey plans would indicate that at least the principal elements of Boutcher's plan were carried out.

11. SRO RHP 270. Boutcher's work ultimately terminated in a law suit in 1738, as Cochrane refused to pay the bill, see Brogden, op. cit., p.359. Relations had been so strained that in 1735 a letter of Cochrane's started: 'I shall begin my letter praying that God may dam you for ever' (ibid.). Later in the eighteenth century this estate assumed its present name of Lamancha; see RCAHM *Peeblesshire*, 2 vols. (Edinburgh 1967) vol.II, p.299. Nothing remains of the formal gardens except a sundial; see ibid., pl.75E.

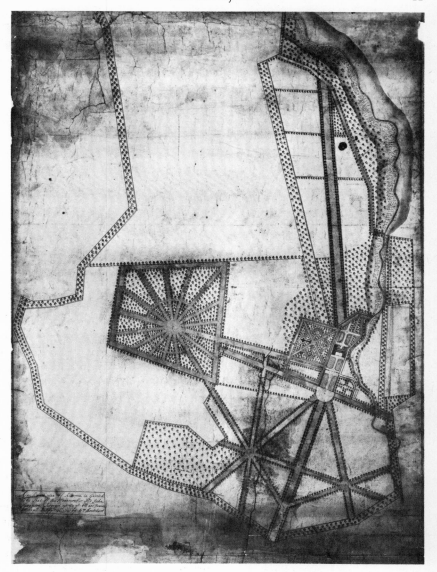

Plate 1. Kilkerran, Ayrshire, improvement plan by William Boutcher, 1721

12. Adam's design for Cally, Kirkcudbrightshire, is illustrated in *Vitruvius Scoticus*, pls.111–13. In 1742, Adam produced a design for the garden; see SRO GD 10/1421/vol. IV f.212. At the same time, its owner James Murray had the lists and prices from 'Messrs. Bain and Boutcher the two principal Nursery Men about Edinburgh' (GD 10/1421/vol.IV ff.205, 205 A and B). For Taymouth see GD 112/21/77–79. The first Earl Fife, then Lord Braco, wrote to Adam in October, 1735: 'I shall be glad you make out the plan of my Grounds confirm to the Lines you took; and though it will be some Time before I can put anything in Execution as to that, yet I wish to have it in my View to do it in the best Manner. *Boutcher* was lately in this country, I have likewise put it on him to make out a plan of my Ground, I want to glean from all Quarters in this matter, and keep by that is best' (*Petition of William Lord Braco* (1743) pp.21–2).

13. For Adam's connection with Newliston, see his bill of 1723 in SRO GD 135/144 f.24. In 1740, Lord Stair's land agent at Newliston referred to 'Mr. Adams' as constructing the 'most spacious farm courts in Scotland' at Milridge on the estate (John M. Graham *The Annals and Correspondence of the Viscount and First and Second Earls of Stair*, 2 vols. (London 1875) vol.II, p.442. There is also his plan for the garden in the Muniment Room, Blenheim Palace (I am indebted to Mr H.M. Colvin for this information). It may be assumed from this that he was similarly employed by Lord Stair at Castle Kennedy where amongst other things he designed a small temple for the bowling green, see *Vitruvius Scoticus*, pl.120, 121. In William Adam's lawsuit with Lord Fife (Braco) in 1743, it was noted that 'Mr. *Adams* made Plans for Lord *Stairs* of several Pieces of work, which he afterwards finished, and was paid for his Plans over and above his Accounts of the work' (*State of Process: William Adams . . . against William Lord Braco* (1743) p.10). The plan referred to was without doubt that produced by Adam at the end of 1735, see note 12. At Marchmont in Berwickshire, the Earl of

scrawled over the design his infuriated comments, 'Moss wher the Divel wont Grow', and that 'no part of this plan execut nor would the Brute Alter it though often desird to do it'. Boutcher was probably safer when confined to the ordered world of the kitchen garden and the selling of seeds.

William Adam's gardening career was remarkably unlike that of the Boutchers. Although they were associated with one another at Taymouth and Cally, and were in competition for the dubious patronage of Lord Fife at Duff in 1735, they approached their business from different ends of a professional scale.[12] Adam was an architect, the Boutchers were nursery gardeners. For Adam architecture was the key to his gardening career, and at Hopetoun, Taymouth, Arniston, Cally, Duff, and Buchanan, where he had started out as a builder, he stayed as a gardener. This pattern was broken only in his work for the Earl of Stair at Newliston and Castle Kennedy, where, between 1720 and 1740, he designed and executed two grandiose gardens for houses that never were – much in the spirit of the avenues at Marchmont, planted in the late 1720s for a house built in 1750.[13] Newliston had to wait longer, and received its small classical house only at the very end of the century from his son Robert. Castle Kennedy, less fortunate, remained a burnt out shell, presiding over some seventy acres of formal gardens, kept in impeccable order, and surviving until virtually the end of the eighteenth century.[14] So impressive a *memento mori* was hardly intended, and Adam had no doubt produced some sort of design in line with the baroque Palladianism of the scheme he illustrated in *Vitruvius Scoticus* for Newliston.[15] But a new Castle Kennedy never materialised and instead Lord Stair employed Adam to alter the adjoining house at Culhorn in the 1740s, and build in the gardens a square temple beside the bowling green.[16] Strange though it may seem, Lord Stair gardened contentedly at both places, laying out vistas down which no windows looked, and building canals and basins that reflected no façade.

Both the undated plan for Newliston, at Blenheim, and its copy of 1759, showed completely formal designs, isolated from the countryside behind their bastioned walls, with even the intended house imprisoned in a horse-shoe cour d'honneur. Only at the extreme eastern edge of the park at Lindsay's Craigs was any natural planting

Marchmont planted the surviving avenues for the new house with Dutch elm imported from France in 1724/5 (SRO GD 158/2515 ff.191, 197). In 1725, he

wrote to his gardener John Bouie (Bowie) 'let care be taken to lay the avenues both east and west', and instructed him 'to begin to plant above the Oval pond and

what trees are ready for it' (ibid., f.303).
These avenues and the new house are
shown in Roy's map; see also Margaret
Warrender *Marchmont and the Humes of
Polwarth* (Edinburgh 1894) p.87. William
Adam produced a scheme for
Marchmont in 1724, which was rejected
by Lord Marchmont as too expensive
(SRO GD 158/2515 ff.119, 173).

14. For Robert Adam's design of
Newliston, see Arthur Bolton *The
Architecture of Robert and James Adam*, 2
vols. (London 1922) vol.II, pp.278–87. In
1793, Lord Stair's gardens were still
reasonably intact for the *Statistical
Account* to report that 'The pleasure
grounds, nearly three miles in
circumference are entirely after his
design, covered with trees of his
planting and much adorned with
artificial lakes' (ibid., VIII, p.74). Castle
Kennedy was burnt out in 1717 and not
rebuilt. When Lord Stair returned to
Scotland on a permanent basis in 1721,
he lived at Culhorn; see Graham, op.
cit., II, p.161.

15. See *Vitruvius Scoticus*, especially
pl.113. This shows the extensive façade
of the house with a main block in a
strongly baroque style but with simpler,
more classical wings, close to those
found in Palladio's grander villas.

16. Adam sent plans down to Culhorn in
1747, see SRO GD 135/139, vol.I f.4. In
March 1754, John Adam had 'made a
search for the plan of the building of
Culhorn among his father's papers, but
can't find it, so he desires you to make
one of your workmen make a sketch of
the site ec. where the entry is proposed
to be, & then he will send a draught' (GD
135/13, vol.I, f.74). For the temple see
Vitruvius Scoticus, pl.120, 121.

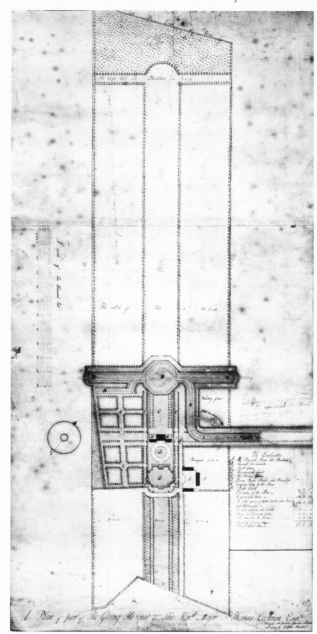

Plate 2. Grange (Lamancha), Peeblesshire,
improvement plan by William Boutcher, *c.*1733

Plate 3. Newliston, West Lothian, 1759 copy after a plan by William Adam, *c.*1725

17. For the 1759 plan, kept at Newliston, see RHP 2178. A further plan RHP 2150, 'A General Plan of the Parks of Newliston', is unsigned and undated but shows in outline Adam's garden; Roy's map of c.1747, shows the informal planting at Lindsay's Craigs but not the two circular 'belvidere' copses.

18. Samuel Boyse wrote this description in his poem *Loch Rian* of 1734, published in his *Translations and Poems, written on several occasions* (London 1738); see *The Works of the English Poets*, ed. Alexander Chalmers, 21 vols. (London 1810) vol. XIV, p.534. Boyse also wrote poetry describing the gardens at Yester, Mavisbank, and Dalkeith, and Stowe and Arlington House in England.

19. Loudon visited Castle Kennedy in August 1841. He did not return before his death in 1843, see John Gloag *Mr Loudon's England* (Newcastle 1970) pp.65 and 211. Loudon's ideas are presumably repeated in the 'Plan of part of the Grounds of Castle Kennedy, shewing how they are in part planned, and how the remainder is proposed to be planted', of 1849 (SRO RHP 4677). This plan is only concerned with the formal gardens around the old castle. For the dates of Roy's survey maps see, R.A. Skelton, 'The Military Survey of Scotland, 1747–1755' *Royal Scottish Geographical Society: Special Publication* (Edinburgh 1971) p.3.

20. Dick Lauder noted that the 'outlines of both lakes are left irregularly sweeping as nature formed them; but, from all that now remains, it is manifest that not one square yard of these seventy-one acres, which divide them from each other, was left unworked upon by the spade' (*Sir Uvedale Price On the Picturesque*, ed. Sir Thomas Dick Lauder (Edinburgh 1842) pp.169–70). He also mentioned 'The original plan for Castle-Kennedy is now before me – but, from various pencil mark upon it . . . I should say that there has been

attempted and it is likely that this too was part of Adam's scheme (Plate 3).[17] Castle Kennedy repeated a similar sort of exclusiveness, except that its site was such that made complete separation of the new garden from the immediate landscape of the Black and White Lochs physically impossible. The two extensive and natural lochs held the peninsula of the castle and its gardens between them like a pair of pincers. For once, the parterres, étoiles, basins and the whole ragbag of formality, seemed incongruous in so fortuitously grand a natural setting. Yet Lord Stair's contemporaries took it in their stride as a nice visual conceit where, 'Through the long vista, or the casual break'/'Glitter the blue canal, or silver lake;'/'Sweetly bewilder'd the spectator roves'/'Midst hills, and moss-grown rocks, and hanging groves,'/'With care the eye examines every part,'/'Too form'd for Nature – yet too wild for Art'.[18] This contrived ambiguity between Nature and Art was probably Adam's responsibility, and he may have gained the effect by perhaps deliberately softening the angularity of his geometry, leaving the edges of the lochs much as they were, and by planting the southern banks in the simplest fashion. This, at least, was apparent in the diminutive scale of General Roy's map of about 1747 and was still evident in Sparrow's view of the late eighteenth century, even before the gardens were restored after a design by Loudon in 1842 (Plate 4).[19]

The gardens that exist today as the result of this restoration reflect, much more than they might have, both Adam's scheme and his incipient naturalism (Plate 5). What was probably his plan was found during the turmoil in the grounds in the 1840s, hidden away in a gardener's cottage by the historian of the picturesque in Scotland, Sir Thomas Dick Lauder, who had 'no mean talent as an architect, artist and landscape gardener'.[20] Its discovery must have made obvious whatever shapes and features had been lost or disguised when the gardens were dismantled and ruthlessly landscaped between 1799 and 1802. Lauder's considerable influence, sensitivity, and respect for Adam, should have ensured a sympathetic reinterpretation of the old

considerable deviation from it in the execution' (ibid., p.170). According to Sir Herbert Maxwell, this plan was found in a gardener's cottage, see Sir Herbert Maxwell *Scottish Gardens* (London 1908) p.79. Dick Lauder practised gardening both at Relugas and The Grange in Edinburgh, see J. Stewart Smith *The*

Grange of St. Giles (Edinburgh 1898) pp.316–26, and 332–56. Relugas, which he acquired by marriage in 1808, and extended in about 1821, was vividly described in Cockburn's poem, 'Relugas' see Karl Miller *Cockburn's Millennium* (London 1975) pp.301–2. Dick Lauder also edited Gilpin's *Forest Scenery* in 1834.

Plate 4. Remains of the gardens and castle at Castle Kennedy, Wigtownshire, by Sparrow, *c.*1789

21. According to a report of 1832 from a factor who had been on the estate for 53 years, 'There was part of Castle Kennedy, called the Wilderness, in which there were various grass walks regularly mown, some clumps of Laurels, ornamental wood, and hedges kept dressed. About 30 years ago the late Earl of Stair thought all this too formal, ordered most of the Laurels and ornamental wood to be cut, disposed that front thrown open, and the intersecting hedges destroyed' (SRO GD 135/139/vol.11). This is borne out by Dick Lauder, op. cit., p.173. Ornamental and forest trees for this landscaping were bought from Joseph Norman, see GD 135/59/49. For the restoration of the garden during 1841 and 1842, see GD 135/50/47.

22. SRO GD 135/48/33.

23. George Dundas succeeded to the estate in 1706 and died in 1762, see *Royal Letters etc. from the Family Papers of Dundas of Dundas*, ed. Walter Macleod (Edinburgh 1897) p.xi. Dundas Castle was rebuilt by William Burn between 1818 and 1820, but there is a view of the old house from the walled garden in 1769; see ibid.

24. NLS Adv.80.6.3 f.12 verso. This manuscript is in the same hand as Mss.80.6.13 and 80.6.14, the improvement diaries from 1707 to 1757 of George Dundas. The source for some of his ideas was Bradley's *A General Treatise of Husbandry and Gardening* of 1724, which he owned and from which he took notes, see NLS 80.6.2.

plan and a brake on Loudon's reforming zeal and the carpet bedding, supplied ironically by Dicksons of Edinburgh.[21]

While Adam's cautious advocacy of the natural was not without precedent in the 1730s, it was surprising to find it in a garden belonging to Lord Stair. Newliston, with its unrelieved contrast between garden and countryside, was probably closer to Stair's heart than the dalliance with nature at Castle Kennedy. He had admired the formality of Stowe and Blenheim, and his taste for such things could not fail to have been strengthened by his spell as ambassador at Versailles. The catalogue of the library at Culhorn, made in 1762, listed works like the *Description of Versailles*, Marot's plans, and gardening books such as Miller's *Dictionary*, his *Gardener's Calendar*, and Switzer's *Hydrostaticks*, all of which he had probably acquired.[22] His ideas on gardening were in many respects in a lower line with those of his Newliston neighbour George Dundas of Dundas Castle.[23] Dundas undertook, probably some time around 1724, a subjective summary of the principal features employed in designing a formal garden, where he listed 'the necessary ornaments in a garden' as '(next to the plants & trees), Fountains, Cascades & Buffets of water, accompanied wt spouts & jets d'eaux, where water is plenty, ponds & canals, wt pleasure boats',[24] and so on in a suitable

Plate 5. The gardens at Castle Kennedy, from the round pond

25. NLS Adv. 80.6.3. f.14, ff.21 verso – 23 verso. Dundas's list of the more popular trees for the pleasure garden comprised, oak, elm, chestnut, lime, beech, hornbeam, maple, ash, sycamore, birch, acacia, plane, aspen, alder, poplar, sallow (willow). He also gave his selection of shrubs used 'to fill up and furnish brushwood at the foot of great trees' such as the whitethorn, hazel, judas, and ozier, with the Lote tree, Bladder Senna, service tree, Cornel, Bitter cherry, and Neapolitan medlar, as more particular. Shrubs used to make the borders of parterres were roses, honeysuckle, syringa, jasmine, jonquil, privet, sweet trefoil, rosemary, and Spanish broom. As 'Evergreens fit for palisades and garnishing the borders of parterres', he listed, Pitch tree, fir tree, pine, cypress, scarlet oak, holly, juniper, phillyrea, pyracanthus, and box (ibid., ff.42–6).

26. SRO GD 10/1421/212.

27. See SRO GD 18/4404 and 4518. Presumably S. Boyse was Samuel Boyse, the author of *Verses, occasioned by seeing the Palace and Park of Dalkeith* (Edinburgh 1732). In this, Boyse showed himself the equal of Clerk's natural and informal ideas, and referred to the 'wild romantick Prospects' of Dalkeith, where 'the steep Precipice with craggy Brow,/Hangs o'er the Deep, and forms an Arch below' (ibid. pp.9, 11). For 'The Country Seat' see A.A. Tait 'William Adam and Sir John Clerk: Arniston and the Country Seat' *Burlington Magazine* (1969) pp.132–40; Stuart Piggott 'Sir John Clerk and the Country Seat', *The Country Seat*, ed. H.M. Colvin and John Harris (London 1972) pp.110–16; and *The Genius of the Place*, ed. Peter Willis and John Dixon Hunt (London 1975) pp.196–203. In March, 1724, Clerk wrote that he 'had perfected my poem of the Country Seat in blank verse' (SRO GD 18/5033). He then regretted he had not written in rhyme, and acknowledged his debt to the *Georgics* and Thomson's *Seasons*.

vein. He also gave the five essential points to look for in choosing the site of a garden – wholesomeness, good earth, water, conveniency, fine prospects – and followed it with an interesting and detailed list 'Of trees proper for pleasure gardens'.[25] In none of these was there any originality, and Dundas, for all his great interest in gardening, was remarkably blind to the natural that preoccupied his contemporary Sir John Clerk and even Lord Stair. In this he was distinct from William Adam too, who must have realised by 1730 that the baroque garden, as created by Bruce and Edward and imitated at Hopetoun or Newliston and on a much smaller scale at Dundas Castle, was an anachronism. The future lay clearly with those that developed the fashionable ideas of naturalism already pin-pointed by his patron Sir John Clerk, and publicly extolled by the latter's amanuensis Samuel Boyse in his *Translations and Poems, Written on Several Occasions*, of 1738.

Adam had always an ambivalent attitude to the natural style, and his career represented no logical progression from formal to informal. Although at heart, and on his own property at Blair Adam and at North Merchiston, he revealed an idiosyncratic mix of the two styles, in public, with his living to earn and his career to advance, he was prepared to follow rather than direct the inclinations of his clients. The Scottish exponents of the informal garden in the 1730s were few, and a fair indication of Adam's uphill battle was the qualification of his revolutionary statement in 1742 that 'the risings and fallings of ground are to be humoured and generally make the greatest beautys in Gardens' with the thoughtful phrase: 'and with the least expence'.[26] But he was fortunate that amongst the few was Sir John Clerk, who was prepared not only to encourage Adam in better and more sophisticated ways, but also, and like most pedants, incorrigibly disposed to instruct. Clerk's instrument for this was his manuscript essay in rhyme, 'The Country Seat', which became Adam's second bible.

Clerk's 'The Country Seat' was completed in 1727 with several pages of notes and alterations and copied by Boyse 'the transcriber' in Edinburgh in 1732.[27] This was the same Boyse – Samuel the poet – who urged its publication upon Clerk in his *Epistle to Sir John Clerk* with the lines: 'would'st thou indulge the Muses' fond request,/Thy Country Seat in all its beauties drest,/Fair as its model, just as its design,/To future ages should distinguish'd shine'.[28] While it had little claim to theoretical originality, echoing as it did the ideas of Shaftesbury, Addison and Pope, it sought attention by applying rather than fashioning theory. For Clerk was prepared not only to define clearly his notions of the different sorts of gardens, but also to discuss their

28. Boyse wrote this referring both to Mavisbank, Clerk's country seat, and to *The Country Seat* of which he was a transcriber, see *The Works of the English Poets*, XIV, p.583. Boyse also saw Clerk as a pioneer gardener who 'Bless'd with such all-improving hands as thine,/Soon would make her (Scotland's) face with new advantage shine' (ibid.).

29. SRO GD 18/4404 f.10. Reid wrote that 'As the sun is the centre of the world: as the Heart of man is the Centre of the man: as the nose the Centre of the face and as it is unseemly to see a Man wanting a leg, one arm and ec. . . . Just so with House Avenues, Gardens, Orchard ec. where regularity or uniformity is not observed'. (John Reid *The Scots Gard'ner* (Edinburgh 1683) p.2). However Clerk, for all his ideas, seems to have used a contemporary edition of Bradley's *New Improvements of Planting and Gardening*, see SRO GD 18/5146.

30. Stephen Switzer *Ichnographia Rustica: or, the Nobleman, Gentleman, and Gardener's Recreation*, 2nd ed., 3 vols. (London 1742) vol.1, pp.xviii–xix. Here Switzer was echoing in practical ideas the sentiments found in Addison, Pope and Shaftesbury, see broadly H.F. Clark *The English Landscape Garden* (London 1948) pp. 11–16; Christopher Hussey *English Gardens and Landscapes* (London 1967) pp.32–5; and Joseph Burke *English Art 1714–1800* (Oxford 1976) pp.39–68.

31. Francis Hutcheson *An Inquiry into the Original of Our Ideas of Beauty and Virtue* (London 1726) p.44.

32. For the equation between liberty of a Whiggish sort and the informal see Nikolaus Pevsner *Studies in Art, Architecture and Design*, 2 vols. (London 1968) vol.I, pp.100–1. In Boyse's *Triumph of Nature* which describes the gardens at Stowe, the political overtones are captured and he gave as a footnote the list of politicians that were in Lord Cobham's view 'Virtue's fav'rites and for Britain's friends' (*The Works of the English Poets*, XIV, p.537).

practicality over a range of situations extending from the formal to the natural. Despite a certain staleness and the cumbersome system of blank verse, the idealised setting Clerk devised for his country house was infinitely nearer the imminent natural landscapes of Kent than the formal garden that, even he, showed a reluctance to cast aside completely. In his desire for 'some little Hills', and wish to see fields 'chequered round', Clerk had resolutely emancipated himself from what were reckoned the joys of gardening in an old fashioned but still popular work such as Reid's *The Scots Gard'ner*, where nature was regarded throughout with a watchful and on the whole distrustful eye.[29] Clerk's position without doubt owed much to a recognition of the ideas offered in Switzer's *Ichnographia Rustica*, of 1718, where its author, dramatically flying in the face of convention, stated that 'if the Beauties of Nature were not corrupted by Art, Gardens would be much more valuable'. It was Switzer who set forth in more or less practical terms the 'Natural Garden', in which 'all the adjacent Country be laid open to View, and that the Eye should not be bounded with high Walls, Woods misplac'd, and several Obstructions that are seen in too many Places, by which the Eye is as it were imprisoned, and the Feet fetter'd in the midst of the extensive Charms of Nature, and the voluminous Tracts of a pleasant Country'.[30] This message was fully grasped by Clerk and appears more cautiously in the work of the Scottish philosopher, Francis Hutcheson, who noted more or less approvingly that, '*Regularity* in laying out of gardens in *Parterres*; *Vistas*, *parallel Walks*, is often neglected to a limitation of Nature even in some of its Wildernesses'.[31] Yet nowhere in Clerk's 'Country Seat' was any association made between the informal and liberty. In this he was unlike Addison and Pope or even Thomson, and saw no need for something like a Scottish equivalent of Lord Temple's Stowe and its political patriotism.[32] The obvious parallel was the later and now destroyed Temple of Fame, set up in the park at Blair Atholl in 1742 as a shrine to literary and philosophical ideas but without any apparent political overtones.[33] In Scotland, freedom in nature did not seem to

33. The Temple of Fame was one of several sculptural groups set up around Diana's Grove at Blair in the 1740s. There is an anonymous plan, 'Insides of the Temple of Fame at Blair' dated 1744, which lists the deities and literary figures whose busts were arranged in two tiers inside the circular building (Blair Castle Charter Room D 2/12(18)). Apart from the obvious figures like Shakespeare and Milton, it contained the seasons and, more eccentrically, 'Flaming boy', but no politicians or statesmen. The temple has not survived though it was seen by Pococke in 1760, having been set up in 1745 (ibid., Box 40, IV 25).

have been indicative or symbolic of freedom in government, any more than the baroque garden reflected overtly dictatorial tendencies. For Clerk, there was no political message in the gardens he described. His various references to Scottish history and freedom were without any political significance, and lines like 'Each bold attempt to free the Scottish Land/Where valiant Bruce or Wallace did command', were offered more as a possible, and elevating, subject for a piece of history painting and less as any insight into the meaning of the informal garden.[34] The key to the landscape movement for Clerk and others like him was not political but emotional and literary. Dalrymple's essay on landscape gardening of about thirty years later showed much the same bias.

Perhaps perversely but understandably, Clerk made more important and original statements about garden design in the notes and revision to his manuscript, where he was freed from the restriction of blank verse. So much so, that in his preface, 'The Author to the Reader', he wrote as his penultimate paragraph that, 'I might add another Apology for the Dress of this Poem', explaining that he had used verse by and large to combine 'ancient and modern Precepts' in the style of the contemporary 'best Poets'.[35] This tended to make his work more literary and cumbersome, and less practical and clear. His additional seventy notes were a means both to modernise parts of his text and to explain others in greater and more technical detail. In this way he expanded 'How wild & shapless Fields may be adorned/With easy Labour and without Constraint' in the text, with a note pleading the cause of naturalism, 'Grounds are not to be forced by levelling but taken as they lye, i.e. plain ground may be made (more plain) or very plain & sloping ground may be made to slope more gradually & equally'.[36] He also reinforced the critical note of 'all these trifling mary knotts', with the more decisive statement that 'This will be best understood upon considering these little Knots that were the Ornament of Parterres 20 or 30 years ago'.[37] In the same way, his couplet, 'The Fountain's margin should not much extend/Beyond what may the falling drops contain', had a note which explained the practical ramifications of the subject; that the diameter of the jet pipe should be proportional to the width of the basin below it, and so on in great detail.[38] Significantly, he added dismissively that 'I would choose rather a plain piece of water rather than one fed by a small paltry jett'. Not surprisingly, Clerk's ideal setting for a country house was largely a natural and informal one, and he was adamant that 'where Nature is wanting, the Defect can never be supply'd'.[39] He recommended a river

34. SRO GD 18/4404 f.16

35. ibid., f.2

36. ibid., f.27, 9 note 61.

37. ibid., f.27 note 62.

38. ibid f.29. Clerk thought that a basin 'of 50 feet Diameter small enough for a Jett Pipe of an Inch diameter, because this will force upwards a very great Quantity of water. At the same time, I think a bason of the same dimensions sufficient for a Conduit of a foot diameter if the water is not to be forced but to fall perpendicularly down from any Figure placd in the middle of the Bason. One of a 100 feet diameter would require a Rivulet to adorn it' (ibid., f.10 note 66).

39. ibid., f.1 'The Author to the Reader'. Similarly, he wrote that 'These Countries which are level low and plain/Have not Variety to entertain/The busy mind, but always are the same' (ibid., f.10)

bank, as at his own Mavisbank, sheltered from the north, with 'little hills', 'flowery meadows Groves and beauteous springs near at hand'. 'Countries which are level and plain' he thought lacked variety, but he turned his back upon the more obvious elements of the later picturesque and sublime that were to fascinate both his own son John and William Adam's Robert. While the sea might produce at a distance and in certain circumstances 'noble prospect', this was only tolerable when 'Neptune's awful frowns/Are hid in Distance'.[40] Similarly, 'Deep rapid Rivers, wide extended Lakes/High tow'ring Rocks and noisy cataracts' were admissible only at the extreme 'Bounds of Sight'.[41] Clerk feared the 'Rocks with tumultuous Noise with eccho (forth)/Loud Peals of Thunder from the Cataract', and was far happier and much more at ease in a landscape where 'spreading trees in many stately Rowes;/Display the Parterres and the shady walks/The sloping Greens, the Bends and water works', were 'never fading charms'. All this held true for Clerk's own riverside villa at Mavisbank – 'by much-lov'd Esca's flow'ry side' – whose creation had no doubt done much to inspire the writing of 'The Country Seat'.

Mavisbank was designed by Clerk in about 1723. It followed his dummy run at Cammo, near Edinburgh, a decade earlier, and the garden appears to have been developed along with the building of the house. Trees were bought for it from Edinburgh and Pinkie between 1724 and 1729, and the garden and park around was sufficiently finished in 1733 for Clerk to view what he had achieved critically, and for it to be praised uncritically around that time by Samuel Boyse.[42] Rather oddly, what seems to have troubled him was not its dated formality but its size and expense, and he wrote in his memorandum that 'I would have made much finer improvement . . . but I chosed to do no more than 2 or 3 men can easily keep in good order at the expense of 20 or 30 li. yearly. . . . Yet the gardens might doe well if improved to the best advantage'.[43] Roy's map of about 1747 shows on a small scale much of what Clerk had completed and this is borne out by Boyse though in the most general way. A cour d'honneur between the two Adam pavilions was treated as a parterre whose diminutive grandeur Clerk explained away in the same memorandum with the disingenuous excuse that 'the smalness of this obliged me afterwards to make two wings'. An undated and incomplete plan for this courtyard showed a *parterre à l'anglais*, with grass in the main compartments, a small border of flowers, and gravel or sanded walks (Plate 6). Both parterre and pavilions were an afterthought about which Clerk had misgivings that can only have been partially smoothed away by

40. ibid., f.9. In a sense, Clerk wanted to have his cake and eat it. He wrote that 'every beauteous Villa should be placed/In open View of Neptunes wide Realms;/Yet shun his Borders with your utmost care' (ibid.).

41. ibid., f.9.

42. SRO GD 18/1767/1 and 18/1766. The nursery at Pinkie just beyond Musselburgh, was Alexander Cochran's and that in Edinburgh William Miller junior. Miller also supplied seeds to Adam and the Earl of Stair at Culhorn, see also 'Memoirs of the Life of Sir John Clerk' *Scottish History Society* XIII, ed. John Gray (Edinburgh 1892) p.132. For a brief account of Clerk at Penicuik and Mavisbank, see William Spink 'Sir John Clerk of Penicuik, Landowner as designer' in *Furor Hortensis*, ed. Peter Willis (Edinburgh 1974) pp.31–40. For Boyse's account, see *The Works of the English Poets* XIV, p.583.

43. SRO GD 18/1770.

44. SRO GD 18/4735/2. This is undated but would appear from its sequence to be of *c.*1729. In it, Adam was dealing with a series of complaints from Clerk about the house and grounds.

45. See SRO GD 18/1767/1.

46. Allan Ramsay 'An Epistle wrote from Mavisbank March, 1740' SRO GD 18/4351; and see *Scottish Select Texts: The Works of Allan Ramsay*, vol. III, ed. A.M. Kinghorn and Alexander Law (Edinburgh 1961) p.261. Ramsay's poems expressed little that was novel and repeated several themes found in 'The Country Seat'. His idea of gardening was still that of the early eighteenth century and his ideal was probably a nature inspired by 'Sachi or Salvater', and certainly one improved by 'Art'.

47. SRO GD 18/4416 f.14. This was dated 1738 but was a version of a similar inscription dated 1728. There were further inscriptions about the grounds including that 'for the walk pedestal at Mavisbank' (ibid., f.13).

48. SRO GD 18/4404 f.26.

49. The wilderness of 1737 seems to have been the first part of the creation of the formal gardens at Blair, see Blair Castle, Charter Room, Box 70, D.1–14. Progress on the gardens was interrupted by the siege of 1745, but was continued after this until the Duke's death in 1768. For a detailed account of these improvements, see Box 40, III & IV.

50. Charter Room, Box 70, D.5.

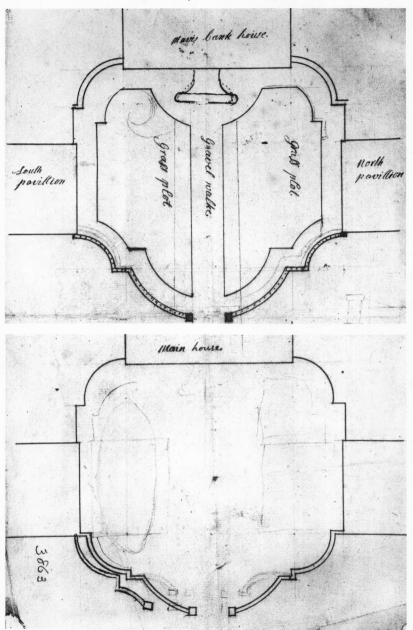

Plate 6. Alternative designs for the courtyard parterre at Mavisbank, Midlothian, by Sir John Clerk, *c.*1725

51. John James *The Theory and Practice of Gardening* (London 1712) p.59. James described his fourth plate as 'containing ten different Groves; the four first figures are fit for places that are oblong, and about an Acre and a half, or two Acres Extent; the six others following, shew what may be done in long slips of Grounds, and narrow Guts of a Garden. These woods are much varied, and though plain, are nevertheless handsomely cut, and well wrought' (ibid., p.56). The Duke was also influenced by what he had seen in London and referred to the Mall at St James's and a walk at Hammersmith as a possible source for the avenues at Blair (Blair Castle, Charter Room, Box 70, D.8).

Adam's assurance that the pavilions 'can be scituat nowhere but some pairt of the prospect of the field must be lost, and I look upon the whole bottom to be a Rurall Garden, and the distant view with watter the best'.[44] This view was taken up in a *patte d'oie* of three broad avenues running outwards from the house with its intervening ground thickly planted, leaving unexploited and to the rear the fort which Clerk as author of the *Dissertatio de Monumentis quibusdam Romanis* of 1750 had dubbed 'a Roman Station'. These avenues were probably formed by the English elms and limes that Clerk had bought from William Miller at Edinburgh for the planting season of November to February 1726.[45] To the south of the house, and connected with it by a winding path through a wilderness studded with inscribed pedestals, were two gardens, circular and rectangular, similar in site and style to Pope's grotto at Twickenham, and a foretaste of the garden that Clerk was to form for himself at Hurley in 1742. This walk was described by Allan Ramsay in his *Epistle wrote from Mavisbank*, of 1740, as one that led 'along the margin of the Burn / Wher fishes will divert your Eye / While jumping up to catch a fly', until it ultimately reached the garden where, significantly, 'art adds life to Nature grace'.[46] At the edge of the water was a Bridge house carrying the following inscription, presumably evocative of Clerk's days at Mavisbank: 'Hic / Libris Interdum / Otiique Honesti Blandimentis/ Rusticatur/Interdum Etiam Muliebriter/Infenso Baccho/Cum Cenis Bibitur'.[47] All this was in keeping with the kind of secret garden described in 'The Country Seat' as 'Where every Goddess and their train / A clear and Secret bathing Place may find / Where Flora with a Knot of gaudy Flowers / May dress her lovely head'.[48] So intimate a mood was, however, less typical among his contemporaries, where the derivative and routine approach obvious in the gardening of the Duke of Atholl at Blair was normal. There, the wilderness to the east of the castle was begun in 1737, with the Duke using John James's *The Theory and Practice of Gardening*, to which he was a subscriber, as his source of inspiration.[49] During his December reading that year, he noted for his gardener John Wilson that James's 'Figure 6th, in the fourth Plate may be very fit for the south division in the wilderness at Blair', and that figure nine might serve for the serpentine walks (Plate 7).[50] Both of these references were to the familiar geometric designs characteristic of the baroque garden – the first to 'Designs of Groves of a middle height', the other to what James described as 'Garden-work very extraordinary, and yet very magnificent in their kind'.[51] Although neither can be positively identified with anything remaining at Blair or shown in Thomas

Plate 7. Plate IV from John James *The Theory and Practice of Gardening, 1712*

52. Winter's survey at Blair remains only in the form of a copy made in 1744 by Charles Esplen (Blair Castle, Charter Room, B.15). However, it is confirmed by a note that the 'inclosures' at Blair were 'surveyed and drawn by Thomas Winter in August, 1744' (Charter Room, Box 40, IV 22). This showed two areas of wilderness, that around Diana's Grove and a further one near the walled garden, though neither accurately after James. An earlier design, attributed to Boutcher senior, is again not sufficiently clear in detail (Charter Room, B.5/3). Some details of the parterre and formal groves are shown in the plan after Tinney's Survey of 1744, given in G.L. Le Rouge *Le Jardin Anglo-Chinois*, pt.II (1766) pl.2.

53. See John Fleming *Robert Adam and his Circle* (London 1962) pp.328, 329.

54. SRO GD 18/4404 f.28.

Winter's survey of the gardens in 1744, the general form the wilderness took reflected such second- or third-hand ideas and betrayed an unimaginative response that would certainly not have been Clerk's.[52]

Clerk's grotto and garden at Hurley, on the Penicuik estate (Plate 8) was, however, a much more advanced design than the riverside 'bathing place' at Mavisbank. Between making the two, he had visited London in 1727 and again in 1733, and when there had visited Chiswick, probably seen Pope's garden with its grotto and subterranean tunnels, and looked at Bridgeman and Kent's garden at Claremont.[53] Their influence certainly lay heavily on Hurley, which Clerk developed with a rock hewn tunnel running beneath Clermount hill and a series of ponds beside the river Esk that reminded him rather fancifully of the Neapolitan Grotto of Posillipo. Inside the hill, he built a small domed chamber, which had inscribed on one wall the tag 'Tenebrosa Occultaque Cara'. In much of this, he was, of course, running counter to the ideas of 'The Country Seat', and even his ponds there were of the sort that 'stagnant lye from latent sources fed', which his verse had dismissed as 'awkward ornaments at best'.[54] But even so, Hurley must have been outstanding, particularly when compared with a water garden such as that formed at Blair, in about 1750, by the Duke of Atholl (Plate

Plate 8. Grotto, Sir John Clerk's garden at Hurley, Penicuik, Midlothian

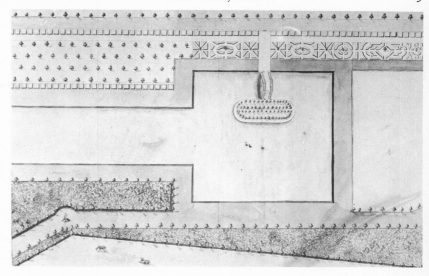

9).[55] There, a series of large, shallow but still ponds were confined within the geometrical setting of a walled garden, and created with their bridged island an almost oriental or willow pattern feeling in so Highland a setting, which may have led to the garden's inclusion in Le Rouge's *Le Jardin Anglo-Chinois* (Plate 24). Such a garden had little meaning, less purpose other than as a spectacular duck pond, and attempted no kind of classical evocation comparable to Hurley. To Clerk, rather than Atholl, such things came as second nature, and he needed little encouragement to take up this kind of mannered and literary style of gardening. His severe classical education and his obsessive antiquarian bent would have sent him, as it did others, in this direction sooner or later. It encouraged a fondness and sympathy for authors like Walton, Temple and Evelyn, that was readily apparent in 'The Country Seat'. It made him appreciate and extol in Latin verse the series of grottoes and cascades on the river at Corby Castle in Cumberland in 1734, as the physical incarnation of those described by Milton in his *Comus*.[56] The tenacity of this form of intellectual gardening was apparent as late as 1787, when Daines Barrington maintained, erroneously, in his essay on the 'Progress of Gardening' that Spenser's Arcady as described in the *Faerie Queene*, was deliberately and at last realised in the 'modern garden' of William Kent.[57] The very lack of such imitative overtones in the landscapes of Brown was for Barrington a

55. This water garden does not appear in Winter's survey of 1744, but is shown in that of the surveyor James Dorrett in 1758 (Blair Castle, Charter Room, A.13). There is an unsigned drawing for the garden at Blair (Charter Room, D.5/45) pl.9. It is possibly the work of John Wilson, the gardener at Blair until around 1763. The garden was restored and altered in 1888, but is now in a derelict condition.

56. See *Furor Hortensis*, p.32 and Clerk's manuscript account of the beauties of Corby, SRO GD 18/4416.

57. Daines Barrington 'On the Progress of Gardening' *Archaeologia* VII (1787) p.130. Barrington acknowledged his debt to Walpole's *Essay in Gardening* of 1771 for 'several anecdotes and observations with regard to the progress of gardening' (ibid.).

Plate 9. Blair Castle, Perthshire, plan of the water garden, *c.*1750

58. See Tait *Burlington Magazine* (1969)
pp.132–40.

59. Two plans, or rather surveys, of the
gardens show what had been intended
and what accomplished. One survey was
inscribed 'General plan of Arniston
House Parkes and Gardens of the
Honble Mr. Robert Dundas Esquire,
1726'. This drawing may be linked with
Adam's design for the house, which
showed double rather than single
pavilions on either side of the main
block; see Arniston Charter Room,

fault, which smacked too much 'of the gardener of Old Stowe', presumably Bridgeman, and too little of 'Poussin or Claude Lorraine'.

A broader and perhaps better parallel with the more liberal aspects
of 'The Country Seat', was provided not by any garden of Clerk's
making but by that of his diligent and imaginative pupil William Adam
at Arniston.[58] Work on the gardens there roughly coincided with the
building of the house, from 1726 until about 1732, and they are shown
in their maturity in Nasmyth's view of the house of around 1800 (Plate
10). Both before and during all this time, Adam was more or less in
constant touch with Sir John Clerk. Although much of Adam's garden
was simplified and brought up to date in the 1750s, the principal

Plate 10. View of Arniston, Midlothian, attributed to Alexander Nasmyth, *c*.1800

Portfolio f.9(12). It is possible that this survey is from Adam's office, which at this time undertook such work; see the plan for Leslie in Fife. A second plan by David Dundas, of 1732, repeated that of 1726 but without the Great Avenue to the north (Arniston, Charter Room, portfolio 'Arniston Plans').

60. William Adam finished the Drum for Lord Somerville in 1726 (Fleming, op. cit., p.49). It is possible that he concerned himself with the garden, which was fully described about 1783. It was then noted that the old cross of Edinburgh was the terminal of the great avenue, installed in 1756, and that the 'avenue opposite the north part of the house is terminated by an ancient like structure, on the very summit of a hill' (see Thomas Whyte 'An Account of the Parish of Liberton in Mid-Lothian' *Archaeologia Scotica* I (1792) p.318). Adam's plan for Hopetoun was signed 'Gull. Adam Arch. delint' and was probably made in about 1721, when work had begun on the gardens, see Hopetoun Muniments 'A General Plan of Hopetoun Park', and Building Accounts, 1721–50. Clerk himself wrote of his avenue planting at Penicuik that, 'Avenue terminat on any object, as a porch or ruine, it will make, in time, a very good "figure"' (*Scottish History Society* XIII, p.148).

61. SRO GD 18/4404 f.26. Clerk, however, felt that the distant view of the city was also a warning to beware 'Her loud harmonious Bells a warning give/To shun such pourfull draughts of rural Joy/As may intoxicate the lazy mind' (ibid.). Allan Ramsay wrote from Mavisbank with less enthusiasm for Clerk's distant view. The prospect of the country from the city was the better one for him: 'Come view with me the golden Beams, /which, Phebus, every Morning pours/upon the plains adorn'd with flowers.' (SRO GD 18/4351 f.83).

elements of his scheme remain today. The plan that he produced about 1726 for the Lord President Dundas, a highly successful lawyer, showed most of the stock props of any formal garden – a bastioned parterre, a wilderness, a great avenue, cascade, and basin – all of which derived from the late gardens of Wise and London or in Scotland from Bruce and Edward.[59] But in his adaptation of these elements of baroque design, Adam broke with as much tradition as he followed. He developed further Bridgeman's and indeed Bruce's introduction of natural elements as at Kinross and Balcaskie into a formal composition, and while at Blenheim or Stowe avenues were invariably closed by a column or fountain, Adam proposed at Hopetoun, possibly at the Drum, and later at Arniston, a more monumental and at the same time harmonious termination for his vistas. At the Drum an old dovecot closed the west avenue and 'three Gothic arches' the east, while amidst the strict geometry of Hopetoun, he noted on his plan that 'The avenue Eastwards from the House carries your Eye over two Myles of the River Forth to the island of Inchgarvie and from thence along 22 myles more to North Berwick Law, Being a high Mount in the form of a Suggar Loaf which terminates the Avenue'.[60] He attempted the same at Arniston, and advocated the bulbous form of Arthur's Seat, some twelve miles away on the edge of Edinburgh, as the ideal closure for the northern end of the Great Avenue (Plate 13). This would also have given the house a fleeting glimpse of city and brought animation and so relief from the early eighteenth-century dread of complete rural isolation. As 'The Country Seat' put it, 'Another noble Prospect may be deem'd/That of the Great Metropolis or Town'.[61] In any event it was a much more lively solution than the dreary circle of fir trees suggested by *The Scots Gard'ner*, and proposed as late as 1756 for the formal design for Kilravock, Nairn.[62]

The various avenues at Arniston established a pattern, at least on paper, that was repeated in miniature in the grounds about the house. The eastern avenue – the principal approach to the house from Gorebridge – had its lines continued by the hollies on either side of the main block of the building and the avenue itself merged into a sanded *allée*.[63] To the south, the axial lines of the Great Avenue were carried into the parterre and beyond to the cascade, giving a set geometry to both building, garden and park. Immediately to the west of Arniston but off axis with the east avenue lay the wilderness, planted with larch and evergreens, whose serpentine and symmetrical paths formed, as at Hopetoun, an *étoile* of some twelve points, with their centre later marked in the 1750s by a stone urn and pedestal designed by James

Adam (Plate 11). This was balanced to the east by the square of the kitchen garden and orchard. In the centre, the parterre was set out, as Adam indicated in the 1726 plan, with three distinct forms of planting: the areas coloured by wash were grassed with an edging of evergreen, the stippled parts filled with flowers, and the east and west compartments planted like the wilderness with flowering shrubs but in a much more formal composition.[64] The salon windows on the south front of Arniston looked down and over the parterre with the view to the south closed by the cascade. Although it has been grassed over, Clerk's 'verdant Mantle edg'd with gold / Or an embroydered carpet all perfumed / With Indian sweets', can with a little imagination be visualised.

The cascade has followed the parterre into oblivion.[65] It was the obvious climax in Adam's or any garden of the period, and some of its spirit can still be evoked in the twisting stream and small rills that flow through the naturalised valley in the style of Kent's Rousham. Unlike many such cascades, that at Arniston was separated from the parterre by a small strip of parkland, and both it and the land around were treated by Adam in a remarkably free manner. The woods of Purvieshill, which fringed the banks of the stream running from the basin, were shown as planted in an irregular and natural way, contrasting with the geometric forms of the woods in the adjacent Fountainhead Park, and with his own use of wood and water at Newliston (Plate 12). Much of this spirit though not the form remains today (Plate 14). The cascade itself was unambitious, especially when compared with his proposed waterworks for Hopetoun, and perhaps closer to the rather dull one designed by Sir John Clerk in 1714 for Cammo or possibly Penicuik.[66] However, the most elaborate and the most simple cascade shared alike a simplicity of method, for both forced water over a series of largely ornamental obstacles. In Clerk's design, the water was to fall over five steps, while at that built for the Duke of Atholl at Dunkeld in the 1740s by his gardener William Clark the same system was followed but on a more generous scale.[67] There a channel eight feet wide discharged water over and down a drop of some six feet. None of these, however, matched the cascades illustrated and praised in Switzer's *Hydrostaticks* of 1729, and were only the puniest of descendants of the great fountains of Le Nostre at Marly and Chantilly.[68] More romantically and naturally, perhaps closer to his suggestion to Lord Milton in 1734 to turn to advantage 'the View of the Fall of Water from the whell of the New Milne' on the Brunstone Burn, the cascade at Arniston evoked a quieter mood – one which the author of the *Epistle address'd to*

62. Reid, op. cit. p.15. For William Taylor's design for Kilravock Castle, see SRO RHP 30778.

63. The destruction of these hollies was reported by Lord Kames as being the work of Lady Dundas, although two survived until 1780; see *The Arniston Memoirs* (ed.) George Ormond (Edinburgh 1887) p.49. The gardens at this transitional stage were seen and described by Pococke as 'Before the house is a fine lawn adorned with single trees and Clumps . . . there are ridings round the whole, which wind in such a manner towards the glyns as to make the circuit thirteen miles: Near the house are beautifull winding walks round some uneven grounds over glyns beautified by the prospect of Chinese and other bridges that make it a most delightfull place' (R. Pococke, *Tours in Scotland* (1887), p.313). Drawings for several of these bridges are in the Charter Room at Arniston; see Tait *Burlington Magazine* (1969) p.135, n.20. Several of these clumps were removed in the 1840s, see James Brown *The Forester* (Edinburgh 1851) p.479.

64. In 1736, flowers were ordered for the 'ground in front of your windows (the parterre)' (Ormond, op. cit. p.89). From the plan it would seem that they were planted in simple beds rather than according to any geometric pattern. The wilderness at Arniston, as in other cases, incorporated formal and informal sections virtually side by side. James Adam's urn is shown in a drawing in the Clerk of Penicuik collection, Adam Album 2, f.19 – 'Vase at Arnistone'.

65. The cascade was destroyed *c.*1764, and the large and small basins were incorporated into the newly built kitchen garden where, in a plan of this time they were marked 'K' and 'I'; see Arniston, Charter Room, portfolio, Arniston Plans. This garden, now a market garden, can be seen in something like its original form in the illustrations to an article on the house in *Country Life* (August 1925) pp.254, 255.

66. At Hopetoun, Adam designed his waterworks for the foot of the west avenue above the existing round pond. In his 'A General Plan of Hopetoun Park', they were described as 'A Bason in the West Avenue, with Right Angular Cannal on each side. The North Cross Cannal having a Cascade of 3 falls into one octogan Bason'. It is unlikely that much of this elaborate design was constructed; see Hopetoun Muniments, Building Accounts, 1721–50. Clerk's drawing was inscribed 'Model of the hewn work of ye Cascade, May, 1714' (SRO GD 18/1775). Clerk acquired Cammo, near Cramond, in 1710 and parted with it in 1722. His improvements there were largely planting, but there still exists a canal which may have been of his making and connected with this cascade drawing (see *Scottish History Society* XIII, p.84).

67. Blair Castle, Charter Room, D.28 The state of the gardens at Dunkeld are shown in a plan of 1748 by William Clark, though it only marks, as A, the classical greenhouse built by Mercer in 1740 and, as K and L, the 'stores' (Blair Castle, Charter Room, B.13).

68. Switzer, op. cit., vol.II, pls.41, 43, 44 and 46.

Plate 11. The wilderness at Arniston, from *l'étoile*
Plate 12. The western canal at Newliston, West Lothian

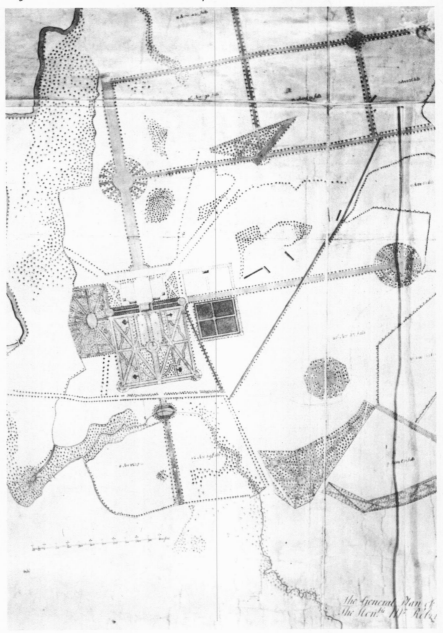

Plate 13. Arniston, improvement plan by William Adam, *c*.1726

Plate 14. Aerial view of Arniston, from Purvieshill burn, 1979

a Friend described tellingly in the language of William Kent:

> Led by the Sound of falling water, next
> Southward I'd gone, and thro' my sounding verse
> Made the cascade's sonorous voice be heard,
> And way'd the surface of the silent ponds.
> Nor should the little rivulet, that yields
> Such show remain unsung; nor its retreat
> Miss'd my attendant verse, as from its pomp,
> Down o'er the steep it hastens to the grove.[69]

69. Anonymous *An Epistle address'd to a Friend* (Edinburgh 1740) pp.13–14. For Adam's letter to Lord Milton see NLS Saltoun Papers, SC55; for Adam's relations with Milton, see Ian Lindsay and Mary Cosh *Inveraray and the Dukes of Argyll* (Edinburgh 1973) pp.62, 64.

70. Adam's designs for Taymouth were illustrated in the prints he made for his posthumous publication *Vitruvius Scoticus*, pls.50–52. For a full building history of the castle see *Country Life* (Oct. 1964) pp.912–15, 978–81; and also John Christie *The Lands and Lairds of Loch Tayside* (Aberfeldy 1892) pp.22–5. Apart from survey plans, there are few surviving drawings for Taymouth: several were certainly sold in the Taymouth Castle Sale of 1922, as Lot 1767, 'Portfolio of ink and pencil sketches, old plans of St. Mary le Bone, Taymouth plans, etc. found in the Library'.

Plate 15. View of Taymouth Castle, Perthshire, with William Adam's wings, by George Barret sen., *c.*1780

Perhaps the most appealing element at Arniston was the sustained concern to capture in its gardens something of the informality and naturalism of the surrounding countryside. Such sensitivity was probably the outcome of Adam's association with Clerk, although his earlier garden at Taymouth Castle in Perthshire showed the awakening of some sort of awareness, if not sympathy, with Pope's genius of the place. Adam came to Taymouth predictably as an architect employed by the Earl of Breadalbane to add pavilions to either side of an old castle, and created a stylistic mélange, as much unscholarly as picturesque, flattered by Barret's view of the 1780s (Plate 15).[70] He stayed to mastermind a landscape setting infinitely superior to his architecture. And while his landscape remained the basis of all subsequent schemes, his classical pavilions disappeared without much regret when the castle was again gothicised some eighty years later.[71] Both this garden and expanded castle are probably shown in a birdseye view of the estate, attributed to the Norie family, and accurately foreshadowed in an unsigned garden plan of 1720, close to Adam's style of draughtsmanship and probably in his hand (Plate 16).[72]

71. See pp.126–7. In April 1746, 'Mr. Douglas the architect' was paid for his plans for the dining room and entrance to the Castle, which would suggest some dissatisfaction with the Adam scheme (SRO GD 112/21/78).

72. This painting is in the National Portrait Gallery, Edinburgh. Its date is based on the payment by Lord Breadalbane 'To a Painter at Edinburgh for a view of Taymouth and his going hither to take it' in September 1733 (SRO GD 112/21/77). The dating of this picture is made difficult by its having been altered sometime before 1754, when it was modernised to match the less formal and more extensive landscape. The 1720 plan of Taymouth shows the castle with Adam's pavilion wings in block plan and the style of the drawing is close to the unsigned plan of Arniston attributed to him; see SRO RHP 721. Adam seems to have had a continuing connection with the Breadalbane family over a variety of subjects and in 1738 worked for them at

Dirleton, in East Lothian (Blair Adam Mss. Adam Letters, vol.1). In 1745, he was paid for setting up a monument to

Lord Glenorchy's son in Moffat, Dumfriesshire, subsequently destroyed; see SRO GD 112/21/78.

Plate 16. Birdseye view of Taymouth Castle, attributed to James Norie, after 1726

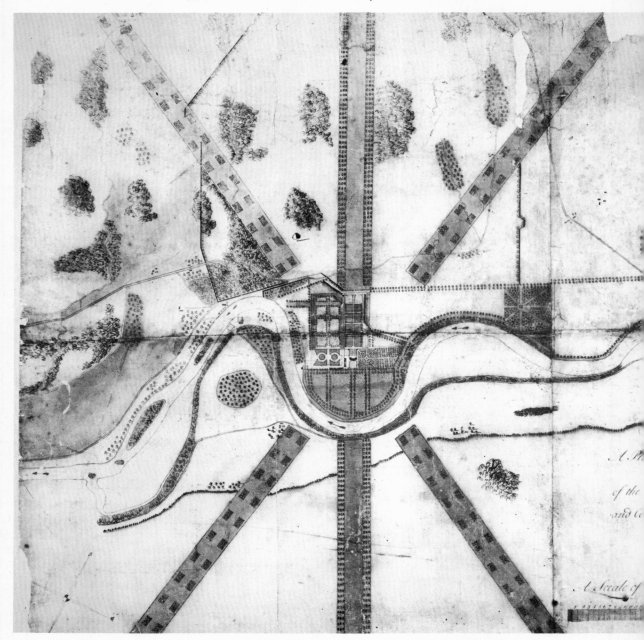

Plate 17. Taymouth, improvement plan by William Adam, 1720

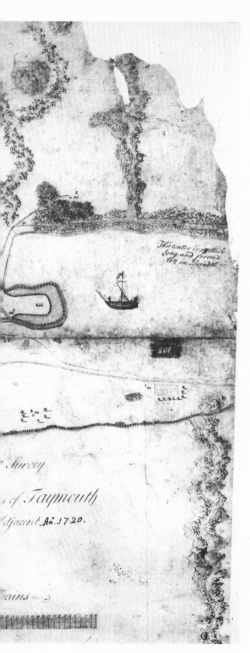

This water is 300 feet
long and grows
65 in breadth

SHIP

.. Survey

.. of Taymouth

..djacent. An 1720.

..ains —

Adam proposed and, as the Norie view shows, executed two main avenues running north and south from the castle, each composed of a triple line of trees (Plate 17). Branching from them was a series of tangential rides formed out of rectangular boxes of trees, rather like those used in the Deerpark at Hopetoun, which made a modified *patte d'oie* both above and below the castle. Adam set a parterre around the house, elaborate towards the east and west, simple on the other fronts of the building. However, these parterres, unlike those at Arniston or Castle Kennedy, were out of step with the axes of the avenues, which apart from the lower portion of the eastern one presented a series of heroic vistas up and down the Tay valley, more truly in scale with the vast landscape than the small, lopsided patches of parterre. The main entrance to the castle was up the lower arm of the east avenue from the point where it was intersected by the public road coming from Killin. This made an unimpressive and unassuming entrance to so grand a composition, as the horsemen and carriage in the Norie view made clear (Plate 16). The unsatisfactory nature of this was unresolved in Adam's plan and continued as an obvious drawback, dividing as it did the rising ground of this part of the park. It was only with the removal of the road to the hillside well above the Taymouth burn, some time about 1754, that the park gained an uninterrupted acreage in front of the castle.[73] While a similar problem re-occurred and was dealt with more successfully at Arniston, his later designs for Makerston (Plate 18), where a straight avenue of 410 feet ran from the gates to the forecourt, and Craigston both showed a full axial approach as the dominant element in his compositions.[74] More satisfactory and precocious was Adam's handling of the harder task of turning Taymouth's irregular setting in a loop of the river handsomely to his advantage, for it anticipated by at least a decade the river walk alongside the Allan at Kippendavie in Perthshire, which was reputedly formed in 1742 and

73. In Adam's plan it was shown below the brook with the great hillside avenues on the other side; in Thomas Winter's plan of 1754 it appeared above the brook and 'The Surprise' terrace but just below the tower; see SRO RHP 961/3. According to Christie, 'about the middle of the last century . . . the public road through the grounds was converted into a private drive to the castle, and a new one was constructed from Kenmure to near the foot of the Balloch burn, where it joined the old road' (Christie, op. cit. p.213; see also p.57).

74. For his unexecuted and undated design for Makerston, see SRO RHP 14094. This showed a straight avenue running into a circular court of 160 feet in diameter. For Craigston plan, see NMR, Edinburgh, Craigston Plan 44, and for its attribution to William Adam see *Country Life* (October 1963) p.947.

said 'to be the first walk of the kind artificially made in Scotland'.[75]

Behind the castle the river formed three small loops rather in the manner of the Glyme at Blenheim. Instead of trying to regularise this prodigious piece of serpentining, or ignore it as Boutcher had done at Kilkerran, Adam followed its pattern, planting the banks, particularly those running westward to Loch Tay, and forming a river walk which twisted and turned with the Tay, and which was kept, according to Pennant, 'with the neatness of the walks of a London villa'.[76] While impressive in itself, and pointing the way to his rather more informal gardens, it made a curious and uncertain contrast with the geometry and convention of the rest of his design. And although it happily merged with the bosquet planted around Adam's temple of Venus, certainly built before 1749 as the Norie view showed, it converged awkwardly with the elaborate formality of the western parterre.[77] All or most of the grounds for this criticism disappeared around 1754, when Thomas Winter's plan suggested or recorded the demise of the parterres and the breaking of the avenues (Plate 29). Yet unsatisfactory though such a juxtaposition may have been, that it was attempted at all was largely through Adam's critical if not ambivalent attitude to the formal garden. While Sir John Clerk and 'The Country Seat' undoubtedly encouraged him to follow a less formal path, it was a way upon which he had already embarked at Taymouth.

Adam was always a ready pupil, and his career as an architect and garden designer was founded on his willingness and ability to learn from others. This was notably true for his patrons, the more discerning or tolerant of whom he was often on terms of considerable intimacy. Sir John Clerk, Lord Milton, the Earl of Stair, the Duke of Hamilton, all in their way helped Adam climb the intellectual ladder. The exception was of course Lord Fife, with whom Adam came to legal blows in 1743. But Fife was notoriously difficult, as well as tasteless, and from him Adam could only have learnt the art of usury.[78] His precise relationship

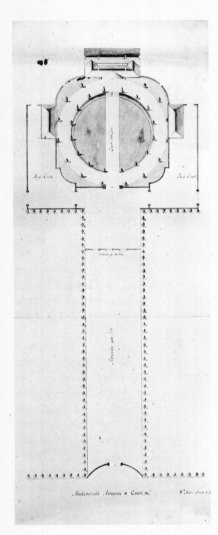

75. For Kippendavie, see Thomas Hunter *Woods, Forests and Estates of Perthshire* (Perth 1883) p.288. Hunter stated it was formed by Mr Hugh Pearson in 1742, who died in 1749, and that 'great havoc was made with the trees by his eldest son' (ibid.). Nothing of his walk is shown in General Roy's contemporary map of this area.

76. Thomas Pennant *Tour in Scotland, 1772*, 3 vols (London 1776), vol.III, p.35.

77. This can easily be seen in the Norie view, where the square temple of Adam's plan is shown standing on a hill and possibly harled white. This temple was probably the west summer house for which a chimney piece was supplied in 1749 by Rochead, who in 1747 had made one for the dining room in the castle; see

SRO GD 112/21/78. It was destroyed in 1830, Christie, op. cit., p.22.

78. For a rather whitewashed account of Lord Fife's character, see Alistair and Henrietta Tayler *The Book of the Duffs*, 2 vols. (Edinburgh 1914) vol.I, pp.108–20. A summary of the involved and costly proceedings, which were never settled in William Adam's lifetime, is given in SRO CS 230A/2/1.

Plate 18. Makerston, Roxburghshire, improvement plan by William Adam, *c.*1730

79. John, 2nd Earl of Breadalbane, 1662–1752, was succeeded by his son John, Lord Glenorchy, the 3rd Earl, 1696–1782. From the surviving accounts of the period, he was obviously in control of the Breadalbane estates from certainly around 1725, see SRO GD 112/21/7. Adam may well have been introduced to Taymouth in the first instance by the young Lord Glenorchy. For a history of the Campbell family at this time see Christie, op. cit., pp.9–15.

80. In 1734, Switzer supplied seeds to Sugnall (see SRO GD 112/21/77), and in the following year payment was made to 'Bridgeman a Gardener for work done in my garden in town' (ibid.) Bridgeman does not seem to have had any further employment with Lord Glenorchy, see Peter Willis *Charles Bridgeman* (London 1978) p.56. Sugnall was inherited by the 3rd Earl through his wife, who was the heiress of the Pershalls of Great Sugnall. They were married in 1730.

81. See SRO GD 112/21/77.

82. SRO GD 112/21/80.

83. SRO GD 112/21/79. The Fort at Taymouth was not shown in Winter's plan of 1754, but must have been built afterwards as payment was made for the lead for its roof in 1765 (GD 112/21/80). There was also a payment to John Baxter in 1759 for plans for a summer house at Taymouth which might be the fort (GD 112/21/79). However, Lord Breadalbane was probably equally interested in the classical and took out in 1763 a subscription to Stuart's *Antiquities of Athens*, whose publication had begun in 1762 (GD 112/21/80).

84. See Bedford County Record Office, Wrest Park Letters, Grey L30/9/139. It is extraordinary that Breadalbane had not met Brown for the latter had worked at Wrest Park before 1771, and Breadalbane knew the house extremely well (see Colvin, op cit., p.147). His first wife, who died in 1726, came from Wrest as a daughter of the Duke of Kent.

with the third Earl of Breadalbane at Taymouth is not clear, but from the length of it – until 1745 at least – there must have been both confidence and trust. Breadalbane, too, had more to offer than the prompt settlement of his bills. As Lord Glenorchy, until his succession to the Earldom in 1752, he controlled the affairs of his elderly father and initiated whatever improvements were undertaken at Taymouth.[79] He had an enthusiasm for gardens and although his taste was no more than conventional, he was always abreast rather than in the rear of fashion. He may have employed the expatriate Switzer at his wife's Staffordshire house, Sugnall, and at his London house in Grosvenor Square he was served by the equally distinguished Charles Bridgeman in 1735.[80] But in neither of these gardens did he attempt anything remarkable, and both were more or less formal. But as an inveterate visitor of gardens from probably 1730 onwards, he could not ignore what he saw or restrict his imagination. This may have encouraged him to try his hand at the daunting prospect of Taymouth in the first place, although his early encounter with the informal style may only have happened around 1737, when he visited Kent's modernised Claremont.[81] After that he made a regular habit of viewing gardens in England and in 1765 saw Walpole's harbinger of the picturesque at Strawberry Hill.[82] The same taste probably took him to Newstead Abbey, in 1752, to see Lord Byron's toy fort on the lake and the stiffly informal landscape of the park. From this may have sprung the idea of the fort at Taymouth, although he seems to have been equally interested in the ecclesiastical gothic of St Mary Redcliff in Bristol, which he saw in 1759.[83] Yet surprisingly enough for such an enthusiast and country house visitor, he wrote in 1770 that he had never met Capability Brown; more surprisingly, he showed little intention to do so.[84]

But if Breadalbane encouraged Adam to look at the new style in English gardens, there were others who must have regarded such an activity as little less than folly. The supporters of formality, both in Scotland and amongst Adam's clients, were numerous and included many even at the end of his career. The large and impressively formal design Adam produced for the Duke of Montrose in 1745 emphasised the strength of the tradition as well as Adam's stylistic dexterity (Plate 19). Once again he was called in to add wings to an old castle and from this commission he seems to have moved outwards to deal with the surrounding landscape.[85] The cardinal elements he had to cope with were the familiar Scottish ones – river, loch, and castle. However, at Buchanan he had not a narrow river valley shut in by the surrounding

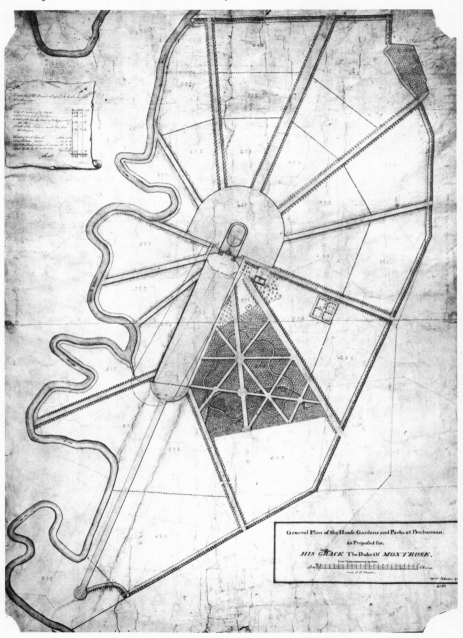

Plate 19. Buchanan, Stirlingshire, improvement plan by William Adam, 1745

85. SRO GD 112/21/79. Adam's design for the new house is shown in plan form in SRO RHP 6150. According to Lady Louisa Stuart, it was a 'wretched old place, to which the Duke has added wings, meaning one day or other to pull down the old front and connect them by a new building' (*The Letters of Lady Louisa Stuart*, ed. R. Brimley Johnson (London 1926) p.137). The Duke of Montrose appears to have also consulted the architect of Inveraray, Roger Morris. Morris was at Buchanan for 'a few days' in 1747, probably on his way to Inveraray (NLS Saltoun Mss. SC 137). Adam and Morris were on good terms.

86. At Inchmurrin the Duke had built a small pleasure lodge beside the ruined castle which he used when visiting the island. This has strong parallels with the pavilions Adam built for the Duke of Hamilton at Chatelherault in *c.*1735, see A.A. Tait 'William Adam at Chatelherault' *Burlington Magazine* (1968) pp.324/5. The visual and utilitarian relationship between Hamilton Palace and Chatelherault was much the same as that between Buchanan and Inchmurrin. However, according to Pennant, there was *c.*1770 little or no view from the house and 'without the least view of so delicious a water' as Loch Lomond (Pennant, op. cit. vol. II, p.176).

87. A plan of *c.*1750 of the house, gardens, and parks, showed little of Adam's scheme; see SRO RHP 6151. However, this survey shows only a pencil and tentative drawing of the house with wings and may well be contemporary with Adam's plan.

88. SRO GD 220/6/33.

89. ibid. However, the walled garden and hothouses were, according to Neill, 'planned and begun about the year 1792, but only finished about 1802' (Patrick Neill *Scottish Gardens* (Edinburgh 1813) p.166).

hills as at Taymouth, but a wide and undulating country opening out to give views over Loch Lomond. Unlike Taymouth again, where the entrance front looked into the flank of the opposite hills, Buchanan was to sit like a sort of spider in the middle of a net of radiating avenues whose breadth varied according to their visual importance. In such a situation, the unsuccessful avenue system that he had foisted upon Taymouth was eminently suitable and could have opened up the whole of the surrounding landscape to well-nigh panoramic views from the castle. Five avenues of varying width stemmed from the bow front of the garden façade, with the vista down the principal one closed in the Bruce tradition by the loch and islands at Inchmurrin.[86] The entrance front was approached by a similar composition of avenues that did little to minimise the awkward geometry of yet another off-axis road to the house. But at Buchanan he handled this better than at Taymouth, and designed two oblique and inner avenues which led the way from the public road to the aligned principal avenue. Above where they met, he set a pair of gates and grille and beyond this a narrow *allée*, together making a vista of nearly half a mile. To the south and immediately below this avenue was the serpentining form of the River Aurick, which he proposed, unimaginatively, to plant out of sight and view from along the walled entrance avenue. The river seems to have played no significant part in Adam's composition, apart from providing a boundary that enclosed with others some 849 acres of the park and gardens. It was, in short, the reverse of what he had done with the river at Taymouth.

Only a portion of Adam's scheme was probably executed, and Roy's map showed only a few avenues at the Loch Lomond end of the park, which may have followed his scheme.[87] They were possibly the work of William Edgar who was 'surveying and planning the high parts of Buchanan' in 1744 and 1745, and working under the superintendence of the Duke's forester John Graham of Duniverig.[88] At that time there seems to have been extensive and continuous work at Buchanan: masons, wrights and carters were employed in the gardens, although, strangely, it was not until 1770 that the sunk fences were made in the park.[89] But whatever existed of Adam's formal design disappeared when the house was rebuilt by James Playfair and the landscape fashioned by him with aggressive informality around 1790. From then onwards there was constant work in the garden and park in a style which predictably demanded that the shrubbery bridge should be built with 'rough stone, like that in the cascade walk, the fewer the stones the better; and rougher the stones, and the less lime

90. SRO GD 220/6/88. Between 1788 and 1791, Playfair designed for Buchanan, a gardener's house, the kitchen garden, a row of cottages, and a tower for the island of Inchmurrin (NLS Adv.33.5.25 f.61). In 1790, he gave a drawing for the approach road to the castle (ibid. f.69).

91. Patrick Graham *Sketches Descriptive of Picturesque Scenery, on the Southern Confines of Perthshire* (Edinburgh 1812) p.150.

92. This was written by Sir John Clerk's daughter, Jackie, during a visit to Finlaystone, Renfrewshire, in March 1751. However, and perhaps characteristically, the best view of the Falls was reckoned that through the trees of the Avenue (SRO GD 18/5474).

93. See Fleming, op. cit., pp.44, 45, 65. An example of this was the Earl of Selkirk, a brother of Adam's patron the Duke of Hamilton, who wrote that 'I am not any wayes sett to solisit for Mr. Addams. I doubt not but att this time when the Towne is full he might get severall people to subscribe there are some who have allready subscribed to him & have been inquering when they are to have his book' (Lennoxlove, Hamilton Mss. 104). The book was *Vitruvius Scoticus*, which was under way in 1726. William Adam designed Dumfries House but it was only begun in 1754. Adam and Lord Stair were at Dumfries several times in 1736 on their way to and from Castle Kennedy (Mount Stuart Muniments, Letters of Countess of Loudoun).

94. See Tait *Burlington Magazine* (1968) pp.316–25. To some extent Adam may have succeeded to Edward's scheme for Hamilton of 1708. Certainly he had proposed an avenue running from the Palace to the edge of the park, where Chatelherault was later built. Edward marked the spot with a gateway a little to the east of the pavilions.

95. ibid., p.320.

that appears the better'.[90] In the end, despite a demesne of nearly 1,200 acres, its lochside setting, and the association of the countryside with robber hero Rob Roy, it bore for a contemporary 'a nearer resemblance, both in its extent and in its ornaments, to an English park'.[91]

At Buchanan, in 1745, Adam offered the bones of a grand and formal scheme, although a little earlier, in 1742, he had written upon the importance of the natural landscape. He also belonged to a circle that sympathised with a Scottish outlook on landscape, one of whose members, in 1751, appreciated that the falls on the Clyde were part of the picturesque and accepted that 'the natural Cascades are so very pretty here that an Imitation wou'd look but trifling'.[92] Yet he always seems to have been disposed to look both ways and to have taken much of his colour from his employer. His architectural career had depended on his ability both to listen and to learn, and the good relations he established with most of his employers, often converting them into patrons, was of the utmost importance in advancing his taste and knowledge, as well as his practice. This was true in his dealings with Sir John Clerk, Lord Hope, probably the Earl of Breadalbane, certainly Lord Milton, and in 1736 the gardening and soldiering Earl of Loudoun was reckoned to have missed the double opportunity of Lord Stair and Adam together at Dumfries House.[93] His work for the Duke of Hamilton at Hamilton and Chatelherault showed much the same sort of relationship as well as revealing Adam's equivocal attitude to the formal and landscape garden.[94] While the Duke's taste obviously ran to the florid staterooms Adam had designed for him at Hamilton Palace, by 1742 his ideas were sufficiently modern for him to appreciate the bleak coast of the island of Arran as one where 'I think for natural Beauties in so wild a place nothing can exceed it, and the help of a little Art might make things here quite magnificent'.[95] This awareness of the natural if not picturesque both on the Duke's and Adam's part in the late 1730s may help to explain the double face presented by the scenographic pavilions at Chatelherault, and made them exceptional (Plate 20). To have a small pavilion as a refuge from a great house was not in itself remarkable even in Scotland. The same arrangement existed in the 1730s at Dalkeith, where another Duke, Buccleuch, escaped from his palace down the park to his 'lovely Smeaton', where 'greatness wearied with its rooms of state,/Finds oft the secret charms of a retreat'.[96] But the formal setting of Smeaton in no way rivalled, though it may have anticipated, the arrangement at Chatelherault, set as it was on the crest of a hill, overlooking a bowling green and down and up a double avenue of trees to the refronted Palace, which in turn offered

96. *The Works of the English Poets*, XIV, p.568. Boyse's poem was dated 1732, and for its publication in 1738 he added the following note about Smeaton: 'A beautiful retreat built at the extremity of the park, below the confluence of the two rivers, and surrounded with fine gardens; to which his Grace has lately added considerable improvements' (ibid.). According to Pococke, who saw it in 1760, the Duke slept there and dined at Dalkeith Palace (Pococke, op. cit., p.312). The building was illustrated (as East Park) in *Vitruvius Scoticus*, pls. 81, 82, and the gardens and avenues shown in the survey plans of 1718 and 1759, SRO RHP 9520, 9521. Unlike Chatelherault, it was axially linked with the gates to the Palace rather than the building itself. Only fragments of the house and avenue exist today.

97. I. Lettice *Letters on a Tour* (London 1794) p.54.

98. This naturalism may have been accentuated when Alexander Nasmyth

'from the central window of the gallery . . . an opportunity of viewing, and, it will be supposed, to the best advantage the castle of Chatelherault, with its towers and pavilions, built of reddish stone, and placed on high ground about a mile distant from our station' (Plate 21).[97] But to its rear, and at the side of the extreme pavilion (which contained the ducal dining room), was an entirely different landscape, as wild and enclosed as the other was formal and expansive. Chatelherault stood here on the brink of a steep ravine and looked over a tumbling river and the park stocked with wild white cattle to the ruined castle of Cadzow (Plate 22). Neither the Duke nor Adam interfered with this piece of the sublime: in planting along the riverside they carefully followed its contours and left the new woods without either avenue or *allée*.[98] The experience for a visitor to Hamilton of walking up

was consulted at Hamilton, around 1800, possibly in the same capacity as he was employed at Dreghorn and Alva, see p.128. For this, see *James Nasmyth, Engineer*, ed. Samuel Smiles (London 1883) p.7. This was to some extent confirmed by Gilpin, who wrote in the 1808 edition of *Observations on the Highlands of Scotland* that 'I am informed

the park, the approach to the house, and the whole scenery around it, are entirely altered and improved, since these observations were made', that is in 1776 (ibid., vol.II, p.57). There was during the period 1779–87, a fair amount of new planting at Hamilton; see Hamilton Muniments, Lennoxlove, F.1./1014 and F.1/1043.

Plate 20. Chatelherault, from Hamilton Palace, Lanarkshire

the hill from the baroque palace below to this side of Chatelherault
must have been dramatic, for here, cheek by jowl, were the two
attitudes to gardening, each expressed in the most extreme manner.

Most Scottish ideas about the landscape garden before 1750 were
represented in 'The Country Seat' and more diffidently in the gardens
of William Adam. Neither theory nor practice showed more than
conventional talent and both relied strongly on the standards of English taste. The journeys to London of Clerk and Adam in the 1720s and
the dispatch there for approval of the latter's plans for Chatelherault
marked a familiar pattern. Nor did there seem to be in Scotland any
feeling for the rightness of a certain garden in a particular setting. At
Buchanan beside Loch Lomond, an old castle was given classical wings
and a setting manufactured out of a series of avenues: the same was
largely true at Taymouth Castle. But in the making of these formal
landscapes, William Adam was unfailingly sensitive to the genius of
the place and always prepared to humour rather than exile it. For this
reason the formal avenues at Hopetoun were to be closed by natural
features rather than by obelisks or temples and, in the same spirit, the
riverside walk at Taymouth was made to follow the lines of the river
rather than fit the geometry of the rest of the composition. But in many
such formal designs, especially on the larger estates, it was virtually

Plate 21. The former avenue, from Chatelherault to Hamilton Palace

impossible to exclude the rude magnificence of the surrounding scenery and in this the door was opened to the natural. That this was appreciated was clear from the attention given to the natural as much as to the landscape garden in Sir John Dalrymple's *Essay on Landscape Gardening*, of about 1756. In this respect, Dalrymple's extended essay was both remarkable and Scottish, and not surprisingly superseded 'The Country Seat' among the Enlightenment as completely as the gardens of Bowie and Robinson overhauled those of William Adam.

Plate 22. Aerial view of High Parks and ravine at Chatelherault, 1979

THE BEAUTIFUL

The informal garden in Scotland should have been more successful and idiosyncratic than its formal predecessor, for it exploited a less complex and demanding range of trees and shrubs and a landscape setting closer to the natural. Inherently Scottish trees, like the Scot's pine, the Dunkeld larch, the wych-elm, and shrubs like the rhododendron ponticum, or a plant like the heather (of which the finest 'heathery' was at Bothwell Castle in 1800), played an important rôle in the informal garden and more than compensated for the rare and exotic, which could never survive in Scotland outside a walled and sheltered garden. In addition, certain of these trees had often a historical or anecdotal value, which made them all the more precious and their landscape meaningful. While Renfrewshire seems to have been forested with Wallace's oak, more pertinently the Corstorphine sycamore was not only a distinct form of Edinburgh tree but had attached to it a macabre and memorable piece of local history.[1] Such trees – like the later Camperdown elm – strengthened the bond between landscape and history of the more romantic sort, and this was later and vividly displayed in Dick Lauder's edition of Gilpin's *Forest Scenery*. But against this, the new landscape gardens when they appeared in the 1750s were something of a disappointment. Initially confined to the lowlands of Scotland they seemed against expectation tame and anglicised. The work of Robert Robinson and the opaque James Robertson were little more than an extension of what they had practised in England and even a Scot like James Bowie offered perhaps an old fashioned reworking of Kent's ideas. More successful, but less demanding, were the associative gardens of the lawyer turned theorist Sir John Dalrymple, whose manuscript *Essay on Landscape Gardening* exhibited a precocious taste for the romantic at the expense of the beautiful.

Sir John Clerk's 'The Country Seat' represented the sophisticated taste of the late 1720s. Its green-fingered successor was Dalrymple's *Essay on Landscape Gardening*, which like 'The Country Seat' was known throughout the later eighteenth century in manuscript form. It

1. For an account of the tree and its history see G.U. Selway *A Mid-Lothian Village* (Edinburgh 1890) pp.6–8. According to Selway, Lord Forrester was murdered under the tree in 1674 by his sister-in-law. The tree, too, was supposed to have bright yellow rather than green leaves in the spring. For a general account of planting in Scotland and the trees used in the eighteenth century, see R.N. Millman *The Making of the Scottish Landscape* (London 1975) pp.141–50; and M.L. Anderson *A History of Scottish Forestry*, 2 vols. (Edinburgh 1967) vol.II, pp.4–52. A report on various trees and 'certain Exotic Plants, which have lately withstood the winter of North Britain; was contained in the work of the 'Committee for . . . Naturalization of Useful and Ornamental Plants', of 1814, printed in *Memoirs of the Caledonian Horticultural Society*, vol.II (1818) pp.355–430. This included notes on various forms of the camellia and magnolia, as well as a tree like the Tulip (Liriodendron tulipifera), which was at Dunkeld in 1755.

2. Significantly, the 1801 edition was tacked on to the end of Whately's *Observations on Modern Gardening*. The Memorandum to the Essay of 1823 stated that it was 'printed from the manuscript of John Dalrymple, Esq., author of an 'Essay towards a general history of Feudal Property in Great Britain'. It was procured from Mr Dalrymple for Mr Shenstone, through the medium of Mr Dodsley, about the year 1760; Mr Shenstone presented it to the Rev. Thomas Evans, afterwards Archdeacon of Worcester; and at the dispersion of the library of that gentlemen in 1815, it became the property of the Editor'. The editor was Bolton Corney, the antiquarian, who died in 1870. The manuscript was not among Corney's manuscripts in the British Museum nor is there another version of it among the Stair Mss. in the SRO. There is a copy among the Spence Papers at Yale, see *Select Letters*, ed. Thomas Hull, 2 vols,. (London 1778) vol.I, p.278, and note 10 below.

3. SRO GD 135/160 f.54. Dalrymple (1726–1810) was at Trinity Hall in 1746 before being admitted to the Scottish bar in 1748, see *DNB*. At this time he considered writing an Epic but never did (GD 135/137 f.13). *An Essay on Landscape Gardening* was instead the outcome of such literary interests. Charles Yorke, the future Lord Chancellor, was, like Dalrymple, interested in legal history, and landscaped the garden of his villa at Highgate in the 1760s, see *DNB*. It may well have been influenced by the receipt of the *Essay on Landscape Gardening* in September, 1760.

4. For Joseph Spence and his interest in gardening see Joseph Spence *Observations, Anecdotes and Characters of Books and Men*, ed. James M. Osborn, 2 vols. (Oxford 1966) vol.I, pp.405–22; vol.II, pp.645–52. The depth of Spence's practical commitment to gardening is fully apparent in his manuscript accounts of gardens and the changes he proposed, see Yale University Library, Spence Mss, Box VIII and IX.

was published anonymously in 1774 as *Essays on Different Natural Situations of Gardens*.[2] A youthful and important work, opinionated though pleasantly tolerant, it can be dated to the 1750s by its reference to contemporary landscape work at Inveraray. Dalrymple himself was never very precise about its birth. He told his fellow lawyer Charles Yorke in 1760 that his 'loose thoughts upon gardening', were thrown 'together at a time when I thought I had some chance of spending more time in England than I now have – upon reading it at the distance of some years I see many things to correct'.[3] This would suppose a time fairly close to 1750 itself, a date more or less confirmed by Joseph Spence, the gardening author of *Observations, Anecdotes, and Characters of Books and Men*, who had a copy of the manuscript before 1757; in gardening terms it would clearly precede Whately's *Observations on Modern Gardening*, which showed a similar interest in categorising landscape in type and scene.[4] In a philosophical chronology, Dalrymple would come before Lord Kames's *Elements of Criticism* of 1762, probably before Burke's *Inquiry into the Origin of our Ideas of the Sublime* of 1756, but possibly contemporary with Hogarth's *The Analysis of Beauty* of 1753. Certainly Dalrymple's practical turn of philosophising has more in common with Hogarth's common sense attitude to beauty and less with Burke's more windy reasoning. Yet it was probably David Hume's 'Of the standard of Taste', from his *Four Dissertations* of 1757, that had the greatest influence upon Dalrymple's gardening theories. He knew Hume, had himself been suggested in 1773 as the continuator for Hume's *History*, and wrote reflectively in 1799 that his thinking had been irrevocably shaped by his reading of Voltaire and Montesquieu, and 'I got nothing New except I found in the conversation of David Hume, Robertson, John Hume, Ferguson, Lord Kames, Sir James Stuart, Smith etc. until Ossian's works were published'.[5] Hume's notion of general standards of beauty as 'drawn from established models, and from the observation of what pleases or displeases', was the purpose of Dalrymple's series of garden categories.[6] His various models and their characteristics were intended as a yardstick with which to measure the natural garden, where one was intrinsically no better than the other. In casting his essay in this form, he was

5. SRO GD 135/148 f.6.

6. David Hume *Four Dissertations* (London 1757) p.218. For the relations between Hume and Dalrymple, never very cordial, see *The Letters of David*

Hume, ed. J.Y.T. Greig, 2 vols. (Oxford 1932). Hume unflatteringly referred to him in 1773 as 'The Knight has Spirit, but not style, and still less Judgement than the other [Macpherson of Ossian]' (ibid., vol.II, p.269).

following in Clerk's footsteps too, for 'The Country Seat' had dealt with its buildings and gardens as a series of architectural forms, appropriate more to the owner's situation in society than his house. This pragmatism was shared by both Dalrymple and Lord Kames to an extent that, like Price later on, they were used as practical guides to improvement.[7] Dalrymple was thought sufficiently important to be sent down to the leading exponent of the beautiful, the poet gardener William Shenstone at The Leasowes, and Kames's *Elements of Criticism* was admired for its author's 'beautiful and philosophical manner', and, more importantly for its arguments against the 'forcing nature in any respect'.

Sir John Dalrymple was, like Kames, a lawyer and improving landlord on his estates at Cranstoun and Oxenfoord. He was an enthusiastic supporter of the arts in Scotland, a patron of Robert Foulis and his Academy, an admirer of Ossian and Macpherson, whose travels he had helped to subsidise, and a long-standing friend of Robert Adam.[8] He was reasonably familiar with the early informal gardens in England, and had developed from them his own gardening essay. His attitude was that of a zealous convert seeking a landscape worthy of conversion. His parish was Scotland, and he described it in 1740 as 'uncultivated but romantick; perhaps not beautiful, yet grand Scenes', worthily and bewilderingly depicted by Ossian with the 'Majesty of Homer & the Tenderness of Sophocles'.[9] His landscape essay was to be the means to such ends and was viewed in this light by Joseph Spence, who wrote that 'improvements in the thought of Gardening are not confin'd to the Southern Part of this Island: it is got into Scotland too as will fully appear by a paper I have receiv'd from a Gentleman there'.[10] In it Dalrymple's gardens were arranged as four models, each inspiring different sentiments which might be roughly equated with the succeeding popular declensions of the sublime, the picturesque, the beautiful, and the dull. And although he appreciated that the 'different dispositions of grounds, distinct from each other', created 'distinct and separate sentiments', his divisions were neither artificial nor doctrinaire, and at the conclusion of his essay he gave warning against such hard and fast attitudes.[11] 'It is but seldom that a situation consistent with a single person's conveniency', he wrote, 'is so precisely and particularly marked as to suit only one of the four situations I have mentioned; on the contrary grounds generally consist of several of these situations, mixed and running into each other'.[12] His reasonableness was decisive and by 1764, he and Kames had created a taste for the natural style in the same way as Spence and Kent had done

7. In Edinburgh Samuel Bard wrote to his father at New York in 1764 recommending Kames 'to your perusal, especially that part of it relating to gardening and architecture, before you go on to improving your place on the north river' (J.B. Langstaff *Doctor Bard of Hyde Park* (New York 1942) p.61).

8. For his patronage of Foulis, see SRO GD 135/137 f.13. He particularly encouraged Foulis to publish his edition of the *Poems on Several Occasions* of William Hamilton. For his support and admiration of Macpherson, see GD 135/160 f.33 and f.56. Robert Adam he recommended to Yorke, as 'the most perfect taste in Architecture painting and gardening I ever knew joined in one man' (ibid., f.11). Dalrymple employed Adam to rebuild Oxenfoord, see p.110.

9. SRO GD 135/160 f.33 and f.44.

10. See Yale University Library, Spence Mss, Box VIII. Spence referred to Dalrymple as a 'very ingenious gentleman of Scotland' (ibid.). His general criticism of Dalrymple's *Essay on Landscape Gardening* was that it was 'a little too systematical', though it showed 'a great deal of taste and good sense in it' (ibid.).

11. Sir John Dalrymple *Essay on Landscape Gardening*, ed. Bolton Corney (Greenwich 1823) p.6.

12. ibid., p.21.

in England. In that year, an Edinburgh medical student wrote to his father in New York recommending Kames and observing 'from what (Gardens) I have as yet seen, I find those the most beautiful where nature is suffered to be our guide'.[13]

Three of Dalrymple's categories for the landscape garden were unremarkable and conventional: flat countryside, a landscape with gentle rise and falls, and the more rugged countryside, were all types of scenery that might be found almost anywhere. These he identified with certain human temperaments, the flat countryside attracting a person with little taste or feeling, the undulating landscape, which he associated with Kent's gardens, appealing to a cheerful temper, while the more romantic hills and valleys often drew the 'man in misfortune'.[14] His remaining situation was one that he particularly identified with Scotland and he described it as 'that of a highland country, consisting of great and steep mountains, rocks, lakes, impetuous rivers etc. Such a place is *Inverary*. The sentiment which a situation like this creates in the breast of a beholder is obviously, and every one feels it, that of grandeur.'[15] With increasing enthusiasm, Dalrymple sensed that this was the sort of landscape that might be sought out by the 'man who is fond of great projects, or great exploits; or who has a high regard for the splendor of his ancestors'. Possibly for this reason it appealed to the 'ancient nobility and gentry of *Wales* and *Scotland*' who, Dalrymple observed, were 'fond, beyond the rest of mankind, of their seats' in this setting.[16]

Dalrymple's most extreme contrast was between the self-consciously man-made and the natural, and this he saw as typical of the immense difference between the informal and the formal. The latter he made his fourth situation – the 'dead flat' – where nature demanded the 'assistance of art to make the chief parts of the garden'.[17] For this reason, he applied there all the trappings of the formal garden to the area immediately around the house where he wished to see '*bosquets*, statues, vases, trees cut into great arches, *jets d'eau*, cascades forced up and made to tumble down an hundred steps, regular basins, peristyles, temples, long vistas, the star plantation etc.'. The other extreme was his first situation, the highland country, where the emptiness of the landscape demanded some sign of human habitation and improvement but on a scale and in a style that accorded with the natural scene. In this his instructions were precise and obviously written with the success of Inveraray, rather than the over-improved 'naturalism' of Dunkeld, strongly lodged in his mind. He wrote of the ideal house that 'The principal should be in the form of a castle. The

13. Langstaff, op. cit., pp.57, 58. Bard also remarked that he would 'by no means follow the Dutch in laying thy Garden upon a Dead Plain', itself Dalrymple's category. He also disliked straight avenues, preferring 'serpentine walks are much more agreeable'. Bard also noted 'that a number of gentlemen here have formed themselves into an association for the importation of American seeds and plants, and would be much obliged to you to recommend a proper person as a correspondent' (ibid., p.58). This was described in the *Scots Magazine* of 1765 as successfully underway with the 'importation of foreign seeds from different parts of the globe, but chiefly from America. A subscription was made, and proper persons employed in different colonies' (ibid., p.395). For this society, see also Blanche Henrey *British Botanical and Horticultural Literature before* 1800, 3 vols. (London 1975) vol.II, pp.638–9. In 1765, *A Catalogue of Seeds from Canada*, was printed which listed 113 specimens (Yale University Library, Spence Mss, Box IX).

14. Dalrymple wrote of the undulating landscape, 'Perhaps instead of all other rules for such a situation, it would be enough to say that *Kent*, who beyond all others loved and made use of it, should be studied and followed'. Dalrymple admired his work at Chiswick and Stowe, but was more critical of his designs for Claremont and Esher (ibid., p.17).

15. ibid., p.6.

16. ibid., p. 7.

17. ibid., pp.7, 20.

elegance and fineness of execution belonging to *Grecian* architecture, would be here totally misplaced. If in that castle, added to the greatness and solid appearance of the main building, there should shoot up in the middle a *Gothic* tower, pierced and of hardy execution, a sentiment similar to the sentiment of terror . . . would still more correspond to the natural genius of the place.'[18] There can be little doubt that this hypothetical castle was Roger Morris's Inveraray (Plate 23). Dalrymple continued that around the highland castle the 'disposition of planting and water should correspond to the same greatness of matter and manner in the buildings'. He wished lakes rather than ponds and the 'rapidity and noise of rivers, should be increased by artificial bulwarks and impediments, as is done at *Inverary*; and the falls of water should, either by the interposition of rocks, or of new streams brought over them, be made to look more like cataracts than cascades'.[19] In the same broad manner, he wished the new plantations to 'cover the whole side and top of a mountain', and that these should be composed of 'great

18. ibid., p.8.

19. ibid., p.9.

20. This is shown very clearly in the survey plan of James Dorrett, made in 1758 (Blair Castle, Charter Room A.13). For alteration of the castle by Winter, see Colvin, op. cit., p.907.

21. For Morris's design see Charter Room D.12/2–5. His scheme is similar to that he was to produce for the hilltop of

Plate 23. View of castle and park, Inveraray, Argyllshire, *c.*1800

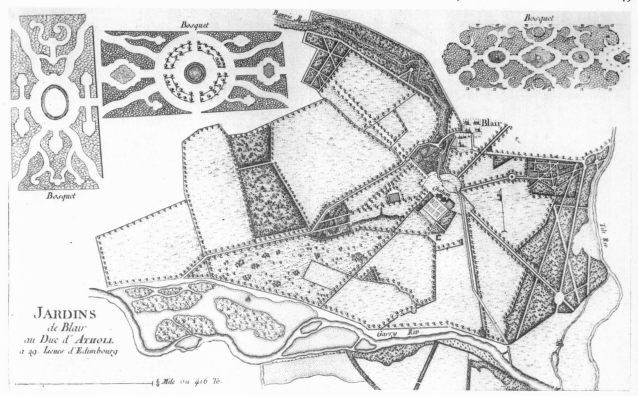

Plate 24. Plan of Blair Castle, Blair Atholl, from Le Rouge *Jardin Anglo-Chinois*, part II, 1766

Duniquoich at Inveraray. The Whim, still surviving, was the only Gothic monument set up at this time at Blair. Its origins lay in a battlemented wall with arch scribbled by the Duke on the list of things to be done at Blair in 1758 (Charter Room Box 40, IV.163). From this emerged the 'Ruin' of 1761 (Charter Room Box 40, IV.194). In 1757 the lawn around the castle was finished and the sunk fence was in the process of completion (ibid., 40, IV.158). In his description of Blair in 1757, the Duke wrote that the castle was surrounded with 'near 1000 acres of inclosed grounds most laid into grass' (ibid., 40, IV.157). It is worth noting that at Gordon Castle, the canal and basin remained until 1779.

forest trees; such of the exotic evergreens as will grow there', whose effect would add 'to the uncouth appearance of the place'; especially when 'they should all be planted irregularly'.

Only Inveraray could have provided Dalrymple with so exact and virtually unique an image. It had few rivals even in the Highlands, for a castle like Blair, situated deep in a mountainous landscape, had turned its back in the late 1740s on this particular category of Dalrymple's. Its remodelling by James Winter after its siege in the '45 rebellion had reduced it to a large and bleak country house, set in a park, which in the 1760s was still basically a formal one as Le Rouge's print showed (Plate 24).[20] Any feeling for the character of the place or its history came slowly. Roger Morris's imaginative design for a tower at Broomknowe above the castle in 1742 came to naught, and it was only in 1761 that the battlemented Whim was set up and the formal *bassin* in front of the

22. See Thomas Garnett *Observation on a Tour through the Highlands*, 2 vols. (London 1800) vol.II, p.46. Numerous sculpture pieces were set up in the 1750s including a winged figure with ball in 1757 (Charter Room Box 40, IV.137). Pennant noted the 'views in front of the house are planted with so much form, as to be far from pleasing', though he admired the picturesque walks beside the river Tilt (Pennant, op. cit., vol.III, p.59).

23. For the history of the castle and the laying out of the new town at Inveraray, see Ian Lindsay and Mary Cosh *Inveraray and the Dukes of Argyll* (Edinburgh 1973). By 1773 most of the old gardens near the castle had gone and a visitor wrote 'The gardens, too, must keep their distance. What have poor Flora and Pomona done to deserve banishment? As for the sheltering Dryads of antiquity, they are all marched off, for no reason that I can think of, but their being grown old maids' (Anne Grant *Letters from the Mountains*, ed. J.P. Grant, 2 vols. (London 1845) vol.I, p.19). However, it was not an entirely clean sweep, and at least three Portugal laurels (*Prunus lusitanica*) planted it was thought in 1695, remained until 1834 at least, see *Gardener's Magazine* XI (1835) p.178.

24. There is a Gothic design for the Mill at Carlundon, possibly by John Adam, of 1757 (Lindsay and Cosh, op. cit., p.130). The Carlundon, or Douglas Bridge, was built by William Douglas. It was a single span and executed in rough freestone, and corresponded to Dalrymple's ideal that a bridge in such a setting should be 'of one vast bold arch, instead of two or three elegant ones; and if it has one or two ornaments it should have no more' (Dalrymple, p.9). The garden bridge was built by John Adam and finished in 1761. It was intended to mark the head of the 'New intended deerpark', which ran up the glen to Carlundon (Lindsay and Cosh, op. cit., p.137).

25. ibid., p.134.

castle filled in and turned to lawn (Plate 25).[21] The sculpture, temples, columns, and obelisks remained, however, to amuse and impress the simple and to be viewed unfavourably by Garnett in 1798 and most other seekers of the picturesque.[22] They were just as dramatically out of step with Dalrymple's highland model, and suited perfectly his description of the quasi formal gardens of the fourth situation – the dead flat (Plate 1). This deepened the visual and intellectual gulf between the two castles, a gulf that was widened further when, as Blair shed its turrets and battlements, Inveraray was aggrandised in a castellated and highland style with a landscaped park that zealously matched most of Dalrymple's conditions.[23] Daniel Paterson's plan of castle and grounds in 1756 accurately recorded its setting at this time (Plate 26). His survey emphasised the river Aray as the principal feature, whose windings through the park sinuously linked the gothic mill and bridge at Carlundon, begun in 1751, with the Garden Bridge below and beside the castle.[24] Beneath the house where the Aray ran into the loch, its banks were canalised and made to flow over a series of shallow cascades formed by Walter Paterson, the Duke's gardener, in about 1756, and admired by Dalrymple a few years later.[25] To the west

Plate 25. The Whim in the park at Blair Castle

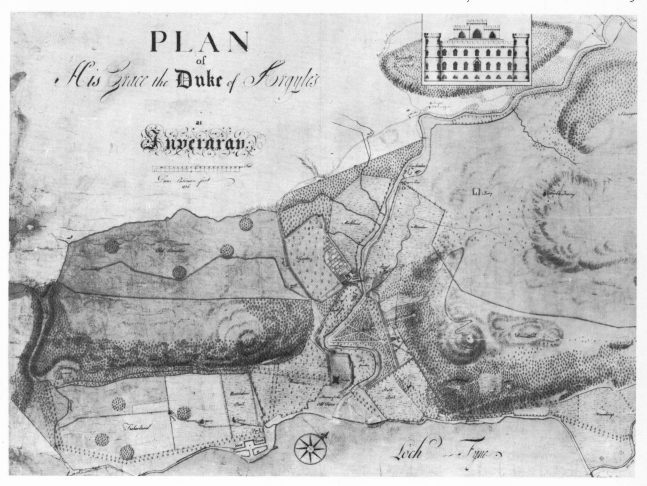

Plate 26. Inveraray, survey plan by Daniel Paterson, 1756

of the castle in the Wintertoun Park, the formal avenues of the old gardens survived in typically Scottish style, and this may have led Dalrymple cautiously to speculate that 'there is so much state in the approach to a great house by a great avenue, that we almost imagine a great avenue to be a necessary appendance to a *Gothic* house'.[26] More direct was Dalrymple's admiration of Roger Morris's lookout tower, of 1748, which he identified as the 'castle on the top of *Dunequeck*' and regarded as having ' a much finer effect than that of a ruin in such a place could have had' (Plate 27).[27] In thinking this way, Dalrymple was perhaps showing his age, for however much he admired the highland situation, its emptiness worried him as much as it had done Sir John Clerk. He preferred the castle's bustle and noise to the desolation and silence of the ruin. As he wrote, 'it has too much the appearance of dead life: that appearance, added to the vastness of the objects, creates . . . despair in the mind, which considers itself as nothing amidst that stupendous and solitary scene it beholds'. Ruins, he thought, emphasised this emptiness and 'whatever buildings are erected should be in conspicuous places, to create a notion of life and populousness'.[28] The tower at Duniquoich, and even better Morris's pigeon house, helped to dispel the incipient melancholy of their Highland setting.[29]

Dalrymple was not alone in allowing the improvements made at Inveraray to catch his imagination, although he was the earliest and most important. Aesthetically and economically, it seemed to have encouraged other landlords of similar and more inhospitable terrain to plant, landscape, and occasionally build castle-style houses. Its most obvious imitator was the sister and rival Campbell house of Taymouth, where the park formed by William Adam in the 1720s was thought thirty years later to be old fashioned and lacking in informality, possibly in the light of Dalrymple's theoretical categorising. Perhaps for this reason, the Earl commissioned around 1757 a pair of views of the castle from either side of the river of which that looking southwards is reproduced here on Plate 28. According to the agricultural improver William Marshall, who was consulted about Taymouth in 1793, the grounds that he saw led him to believe that they had been formed around 1750. Certainly they matched the descriptions given in the 1760s by Bishop Pococke and the poet Thomas Gray.[30] What was significant in both Pococke's and Gray's accounts, and to some extent in Marshall's, was the informality of much of the landscape and especially the absence of the various parterres beside the castle – so much so that Pococke referred to their former site as 'a fine lawn of uneven ground adorned with single trees'. All of them, however, praised the

26. Dalrymple, p.10.

27. ibid., p.11. The tower at Duniquoich was begun in 1748 and finished shortly afterwards (Lindsay and Cosh, op. cit., p.127). Nasmyth, according to Loudon, produced a scheme for fortifying it with 'ramparts and bastion', which reflected a complete and surprising lack of understanding of the building's stark rôle in the landscape; see Loudon *Encyclopaedia of Gardening* (1824) p.1093. Nasmyth was at Inveraray around 1800; see Lindsay and Cosh, op. cit., p.254.

28. Dalrymple, p.11.

29. The pigeon house was built in 1747 by William Douglas. Harled and painted white, it 'created a notion of life and populousness' sought by Dalrymple, p.11.

Plate 27. Roger Morris's tower at Duniquoich, Inveraray

river avenues, Pococke describing the bank nearest the castle as 'a fine walk of lime trees of great size', and on the other side as having 'a beautiful broad walk, with a fine summer house at the west end and an open Cross house at the other'.[31] Gray was more impressed by the mountain terrace behind the castle – The Surprise – that ran parallel but above those of the river (Plate 28). He wrote that, 'on the mountain's side runs a terrass a mile & 1/2 long . . . from several seats & temples perch'd on particular rocky eminences you command the Lake for many miles in length, wch turns like some huge river, & loses itself among the mountains, that surround it'.[32] Disappointingly, Pococke made no real criticism of what he saw, and acted throughout his tour as a sort of eighteenth-century camera, recording without comment. Gray was more critical. He concluded his description of the grounds in 1765 with the sarcastic judgement that: 'of the Earl's taste I have not much more to say. it is one of those noble situations, that Man can not spoil: it is however certain, that he has built an inn & a town just where his principal walks should have been, & in the most wonderful spot of ground, that perhaps belongs to him'.[33] No doubt it was true, but both Pococke and Gray underestimated the act of faith and imagination,

30. See Pococke, op. cit., p.235, and *The Correspondence of Thomas Gray*, ed. P.J. Toynbee and L. Whibley, 3 vols. (Oxford 1971) vol.II, p.893.

31. Pococke, op. cit., p.235. The 'open Cross house' was presumably Maxwell's building which appeared some time after 1754. It is shown in a view of the house of that time and in Langland's 1786 survey of the park as a pedimented building of three bays (SRO RHP 961/2).

32. *Correspondence of Thomas Gray*, p.893.

33. ibid.

Plate 28. Birdseye view of Taymouth Castle, Perthshire, *c*.1757

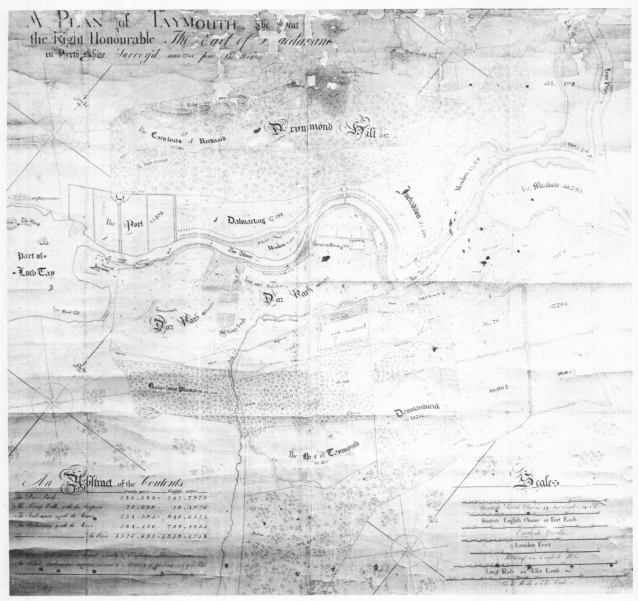

Plate 29. Taymouth, survey plan by Thomas Winter, 1754

limited though they may have been, needed to make a garden on this scale in the first place. Much of what they saw in the early 1760s survived until 1786 at least, when George Langlands made his survey of that part of the Taymouth estate. But the writing for this style of garden was already on the wall, and in 1776 the connoisseur of the picturesque William Gilpin had proscribed the whole scene with the damning sentence 'capable of great improvement: but when he saw it, nothing like taste had been exercised on it'.[34]

The river terraces were either planted or incorporated by William

Plate 30. Aerial view of the park at Taymouth, 1979

35. SRO RHP 961/3. This was shown in Roy's survey and marked by Winter as 'The Surprise'. It ran parallel to the Taymouth burn at the east side of the river between the Fairy Temple, later Apollo's Temple, and that of Aeolus. Apollo's Temple was in ruin late in the nineteenth century, when the metal cast of the god, which surmounted the building, was 'lying at the base with dismembered limbs' (Christie, op. cit., p.22). The Surprise adjoined a further Nutting walk, planted around 1762 with larch that survived until a gale destroyed them in 1829 (ibid.).

36. Gilpin *Highlands*, vol.I, p.158.

37. Dalrymple, op. cit., p.14.

38. ibid.

39. ibid., p.15, see William Marshall *Planting and Rural Ornament*, 2 vols. (London 1796) vol.I, p.392.

40. ibid., p.14.

41. Pococke, op. cit., p.235. This building may be the forerunner of the fort built by Paterson in 1765 above The Surprise; see GD 122/21/80 Accounts 1762–70, and 1764–70. The architect, John Paterson, was later called in to rebuild the castle in 1801. The building Pococke described was not shown in Winter's survey of 1754, though it does mark the tower, which he described as a 'round tower, the walls of which are about three feet thick, and the room 18 in Diameter, and there is a way up to the leads, the top being finished with Battlements' (Pococke, op. cit., p.236). This was marked in Langlands plan of 1786. Apart from those two buildings all the rest were classical of sorts, excepting the Chinese bridge described by Robert Heron *Observations made in a Journey through the Western Counties of Scotland*, 2 vols. (Perth 1799) vol.I, p.249.

Adam into his design of 1720. The upper terrace on the mountainside, which Gray so admired, was shown in Roy's map of about 1747 and was in existence when the gardener-surveyor Thomas Winter made his plan of Taymouth in 1754 (Plate 29; cf Plate 30).[35] A little later, the second panoramic view of Taymouth was painted showing the terraces, the Surprise Walk, and a bewildering number of temples, to which Gilpin later took exception as being tawdry and inelegant.[36] Both river terraces relied for their effect on the serpentining of the Tay, the wide views down the Loch to Killin, and the steep perspective formed by the surrounding mountains. The atmosphere of this sylvan Gaeldom was close to what Dalrymple called his 'Second Situation' where 'the sentiment to be created by it, is that of composure of mind, and perhaps even of melancholy'.[37] He contrasted this with the highland scene of Inveraray, and thought that 'in a romantic retired situation, the parts not being so great, there is no disproportion betwixt it and the single inhabitant'.[38] In such a landscape, he sought a more formal planting where the trees formed the occasional straight walk whose 'dimness and length, composes the mind at once to meditations'. Essential to this mood was the river: 'to these solemn walks the river should be made to contribute a solemn silence. For this reason it should be protected from the winds, all obstructions should be removed from the course of its current, and it should be deepened, and made to run more smoothly than it is naturally inclined to do. It should be made to lose itself at the end in a thick wood: the fancy naturally pierces into these recesses, and follows the river with awe in its unknown course. For the same reason, this silent river should be shaded with trees hanging over it.' Dalrymple also approved of the plethora of temples that were scattered the length of these terraces and which Marshall, tongue in cheek, later claimed were essential in the uncertain Scottish climate.[39] In the ideal highland situation, Dalrymple felt such buildings were desirable, 'to call the mind to life and motion; but in this romantic situation on the contrary, it is proper, in order to compose the mind, to remove it in a good measure from both'.[40] To this end, he suggested that 'views of ruins are much more proper for this situation, than those of houses intended for use'. He also stipulated the gothic style for them, and similarly advised their execution in 'stone of a dark colour, or brick'. None of the temples and pavilions at Taymouth matched closely this ruined or gothic quality, except perhaps the anachronistic fort on the mountain terrace, which Pococke described as 'a fortification designed as an object for prospect', and which may have been rebuilt by John Baxter in 1770.[41]

Like many features in the Scottish landscape garden, these terraces were a naturalisation of the more malleable elements of the formal garden. Much the same had happened to the riverside gardens at Dunkeld where the walk along the river, shown stiffly in William Clark's plan of 1748, had a decade later become naturalised enough to link harmoniously a series of simple, rock grottoes and small cascades, and catch the sharp eye of the artist John Claude Nattes (Plates 31 and 32).[42] But Taymouth was bigger and better, and with the hillside Surprise Walk an unexpected and contrasting element was introduced among the natural and luxuriant beechwoods. The Surprise provided a viewing platform looking down to the castle and deerpark, and scanning westwards along the loch and to the river in the east, in the manner of the Rievaulx Terraces at Duncombe Park in Yorkshire or those at Muncaster Castle.[43] To create this wide view, Winter's plan of 1754 suggested the removal of the 'highway' to its present position, higher up Drumandurick and behind The Surprise, and so integrating park with walk as a private Arcady.[44] It was, moreover, only part of the general activity at Taymouth during the fifties and sixties that marked the decisive transition to an informal landscape.[45] But the pursuit of naturalism cannot have got out of hand for Breadalbane's taste while open was also cautious. The various temples scattered down the walks and marking the terminations of vistas remained and were perhaps added to, the lead statues of Mars and Venus were set up as late as 1764, the menagerie of Guinea fowl and Muscovy ducks maintained, and the terraces themselves cannot have varied too greatly from those conventionally described in Switzer's *Ichnographia Rustica*, of 1718.[46] Only in the scale of the magnificent and natural sweeps of the wooded Tay at this point did these terraces evoke the rival informality of the Rievaulx Terraces at Duncombe. As the professional improver William Marshall wrote in his *Planting and Rural Ornament* of 1796, the curving riverside avenues of limes near the castle had a 'licence' which 'a century ago, must have been audaciously heretical'.[47] For all this,

42. Clark's plan of 1748 is at Blair Castle, Charter Room, B.13, The Hermitage, 1757, the Chinese temple, 1753, the thatched Swan House, 1755, were all part of the naturalising of the river landscape (Charter Room, Box 40, II.27/31, Box 40, IV.1/82, 97). Pococke gave a lengthy description of the garden as it was in 1760, Pococke op. cit., pp.229–31, and Nattes views were made in 1799 (NLS 5204 f.9). For Nattes, see Martin Hardie *Water-colour Painting in Britain*, 3 vols. (London 1967) vol.II, p.133.

43. For Winter's career as a landscape gardener see App. III. For an account of the terraces at Duncombe Park, see Christopher Hussey *English Gardens and Landscapes* (London 1967) pp.140–6.

44. See SRO RHP 581/3. The position of the old road is shown in the view of *c*.1733, see p.33, pl.16. In Winter's plan the old highway was given a lodge at its eastern end and converted more or less into an estate road. The new public road was above The Surprise Walk and just beyond the fort. This situation prevailed during Pococke's visit in 1760, and he described how he crossed the estate road and went uphill to The Surprise, which he thought had 'the most retired and quiet look that I ever saw' (Pococke, op. cit., p.236).

45. Payment to Stewart, the Earl's gardener and his workmen was running at about £116 per year at that time. Stewart's own salary seems to have been about 27 or 28 per year, see SRO GD 112/21/80, Accounts 1762–70. The end of this period was perhaps celebrated by a series of landscapes executed by James Stuart who appeared at Taymouth in 1765 when he was engaged 'for copying two landscapes of views at Taymouth', for five guineas. According to Gough, 'Mr. Stuart exhibited at Spring-gardens, 1765, three paintings of the cascade at the Earl of Breadalbane's seat at Teymouth, the Duke of Athol's seat at Dunkeld from the E. and the cathedral of Dunkeld. In 1767, part of a lake of 8,000 acres belonging to the earl of Breadalbane, and a waterfall fifty feet high, seen from the hermitage in the duke of Athol's gardens at Dunkeld' (Richard Gough *Anecdotes of British Topography* (London 1768) p.651). By 1769, he appears to have become some sort of artistic mentor to Lord Breadalbane and bought pictures on his behalf including 'Ruins & figures by Both' for £5.15.6. The 3rd Earl of Breadalbane was interested in the landscape movement. On his travels to and from London, he visited gardens and collected plants, saw Strawberry Hill in 1765, and in October, 1763, commissioned from 'Norie a Painter for two Views of cascades at Breadalbane' for seven pounds (ibid.). This was probably Thomas or John Norie, both Scottish decorative artists.

46. Switzer listed four types of terrace of which that 'cut out of a large hill' came near The Surprise at Taymouth (Switzer, op. cit., vol.II, pp.154–9, pl.26). Nearest to the river terraces was his idea of a canal walk which he claimed was 'the beautifullest of all fences' (ibid., p.165). According to Batty Langley *New Principals of Gardening* (London 1728) statues of Mars and Venus were intended for open lawns and large centres (ibid., p.20). It is probable that these statues were set up in the area west of the castle and beside the river. The animals at Taymouth seem to have been a conventional taste: they were pheasants, doves and turtles, at Dunkeld, and swans and wild duck at Blair Atholl, see Pococke, op. cit., pp.227, 230; and SRO GD 112/21/80, Accounts 1762–70.

47. Marshall, op. cit., vol.I, p.388. Marshall attributed the then existing gardens to the 'late Earl', which would be the 3rd who succeeded in 1752 and died in 1782. He remarked on the 'superior talents' the grounds revealed, 'considering the day in which they were done (near half a century ago in the early dawn of rational improvement)' (ibid., p.389). Marshall also seems to have known that there had been a 'sumptuous garden stretched out in straight lines, from the front of the house' (ibid., p.388). If this was the case, then it was a modified version of the gardens shown in the 1720 plan, which had vanished by 1754.

Plate 31. Dunkeld, Perthshire: 'Ferry from the Cascade' by J.C. Nattes

48. ibid., vol.I, p.393. This suggestion was given earlier in 1779 by John Clerk of Eldin who wrote that the walks were 'so close shut up that you do not see the fine river nor even ye Lofty plantation upon the Hills' (SRO GD 18/2118). Marshall also suggested more radical improvements which included enlarging the house which was put into effect with Paterson as architect. The house was rebuilt again by the brothers Elliot between 1806 and 1812, and work carried out on making new east and west approaches, and forming the lawn between the castle and river; see SRO GD 112/12 Box 1, and 112/74/20. For a while in 1804, Lord Breadalbane considered rebuilding the castle on the site of the Venus Temple, see James Macaulay *The Gothic Revival, 1745–1845* (Glasgow 1975) p.195.

49. Loudon *Country Residences*, vol.II, p.590.

50. *The Letters of Sir Walter Scott, 1817–1819*, ed. H.J.C. Grierson, vol.5 (London 1933) p.302. Around this time, further parts of the eighteenth-century gardens were destroyed. In 1830, the Temple of Venus was replaced by a dairy, and the Octagon (or Mary's temple) removed in 1836. The porter's lodge on the north side of the river and beside the bridge was demolished around 1799, and the Star Seat, east of the Castle of Inchadney, replaced by the Battery in 1829 (Christie, op. cit., pp.22, 23). A view of the latter in action was painted by Octavius Hill before 1840 as 'Feu de Joie', see Lot 356, Sotheby's, Gleneagles, August, 1976.

Marshall still proposed in his improvements of 1793, the clumping of these terraces by a series of openings cut through the beeches and limes 'so as to give additional feature to the views from the house and, at the same time, to disclose the house to the walks, in the best point of view; as well as to display the beauties of the terraces to each other. But most of all, to sever these screens, in such parts, as command picturable composition: and this most especially where the river, or the lake, forms a middle ground to mountain distances.'[48] There was apparently enough of this done to alarm the champion of formality and, when it suited him, preservationist Loudon, and cause him to protest in his *Country Residences* that the lime avenues 'ought to be carefully preserved'.[49] It was in vain, for though the river avenues survived as Marshall's clumps, by 1819 the lime avenue between the castle and the river had gone, 'cut down by the present Lady Breadalbane'.[50] What might have been done to avoid either Marshall's openings or Lady Breadalbane's wholesale destruction was later suggested by Sir Thomas Dick Lauder. With the true spirit of the picturesque, he recommended that 'where pleasure walks have been so confined by trees, that the romantic river, or the wide spread landscape has been hidden from view, instead of cutting open a formal breach in the wood,

Plate 32. Rock grotto at Dunkeld House

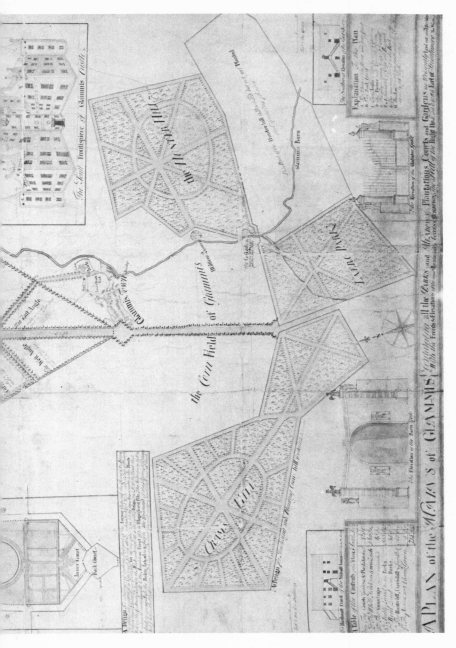

Plate 33. Glamis Castle, Angus, improvement plan by Thomas Winter, 1746

51. See William Gilpin *Forest Scenery*, ed. Thomas Dick Lauder, 2 vols. (Edinburgh 1834) vol.I, p.51.

52. For a short account of Winter's career, see Ian H. Adams 'The Land Surveyor and the Scottish Rural Landscape' *Scottish Geographical Magazine*, vol.84 (1968) p.250; and for his work at Monymusk, see Monymusk Papers, *Scottish History Society*, ed. Henry Hamilton (1945) pp.100–18. So extensive were the plantations at Monymusk, that Lady Grant complained in 1770 that 'she thought Planting was his Folly, and that people ought to take care, lest their concern for Posterity should hurt themselves' (*The Letters of David Hume*, vol.II, p.226).

53. For Glamis see pp. 133–7. At Castle Grant his work was concerned with the formal gardens beside the castle and planting on the estate generally. In the policies he formed a beech avenue probably to the home farm, and at Dun Brae above the castle a 'row of a lesser size (beech) and ash alternatively' (SRO GD 248/171/2). For his design for Easter Moy for Major George Grant, see SRO RHP 9018. This drawing was the companion to a survey plan made of the place in the same year, RHP 9017. In 1747, Winter also appears to have been working for an unidentified 'Sir Robert' as well as for Sir Henry Innes, at Innes, near Elgin (SRO GD 248/173/2). Innes was a relation of the Grants of Castle Grant by marriage.

54. For Taylor's plan for Kilravock Castle, see SRO RHP 30778. It was unexecuted. Like Winter's design for Glamis, this carried a lengthy explanation of his scheme, which laboriously pointed out that his proposed wilderness would give 'severall views, pointing on remarkable places, for terminations, some of them verie extensive', and which would open up 'a large country to the eye, besides verietys walles, cut out, especially solitary walks, which is veried and

resembling the port hole in a ship's side, or an embrasure in a wall, we have often found the advantage of leaving trees most fit for our purpose, and breaking it rudely down with the hatchet into a picturesque form'.[51]

Between William Adam's departure and the compilation of William Marshall's list of improvements, no gardener of any importance seems to have been associated with Taymouth. The exception was possibly Thomas Winter, although his role was an ambiguous if not ambivalent one. As a surveyor turned gardener, his plan of 1754 may have been as much a record of what was there as his suggested improvement. Before 1746 he was essentially a surveyor, having come from Norfolk twenty years earlier to work for Sir Archibald Grant at Monymusk.[52] Then he branched out on his own and in 1746 made an improvement plan for Glamis (Plate 33), and in 1747 and 1748 smaller garden plans for Easter Moy and Castle Grant.[53] In all of these he showed a conservative taste, respectful of precedent and the past, enviable virtues but hardly uncommon ones at this time and apparent in the 1756 scheme for Kilravock, Nairn, by another highland gardener William Taylor.[54] But Winter's Taymouth drawing was outstanding in its careful, almost graded, informality, conditioned as much by the physical past as by the designer's respect. Such sensitivity had been characteristic of his scheme for Glamis, where he expressed in his commentary an exemplary appreciation of its unfashionable architectural gardens and a tactful concern to improve their setting. He worried over the main approach from the Gladiator Gate to the castle, and wrote that 'altho att present it is Very Great Being above Ten hundred feet Wide and a Strip of Planting of the same Breadth on Each Side. Yet in my opinion, it is not by far answerable to the House but on the contrary Eclipses it Much'; and so on in the same vein.[55] To remedy this, Winter put forward an abortive design of his own for the castle's foreground to be enlivened and dominated by a circular basin, lavishly

delightful, to a thought full, virtuous mind' (ibid). Taylor flourished from about 1756 to 1779, see RHP 31 and RHP 2741/1 and 2; and Ian H. Adams *Descriptive List of Plans in the Scottish Record Office*, 3 vols. (Edinburgh 1970) vol.II, p.viii.

55. See SRO RHP 6493; the original is in the Charter Room at Glamis. At this time, a series of plans and elevations of

the castle were made by Lieutenant Elphinstone for the Duke of Cumberland, presumably with the idea of fortifying it for the future (British Museum, King's Maps, XL1XA2). At this time, too, Sandby made his idealised drawing of the castle which was later published. There was a further scheme for Gothicising the castle in 1763 that was not, apparently, executed (Glamis Charter Room plan).

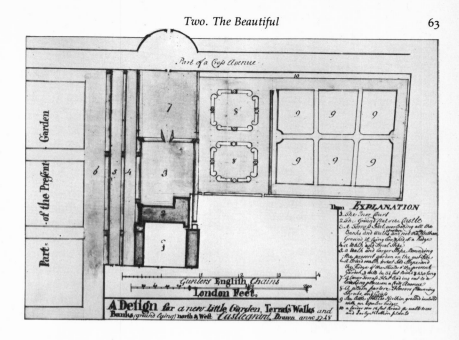

Plate 34. Castle Grant, Morayshire, design for formal garden by Thomas Winter, 1748

56. See John James, op. cit., p.217 and pl.L, fig.1. None of this was executed as Thomas Gray's visit to the castle in 1765 made clear. Gray wrote that he approached the castle along a 'double & triple avenue of Scots firs 60 or 70 feet high under three gateways' (*Correspondence of Thomas Gray*, vol.II, p.888). This was repeated in Pococke's account of the castle, who compared the avenues with those in St James's Park, London (Pococke, op. cit., p.218).

57. SRO GD 248/173/2.

58. ibid. A similar sort of garden was proposed about this time for the Earl of Fife's Rothiemay in Banffshire. There an annotated design for the wilderness, beside the bowling green, showed it planted entirely with fruit trees, some 228 of them, and with gooseberry and currant bushes (SRO RHP 31, 455).

59. SRO GD 248/173/2.

fed by four others, which together might balance the architectural grandeur of the building. This proposal was in line with the plain cascade illustrated in James's *The Theory and Practice of Gardening*, and caught admirably, perhaps intentionally, the old fashioned and fantastical air of the castle.[56] Yet his approach to design was practical, almost naive and he was always ready to sacrifice the conventions of style to the more prosaic demands of good gardening. From this standpoint he wrote to Sir James Grant in 1748, describing and enclosing a design for a more or less formal garden at Castle Grant, which was to be constructed as a series of embankments with a flat terrace 'overlooking all the Banks and Walks and parterre and not the new Kitchen Ground', all set out according to the English fashion in 'London Feet or Gunter's English Chains' (Plate 34).[57] Typically, he added 'I know that the People of Modern Tast will be Ready to Object that it is to near the House to have any Kitchen Ground', and so he proposed to disguise it with a practical and apposite 'Espalier Hedge'.[58] The same sincere humility was apparent in his request for paper and colours for any further surveys, and his apology that his garden plan would have been drawn 'Larger and more Elaboratly. But that it was to come by Post'.[59] This very attitude marked him out as one of the last of his sort to gain high patronage. The future belonged instead to a more ambitious kind, sophisticated, argumentative, less practical, rarely pedestrian, who were never committed to a family or particular area as Winter had been.

With the exception of his putative work at Taymouth, Winter had shown, like his Highland patrons, a wariness of the new landscape taste – the Scottish *furor hortensis*. This was not true in the southern half of the country where the Enlightenment of Edinburgh had embraced it as appropriate to the culture of North Britain. No doubt the less spectacular beauties of the Lothians and east coast encouraged such an experiment, for they were often topographically close to their models in the English countryside. Not altogether surprisingly, it was here that perhaps the first two landscape gardens in Scotland appeared, at Alderston near Haddington, and at North Merchiston on the edge of Edinburgh. John Adam, the eldest son of William, remodelled about 1755 his father's garden at the latter after the fashion of Shenstone's The Leasowes, and a few years earlier Sir Thomas Hay had employed 'Mr. Bowie', probably James, to cast his garden at Alderston 'in a natural way'.[60] While John Adam was his own master, Bowie was a professional gardener with a nursery at Stoneyhill, near Musselburgh, and a practice which extended across the border as far as Yorkshire. His style was Kentian, and the less adventurous of Dalrymple's models: his ideas advanced compared with William Adam, less so with John. This was certainly Sir Thomas Hay's view, for he excluded William Adam (and his work at Arniston which he would have known at first hand) when in 1752 he pressed Bowie's claims, as the 'only person that I have met with in this part of the world that has a good fancy in laying out ground in a natural way', upon his kinsman and

60. For Adam's work at North Merchiston and its relationship with William Shenstone's The Leasowes, see pp.95ff.; for Hay's patronage of Bowie see NLS Acc. 4862/Box 98/F.1. The identification of Bowie with Stoneyhill was made in John A. Inglis *The Family of Inglis of Auchendinny and Redhall* (Edinburgh 1914) p.93. In an advert that appeared in the *Edinburgh Evening Courant* for 1757, William Bowie advertised as a 'Nursery and Seedsman at Stoneyhill'.

61. NLS Acc. 4862/Box 98/F1. Presumably Bowie must have performed successfully at Alderston which had led Hay to 'recommend him to your Lordship'. This would date his work there as before 1752. On Hay's death, Alderston became Smeaton Park, but reverted to its old name some time after 1788; see George Barclay 'An Account of the Parish of Haddington', *Archaeologia Scotica* (1792) vol.I, p.43. Hay must have had some real interest in gardening as his subscription to Boutcher's *Forest Trees* of 1775 indicated. Of the other houses in the area, Bowie may have been responsible for landscaping the park at New Mills (later Amisfield) built by Isaac Ware for the Charteris family. It was described in 1760 by Pococke as having avenues 'with a wood on each side, and the lawns with clumps and single trees. There is a bowling green and a summer house, and a fine walk by the river, and a most beautifull kitchen garden that way' (Pococke, op. cit., p.318). Only the summer house has survived; the kitchen garden was rebuilt in 1785.

62. NLS Acc. 4862/Box 98/F1. These are perhaps worth quoting in full: 'Remarks on the ground and River at Yester'. (1) On the hill before the house a few Trees to be taken out and a variety of Flowering Trees and shrubs planted to ornament it in a natural way with an easy walk up to the Top where is a proper place for a Bowling Green and a Gothick Temple. (2) An oblique View from the South and East front of the house. (3) In the park above the house a Convenient Place to make an irregular piece of water which would form a Cascade with a fall of 14 feet. (4) Another Cascade at the North East front of the house facing the walk from the Gates, the fall 12 feet. (5) The approach to the house to be inlarged and the road continued through the old orchard at the extent of which a Grand Gate with a fall of water on each side at a proper distance, the fall 7 feet. (6) A cascade where the mill race is now, fall 18 feet. (7) The ground by the sides of the chapel to be raised higher and planted with evergreens, the Chapel to remain and parted from the rest of the ground by a fence rudely formed, so that it may be of a piece with the antiquity of the place at present. (8) The arches which are already made to be faced over with large stones naturally disposed, the lower one to form a grotto, the upper one a rude Cavern. (9) The ground on the south front of the house to be concaved with some variety of Trees planted round.

Bowie, not unnaturally, had been most impressed by Yester, and according to Hay was 'vastly pleased with the house and ground about it and thinks your Lordship with no great expense might make it both Magnificent and pretty' (ibid.).

neighbour the Marquess of Tweeddale at Yester.[61] Bowie visited Yester twice, then sent in his plan accompanied by his written proposals, which alone survive in a summary by Sir Thomas Hay. There were nine points in this memorandum, which achieved a nice balance between the natural and the contrived.[62] Bowie first recommended that, 'on the hill before the house a few Trees to be taken out and a variety of Flowering Trees and shrubs planted to ornament it in a natural way with an easy walk up to the Top where is a proper place for a Bowling Green and Gothick Temple'; in his third, he advised 'an irregular piece of water' matched by 'a Cascade with a fall of 14 feet'.[63] More informed and closer to the Kentian style, was his idea of raising the ground on either side of the chapel, planting it with evergreens, and giving it a fence, 'rudely formed, so that it may be of a peice with the antiquity of the place at present', which was shown in Robertson's print of about 1790 (Plate 35).[64] Such ideas, Dalrymple would have associated with his third situation – that inspired by Kent.

In proposing this landscape for Yester, Bowie made only the occasional reference to the late seventeenth-century gardens that surrounded the house, rebuilt by William Adam and rapturously described by Boyse in his *Retirement: A Poem*. More prosaically and pictorially they are shown in de Witt's series of views of the 1690s (Plate 36). Bowie's approach road to the building was the existing one enlarged, and made to cut through 'the old orchard', with a 'Gate with a fall of water on each side' at its close.[65] More ambitiously, he intended to plant randomly the south prospect with a variety of trees, and no

63. ibid.

64. ibid. The surviving chapel was St Bathan's Collegiate Church, which lay a little beyond the house to the west. This was romantically described by Boyse in *Retirement: A Poem* as, 'An ancient chapel rears its spiry head/ Close by the margin of the winding flood' (*The Works of the English Poets* XIV, p.578). For the building history of Yester and its gardens see John Dunbar 'The Building of Yester House, 1670–1878', *Transaction of the East Lothian Antiquarian Society* XIII (1972) pp.20–39; see also *Country Life* (August 1973) pp.430–4.

65. NLS Acc. 4862/Box 98/F1. This can be seen in a view of the house from the north east by James de Witt of *c.*1695, formerly at Yester House. The former approach was also described by Boyse as 'with easy steps the avenue I gain / where, to the left, the brook its passage steals,/And in its rocky bed its stream conceals; /Now gently purling forms a soft cascade' (*The Works of the English Poets* XIV, p.579). Boyse's description, though fanciful in language, proves that the formal gardens existed almost intact until the middle 1730s.

Plate 35. View of Yester House and chapel, East Lothian, from an engraving by George Robertson, *c.*1790

Plate 36. The parterre at Yester, from a view by James de Witt, *c.*1695

Plate 37. Aerial view of Yester, showing approach from Gifford, 1979

doubt in the ensuing upheaval, whatever remained of the formal garden, its statuary and fountains passed into oblivion. It would certainly have happened sooner or later, and its disappearance had already been contemplated when John Adam completed his father's work on the house in 1751.[66] And although its removal was neither so sudden nor as dramatic as in some cases, it was nonetheless remarkably complete (Plate 37). So much so, that when the assiduous Pococke visited the house in 1760, he saw a landscaped park with only the odd cascade or shell grotto hinting at a less informal past.[67]

But Bowie must have had other successes elsewhere in southern Scotland, beyond Yester and his problematic association with Alderston. In 1758, he designed a classical, walled garden and possibly a series of riverside grottoes at Redhall in Edinburgh, and ten years later, his family reappeared at Bothwell House, Lanarkshire, where the gardens were being laid out between 1759 and 1782.[68] There a W, probably William, Bowie gave the Duke of Douglas an impressive but undated design for the kitchen garden, with the various hothouses and the gardener's house turned into an accomplished architectural composition, classical and casually battlemented, which was paralleled by similar work for the Earl Fife at Duff House in Banff.

This vast classical building had stood incomplete and abandoned since the lawsuits of the 1740s until the succession of a new Earl in

66. NLS Acc. 4862/Box 49F.1 and F.2. In 1751, John Adam had suggested a 'Temple in the island, with a Rail form'd in the Chinese manner for a bridge, or passage over the River, from the terrace to the temple' (ibid., F.2). His sketch, which was enclosed, has not survived. For John Adam's interest in gardening see Fleming, op. cit., p.363, and pp. 97ff. In 1760, Pococke saw Adam's temple and possibly Bowie's landscape, and gave the following description: 'the lawn behind the house is fine, with large trees interspersed, where the sheep feed, and there is a terrace round it; on one side is a hermitage and on another a summer house in a little island; beyond this is the park' (Pococke, op. cit., p.316).

67. ibid.

68. See Inglis, op. cit., p.93, and SRO RHP 7. Bowie was employed at Redhall by George Inglis, who paid him £229 for 'making a Garden for me at Redhall conform to a plan and Estimate to which my letter is subjoined (Inglis, op. cit., p.93). The garden was altered in 1831, when an ornamental railing and gate were inserted (ibid., p.191). A surviving survey of the mid-eighteenth century for the Damhead at Redhall may be connected with Bowie's grottoes; see SRO RHP 1759. RHP 7 for Bothwell House is signed W., presumably William Bowie. What relationship he had with James Bowie is not known and whether the Bowie consulted at Alderston and Yester was James not William is hard to say. On account of James's Edinburgh connection, he was the more likely. Neill wrote that the garden between the old castle and house was 'laid out in the late Duke of Douglas's time about 1759, but only finished in 1782' (Neill, op. cit., p.170). He referred of course to the walled gardens and hot houses rather than to the landscape. In 1759, the interior of Bothwell was remodelling and a colonnade being built 'to the intended Pavilion'; see Douglas Estate Office, Metal Box, Misc. Papers, 1462–1824. A plan of the policies at Bothwell of 1781 showed parkland through which ran a formal avenue; see SRO RHP 21956. The house was again totally rebuilt by James Playfair in 1789. In 1799 Stoddard referred to the old castle ruins as 'kept in a state of readiness', and Sismond referred to 'a good ruin but dressed rather too youthfully – taken from the bed of rubbish carefully dusted, scoured with soap suds and a brush, then placed on top of a bundle of neat turf, with a grand walk all around' (Louis Sismond *Journal of a Tour and Residence in Great Britain*, 2 vols. (Edinburgh 1815) vol.1, pp.282–3. Loudon illustrated in his *Encyclopaedia of Gardening* a wooden, roofed garden seat as typical of those at Bothwell; see ibid. (1834) p.617, fig.629. It is possible that Thomas White was also consulted at Bothwell.

69. According to William Adam's lawsuit with the then Lord Braco, in 1743, the 'Pursuer (Adam) also made a Plan of the Grounds about the new House, and a Burial-place, and of a Temple in an island of the *Divern* . . . which Temple was accordingly built' (*State of Process, William Adams . . . against William, Lord Braco* (1743) p.9). In Roy's map of 1746, Duff House was shown in an empty landscape, but by 1782 there was 'a fine shrubbery, not very broad but extending a mile and a half in length' established there; see Francis Douglas *A General Description of the East Coast of Scotland* (Paisley 1782) p.296. In 1763, Lord Fife built the bridge over the Deveron and the Eagle Gates, and contemplated building the missing wings at Duff, see Alistair and Henrietta Tayler *Lord Fife and his Factor* (London 1925) pp.17 and 23; and *Vitruvius Britannicus* (1771) vol.v, pls.58–60.

70. See SRO RHP 31,394. This plan is undated and without title and might be for any of the several properties owned

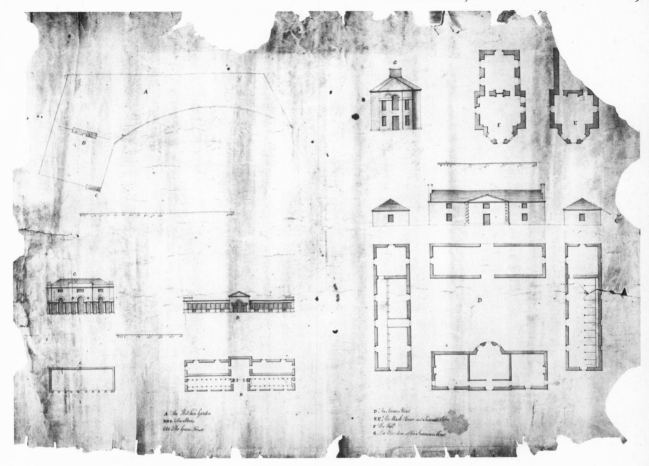

Plate 38. Designs for gardens and buildings at Duff House (?), Banffshire, by William Bowie, *c.*1750, showing 'G' the Summer House

by Lord Fife. However, the garden and offices do resemble those surviving at Duff, as does the temple the larger building of the plan. In 1767, William Reid wrote to Lord Fife saying that he had 'near finished the planting in most places at Duff House', with clumps and belts, and that the riverside walk was formed from the 'Bridge at Banff to the Bridge att Alva' (Aberdeen University Library, Ms.2226/275/6). The informal and eminently picturesque qualities of this walk certainly sustain Bowie's reputation in 'the natural way'.

1763.[69] To this new era belongs an undated sheet by Bowie of designs for temples, farm buildings, and a walled kitchen garden. The last corresponds fairly well with that surviving behind Duff House, which was planted with fruit trees from France in 1767—a reasonable date for Bowie's activities there. The square, classical temple marked as 'G. the Summer House' on the same drawing probably also exists as the derelict hillside building at the Alvah end of the park (Plates 38, 39). It was linked to the house in the 1760s by the largely surviving 'small walk made along the watter side', grander but probably similar in mood to Bowie's grottoes beside the river at Redhall (Plate 11).[70]

Although the landscape at Duff is now despoiled and in decay, Cordiner's pretty gouache of the 1770s admirably catches its contrived naturalism in a scene where Lord Fife's coach and six crosses the Alvah bridge with on one side a Gothic tower and on the other a small grotto and garden, before beginning its two mile descent to the house (Plate 40). Lord Fife hung this picture above the library fireplace at Rothiemay, another of his houses. The little that can be pieced together of Bowie's work here, together with his Redhall garden, and designs for Bothwell and Yester, add up to a fairly slim testimony for a gardener sufficiently renowned to share with William Adam the accolade of the pioneer of the natural way.

  In the next decade, that of the sixties, the two most distinguished landscape gardeners were James Robertson and Robert Robinson. Between them, they carved up the lowlands and the east coast of Scotland as far as Inverness in a series of tame gardens, most of which belonged to Dalrymple's third situation, 'that of a champaign rich country, full of gentle inequalities'.[71] For Dalrymple and probably for these two designers, the rules for such a situation were basically those devised by Kent, 'who beyond all others loved and made use of it', and who, he earnestly believed, 'should be studied and followed'.[72] This

71. Dalrymple, op. cit., p.19.

72. ibid.

Plate 39. Ruined temple at Duff House

was probably the way to assess the garden at Prestonfield House, near Edinburgh, where in 1764 Joseph Spence and the botanist William Walker seem to have collaborated in devising if not executing a new park for Sir Alexander Dick.[73] The tight little clumps that interested Spence there, 'grovettes' as he called them, survived into the 1860s. The landscape itself was described in Alexander Dick's doggerel of 1784 as begun in 'fifty-three' with 'The Brook taken in and a Fishpond extended/My Clear burn, fine stream, cascade, little grove,/And Orchard and Kitchen-ground which fertile prove/My fishpond completed, so well grac'd with the swans,/Concealing the bounds shows beyond all my plans/The view of Craigmillar surmounts all the rest'.[74] These and other remnants of Robertson and Robinson's work justify Dalrymple's contention that this type of garden was typically an English one. Although Robinson was prepared to get himself up as some horticultural Ossian in 'a highland dress with a large plaid of the same dimensions and form of Fingal's, and to crown the whole with a large Bonnet', while surveying in the Cairngorms, rarely did his landscapes match the sublimity of his mentor's poetic descriptions.[75] On the other

73. For Spence's involvement at Prestonfield, see Yale University Library, Spence Mss., Box IX. He may have been involved with other Scottish gardens, especially after his Scottish tour of 1760.

74. 'On Preston field and its Garden/A Song/1784' (SRO GD 331/16).

75. SRO GD 248/178/2.

Plate 40. Duff House: 'The Bridge of Alvah' by Charles Cordiner

76. Loudon *Encyclopaedia of Gardening*, p.82. Apart from his work at Duddingston, which is documented by both Loudon and Sir Walter Scott, there is no real evidence of Robertson's further career. Confusion was made by Loudon's mixing Robertson with Robinson in the note he gave of Duddingston in the 1822 edition of the *Encyclopaedia*; see ibid., p.1250. The account given of him in Steuart's *The Planter's Guide* of 1828 follows Loudon, and only adds that his Christian name was James; ibid., p.46. It is not entirely impossible that Robinson was in fact Robertson. Against this, there was a George Robertson who was alleged to have been his nephew and who worked at Bargany in Ayrshire, see pp. 167–71. Similarly, the tale that he left Scotland for Ireland may be borne out in Samuel Hayes *A Practical Treatise on Planting* (Dublin 1794) p.42. According to Hayes, Robertson introduced the planting machine into Ireland (ibid.) There is also an account of him as working at both Castletown and Carton, in County Kildare, in the *Transactions of the Royal Irish Academy*, but this was largely an embellishment of Hayes; see Edward Malins and Desmond Fitz-Gerald *Lost Demesnes, Irish Landscape Gardens 1660–1830* (London 1976) p.71.

77. Loudon *Encyclopaedia of Gardening*, p.82. He was probably well informed about Duddingston from his master John Mawer who had been 'formerly gardener and steward to the Earl of Abercorn'; see J.C. Loudon *Encyclopaedia of Agriculture*, 2 vols. (London 1831) vol.II, p.1179. Mawer died in 1800.

78. Richard Payne Knight *The Landscape* (London 1794) p.33.

hand, it seems likely that Robertson did not even try, and according to Loudon he scattered the lowlands at Livingston, Hopetoun, Dalkeith, Dalhousie, Niddry, The Whim, and Moredun, with better or worse imitations of his work at Duddingston House, Edinburgh, of about 1765.[76]

Loudon who had known Duddingston thirty years later in the 1790s, described it as a 'perfect specimen of Brown's manner', and by this he meant that there was little good that he could say about it.[77] The park contained nearly 200 acres and was isolated from the rest of the countryside – and any view of it – by continuous planting around its periphery (Plate 41). A stream was cut through its flattened surface and made to serve, according to Loudon, 'a string of wavy canals on different levels, joined by cascades'. Along its bank was placed a series of temples and seats, and it employed Knight's stock device of 'the thin, fragile bridge of the Chinese;/Light and fantastical, yet stiff and prim,/The child of barren fancy turn'd to whim'.[78] While the garden's importance as a pioneer with Yester cannot be overlooked, its fatal influence should not be forgotten.

Robertson's apparent refusal to come to terms with the landscape within which he worked seemed to have rankled in Scotland not long after Duddingston was finished. Sir Walter Scott, whose family were professionally connected with its owners, the Abercorns, reported a conversation that allegedly took place between Robertson and the then Earl of Abercorn. Robertson justified to his client the exclusion of both

Plate 41. Duddingston Park, Edinburgh, showing Chinese Bridge, from a print by R. Scott, *c.*1770

79. Scott unflatteringly described the park as 'A brook flowed through the grounds, which, by dint of successive dam-heads, was arrested in its progress, twisted into the links of a string of pork-sausages, flung over a stone embankment, and taught to stagnate in a lake with islets, and swans *quantum sufficit*' (Sir Walter Scott 'On Landscape Gardening' *Quarterly Review* vol.xxxvii (1828) p.316). Scott reported that 'some advantage might have been gained by looking out from some point of the grounds on Craigmillar Castle, a ruin beautiful in its form and interesting in its combinations with Scottish history; and the professor of landscape-gardening was asked, why so obvious a resource had not been made something of? He replied, with the gravity becoming such a character, that Craigmillar, seen over all the country, was a common prostitute'.

80. Ainslie's plan was redrawn in William Baird *Annals of Duddingston and Portobello* (Edinburgh 1898) p.89. After the death of the Earl of Abercorn in 1787, the garden seems to have been run down, with the Abercorn family living in England at Bentley Priory. According to Baird, statues were taken from the garden to be set up in the new bridge at Ayr in 1787; Baird, op. cit., p.87. A plan made in 1827 does, however, still show the principal aspects of the landscape (SRO RHP 10567).

81. Invercauld Mss, Plans. Invercauld in the eighteenth century was distinguished for its larch, and Loudon noted in his *Encyclopaedia* that it was 'famous for its pine-forests, the timber of which equals that of Norway' (ibid., p.1093); see also correspondence between Pennant and Dr Hunter, Invercauld, Box 21. Robinson made his plan of Careston for George Skene, see SRO RHP 31, 443. It developed the existing landscape with an old quarry forming his 'small sheet of water', the greatest change being the elimination of the southern avenue. For a survey of Careston in 1753, see RHP 31, 444. Much of Robinson's plan seems to have been

a view of Duddingston Loch and Craigmillar Castle with the condescending logic that they were too visible and therefore too common a sight.[79] Such a lack of imagination was fully apparent in Ainslie's survey plan of the estate, of 1770, where Robertson's cold-shouldering of what Scott clearly regarded as two parts of a historic landscape, emphasised an artificiality that Dalrymple identified with the '*English modern gardens*'.[80] For this reason it was both a mile- and grave-stone; for the same reason it was detested by Scott and Loudon as 'the model of all future improvements in Scotland till within the last twenty years'. Yet Robertson had to be given grudgingly his due and appeared as 'a man of considerable taste and acquirement' in the *Encyclopaedia of Gardening*.

At no time, however, did Robertson have undisputed control of the practice of landscape gardening in Scotland. Nor was he alone in claiming association with Capability Brown, for, in March 1760, Robert Robinson advertised in the *Caledonian Mercury* as the 'late Draughtsman and Executor of the Designs of Lancelot Brown, Esquire, who was prepared to undertake garden and policy designs'. Four years later, in January 1764, he placed a similar advertisement in the *Edinburgh Advertiser*. How necessary or successful these public solicitations were is hard to say. Certainly Robinson's first Scottish commissions, in 1761, followed the *Caledonian Mercury* advertisement and he seems by then to have been established in the north east, making a small improvement plan for Careston Castle, near Brechin, in that year and carrying out an unambitious survey for planting at Marlee on the Invercauld estate in Aberdeenshire.[81] They were hardly the stuff of a reputation, but were followed by more rewarding work, for Sir Alexander Ramsay, possibly at Fasque, at Pittencrieff near Dunfermline, at Monymusk and Crathes Castle, all in 1762, and two years later at Castle Grant, Banff Castle, and Glamis.[82] He was evidently sufficiently agreeable, and his work sufficiently satisfactory, to be rated at Monymusk as a

carried out as was shown by the 1863 Ordnance Survey. George Skene had a good local reputation as an improver and plantsman; see *New Statistical Account* (1845) vol.i, p.530.

82. SRO GD 248/178/2. In this letter of September 1762, Sir Archibald Grant of Monymusk wrote that payment of Robinson depended 'intirely upon the Time he consumes, and *the Nature* of the work he is Employed in; whether

Surveying, Planning or *Overseeing*; tho in some instances he has *Given in an Account* (as in Achoinany's case, where he got *Twenty Guineas*) in General he has *taken what was offered him*. Sir Alex. Ramsay gave him Twenty guineas; We the same; Capefield 12 *Guineas*, Pittencrief *ten*'. Capefield and Achoinany have not been identified. For Crathes see GD 248/178/2. He was at Banff Castle in May 1764 (GD 248/346/5). For Monymusk see GD 248/178/2.

Plate 42. Castle Grant, Morayshire, improvement plan by Robert Robinson, 1764

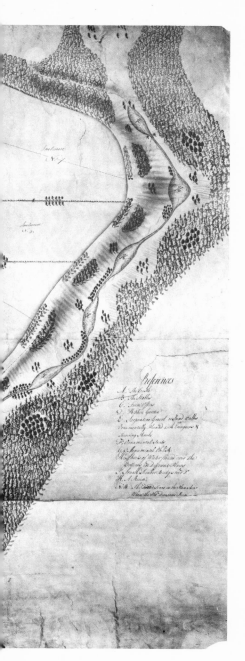

'Companion and Gentleman; is very Entertaining, and far from being forward . . . Is well accomplished and well bred'.[83] Lord Deskford at Banff wrote in much the same vein, 'what I have seen of this Man's doing, I have formed a good enough Opinion of his taste'.[84] It was only later that he was found by Sir Archibald Grant of Monymusk to be a 'Bad Economist and needy, and aimes chiefly at the next payment'. After the spate of commissions in the north east, his career as a gardener and his travels became more erratic. Though he was in the north at Cullen in 1766, it was shortly followed by Paxton in the Borders, then The Inch at Paisley in 1777, Balbirnie in Fife in 1779 and Archerfield, East Lothian, around the same time. In his designs for these properties, irrespective of geography, he seems to have stuck fairly closely to the formula of his rival at Duddingston, and rung all the familiar variations upon lake, clump and belt. But where possible, he does appear to have made some concession to a local if not Scottish spirit, and to have shown some sort of picturesque feeling in his proposals for the river valleys at both Glamis and Paxton. But these tended to be lucky accidents, or were suggested by the taste of the proprietor, rather than deliberate attempts to design in such a manner. In this way, and in most others, there was little stylistic variation between Robinson's work at Castle Grant in 1764 and at Balbirnie more than a decade later (Plates 42 and 44). The accepted convention of the improvement plan possibly exaggerated this sameness. The surviving portions of his landscapes at Paxton, and to a lesser extent Balbirnie, show a more richly picturesque taste than either of his plans suggested, and this may well have been true of other schemes (see Plate 46). Yet, a design such as he produced for Castle Grant seems a deliberate attempt to make an eye-catching pattern on paper (Plate 42).

At Castle Grant there was every reason for Robinson to produce more than a standard design. His client Sir James Grant had, like his contemporaries the Earl of Breadalbane and Duke of Argyll, a deep

---

83. SRO GD 248/178/2.

84. Deskford also noted that he 'calls himself Architect and layer out of Pleasure Grounds' (GD 248/346/5), and in the list of subscribers to Boutcher's *Forest Trees*, he was 'architect' only. He certainly preferred to be thought of as an architect, and he instructed that he was to be written to as such in Edinburgh.

For his architectural career, see Colvin, op. cit., pp.701–2. According to Lord Seafield, 'one Robinson, the brother to the man who surveyed your grounds at Castle Grant, is the person who works about the king in all the designs in architecture which the king invents or directs himself' (William Fraser *The Chiefs of Grant*, 3 vols. (Edinburgh 1883) vol.II, p.445).

interest in landscape, especially in Highland scenery, and in gardening. In 1761 he was, of course, young, his taste immature, and his knowledge of gardening slight – sufficiently so for Lord Deskford to offer him such basic wisdom as 'think of the Disposition of your Grounds and Plantations. Trees take a great while to grow and nobody ever regrets of having begun to Plant Early, especially in this country where everything must be raised from seed . . .'[85] But he learnt rapidly, and displayed in the 1760s an interest in Robinson as well as an artist such as Alexander Cozens and, a decade later, in the water-colourist William Tomkins. Grant subscribed to Cozens's *Characteristics of Landscape*, and received from Tomkins in 1778 a list of drawings that might interest him.[86] All the twenty-four views suggested were local ones, mostly topographical and invariably picturesque. The range was predictable, even parochial, and included 'A View of a Large fall water of Divack in Urquhart in the County of Inverness upon the Estate of Sr James Grant Bart.,' as well as a 'View of Craigelachie with lock [sic] of Water Storms of Rain in the Distance Beauty full'.[87] Such enlightened taste and Robinson's expertise should have resulted in a promising scheme for Castle Grant. Unfortunately this was not so. Robinson had worked with the incompetent land surveyor Charles Tennoch at Castle Grant some time before June 1763, and had then ingratiated himself with the Grant family.[88] When he returned to the castle in May 1764, he found his client had left for London leaving no instructions about the new garden. It was hardly the most propitious of situations but Robinson made the best of it, assuring Grant that 'in your absence you may depend on my applying any little skill I have, both with regard to the utility and ornament of this place, at the same time should have been very happy in your presence here, it being always satisfactory to advise with the proprietor'.[89] It was a predicament which Grant had been warned to avoid by Robinson's patron at Monymusk, Sir Archibald Grant. He had taken the 'liberty to suggest that it would on many accounts, be proper that you concert with Mr. Robinson the Plan of his Operations *on the Spot*, before he commits his thoughts to paper (Except in a rough Sketch to Explain his Ideas). Especially as to what regards the Policy; which, I imagine will save Time and expence by Ascertaining the *Disposition*, the *Taste* etc., suited to your views.'[90] By June, Robinson had left Castle Grant for Edin-

85. SRO GD 248/672/4. He also recommended that Grant in London took a tour of two or three days through London gardens and especially 'the Chelsea Physic gardens and Mr Gray's Nursery at Fulham'. He also suggested a talk with the Duke of Argyll (ibid.). Sir James Grant succeeded in 1771, but had been effectively involved in the Estate since 1761. He was something of an amateur artist; see 248/178/2. For an account of his career and his time in Rome in 1760, see Fraser, op. cit., vol.I, pp.442–61.

86. In 1766, Cozens wrote to Grant thanking him for the 'drawings which you were so kind to commission' (GD 248/345/2). Cozens also sent him his prospectus for his 'Characteristics of Landscape' (ibid.). Although Grant presumably admired Tomkins work, he nonetheless wrote to him suggesting that some of his proposed views 'will look very tame one cannot put so much spirit in water couler as in Oyls couler that will be of great want of Beauty in Rock and waterfalls and richness of trees' (GD 248/227/3). Tomkins also had the Earl Fife as a patron at this time. He painted for Lord Fife in 1767 a view of Rothiemay and one of Mar Lodge (Gough, op. cit., pp.639–40). A group of such pictures were hung at Fife House in London, see *Catalogue of Paintings and pictures in different houses belonging to James, Earl of Fife* (London 1807) p.92.

87. See SRO GD 248/496/4. This Tomkins noted 'all the Views I have of Sr. James Grant Bart'.

88. In June 1763, Robinson with Tennoch was paid £21.4.9 (GD 248/250). For Tennoch the surveyor, see Adams, op. cit., vol.III, p.xxii who refers to him as 'one of the worst land surveyors of the period'. He had been instructed to go to Castle Grant since 1762 (GD 248/178/2). Certainly Grant had intended doing something about improving the Castle since 1761 when Lord Deskford wrote that 'I intend to be at Castle Grant this year when you form your plan for laying out your Ground within sight of the House' (GD 248/672/4). There is an undated letter from Sir Archibald Grant to Grant recommending a complete survey of the estate; see Fraser, op. cit., vol.II, p.442.

89. SRO GD 248/178/2.   90. ibid.

Plate 43. View from the court at Castle Grant

91. He wrote to Grant in July 1764, a rather petulant letter complaining that he had 'met with no particular instructions' and had 'made out the plan I thought most suitable to the place'. He added that he had written to Grant 'on my arrival at Castle Grant but my not being favoured with your reply while there delayed writing you again till I came home, expecting to meet with you here' (GD 248/250).

92. SRO GD 248/346/6.

93. For Adam's work there, see SRO GD 248/176/177, 178/2. The north front of the house was probably John Adam's work. Robert Adam also designed a house for Lady Innes at Elgin in 1766 (GD 248/250). This presumably passed to Sir James Grant and there is a plan for the garden there with notes by Grant. It was unimpressive, with two enclosures in front and rear, and a serpentine approach (GD 248/473).

94. SRO RHP 13947. This plan, which is not entirely finished, was that referred to when Grant asked Robinson to send on his sketches and rough draft (GD 248/208/2 f.35), in December, 1764. The then existing setting of the castle is shown in RHP 8947.

burgh without seeing either its owner or being given any further directions.[91] Not unexpectedly his Improvement Plan of the following year, for which he charged £31 10s and a further £16 for expenses, was thought 'very extravagant'.[92] Yet for all this, it was little valued, and it remained permanently on the shelf.

At Castle Grant, Robinson was faced with a U-shaped and rather nondescript building. Both John and Robert Adam had been employed there from 1753 till 1765 but with little aesthetic result.[93] Its setting was largely a formal one, with Winter's terraced gardens on one side, a long avenue running southwards from the castle to the Milltown area, and a small canal and basin asymmetrically placed beside the castle. From the courtyard, the castle looked south towards Grantown, founded by Sir James in 1766 (Plate 43). In proposing his landscape, Robinson wished to eliminate both garden and avenue, banishing the former to the home farm, and substituted in their stead a curiously symmetrical informality.[94] The castle was to be set in a figure of eight, with a lawn to the north and south, and roads or paths sketching the outline of the number (Plate 42). This mathematical style was further and unduly emphasised by the geometry and symmetry of Robinson's planting, particularly on the south lawn, where one side was virtually a mirror

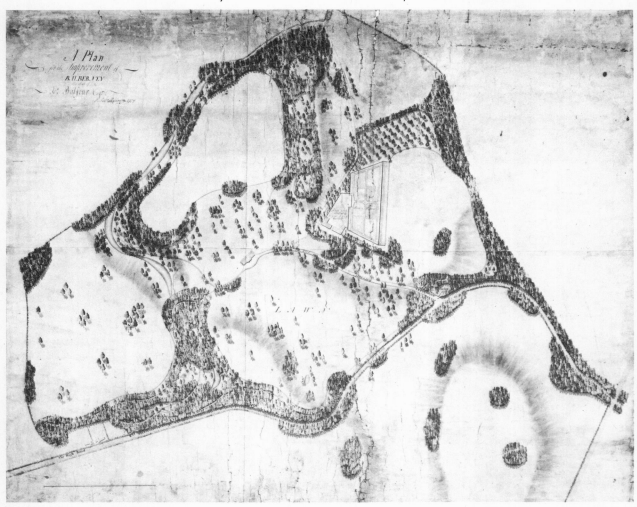

image of the other, with hardwood trees sharply defining the edge of otherwise coniferous plantations. The contrast between Robinson's paper pattern and the informality of the rest of the woodlands seems to have been quite deliberate, though it could hardly have been successful. It was not of course new. Such a formula had emerged earlier and on a smaller scale at Careston in 1761, and was to reappear in his more open scheme for The Inch of 1777 and, less strongly, at Balbirnie, in

Plate 44. Balbirnie, Fife, improvement plan by Robert Robinson, 1779

1779. Yet such an approach can hardly have found much favour with Sir James Grant, whose picturesque sensibilities must have been appalled at the largely formal vista running from the lawn to a Monumental Obelisk, marked 'G' in Robinson's plan. Fortunately, he showed greater imagination and more freedom in his use of water. As

Plate 45. Aerial view of the park at Balbirnie, 1979

at Balbirnie, his two lakes and various ponds were to be hidden in the woods directly below the south lawn, with the course of the stream that fed them charted by a series of semi-circular glades, invariably with a clump of trees in their centre. The water sources were the small burns of Allt an Fhithich and Allt a Bhacain, which can only have supplied the smallest head of water, for Robinson noted that his shallow lakes were to be 'sheets of water floated over the Bottoms in different Places'. As a scheme it was a stiff and lack-lustre essay in the Kentian tradition, and certainly inferior both to his ambitious design for Glamis and his more intricate essay at Paxton (Plates 90 and 46).

Sir James Grant's probable disappointment with Robinson's work would have arisen, paradoxically, from his own growing interest in the landscape. His taste was illustrated by the surviving side of a correspondence between him and the literary and green-fingered Dean of Ripon, Robert Waddilove.[95] Like Lord Deskford, the Dean encouraged Grant to plant, reminding him in 1764, just after his marriage, to 'Plant Oaks for your D'rs fortune, a 1,000 for every child that is born – I have some acorns for you, and I would have you read Evelyn's Sylva'. Some time after that he gave a prosy improvement plan for Castle Grant, which was an ambitious but ill-co-ordinated fusion of formal and informal ideas. He suggested an artificial cascade planted with wild flowers and a series of winding walks over the hills, to be contrasted with 'little bits of Parterre', in a way that Repton would have favoured. But Waddilove was conscious that some of his ideas at least must have seemed out of date and ill-accorded with Rousseau's pursuit of the simple and natural.[96] But for all this, neither Waddilove nor Robinson prevailed upon Grant, and a survey of the castle made in 1810 showed the formal landscape still intact, and little new apart from the continuation of Thomas Winter's commercial plantations.[97] Nor were any of Robinson's practical ideas on the siting of the kitchen garden or the location of the offices taken up. Other plans were made by George Taylor for a new garden and related buildings in 1771, and a still further garden scheme given by Lewis Sinclair in 1803.[98]

Robinson's work at Balbirnie showed no real extension of the ideas displayed at Castle Grant, only a certain ease and flexibility in

95. For Waddilove's career see *DNB*. Waddilove seems to have taken upon himself to supply Grant with nursery catalogues. He wrote in September, 1764, 'from the Catalogues I have sent you, if your Gardeners know any thing – but they seem to me capable of being instructed by an old Riders Almanac – I wish you would give them Whitmill's Gardeners Calendar. It is smaller than Millars, and will be of more service' (SRO GD 248/178/2).

96. SRO GD 248/680/8. This was contained in description of 'Numa's Fountain at Castle Grant'. Its site was to be where 'the turning Room now is, if not I wd propose some other cover'd building in the form of an Hermitage fitted up similarly and Books etc. in it'. From this he expanded outward to the gardens, advising a cascade, a bowling green, 'an elegant Farm and neat Farm house and Dairy' (ibid.). He referred to Rousseau as 'spight of Mr. Rousseau's Criticism, I would in another part of this Elizium have an aviary but it should be something like that at Kew'.

97. See SRO RHP 9012. For Winter's work at Castle Grant see pp. 62–4. In 1764/5, William Forbes the factor at Castle Grant wrote to Sir James reporting the planting of firs, etc., at Grantown Park, and then – more importantly – gives this account of improvements being made at Castle Grant: 'I have set so many hands to the levelling about the House and I hope to get the Access on the west side made easier and the Road that goes Down the Back of the Garden stoped and turned' (SRO GD 248/250). Forbes also reported buying flowering shrubs and evergreens in Edinburgh (ibid.). In all of this, they seem to have been following the existing garden pattern and being directed by a 'Mr. Date'. For several descriptions of the house and estate in the late eighteenth century, see Fraser, op. cit., vol.I, pp.447–50. In 1784, the Earl Fife remarked only, and critically, upon a new approach road (ibid., p.483).

98. Lewis Sinclair, who worked as both planter and surveyor on the Grant estates, designed in 1803, a 'Plan of the New Garden at Milltown, Castle Grant', which was to contain fruit trees sent up by Lee and Kennedy of Hampstead in 1802 (GD 248/702/2). For Sinclair's work see 248/713/1 and RHP 13912. Taylor's plan for the garden and offices at Castle Grant was sold at the Cullen Sale, Sept. 22nd., 1975. Lot 591 – Christies. There remains too a late eighteenth-century plan for a hothouse; see RHP 9057.

their deployment (Plate 44). Once again the house was set in a sort of figure eight, with areas of lawn above and below the building and a small stream made to wind through a series of woodland glades, encountering the odd temple and pond on its way. That much of this happened was obvious from Thomas White junior's scheme of 1815 to substantially enlarge Robinsons's park.[99] Significantly, however, White rid Balbirnie of any trace of Robinson's geometry and made an open and truly landscaped scene instead of a series of more or less inviolate enclosures (Plate 45). But at Paxton, Robinson appears to have chosen finally to break the mould (Plate 46). Possibly so radical a decision was forced upon him by the nature of the ground. Here the house was impressively set at the extreme end of the park virtually on top of the steep Scottish bank of the Tweed and without a background of rolling parkland to soften the stark architectural silhouette of the mansion (Plate 47). It was also a smaller scheme than most, and perhaps for this reason it was carried out. A rather diagrammatic plan of the Paxton estate in 1776 showed most of the basic elements of his design: the sunk fence that formed the boundaries of the inner park, the serpentine approach road, and the bridge that was certainly finished by 1767.[100]

In general terms, however, Robinson's design belonged to the 'champaign' landscape typical of Dalrymple's third declension and equally so of the English style. Nevertheless, Paxton's situation on the Border perhaps encouraged Robinson to make some concession to local landscape if not to local pride. His solution was broadly characteristic: the small park about the house – the 'Lawn' in Robinson's reference key – was composed of two unequal areas that were cut by the approach road to the house. Around its circumference wound the familiar walk, solidly planted on one side, partially open on the other, with views inwards to both a Rotunda, proposed for the lawn, and the house itself. Where it ran along the top of the river bank, just below the garden front, Robinson advised 'A Gravel Path ornamentally planted with flowering shrubs along the top of the Banks of the Tweed'.[101] Much of this walk has survived, running inland from the river and along the top of the stone sunk fence of the park. But in all this, there was nothing memorable or remarkably Scottish. It was in some respect Duddingston again, for the best and only outward view from the lawn – east over the river to the Northumbrian coast – was blocked by the house itself. It was beyond this area, in the valley of the Lynn burn and the approach road to Paxton from Berwick, that Robinson showed individuality and some feeling for the Scottish terrain. The fields

99. His plan for Balbirnie was fully finished and titled 'A Plan for the Improvement of Balbirnie the seat of John Balfour, Esq. Robt. Robinson 1779'. For both White's and Robinson's plans see SRO RHP 24, 334 and 24,335. A certain amount of planting was carried out at Balbirnie in 1779; see SRO GD 228/264. In the 1780s more ambitious plantations were formed with trees supplied by Dicksons in Edinburgh, and by John Richmond, presumably also of Edinburgh; see SRO GD 228/237.

100. For the plan of 1776, see SRO RHP 6145. The bridge and walled garden shown in this plan were mentioned in a 'Survey of Mensuration of Mason Work' in 1767 (SRO GD 267/16/9 ff.34–5). This survey showed the house standing in a park bounded by a sunk fence but virtually treeless. Robinson referred in his plan for Paxton to Patrick Home of Billie, by whom it was commissioned. He gave no date for the design. Patrick Home succeeded to Billie in 1754 and to the larger estate of Wedderburn in 1766. He died in 1808. It is probable that Robinson made his plan between 1754 and 1766 when Paxton was still the centre of Home's interest. For a genealogy of the Home Family, see *Historic Manuscripts Commission: Report on the Manuscripts of Colonel David Milne Home* (London 1902) pp.8–12.

101. See Note H on Robinson's plan at present at Paxton House. Presumably further details for the planting of this area were contained in his 'loose paper', which has now disappeared.

Plate 46. Paxton House, Berwickshire, improvement plan by Robert Robinson, *c.*1766

running down from the road to the Lynn remained planted in the Scottish fashion with strips of trees dividing one from the other, forming in this way a straight avenue to the bridge over the burn. From there the road looped across the lawn to the gravel circle in front of the house. The steep banks of the Lynn – an area Robinson patriotically designated the Glen (Plate 48), in the spirit of Repton's 'Loch' at Valleyfield – were treated with considerable naturalism and contrasted with the shaven and clumped appearance of the lawn to the immediate south. In this valley, he intended several small footbridges, possibly the predecessors of the present ones, and near the site of the existing

Plate 47. Aerial view of Paxton, beside the Tweed, 1979

102. Much of the layout of Paxton was altered in the 1780s, when the walled garden was extended, and in 1789 the stables built according to a plan of Ninian Home. Patrick Home's brother and ultimate heir George Home seems to have looked after the Paxton section of the triple estates (SRO GD 267/1/1 and 1/2). All the Homes at this time showed an interest in gardening and improvement. In the library at Paxton are copies of Miller's *Gardener's Dictionary* of 1752, Whately's *Modern Gardening* of 1770, and in 1782 George Home was having bound Boutcher's *Forest Trees* (GD 267/1/1). Further work was undertaken in the park in 1815, when the east and west lawns were drained, and an 'invisible fence' was made in front and behind the house (GD 267/7/16). Much of this work went hand in hand with similar activities at the fraternal house of Wedderburn.

103. See SRO GD 267/539/1.

104. Adam's bridge over the Smale Burn was built in 1744 and repaired by John Adam in 1749 (SRO GD 248/951/5). For some account of the gardens at Cullen at this time see, GD 248/680/6. Peter Charles, the gardener then, was instructed by Lord Findlater to plant American oaks, chestnut, walnuts, etc., and references were made to a Chinese Bridge, a little Mount, and the formation of a kind of shrubbery. A survey made by Peter May in 1764 showed the policies at the time of Robinson's arrival in 1766, see pl.50. In 1770, Charles was instructed by Lord Findlater that he wished 'a few scattered Trees to be planted in the Glen' (GD 248/680/6). This glen or den was described by Douglas in 1782 as 'the sides of the den are covered with all kinds of trees and flowering-shrubs, through which serpentine gravel-walks have been made. The semi-circular hollow under the windows is laid out in a grass plot . . . lately made out *a fine ride* round the whole policy' (Douglas, op. cit., p.304).

rustic cottage suggested, in vain, 'A Monumental Obelisk'. The burn itself he made into a series of pools fed by stretches of fast, straight water. While this end of the park is nowadays wilder and less kempt than Robinson envisaged, the cathedral-like atmosphere of a crepuscular woodland glen, with tall trees reflected in still water, must have been much as he intended even without his proposed obelisk.[102] It may have encouraged him to repeat the idea of a burn valley at Cullen, where he was consulted in 1766.[103] Although little is known of his work there, the gardens were certainly naturalised about this time, especially in the gorge-like glen immediately behind the house and below William Adam's bridge (Plate 49).[104] This much is clear from Peter May's survey of 1764 (Plate 50). The simplicity and sense of scale apparent in both these valleys made his further and unexecuted project for the Glamis burn a lost opportunity, and one heightened by the failure of later gardeners, like White at Scone and Repton at Valleyfield, to deal sensitively with the Scottish glen.

Both Robinson and Robertson shared, unequally, a Kentian vision where, as Dalrymple had it, 'great verdure, cultivation and populousness' inspired 'a cheerful gay temper'. They paid in their landscape gardens little more than lip service to the ideals of their stated mentor Brown. Robertson's alleged departure to Ireland, where the informal and dull landscape at Carton in County Kildare has unflatteringly been attributed to him, and the bankruptcy and collapse of Robinson in

Plate 48. The entrance to the Glen at Paxton

1. Aerial view of the park at Blair Castle, Perthshire, 1979

105. According to Loudon, and Steuart's *The Planter's Guide*, Robertson left for Ireland, handing over his practice to 'his nephew George, and James Ramsay, one of his most promising pupils (Steuart, op. cit., p.44). His Irish patrons were supposedly the Duke of Leinster at Carton and Mr Conolly at Castletown. The improvements undertaken by the former in the 1760s may be Robertson's work. A view of the gardens at this time is given in the catalogue: *Irish Houses and Landscapes* (1963) pp.22–3; and an account of the formation of the park in Arnold Horner 'Carton, Co. Kildare' *Bulletin of the Irish Georgian Society* XVIII (1975) pp.45–103; see also Malins and Fitz-Gerald, op. cit., p.71. For Robert Robinson's bankruptcy, see SRO CS 17/1/1 p.152. In this action, Robinson's creditors sued Alexander Spiers of The Inch for non-payment of the improvement plans made in 1777.

106. Robinson produced two plans for The Inch both of 1777, which are at Houston House, Renfrewshire. The more finished and signed plan shows the outer lawn running to the Clyde's edge with three clumps of trees beside the water – one at either corner of the lawn and a smaller one in the centre. This corresponded more or less with the survey plan made by David Owen in 1786, and presumably followed Robinson's design.

107. For Loudon's attribution to Ramsay of both Cally and Gosford (as Wemyss House), see *Encyclopaedia of Gardening*, p.1251. Gosford was bought by the Wemyss family in 1784, and the mausoleum and Ramsay's plantations are shown in Forrest's map of East Lothian. Again, according to Loudon, his nursery was at Leith Head, presumably Leith, and he died, erroneously, in 1794 (ibid., p.79 and *Edinburgh Encyclopaedia* XII p.543). For his complementary career as an architect, see Colvin, op. cit., p.671. His design for Hermand, Midlothian (NLS Ms.5177) was possibly carried out by Lord Hermand, though little was visible by 1852; see

1782, left the field open to others who were prepared to apply Brown's principles with greater informality and understanding.[105] Certainly Robertson's nephew George, to whom he had left his practice, attempted in his 1774 plan for Bargany in Ayrshire, to merge the elements of an older, more formal garden into a park landscape (Plate 51). This transition was most obvious and least effective in the woods surrounding the bowling green where the irregularity of the concatenation of small lakes, altered by W. S. Gilpin in the 1820s, was at odds with the stumps of the radiating avenues. He was more successful in handling the planting along the river Girvan, where thick shelter belts beyond its banks and individual trees beside it, transformed the periphery of the park into a lake-like composition, as well as creating an effective middle distance. This was a much better solution than Robinson's weak and precisely balanced clumps beside the Clyde at The Inch (Plate 52).[106]

Robertson's putative partner James Ramsay worked in much the same vein, more competent in the small scale of his designs for Hermand and Rednock, both of 1796, than in his fussy planting around the mausoleum at Gosford, East Lothian, of about the same date.[107] The simplicity and almost diminutive scale of his work on the classical offices at Rednock and in the landscaping he carried out along the banks of the Rednock Burn, showed a willingness to think and work small (Plates 53 and 54).[108] It remains virtually, almost uniquely, intact as a textbook example of a small landscaped estate of the late eighteenth century (Plate 55). Its success makes a striking contrast with his work at Cally, where he seems to have failed abysmally to heighten or even match the superb natural setting of the house, which had generated William Adam's axiom on informality. The laudatory description of the estate written by Robert Heron around 1790 made Cally seem a marvel of which there could be no criticism. For Heron and others like

Ferguson, op. cit., p.152. At Rednock, Perthshire, his plan was superseded by a more extensive scheme of improvement for General Graham Stirling, see SRO RHP 24993 and the account in the *New Statistical Account* (1845) vol.X, p.1108. The design he made for the stables in 1797 was carried out but to a modified plan (Rednock, Album of Plans). Ramsay's two landscape plans showed a much freer hand than his contemporaries and possibly a more casual approach with greater emphasis on artistic rather than surveyor-like qualities.

108. At Rednock, his walled garden, icehouse, and much of the planting around the house and burn have survived. His approach road was changed, however, when a new lodge and road were built by Mcfarlane in 1838; see Rednock, Album of Plans. His whole design sympathetically incorporated much of the existing landscape shown in McArthur's survey of 1772 (ibid.). It was enthusiastically described in 1806 having had 'almost all ornamental improvement which art can bestow' (Graham, op. cit., p.40).

him, the landscape garden in Scotland appeared to have sprung mature and sophisticated, like Athene from Zeus's head. It was for them faultless, for it encouraged agriculture, husbandry and above all planting on a vast scale, which together created an effective visual landscape far beyond the park wall or the windows of the mansion house. They were indiscriminate in their praise not so much of the beautiful and picturesque as of the miraculous new countryside. Such

Plate 49. Aerial view of Cullen House, Banffshire, 1979, showing William Adam's bridge and wilderness garden

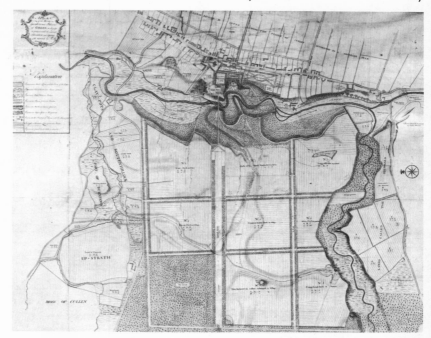

109. Heron *Observations made in a journey through . . . Scotland*, vol.II, p.213. Ramsay's work was probably carried out before 1789, when the Gothic temple, described by Heron, was being built; see SRO GD 10/1291/1189. It has survived restoration by the Forestry Commission, in 1974.

110. Loudon's account of Cally was given in his *Gardener's Magazine*, where he wrote: 'The situation of the house, near an estuary formed by the mouth of the river Fleet, is very fine; but, unfortunately, the entrance front is on the wrong side, and none of the windows of the principal rooms look towards the river'. He also found the trees in the park 'in many places too formal and unconnected', but he concluded 'The scenery about the house, and the views, from its entrance front, of the richly wooded country beyond the river, with the mountains and their rocky summits on the one hand, and the sea on the other, are unequalled by any thing of the kind in this part of the county' (ibid., IX (1833) pp.7–8.)

enthusiasm led Heron to write that 'Every deformity within these grounds is concealed, or converted into a beauty by wood. Everywhere, except at proper points of view, these environs are divided by belts of planting from the highways and the adjacent country. Many fine swells diversify the scene. These are crowned with fine clumps of trees. Within the extent of the pleasure-grounds is a house occupied by a farm-servant, which has been built in the fashion of a Gothic Temple.'[109] More prosaic and professional was Loudon's judgement, some thirty years later, that the entrance front faced the wrong way and ruined the best view, while the main approach spoilt the surprise of a superb view over Gatehouse Bay.[110] Ironically, when so much has changed at Cally and Ramsay's gimcrack tower has disappeared in twentieth-century plantations these faults still remain obviously true (Plate 56). Whatever Heron may have thought, Ramsay had ignored the character of the coastal setting and preferred instead to cultivate a sylvan landscape, conventionally ornamented with lake and clumps, that turned, old-fashionedly, its back on its greatest asset, the sea. In this he foreshadowed Repton's mistakes at Valleyfield, where he

Plate 50. Cullen, survey by Peter May, 1764

111. Ardchattan Priory, Valleyfield Red Book, 'Pleasure Grounds'.

112. In the 1760 *Caledonian Mercury* Robert Robinson was 'late draughtsman and Executor of the Designs of Lancelot Brown, Esq'. There is no known connection between him and Brown; see Colvin, op. cit., p.701, and Dorothy Stroud, *Henry Holland* (London 1966) pp.124–5. In the latter, the far from happy relationship between William Robinson, Clerk of Works (and Robert Robinson's brother) and Capability is cited. Scott referred to White at Allanton as 'pupil of Browne' and both Steuart and Loudon repeated that Robertson was a pupil of Capability Brown; see *The Planter's Guide*, pp.45–6, and *Encyclopaedia of Gardening*, p.34. The only Scottish garden attributed to Brown is Ardgowan in Renfrewshire; see Maxwell, op. cit., p.28. It is much more likely to be the work of Gilpin; see W.S. Gilpin *Practical Hints upon Landscape Gardening* (London 1832) p.10. Ardgowan was built in 1806 and altered by Robert Burn around 1840, when the gardens and park were relandscaped; see Glasgow City Archives, Ardgowan plans.

explained away his proposed 'Loch' with the note that 'with respect to its vicinity to the Firth of Forth, it should evidently rather be measured by the size of the valley and of the river, than by the Forth'.[111]

Both the elusive Robertson and Robinson were designers who worked in a modified Kentian manner while claiming some sort of pupillage with Capability Brown. It was a profitable distinction, presumably sufficiently widely appreciated in Scotland in the 1760s for it to be the key to preferment and opportunity. But apart from this and the willingness of later historians like Sir Walter Scott, Sir Henry Steuart, or even Loudon, to see his shadow everywhere, Brown had no definite connection with any Scottish garden or gardener.[112] No client employed him simultaneously in Scotland as well as England and even his style of the beautiful, 'prim-roll'd gravel fring'd with green', as John Matthews called it, had been anticipated by Dalrymple who was, moreover, an important, perhaps self-important, luminary in the artistic world of Edinburgh. Lip-service was undoubtedly paid to his name, but rarely can any positive identification be established. His vicarious influence on the planting at Galloway House in Wigtownshire was probably quite typical. The heir and active manager of the estate in 1764 was Lord Garlies, later Earl of Galloway, a noted improver and planter, as well as architect of the estate village at Garliestown. In November of that year, he wrote from England that he had been staying at Fisherwick in Staffordshire, where there was 'one

Plate 51. Bargany, Ayrshire, improvement plan by George Robertson, 1774

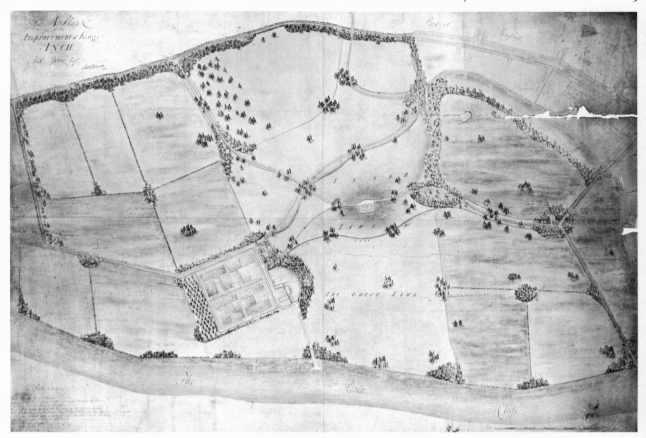

113. SRO GD 99/Box 151. For Brown's work at Fisherwick, see Stroud, op. cit., pp.151–3. For Lord Galloway's standing as an improver the *Statistical Account* of 1791 recorded, 'The Earl has studied the volume of forest trees, and the different ways of raising them and treating them . . . His Lordship's designs are great; and he is accomplishing much, by planting at the rate of 200,000 trees every year' (*Statistical Account*, I, 1791, pp.243–8). The park and gardens at Galloway House were redesigned in c.1850; see SRO RHP 24,712 and 24,713.

114. SRO GD 99/Box 151.

of the finest Parks I ever saw, and with the great Sums of Money he (Lord Donegal) is laying out, & with the assistance of Mr. Brown, it will be in a few year a Compleat Thing'.[113] Lord Garlies was also greatly impressed by Brown's transplanting machine, which he saw at work, and was encouraged to try moving 'some trees with the greatest care in a similar way' at Galloway House.[114] The planting that he was engaged upon then and later presumably reflected Brown's influence. But it went no further, and while Lord Garlies, like Lord Breadalbane, was near to Brown, interested in gardening and admired his work, no commission was apparently offered or accepted. Brown's dictum that Ireland would have to wait until he finished England seems to have applied to Scotland too.

Plate 52. The Kings Inch, Paisley, improvement plan by Robert Robinson, 1777

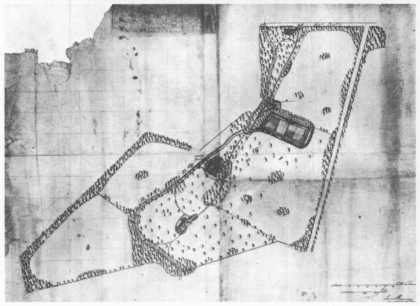

Plate 53. Ramsay's stables at Rednock, Perthshire, from the park
Plate 54. Rednock, improvement plan by James Ramsay, 1796

Both Dalrymple and later Loudon shared a fondness for a mixed landscape that could balance formal with informal elements. But the period between Dalrymple writing in the 1750s and Loudon's debut as a gardener around 1800, was much more doctrinaire. The formation of a landscaped park at this time inevitably meant the destruction of older gardens and in the process their historical character. Such a situation prevailed at Duddingston, where all the natural advantages of its

Plate 55. Aerial view of Rednock, 1979, showing walled garden and approach by the side of the burn

setting were deliberately neglected in favour of a fashionably stock solution. It was not the only example. In the flush of enthusiasm for informality, Dalrymple's axiom that 'the taste of the gardener will be shewn, in proportioning his distribution and assemblage to that particular degree of resemblance, which the part he is then laying out bears to one or another of the four capital situations' was forgotten. The empirical and fortuitous equation, which combined distinct parts taken from the formal garden with the wild landscape and its domestic often castellated architecture, was unrecognised. It was left to the succeeding generation, to the sons of the pioneers, Robert Adam, himself a protégé of Dalrymple's, and John Clerk of Eldin, to make and exploit this discovery.

Plate 56. The Gothic temple at Cally, Kirkcudbrightshire

THE PICTURESQUE

A latent interest in the picturesque was to be anticipated in Scotland. It was, after all, the home of much that was admired in this way from the time of Gray and Gilpin – so much so, perhaps, that its unique combination of mountain and loch was often overlooked or despised by proprietors who, perversely and arduously, pursued the rarer, man-made landscape of the beautiful. The picturesque in Scotland was, as elsewhere, associated with a variety of architectural forms, from the cottage *orné* at Langholm, the model farms of Kinrara and Dunira, to the hybrid style of the late Adam castles. This combination of building and setting constituted the real attainment of picturesque. In Scotland it was a wider fusion, seen at its best and boldest in the watercolours of Robert Adam and his sketching companion John Clerk of Eldin, where they anticipated visually much that was said at length in Knight's *The Landscape* and, more pertinently and locally, in Sir James Hall's *Essay on Gothic Architecture*. Their drawings reveal a conscious relationship between the castles and towns they selected to draw and the legends and often romantic periods in Scottish history with which their subjects were associated. This awareness seemed almost the birthright of the Adam family and was shared, though not equally, by the other brothers John and James, both of whom farmed and gardened, John at Blair Adam itself and North Merchiston, James in Hertfordshire and vicariously in his *Practical Essays on Agriculture*.

North Merchiston, on the edge of Edinburgh, was bought by William Adam in 1730.[1] Its walls enclosed a park of twenty-eight acres laid out by Adam in a series of radial avenues, with the principal walk aligned to the modest house that had come with the property. The vista towards the other end of this walk was closed, as at Arniston, by a view of Edinburgh Castle and the tower of St Giles' Cathedral. It was this pleasure ground with its pleasant old-fashioned house that John Adam inherited on his father's death in 1748. It was in James Adam's mind when he wrote to his sister from Rome in 1761 that 'John proposes making himself very fine in a new house and is adorning it with all those figures of architecture that are known on the other side of the

1. William Adam *Blair Adam*, 5 pts. (1834) pt.I, p.114.

Plate 57. Scene at Merchiston, by James Adam

2. SRO GD 18/4895.

3. *Blair Adam*, pt.I, p.114.

Tweed'.[2] According to John's son William, the author of the privately printed *Blair Adam* of 1834, the plantations there 'were, with the exception of one avenue, which was preserved, and the circle which my Father converted into a Bowling Green, all thinned out and grouped, so as to answer bending lines of walk and shrubbery. The fields were inclosed and separated, for the purpose of pasture, or other produce. Pieces of ground, hidden by a holly hedge, and by little plantations of shrubs, were used for production of vegetables and small fruit. The spaces between the fields were occupied with walks; the useful subdivisions, by hedges; and in some places tasteful and well contrived intricacies gave an interest which was extremely pleasing. The external objects being cheerful or picturesque, rendered it what I have described, and produced another effect, namely, its extent was supposed to be four times what it really was'.[3] According to William Adam again, these significant changes were made before 1760, possibly in 1756, and were the important harbingers of the mature landscape style. They are fairly well in evidence in a pen sketch by James Adam called 'Scene at Merchistone', drawn by him before his departure to Italy in 1760 (Plate 57). In it, John Adam and his family are grouped around a rustic bench in a sylvan landscape that is obviously both new and informal. Such improvements, Adam maintained, were virtually contemporaneous with the creation by the poet William Shenstone of the better known but equally small-scale landscape of The Leasowes. Adam wrote: 'I think it may be said, however, that the Leasowes stamped and extended this mode of treating plantations and adorning grounds; and it is clear, from Johnson's biographical account, that Shenstone could not have advanced far in this until after 1748. I know my Father visited Shenstone at the Leasowes; but the particular date of that visit I cannot ascertain. He had by that time laid out his grounds at North Merchiston, near Edinburgh, and they were far advanced before that visit. North Merchiston was the most splendid Ferme Ornée that can be imagined; its fame had reached Shenstone before my Father visited him; so that the establishment of the new manner of laying out grounds must have been fixed, to a considerable extent, before 1756'.[4] In this assessment and stylistic chronology, William Adam characteristically ignored Bowie's contemporary work 'in the natural way' in the Lothians, even though Bowie was his father's partner at Yester.

John Adam made two documented journeys to England; that in 1748, for which his travel sketchbook survives, and a further trip in 1759.[5] It was during the latter that his interest in gardening came strongly to the fore. Amongst the sights he saw and drew were the conventional ones, like the gardens at Claremont and Stowe; but apart from them he paid particular attention to the smaller more intimate style, of Painshill and, especially, of Woburn Farm. He not only approved of the last but appreciated its significance, and wrote accordingly that it was 'in general an elegant fine thing and justly merits praise for its being the first thing in that free way or among the first, done in England'.[6] But in neither of these journeys made before the perhaps critical date of 1760 was there any mention of The Leasowes. Yet he seems to have grasped that by seeing Woburn Farm he had encountered the heart of the new style and the ultimate source for both The Leasowes and his own North Merchiston. According to Richard Graves, Shenstone's eighteenth-century biographer, the ideas of Woburn Farm had rapidly spread to two other gardens, Warlies in Essex and Mickleton in Gloucestershire, and it was from them that The Leasowes evolved.[7] Some similar but wider sort of evolution may explain North Merchiston and William Adam's contention that it anticipated, rather than followed, Shenstone's ideas. In this way, William was justified in writing that his father had visited The Leasowes, presumably some time after 1760, when his garden in that 'mode' was already completed.

No detailed contemporary plan of Merchiston has survived. The

4. ibid. p.95 Laurie's plan of Edinburgh of 1766 shows little of these improvements beyond six fields with their boundaries planted with trees. That it anticipated rather than followed The Leasowes was confirmed by Sir Thomas Dick Lauder, who wrote that 'From the intimacy that subsisted between Mr. Adam and Shenstone, whom he visited at The Leasowes, it seems to be doubtful whether the poet's formation of that celebrated place was not materially assisted, if not suggested by the hints he received from his Scottish friend' (Dick Lauder, op. cit., p.209). James Adam visited the Leasowes with John Home in May 1758; see Marjorie Williams *The Letters of William Shenstone* (Oxford 1939) p.482; and Fleming, op. cit., p.253.

5. See Fleming, op cit., pp.82 and 263; for this sketchbook of 1748; see *Catalogue of the Drawings Collection of the Royal Institute of British Architects* A (Harmondsworth 1969) p.15. There are further related drawings by John Adam at Blair Adam.

6. Fleming, op. cit., p.265.

7. For an account of Woburn or Wooburn Farm, see R.W. King 'The Ferme Ornée: Philip Southcote and Wooburn Farm' *Garden History* II, no.3 (1974) pp.27–60; and more succinctly H.F. Clark *The English Landscape Garden* (London 1948) pp. 48, 49.

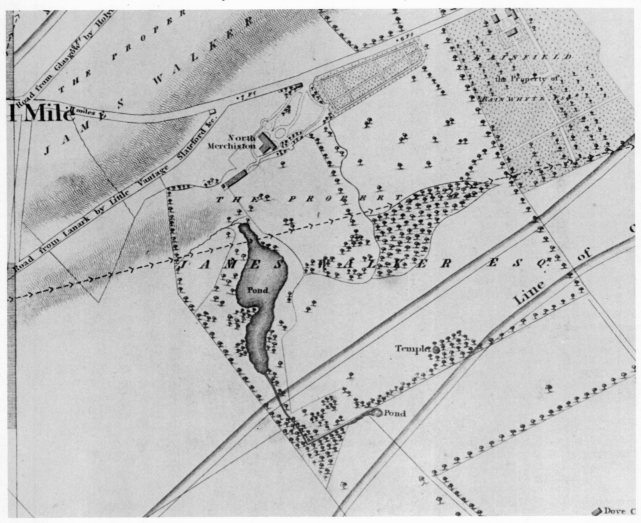

poor best is that published in Kirkwood's 'Plan of Edinburgh' of 1817, by which time the property had already passed out of Adam hands with the pictures from it being sold in the 1790s.[8] Kirkwood's plan showed a T-shaped house, with the kitchen garden adjacent to it at the extreme and northern end of the property (Plate 58). To the south and west lay the rest of the small park, roughly divided into two by an

Plate 58. North Merchiston, Edinburgh, from Kirkwood's map of 1817

irregular belt of trees running east and west, which also edged part of a large lake that fed a round pond. Close to the south boundary was placed a small circular temple, screened by trees. This landscape was seen and admired by Joseph Spence during his Scottish tour of 1760. He noted in his journal that he had called at Mr Adam's and 'saw his garden laid out and planted in the modern way: there are a great many pretty parts in it; particularly the water, Island and Rock that is now in making. T'is a (bad) winding walk round Fields and the ground slopes happily; but ye Fence (which he seem'd willing to be pleased with) is much too apparent'.[9] The scale and the simplicity of all those elements, were without doubt closer to The Leasowes than the 116 ornamented acres of Woburn Farm. Merchiston conspicuously lacked the rich variety of architectural ornaments that studded Woburn, and probably avoided the 'too many clumps of shrubs and spots of flowers', that John Adam had seen and criticised there in 1759.[10] It was close in this nakedness to The Leasowes, where comparative poverty had trimmed Shenstone's sails, and replaced the customary plethora of temples and pavilions with a common field path, which linked a variety of natural scenes – cascades, lawns, dells, a lake, groves of trees, hills and rural valleys, even a lover's walk – all with constant and wide prospects over the surrounding landscape. North Merchiston never matched the variety or sophistication of The Leasowes, nor equalled Shenstone's rich vein of poetic allusiveness, although characteristically and ambiguously William Adam claimed in 1838, that it was 'more extensive and more decorated in some parts but in others full of the simplicity which distinguished Shenstone's pleasing and agreeable residence'.[11] But compared with other Scottish gardens of the 1750s, it must have seemed startling in its simplicity, and it was probably this quality that led to its popularity with the erudite Mrs Montagu and others, and to its imitation (Plate 59).

At both Blair and North Merchiston, John Adam was his own client, for he rarely worked as a gardener outside the wide family circle unless as an extension of his limited architectural practice, as at Balnagowan in 1762. He did suggest at Yester, where he took over from his father, an island temple in the garden in 1751, with a 'rail form'd in the Chinese manner for a bridge, or passage over the River', but his real and happiest rôle was to exhort rather than direct in such matters.[12] In 1756, he toyed with the notion of publishing a series of designs, 'drawn out applicable to gardening, with ruins, temples, cascades and groups of trees', which had been concocted previously by his brother Robert.[13] Such a collaboration was hinted at in a letter from

8. It was presumably sold after John Adam's death in 1792 though the property had been on the market since at least 1785 (Blair Adam Mss. 4/213). It became with most of the surrounding land the property of James Walker, Esq., of Dalry House before 1817. Dick Lauder wrote in 1842 that it had been 'much demolished by having its timber greatly diminished, and the Edinburgh and Glasgow canal carried directly through it, so as to subdivide it' (Dick Lauder, op. cit., p.209). In 1797, John Adam's sister described some of the pictures removed from Merchiston as including works by Berghem, Pannini, Wooton, Mercier, Vandois, Vogelson, and Pellegrini. These were still on their hands though others had gone 'from Merchiston, viz. 35 in all' (Blair Adam Mss, General Correspondence, 1797).

9. Yale University Library, Spence Papers, Box v.

10. Fleming, op. cit., p.265.

11. NLS Ms.11916/79. In this letter to the Earl of Minto William Adam changed the chronology of North Merchiston. It was now 'upon the plan of the Leasowes' rather than anticipating it.

12. See NLS Acc. 4862/Box 49/F2. Adam also proposed a canal for Yester in March of that year (ibid.).

13. Fleming, op. cit., p.363.

14. Blair Adam Ms.4/10.

15. Fleming, op. cit., p.363.

Robert to John, where the former rejoiced 'with you extreamly that the Blair looks so well & that you was so happy at it and should like much to spend a few weeks there Dictating (if youl excuse the phrase) some Italian beauty which the length of my pictoresque genious could suggest or the continuance of my Sojourn in this country intitle me to propose to you'.[14] But the scheme fell through because of Robert's characteristic determination to put his ideas into practice first, and then consolidate his reputation by publication. He wrote with customary modesty that, 'if ever I should have the fortune to execute a dozen of temples and lay out a set of gardens, which are approved of and admired by the world, then is the true time to publish them'.[15] Regrettably the project was abandoned and each went his own separate way in gardening, John at North Merchiston and Blair, Robert in the fantasy landscapes of his drawings.

The same informal taste that characterised North Merchiston was evident in John Adam's work at Blair (Plate 60). But Merchiston was a villa whereas Blair was an estate, and as such expected to earn an income and contribute from its plantations to the later fortunes of the family. It was needed. Once again its historian was John's son, William, who chronicled his father's dedication to the estate and landscape, and his love of planting. He wrote that his father had started work in 1750, two years after his succession, by preparing a nursery for raising trees from seed on the estate, and the following year 'planted

Plate 59. Print of The Leasowes, Worcestershire, *c.*1770, from Paul Sandby
The Virtuosi's Museum

16. *Blair Adam*, pt.I, p.94. There is a further manuscript account of Blair Adam, 'Description of Blair-Adam Garden', which was 'written by Andrew Mackenzie Landscape Gardener while at Blair Adam, 1838 till 1855' (Blair Adam Ms.4/48). This account contained lists of the plants and trees, but gave little further information about the history of the gardens.

17. *Blair Adam*, pt.I, pp.97, 98; see pt.III, Appendix no.1, p.4; and also 'List of Plants received from Inveraray 1757', Blair Adam, Ms.4/90.

18. See *Blair Adam*, pt.II, p.5. In the garden at Blair Adam, William Adam erected a memorial in 1833, which carried the inscription that John Adam completed this garden 'which has been preserved without change of design, or alteration of effect, except what growth had produced' (ibid., frontispiece). The memorial was designed by Henry Westmacott whose 'taste and picturesque eye is well known', see NRA *List of Blair Adam drawings* (1972) pt.I. It was designed by James Loch, the notorious improver and cousin of William Adam. At the end of this volume was a lithographic view of the garden of J.B. Kidd, a view northwards up the broad grass walk, and a plan of the garden. There are further drawings related to these in the Blair Adam Collection. The shrubs in this Section of the garden which were planted by John Adam were 'Arborvitae, Box, various sorts of *Cedars*, Juniper, Swedish Juniper; Irish Yew, Ilex Carolina, Bird-Cherry, (which is almost an evergreen), Portugal Laurel, Bay, Laurel-Bay, Hollies, Laurentines, Pericanthia, etc . . . in all twenty-seven different sorts of evergreen shrubs' (*Blair Adam*, pt.II, pp.10, 11).

the largest of the fir'.[16] In this formidable task, his inspiration was probably not the decorative naturalism of Woburn Farm or even The Leasowes, but the tough husbandry of the Duke of Argyll whose work at Inveraray and The Whim he knew at first hand. While William acknowledged his father's debt to his former school friend Doctor Hope of Edinburgh, 'an excellent arborist', from whom he had obtained many trees of botanical interest, it was from Duke Archibald that 'he gained more than from any other person, both by the instruction he was capable of conveying on that subject (for his Grace was a superiorly skilled planter) and from the opportunity he gave my Father, of taking from his nurseries the most useful and best trees, for the propagation of the fir tribe: so that the most ancient larches, spruces, and silver firs to be found on the Estate of Blair-Adam, were sent by the Duke of Argyle'.[17] In Inveraray fashion, and on ground almost as poor as that of Loch Fyneside, John Adam had ambitiously planted 540 acres by 1784, when the crash of the Adam fortune made such schemes irrelevant. With less concern for shelter and profit, he laid out a walled garden in 1755 that was a curious mixture of shrubbery and pleasure ground, with the plants and trees typical of the Scottish kitchen garden (Plate 61).[18] The fruit trees were grown in espalier fashion on the walls, with soft fruit planted in front or trained on a trellis, which made a further boundary for this garden. The paths were straight, with gravel and grass walks, while in the upper part the shrubbery was provided with serpentining walks. The intended effect was a sort of winter garden, evergreen with a few silver firs,

Plate 60. View of Blair Adam, Kinross, from Adam Blair Adam, *1834*

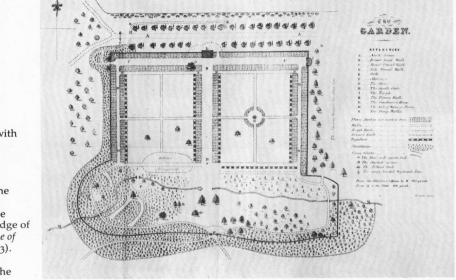

19. For John Adam's direct concern with the garden, see 'Memorial for Adam Livingston' and 'Memorial for James Flockhart', both contained in his gardening notebooks (Blair Adam Ms.4/90). He probably belonged to the Association for importing American plants and seeds founded in 1760, see p.47 n.13. For his theoretical knowledge of gardening and planting, see *Catalogue of the Library at Blair Adam* (London 1883).

20. John Adam continued to add to the estate after his succession in 1748. In 1754 he purchased Dullomuir, and in 1774 Kinnaird. In addition he owned the estate of Woodstone in Kincardineshire, which he had acquired around 1769, having consulted Lord Findlater and Peter May on its purchase; see SRO GD 248/982/1. According to George Richardson, 'The house, with a few trees around it, is but mean and incommodious, see George Richardson *General View of the Agriculture of Kincardineshire* (London 1813) pp.170, 171. For John Adam's Court of Offices, see Blair Adam Ms.4/90. This included several schemes all showing a square block with a circular centre; see Exhibition Catalogue *Robert Adam at Home* (Edinburgh 1978) p. 10. The original design was to have had an entrance front some 144 feet wide (ibid.).

21. For these, see the reports of Thomas Henderson, Mr Brown and Mr Bruce, all made between 1772 and 1789 (Blair Adam Ms.4/88). In Brown's report of 1772, single rows of trees and the various clumps were valued at £289, and the other woods at £509 (ibid.).

Weymouth pines, hemlock spruces and other trees, some specially imported from America, to give the garden both scale and variety (Plate 62).[19]

These improvements went hand in hand with more prosaic but profitable developments on the estate – the one to some extent justifying the other. Poor land was drained and cultivated, a bleaching mill was set up in Dullomuir with the usual premiums for the best spinners and weavers, and the more promising of the tenant farmers were encouraged to modernise their methods with trips to Norfolk and London. The cottages at Dullomuir were designed by John Adam around 1771, and at this date a new Court of Offices was begun as part of an ambitious but never completed, scheme to the west of Blair Adam.[20] Coal, too, was still mined with diminishing return on the estate, and in 1774 the rather incongruous pit, which sat next to the front door of Blair Adam, was finally closed. But for all this and other enterprises, trees still constituted the most obvious and, in the long run, the most profitable part of improvement at Blair Adam. It was just as well, for with the decline in the Adam family fortunes in the 1770s and 1780s, the woodlands were looked at with an accountant's eye, were constantly surveyed and valued, and produced succeeding schemes for their management.[21] Yet, in investing so heavily in timber,

Plate 61. The walled garden at Blair Adam, from *Blair Adam*

John Adam was literally following his father's path. In the woods around the house, he extended and continued William Adam's formal avenues, matching the North Avenue, of 1737–8, with a new South Avenue in 1763.[22] It was where they intersected the Broad Avenue, just east of the existing house, that the new Blair Adam that Robert had planned in 1777 and John had set his heart on was to have been sited (Plate 63).[23] It was never built and the old house, patched and extended, hobbled into the nineteenth century.

Apart from these variations on his father's work, most of John Adam's plantations were made, south and west of the existing house, on the rocky slopes of the Kiery Craigs and the Arlicks. The woods there were largely of larch and pine, and their landscaping was limited to small winding paths. That of The Hill, a plantation directly behind Blair Adam itself, gave a shifting and panoramic view over the Lomond Hills with a distant glimpse of Loch Leven, a scene much admired by Sir Walter Scott.[24] Perhaps the most picturesque of all these woodlands was the Glen, planted between 1762 and 1763, where a path led up the steep course of a small burn, adapted from the former basin of the South Avenue, and opened up a series of woody prospects. This was the soul of John's picturesque landscape. He constantly returned to this Glen, designing bridges and obelisks and creating an evocative day-dream for dramatically high-lighting its slopes with a castle, watch tower, and classical ruins (Plate 64).[25] In all of this John Adam was consciously improving and revising the paternal landscape against the prevailing tendency to destroy and eradicate the formal. He developed in the process, according to his son, a 'taste which, with such decision, made art embellish nature, without breaking down the works of mere art where those works should prevail'.[26] He attempted in this way to fashion from the old, the kind of augustan rural retreat that had been discussed by both Dalrymple and Sir John Clerk. His son christened the new landscape at North Merchiston a *ferme ornée*, and at Blair Adam a *terre ornée*.

James Adam's feeling about landscape was similar to that of his brother John. It was practical, theoretical and had more than a whiff of Rousseauesque simplicity and self-sufficiency, together with a liberal dose of theory from Arthur Young's *Rural Economy* of 1770. In his *Practical Essays on Agriculture* James Adam looked nostalgically back to the stout yeoman farmer of Virgil and his small-holding where, 'The Husbandman who plows his fertile land; / From troubles free, enjoys a sweet repose; / With food supply'd by nature's bounteous hand'.[27] His ideal was a natural landscape, rather like his brother's, but one where

22. *Blair Adam*, pt.i, p.99. The South avenue was composed largely of oaks with off it a fine Spanish chestnut; see pt.iii, pp.88–89 and 36–7.

23. ibid., pt.i, p.112. There are several schemes for additions to Blair Adam in the Blair Adam Collection, and also in the Soane Museum, vol.45, ff.86–89. There are, too, several plans at Blair Adam showing this building and others in the park landscape.

24. The Hill of twenty-two acres was planted in 1754/5; see ibid., pt.iii, pp.50–63. For Sir Walter Scott's admiration of this landscape, and the meetings of his Blair Adam Club, see ibid., pt.i, pp.i–xxxi. According to Sir Thomas Dick Lauder, who knew William Adam, it was Scott who suggested the writing of the Blair Adam book (Dick Lauder, op. cit., p.207).

25. The Glen of sixty acres had the lower part planted in 1762/3 and the upper in 1784/5 (ibid., pt.iii, pp.71–8). It is now lost in Forestry Commission plantations. For John Adam's designs for this area, see *Robert Adam at Home: Catalogue* (1978) pp.10–14.

26. *Blair Adam*, pt.i, p.98.

27. James Adam *Practical Essays on Agriculture*, 2 vols. (London 1789), vol.ii, p.515. Adam prefaced his translation with the following note: 'I proposed to have given Dryden's translation of these beautiful lines, for the information of any English readers; but upon looking over it, although far from a liberal one, yet I found the necessary adherence to ancient mythology and to ancient customs, rendered it not altogether intelligible . . . I therefore flattered myself that I could, perhaps, give a better idea of the pleasure of *our* country life, by attempting an imitation of this divine poet, and, such as it is, I venture to lay it before my reader' (ibid.).

the husbandman rather than the gardener dominated. The advice he gave in his *Practical Essays* was largely drawn from his experience as a small farmer in Hertfordshire, and passed on in Arthur Young's style.[28] He had tried there various forms of husbandry with both crops and animals, and appeared to find as much, if not more, satisfaction in a well-tilled field as in a landscaped park. The countryside had 'in my eyes', he wrote, 'far superior beauties, to the most boasted exertions of art, where silent groves are reflected by artificial rivers, and whole parishes are depopulated to pale around the boundless park, in order to indulge the sullen pomp of sequestered grandeur'.[29] Adam also felt that a large part of the rewards of husbandry was simply the energy spent in their attainment. He idealistically and wholeheartedly recommended rural life and, 'laying aside the enthusiasm of the poet', objectively pointed out 'the many and great advantages, in point of health, which persons employed in agriculture have over those engaged in other pursuits'.[30] In this and similar stances he fell into the

28. Although Adam never referred to his Hertfordshire property by name, he did mention it if only obliquely: 'In this county, it is the grand resource, to which we apply' (ibid., vol.I, p.13), and again: 'Some neighbours of my own' (ibid., vol.II, p. 508). These occurred where he was discussing the agriculture of Hertfordshire.

29. ibid., vol.II, p.512.

30. ibid., p.521.

Plate 62. Aerial view of Blair Adam, from the walled and winter garden, 1979

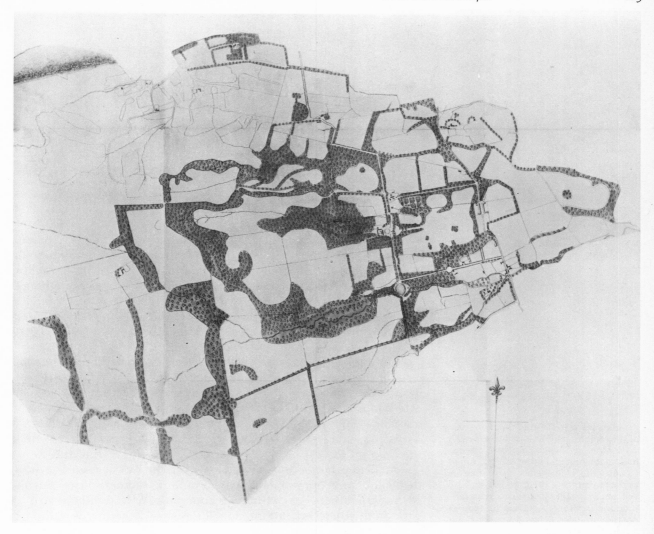

category of what the agriculturalist William Marshall had termed in 1778 as 'The Aerialist'. Although Marshall himself had forsaken the town for 'Rusticity', he had ungenerously little good to say about others who had done much the same.[31] His Aerialist was no exception: he was 'volatile, speculative and credulous – and habitually bookish – He has read the *Tours* and seen the *Patent Plow*! and sallies forth

Plate 63. Plan of the park at Blair Adam, *c*.1775, from *Blair Adam*

31. Marshall also claimed that his writing of the *Minutes* had led him to an '*Analysis of the Means of Human Existence*', and this had 'made him still more anxious for a Country life – He wishes to improve and perfect by practice the theoretic sketch' William Marshall *Minutes on Agriculture* (London 1778) p.2. A similar attitude had possibly induced James Adam to take up farming in Hertfordshire.

32. ibid., p.12.

33. ibid., p.151.

34. See Adam, op. cit., vol.II, pp.502–3.

35. ibid., vol.II, p.503.

Knight-errant of Agriculture, to rescue her from the hands of Barbarism and Boors'.[32] While this was an extreme view that only partially described James Adam, it was intermittently true of his reforming attitude to farming, and in the *Practical Essays*, there was something of 'those Pompous Displayers of Learned Trifles', whom Marshall deplored as 'faint-warbling through the Grove of Letters, to the injury of *Natural* and *Scientific Knowledge*, and the annoyance of *English Literature*'.[33]

James Adam's attitude in such concerns was perhaps more intellectually extreme and doctrinaire than that of the rest of his family, and it contrasted notably with his brother Robert's. While he, and to some extent John, took a thoroughly romantic view of the landscape and its buildings, James was seriously interested in improving the design of farms and cottages for what they were rather than how they looked. In the *Practical Essays*, he wrote that this branch of architecture was a 'useful field yet unoccupied', and bewailed the lack of a sensible study that 'should not only contain designs of the dwelling-houses, but also of the farm offices, or out-houses adjoining'.[34] He rightly turned his back on the thatched and mullioned ramshackle buildings of the picturesque movement, where appearance was all, and particularly his brother's designs in the genre, and went as far in the other direction as to recommend so utilitarian a material as 'rough iron' in their construction.[35] By the time the second edition of *Practical Essays* appeared in 1794, the situation had been remarkably improved by the appearance of Marshall's own series of *General Views of Agriculture* on a county or regional basis. But there was still a market for romanticism. In Malton's

Plate 64. Scheme for the Glen at Blair Adam, by John Adam

An Essay on British Cottage Architecture of 1798 the preservation of the cottage was disingenuously argued as part of 'the peculiar beauty of the British picturesque'.[36] It figured in Malton's and other susceptible imaginations as 'a small house in the country; of odd, irregular form, with various harmonious colouring, the effect of weather, time and accident; the whole environed with smiling verdure, having a contented, chearful, inviting aspect, and door on the latch, ready to receive the gossip neighbour, or weary, exhausted traveller'.[37]

This aspect of Malton's reading of the picturesque was fairly close to Robert Adam's. His taste in garden design had moved during his career from a classico-literary informality to one of increasing naturalism and romanticism. At the outset, his attitude to the landscape garden had been made clear in the abortive scheme, of 1756, to publish some of his designs. This enterprise was sufficiently public property for Dalrymple to describe Adam in 1761 as 'the best Gardner & Painter I had ever known joined in one person'.[38] The ghost of this project may be disinterred in the thirty-nine capricci of ruins, temples, cascades and trees, in the Pierpont Morgan Album in New York (Plate 65). These, and many others like them, show an undulating landscape that is hardly more than an excuse for a series of loosely connected, architectural vignettes of ruined antiquity. They were in every sense a realisation of the contemporary and fashionable melancholia found in the canvasses of Hubert Robert and Fragonard, and were probably directly inspired by an Italian composition like Marchionni's Tempietto Diruto in the new gardens of the Roman Villa Albani, of around 1760.[39] While in these the mood was certainly one of acute nostalgia, it was of a wistful rather than intellectual kind where the various ruined scenes evoked a mellow classical past. The defect of both this sentiment and these drawings was monotony – an endless variation on much the same theme at much the same intensity – where the landscape seemed not only some timeless Elysium, but one undergoing extensive archaeological excavation. This may have induced him to abandon, by 1780 at least, such a barren landscape for the more dramatic scenery of the picturesque and gothic. There the 'lofty mountains, and rocky and lonely recesses – tufted woods hung over precipices – lakes intersected with castled promontories – ample solitudes

36. William Marshall wrote both county and regional 'General Views of Agriculture', which were published by the Board of Agriculture. For the practicality of his scheme, see his work on Taymouth, and his *General View of the Agriculture of the Central Highlands of Scotland* (London 1794), on which it was based. James Malton *An Essay on British Cottage Architecture* (London 1798) gave 14 designs for cottages, all in the picturesque tradition, ranging from 'Dwellings for the Peasant and Farmer', to 'Retreats for the Gentleman'. Although there are earlier excursions into agricultural building in Langley and others, these were designed as eye-catchers rather than practical buildings. The first decade of the nineteenth century saw numerous such works, like Gandy's *Designs for Cottages, Cottage Farms and other Rural Buildings* (London 1805), and, more seriously, Richard Elsam *Hints for Improving the Condition of the Peasantry*, of 1816.

37. Malton, op. cit., p.1.

38. SRO GD 135/160 f.60. Dalrymple had written in the same vein in 1758: 'you will find in him joined the most perfect taste in Architecture painting and gardening I ever knew joined in one man' (ibid., f.11).

39. ibid. For the relationship between scattered groups of Adam drawings and his and John's projected garden publications, see John Fleming 'An Italian Sketchbook by Robert Adam, Clérisseau and Others' *Connoisseur* (1960) p.194. This Album passed from the Collection of Mrs J.P. Morgan to the Library in 1954; see The Pierpont Morgan Library *Review of Acquisitions 1949–1968* (New York 1969) p.129; and John Harris *A Catalogue of British Drawings for Architecture etc.* (Upper Saddle River 1971) p.10. The villa Albani was begun by Marchionni in 1751, but work on the

Temple of Diana and the Tempietto Diruto was only under way in 1761; see Joachim Gaus *Carlo Marchionni, ein Beitrag zur römischen Architektur des Settecento* (Köln 1967) pp.24–7. Like much of the villa, the ideas were those of Winckelmann and Albani. Adam, through Clérisseau, would be well aware of what was afoot, and it is to this circle that the Morgan album belongs.

40. This was Dick Lauder's
characterisation of the ideal Highland
landscape; see his *Forest Scenery*, vol.I,
p.11, where he gives an impartial essay
of his own 'On the Nature and Principles
of Taste'. It was contrasted unfavourably
with the quiet and tame 'English
landscape', seen as a place of 'green
meadows, with fat cattle – canals, or
navigable rivers – well fenced, with
cultivated fields – neat, clean, scattered
cottages – humble antique church, with
churchyard elms, and crossing
hedgerows' (ibid., p.10).

of unploughed and untrodden valleys – nameless and gigantic ruins –
and mountain echoes, repeating the scream of the eagle and the roar of
the cataract' all seemed irredeemably and intrinsically Scottish.[40]

Robert Adam's later landscape drawings probably fulfilled several
purposes. In some respects, they served as a form of escapism from the
rigours of his wide architectural practice and the tyranny of the drawing board. They show a consistent attempt to balance architecture with
landscape, each at its most dramatic and complementary, cast
altogether differently from the standard Capability Brown design. In
their realisation, these compositions followed certain immutable laws,
and showed an almost obsessive preoccupation with the moods of the
most elemental features of the picturesque. His drawings were a
kaleidoscope: its pieces were the cliff-top castle sliding into ruin, the
waterfall pouring into a deep lake with towering mountains above,
and always poor suffering humanity, puny in such a heroic setting
(Plate 66). These *stuffage* figures, invariably present, often in shadow
and never very good, symbolised for the picturesque and Dick Lauder

Plate 65. Capriccio by Robert Adam, from his Garden Sketchbook

41. ibid., p12.

'the weakness and insignificance of perishable man, whose generations thus pass away into oblivion, with all their toils and ambition, while Nature holds on her unvarying course'.[41] In this way, Adam's most familiar composition was one where his small figures were little more than foreground incident, moving inwards along a causeway that twisted towards a castle that towered above them on a rocky outcrop. The viewpoint he selected – typical of the *vedutisti* – was usually above the foreground, and roughly parallel to the middle, with the distant mountains closing the design. The melancholic mood of these drawings was emphasised by Adam's fondness for a tinted ink wash, where tones of brown and blue grey predominated with only a minimal amount of penwork apparent. Because of this, many of his water colours were a succinct expression of his ideas as a picturesque designer, ever concerned with movement, light and variety. There was often only a small and formal divide between them and his real architecture.

Not surprisingly, some of his cottage drawings can be readily seen as the source for actual projects, like his cottage *orné*, an irregular and tactile hotch-potch of 1789, high in the woods above his new castle for

Plate 66. Landscape with castle, by Robert Adam, *c*.1785

42. Two watercolours in the Blair Adam Collection are inscribed 'Mrs Kennedy' and dated 1789. See NRA *Blair Adam Drawings*, pt.1, nos. 88, 89. The thatched cottage was possibly that just above the Castle and marked in the Ordnance Survey of 1856. Several good examples of Adam's cottage compositions are in the Department of Prints and Drawings of the National Gallery of Scotland; see Keith Andrews and J.R. Brotchie *National Gallery of Scotland, Catalogue of Scottish Drawings*, (Edinburgh 1960) pp.10–15.

43. See SRO GD 18/4981 f.134. The history of these parts of Culzean has never been properly settled. There is a good drawing of the old tower house of Culzean with impressively classical stables beside it (NGS. Prints and Drawings, RSA 1424). The latter may well have been erected in the 1750s, when a certain amount of building was going on; see GD 25/9/Box 14, and it approximates to what exists there at present. This drawing also shows the ruined outworks of the tower house that Adam may well have incorporated into his causeway design, see 'Colean Castle before it was altered. Ayrshire No. 31'.

44. These two drawings for the causeway are in the Ailsa Collection at Cassilis, nos.16 and 17, Architectural Portfolio. The drawings were evidently composed in London using a survey sketch. probably sent up by Hugh Cairncross, Adam's Clerk of Works at both Dalquharran and Culzean; see letter from Adam, SRO GD 27/7/Box 2. Accounts 1786–1790. The note on drawing 17 refers to 'the Ground according to your Sketch'. There are further drawings for Culzean in the Soane Museum; see Bolton, op. cit., vol.II index, pp.8–9, and one in the Blair Adam Collection that shows the house before the construction of the causeway, NRA *Blair Adam Drawings*, pt.1, no.62.

his sister and her husband at Dalquharran in Ayrshire (Plate 67).[42] The parallel can be stretched to his more ambitious castellated compositions, and further to several of the castle-style houses he built in the 1780s, especially in Scotland. So much so, that some of his perspective views for Culzean and Oxenfoord were distinguishable only from his imaginative sketches by their greater attention to architectural detail and firmer composition. Culzean was itself a further variation on the theme of the cliff-top castle (Plate III). The sea pounding at its base, the view westward to the Ailsa Craig in the revised tradition of his father, the approach on the landward side by an elevated and fortified causeway, made Culzean a commission that allowed Adam, as Clerk of Eldin pertinently remarked, to 'indulge to the utmost his romantic and fruitful genius'.[43] An anonymous sketch of the gaunt, old tower approached by a track showed a very Scottish balance between building and setting that certainly caught Adam's imagination (Plates 68 and 69).

In two of his drawings of 1780, the decaying walls and towers of the old buildings were a positive force that inspired the sad splendour of the castle as well as the evocative and artificially ruinous causeway.[44] The latter was an essential visual and architectural foil to the castle. Its orientation was contrived so that its vaulted arches disguised the full impact of the building and revealed it only through a succession of half

Plate 67. Watercolour of Dalquharran Cottage, Ayrshire, by Robert Adam, *c.*1790

11. Aerial view of Duff House, beside the Deveron, Banffshire, 1979

45. For Adam's drawing for Findlater, see A.A. Tait *Catalogue: Robert Adam – the Picturesque Drawings* (Edinburgh 1972) pl.7; and, but unidentified, A.P. Oppé *English Drawings, Stuart and Georgian Periods, at Windsor Castle* (London 1950) p.24. It probably parallels an album of designs, twenty-three in all but only eleven extant, which Adam made for Lord Seafield in 1783; see SRO RHP 2544; and also Bolton, op. cit., vol.II, Index, p.13.

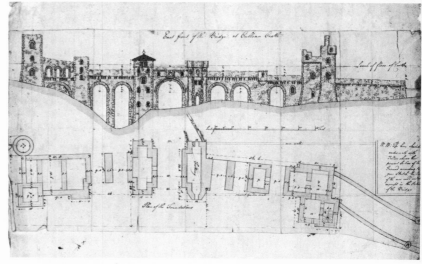

Plate 68. Culzean Castle, Ayrshire, before alteration, *c.*1760, artist unknown
Plate 69. East front of the bridge at Culzean Castle, from Robert Adam's office

46. According to Sir Thomas Dick Lauder, who was very well informed, 'the alterations and improvements on the grounds of Oxenford Castle have been very great since we first recollect them in the days of our youth . . . The boundaries of the park are now so extended as to enclose a very large park . . . Following the example set by his ancestor, Marshall Stair at Castle Kennedy, in Wigtonshire, the noble proprietor has cut the lawn behind the house into terraces and slopes, in the old style of landscape gardening'; (Thomas Dick Lauder *Scottish Rivers* (Glasgow 1890) p.291). Dick Lauder was writing in 1847. *Scottish Rivers* had first appeared in Tait's *Edinburgh Magazine* in that year and referred to the eighth Earl, who had succeeded in 1840. The view showing this causeway is attributed to Clerk of Eldin and would be after 1780 (Clerk of Penicuik Collection, H2450). It is not shown, however, in any of Adam's views of the castle.

47. See *Gentleman's Magazine* (1792) p.673, which reads 'His talents extended beyond the line of his own profession: he displayed in his numerous drawings in landscape a luxuriance of composition, and effect of light and shadow, which have scarcely ever been equalled' (ibid.).

48. See SRO GD 18/4981 f.134.

49. William Angus *The Seats of the Nobility and Gentry . . . Select Views* (Islington 1787). Amongst others, it contained Alexander Nasmyth's view of the bridge and house, built by Sir Thomas Miller, at Barskimming and dated 1791, and that of Dalkeith by Barrett of 1788. Apart from this drawing and its Oxenfoord engraving, Adam was probably deeply involved with the prints made by John Clerk of Eldin. They seem to have co-operated widely and the almost identical views they made of Crossraguel Abbey, in Ayrshire, suggests close collaboration over a number of years (see Tait, op. cit., no.7). According to the Bannatyne Club,

views until the forecourt had been reached. A similar though smaller and less imaginative design was produced nearly a decade later for Findlater Castle. There Adam proposed to echo his father's Cullen bridge with a castellated one, doubling as a banqueting house, which was intended to lead from the castle into an ambitious landscaped park.[45] There was at least a third and similar causeway, possibly designed for the river at Oxenfoord, which appeared hazily amongst the trees in a view of the castle he re-built there for Sir John Dalrymple (Plate 70). It was much the same donjon composition as its Culzean contemporary but veering closer in style to the gothic than the Adamitic romanesque. If it existed, it cannot have been for long, for the park at Oxenfoord was remodelled and expanded in the 1840s to what remains today (Plate 71).[46]

The importance of these drawings was fully realised by Adam's contemporaries and was noticed in his obituary in the *Gentleman's Magazine*. They were praised as showing 'in his numerous drawings in landscape a luxuriance of composition, and an effect of light and shadow, which have scarcely ever been equalled'.[47] While the writer was obviously thinking of the imaginative watercolours, the more prosaic perspective views seem to have attracted almost as great a following. Clerk of Eldin in his account of Adam's career wisely made a distinction between 'his many architectural drawings finished by his

Plate 70. Oxenfoord Castle, Midlothian, showing bridge and causeway, by John Clerk of Eldin, c.1780

Clerks' and the 'infinite number of Valuable pieces, washed with water-colours, as well as what he has executed in Charo Obscuro, with Indian ink studied intirely for the General effect'.[48] Adam had also a commercial market for some at least of his topographic views, and among the work of the various contemporary artists whose drawings together make up the plates of Angus's *Seats of the Nobility and Gentry* was included a view by Adam of his own Oxenfoord Castle.[49] Although it lacked the immediate appeal of his other drawings and particularly of his watercolours of Oxenfoord (Plate 72), it managed to

'In the year 1786, a set of these Etchings, at the suggestion of the Earl of Buchan, was presented to George the Third . . . It consisted of sixty-two etchings by Mr. *Clerk,* some of them slightly tinted by his brother-in-law, Robert Adam, accompanied with descriptive notices of the Views' ('Views in Scotland' *Bannatyne Club* (1855) pp.xii and xiii).

Plate 71. Aerial view of park and causeway bridge at Oxenfoord, 1979

incorporate his stock motifs: the castle above the river, the distant church spire amongst the trees, the fisherman in the foreground (Plate 73).[50] But it was tame and tired, and not greatly different from similar drawings by Sandby or later Nasmyth, both of whose work was included by Angus. Nor was it unlike the work of Clerk of Eldin in either technique, choice of subject, or the ability to use the picturesque to sugar the pill. The majority of Adam's architectural rivals had, since Kent, employed some sort of landscape composition to make an enticing perspective of a proposed building. Some, like Wyatt, went as far as to employ an artist specially for this purpose; others, like Henry Holland, actually designed the garden immediate to the house.[51] In Scotland, James Playfair's drawings for Ardkinglas in Argyll and elsewhere showed a lively appreciation of the decorative advantages of landscape. It was Playfair's habit to produce along with the more conventional drawings what he termed a 'Landscape' plan or 'Landscape perspective', for which he charged both separately and often as much as three guineas.[52] In his proposals of 1790 to replace the old castle of Ardkinglas with a 'Marine Pavilion' he included such a 'Landscape', showing both the old and new houses and explaining his scheme with notes (Plate 74). Together they made an unsatisfactory and diminutive essay in the picturesque, where the old castle was

Plate 72. Oxenfoord, from the park, by Robert Adam, c.1780

50. There are two large watercolours of Oxenfoord, see NRA *Blair Adam Drawings*, pt.I, no.9 and pt.II, no.418. That they have no counterparts in the Soane Museum (see Bolton, op. cit., vol.II, Index, p.25) possibly means that they were associated with Angus's *Views* in some way. Sir John Dalrymple was a long standing patron of Adam as well as a friend which might also explain the drawings survival at Blair Adam.

51. James Wyatt's draughtsman was Dixon, and Wyatt prided himself, perhaps defensively, on his 'inability to draw'. For Holland's work on the gardens at Dunira, see pp.122–3. According to Loudon, Holland was firstly an architect, 'though he generally directed the disposition of the grounds when he was employed in the former capacity'; see 'Landscape Gardening' *Edinburgh Encyclopaedia* XII (1830) p.538. In 1800, Holland wrote to William Adam asking for a list of 'the great nurseries in Scotland'; see NRA List 0063, p.31.

52. NLS Adv. 33.5.25 ff.44, 53.

53. Knight, op. cit., p.12. For Playfair's proposed work at Ardkinglas, see Colin McWilliam 'James Playfair's Design for Ardkinglas' in *The Country Seat*, eds. Howard Colvin and John Harris (London 1970) pp.193–8; and NLS Adv. 33.5.25 f.73 verso. These drawings are in the present Lorimer house at Ardkinglas, and a similar set of drawings in the Soane Museum.

54. For Ardkinglas, see *The Country Seat*, pp.193–8; for Urie, see NLS Adv. 33.5.25 f.43.

55. See SRO GD 151/11/32. Playfair's letter was dated September 1785 and written to his patron Robert Graham. For an account of this gaudy pavilion, see David Irwin, 'A "Picturesque" Experience: The Hermitage at Dunkeld' *Connoisseur* (1974) pp.196–201.

hidden but the new pavilion given open, even staring, views over Loch Fyne, entirely and adversely ignoring Knight's dictum that the 'greater art' was 'To lead, with guile, the prying sight / To where component part may best unite, / And form one beauteous nicely blended whole / To charm the eye and captivate the soul'.[53]

Playfair probably paid more attention to an ideal rather than real picturesque. He was always aware of its possibilities but not its capabilities. In this way he drew at Ardkinglas his client's attention to the setting as 'a much more picturesque prospect than any other', and at Urie, in 1789, suggested that the existing and 'most picturesque' castle demanded that 'whatever is done be in the style of a castle'.[54] But all the same he was prepared to learn humbly. At Dunkeld he freely acknowledged that he followed the painter Charles Steuart, 'Mr. Stuart did design the ornaments on the hermitage at Dunkeld. He informed me of his ideas. I made the drawings he is altogether unacquainted wt the detail of Architecture. But he certainly gave the idea, altho' he did not absolutely compose the architecture'.[55]

By turning his back on the hackneyed and pictorial solution of the sort shown in the plans for Ardkinglas, Adam relied on the illusionism given by a perspective view to boldly establish a rapport between building and setting. The drawing came to life in the way that even a highly ingenious plan, like that of Mount Melville of 1796, failed to do

Plate 73. Oxenfoord, from William Angus *The Seats of the Nobility and Gentry*

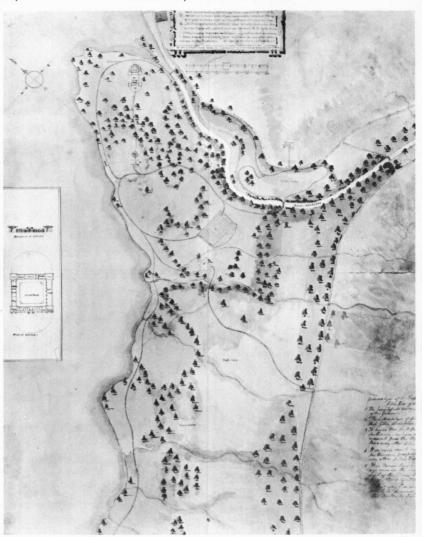

56. This plan dedicated to General
Melville was noted 'a word to the wise'.
It is in the Mellon Collection at Yale. The
ideas of morality it shows are certainly
closer to philosophy than landscape
gardening, and Le Charron may have
based his scheme loosely on a reading of
Montesquieu's natural laws. Its designer
may have been the soldier-author, the
Baron Le Charron, 1759–1837. General
Melville, 1723–1809, was a botanist and
antiquarian as well as a soldier. The
grounds at Mount Melville were laid out
in the 1820s by John Nicol (see App.III)
after the house had been rebuilt by
Gillespie Graham between 1821 and
1828; NLS Adv. 33.8.4.

(Plate 75). This scheme by the Chevalier Le Charron, for all its richness
of imagery and invention – it showed an estuary into which ran two
rivers, one leading from the Gulf of Despair, via revolution, jealousy,
luxury and bad education to the 'Source of the torrent of human
passion', while the other flowing from the 'Source of Happiness',

Plate 74. Ardkinglas, Argyllshire, improvement plan by James Playfair, 1790

through mildness, valour and truth, to the island of happiness – had little to offer but the charm and interest of a map.[56] While pretty, it was without purpose. The landscape it delineated was closer to Le Rouge's eighteenth-century China than Scotland, and its composition, which mixed plan and perspective, was thoroughly old fashioned by Adam's or even Playfair's standards. Although Adam's own technique may have stretched back to the capricci and topographical drawings of the 1750s, it was entirely subsumed by the conventions of the picturesque. But it must be said that however personal Adam's interpretation of the last may have been, it was never a strictly original one. A great many of his ideas, and even his technique with pen and watercolour, were

Plate 75. Moral plan dedicated to General Melville by the Chevalier Le Charron, 1796

57. For an account of Clerk's work in this field, see *Bannatyne Club*, pp.viii–xiv. In the Clerk of Penicuik Collection, Clerk Album H.2430, there is a watercolour noted by Clerk, 'J. Clerk after R. Adam'. Similarly there are several Clerk drawings in the Blair Adam Collection, see NRA *Blair Adam Drawings*, pts.I and II. As a topographical artist Clerk was the better, and certainly his early drawings of *c.*1760 are superior to those of Adam done during this period in Italy; see Fleming, op. cit., pls.50 and 51; see also *Catalogue of the Drawings Collection of the Royal Institute of British Architects A* (Farnborough 1969) p.17. For James Adam as a topographical artist, see Andrews and Brotchie, op. cit., p.9.

58. Clerk of Penicuik Collection, Clerk Album H.2439. In the Blair Adam Collection, there is a series of drawings possibly by Robert Adam of Welsh Castles – Neath, Margam, Oystermouth – made during a sketching tour in south Wales, possibly in 1777, see NRA, *Blair Adam Drawings*, pt.1, nos.76–83. For the Castle of Eudolpho drawing, see *Exhibition Catalogue: John Clerk of Eldin, etchings and drawings* (Edinburgh 1978) p.18.

paralleled in the work of his brother-in-law, John Clerk of Eldin. So much so, that it is difficult and perhaps unnecessary to determine who came first.[57] Certainly nearly all Adam's surviving compositions of this sort belong to the late 1770s, and were quite distinct from either his classical garden compositions of the 1760s or his more youthful and blatantly gothic confections. Clerk's entry into this stylistic world appears to have been earlier, possibly as far back as 1766, when he produced a view of Aberconway Castle that was remarkably close in feeling to the later Adam drawings and his own 'Castle of Eudolpho' in the Clerk of Penicuik collection (Plate 76).[58] Their mood was repeated outstandingly in a series of oblong panoramic views of the early eighties, of which that of the Tay at Dunkeld, in the Penicuik collection, with its misty light and gravelly colours, was a running mate to Adam's castle watercolours. But the difference between the two men was a broad one. Clerk undoubtedly worked up his drawings, had his own stock repertoire for the foregrounds, and remained a topographic artist, a delineator, wedded to the truth as he saw it. Adam was no such thing. For him, the Scottish castle with all its historical associations that he and Clerk drew over and over again, was an inspiration rather than a set piece of Scottish heritage. He was separate in this from the topographers, however brilliant, like Paul Sandby, or those of an exclusively antiquarian bent, like Cardonell and Cordiner, who had

Plate 76. Watercolour of Aberconway Castle, North Wales, by John Clerk of Eldin, 1766

made a similar association between the Scottish past and the picturesque landscape.[59] He anticipated the emotional style of Turner's plates
to the *Landscape-Historical Illustrations of Scotland*, of 1836/8. He
undoubtedly made possible Dick Lauder's certainty that 'the old Scottish house, with its square tower and bartisan, plain windows, hanging
turrets, round towers and lofty sugar-loaf roofs . . . intimately associated with Scottish scenery', was invariably 'quite out of harmony with
English landscape'.[60]

While Clerk set his topographical drawings in a picturesque version of the surrounding landscape, where a building often played a
minor role, Adam concocted both landscape and castle from his imagination. The buildings and landscapes that he and Clerk drew in each
other's company, were for Adam an ideal to be pursued in his architecture. His later Scottish castles at Culzean, Airthrey, Dalquharran, and
Seton, or his unexecuted design for Barnbougle, of 1774, in which the
old castle was the pivot for the new castellated design, were part of this
eclectic and picturesque landscape, where forms and motifs were
closely identified with an intense feeling for the Scottish past. So much
so, that his perspective views of the final design for such commissions
were set in a countryside as much Adamitic as Scottish. The reality was
of course very different, and apart from his work at Culzean, and
possibly Dalquharran, the actual landscape created was rarely his
work. Clerk's only attempt to cast what he saw and drew into building
was the cottage *orné* he erected in his own grounds at Eldin near
Edinburgh. Clerk had acquired this property in 1776 and built there
what he called Adam's Hut, after his brother-in-law, a few years
later.[61] His design was fairly typical of, and almost a parody of, those
he and Adam sketched (Plate 77). His surviving drawings differed
from the etchings he made of it. They showed a cottage, cruciform in
plan, with a round tower at one end, thatched, and with irregular
latticed windows, all reminiscent of Mrs Kennedy's *bijou* at Dalquharran (Plate 67). This seems to have been the occasion where he followed
Adam in making his drawings serve a purpose. For Clerk, even in his
sketching tours about the Scottish countryside, preferred to avoid the
new, and rejoiced only in the old, seeing his castles with their 'lofty
tower and pendulous turrets and battlements', as uniquely and 'sublimely picturesque and beautiful'.[62] His journal of one such tour,
undertaken in 1779, neglected any new gardens and plantations apart
from the odd reference to Cullen, or critical comment about
Taymouth.[63] Clerk had probably the smaller imagination. Certainly
there was little that was remarkable about his ephemeral Hut at Eldin,

59. Both Clerk and Adam sketched with Sandby in Scotland in *circa* 1750, and there is a copy by Clerk of the Sandby view of Castle Duart, Mull, NGS D.4381. There is also a Sandby drawing of John Adam's son William and Clerk of Eldin dated 1752, see Oppé, op. cit., p.57.

60. Dick Lauder, op. cit., p.368.

61. For his etchings of this building, see *Bannatyne Club* plates IX, XVII and XVIII. There is a sheet with a series of plans and elevations for this 'Hut' in the Clerk of Penicuik Collection, Clerk Album H.2454. Further drawings connected with it are in the Blair Adam Collection, see NRA *Blair Adam Drawings*, pt.I, no.35.

62. John Fleming 'A "Retrospective View" by John Clerk of Eldin' in *Concerning Architecture*, ed. John Summerson (London 1968) p.77.

63. See SRO GD 18/2118. This notebook was dated August 1779. There is another illustrated with pencil sketches in GD 18/4678b, and one further, undated and of Ayrshire, in the Clerk of Penicuik Collection.

which expressed more a feeling for false simplicity than an Adamitic taste for architecture in decline.

As much part of the Adam and Clerk picturesque parcel was the whole run of cottages and lodges, more or less *ornés*, that appeared in the closing decades of the eighteenth century. They varied in quality and purpose, and ranged from the supremely ephemeral, thatched ducal tea-house at Dalkeith Palace (Plate 78) to the more substantial descendants of the highland hunting lodge, like Mar or Glenfiddich. While the latter remained true to their original purpose, they exploited to the full their picturesque, if not sublime, settings. Remoteness and inaccessibility, which in the past had been a liability, became a positive advantage to be revelled in by the picturesque spirit and recognised by even the most staid.

The dull, second Lord Fife, who used Mar Lodge principally as a place to shoot, wrote of its charms in 1791 as being superior to any in Switzerland, showing as they did 'nature in greater magnificence and variety'.[64] But the more obvious and familiar sort of cottage *orné* was found below the highland line and better suited to the less dramatic

64. Alistair and Henrietta Tayler *The Book of the Duffs*, 2 vols. (Edinburgh 1914) vol.1, p.187.

Plate 77. Plans and elevations of Eldin Cottage, Midlothian, by John Clerk of Eldin

65. For a description of the Cottage at Langholm, see Louis Sismond *Journal of a Tour and Residence in Great Britain*, 2 vols. (Edinburgh 1815) vol.I, p.262. Sismond made his journey in 1810/11. The 'boor' or bower was built on a rock above the river Esk with 'a beautiful flower garden'. In the floods of 1816 it collapsed and was carried downstream and destroyed (*Gardener's Magazine* VII (1831) p.554). According to the *Statistical Account*, The Retreat was built by the Earl of Wemyss 'about 12 years ago' (*Statistical Account*, 1792, XII, p.66). Its woods and romantic dells were admired by Loudon in his *Encyclopaedia of Gardening*, p.1088. It was circular and thatched, more or less as it is today. For Dunira see pp.122–4, and Lynedoch see p.124.

66. See Charles Cordiner *Antiquities and Scenery of the North of Scotland* (London 1780) p.24; and *Remarkable Ruins, and Romantic Prospects of North Britain*, 2 vols. (London 1788–95) vol.I, up.

landscape of the lowlands, where architecture and landscape were evenly matched. There was for all of them a reasonably straight-forward descent from North Merchiston and the Edinburgh villas of the 1760s. Several, like the Duke of Buccleuch's 'boor', perched on a rocky bent of the river Esk outside Langholm in Dumfriesshire, repeated in extreme the villa philosophy of simplicity. Others, like The Retreat of about 1780, beside the White Esk in Berwickshire, Lynedoch Cottage in Perthshire, and more grandly Dunira in the same county, were all designed for a less simple and more comfortable rural existence in splendid scenery.[65] While the setting and life led in these buildings may have varied within the picturesque canon, they were all very much the children of their builder, indulged and cherished, and rarely long survived their parent's death. None, except The Retreat, remained either unaltered or rebuilt. Two were drowned.

Mar Lodge was a small classical building bought by Lord Fife in 1735. It was set in a landscape profusely ornamented in Taymouth style with garden buildings that included a small home farm. In 1776, Cordiner visited Mar and recorded a gothic tower beside the river, with 'on rugged parts of the hills, a bower, a high obelisk, an hermitage at Glen Corriemonlzie' (Plate 79).[66] These transitory monuments can only have been at cross-purposes with the surrounding landscape and were more appropriate to the riverside Elysium of Dunkeld than the

Plate 78. View of thatched tea-house at Dalkeith Palace, Midlothian, *c.*1799

67. John Stoddart *Remarks on Local Scenery during the Years 1799 and 1800*, 2 vols. (London 1801) vol. II, p.173.

68. See John Plaw *Rural Architecture* (London 1796) pl.52 and 53, and Cordiner op. cit., vol. I, pl. 'Hunting-Seat in Glen Fiodich'.

69. NLS Ms.5205 ff.17, 27; for the surveys of the 1830s, see SRO GD 44/49/24.

70. Cordiner, op. cit., vol. II, up.

forest of Mar. They were eminently characteristic of the pompous taste that the first Lord Fife had shown at Duff House. Not unjustly, such fripperies were marked down by Stoddart before 1800 as giving variety but only at the heavy 'sacrifice of Sublimity'.[67] This was never the case with Mar Lodge's near neighbour the Duke of Gordon's cottage at Glenfiddich or, more distantly, the Duchess's Kinrara, both of which lacked any such garden buildings apart from a simple monument at the latter. The English architect John Plaw gave a design for Glenfiddich around 1796 which, though unexecuted, captured in the bungalow style of the bows and arcades the casual air of the long rambling building shown in Cordiner's view. (Plate 80).[68] It remained in this haphazard way, without much embellishment or alteration, until the 1830s at least.[69] Possibly much of its simplicity was due to its rôle as an appendage of Gordon Castle to which it was usefully, though bizarrely, linked by an extraordinary hunting telegraph, which caught Nattes's sharp eye in 1799 (Plate 81). Its character as a sort of ducal bothy was obviously part of its charm: 'To leave the entertainments of the palace, and the gay scenes of festivity and convivial splendour; and to woo tranquillity in the shades of a vast and various scene of majestic landscape, is a transition in life, to minds of superior sensibility, oft-times the most eligible and pleasing'.[70] Little of this was true of Kinrara, which was agrarian rather than sportive, and more closely associated with the Duchess rather than the Duke of Gordon. Taken over by this extravagant and wayward Duchess about 1798, it was at

Plate 79. Mar Lodge, Banffshire, and cascade, from Charles Cordiner *Antiquities and Scenery of the North of Scotland*, 1780

71. Stoddart, op. cit., vol. II, pp.154–6. In 1798, Mrs Grant in her *Letters from the Mountain* described the Duchess as setting up 'a wooden pavilion' at the time (ibid., vol.II, p.142). A plan for enlarging the house was given in 1804, by John Smith and additions to it were carried out in 1805 by the London architect John Sanders, who had also worked at Gordon Castle (GD 44/51/279, and RHP 2498). Further work was carried out in 1810 (GD 44/51/281) and the house took its ultimate form in 1814 (GD 44/48/70). There are also drawings for this period in SRO RHP 31,786–31,788.

the outset a fairly small building described by Stoddard in the following year as a 'mere Highland farm', which awaited 'further architectural embellishment for which she (the Duchess) had received several architectural designs' (Plate 82).[71] He also maintained that the Duchess intended 'the establishment of a village at a little distance', which never materialised, although a garden formed 'in a hollow of the hill',

Plate 80. View of Glenfiddich, Banffshire, from *Antiquities and Scenery*
Plate 81. The Hunting Telegraph at Gordon Castle, Morayshire, by J.C. Nattes, 1799

72. Stoddart, op. cit., vol. II, p.156.

73. For gardening accounts at Kinrara, see SRO GD 44/34/55 and 44/51/279. The gardener at Kinrara at this time was David Cameron. Its setting was much admired in James Robertson's *General View of the Agriculture of Inverness* (London 1808) p. ix, and its layout apparent in a survey plan of 1838 (SRO RHP 2499). Robertson noted the sheltered garden, which grew 'turnips and other crops'.

74. See Cyril Matheson *The Life of Henry Dundas First Viscount Melville* (London 1933) p.97. His views on farming and country life were contained in a memorandum of 1802 'on the subject of a gentleman farming a part of the whole of his own property'. Prior to Melville's retirement his affairs and building at Dunira had been looked after by Sir William Murray of Ochtertyre.

75. See Matheson, op. cit., p.324.

76. ibid.

77. Holland's plans for Dunira are dated 1798 and show an existing U shaped house (see Dundas Mss. Comrie House, 'Plans and Estimates for Dunira 1803–1809'). This first building must have appeared after 1770, when a survey of Dunira then showed only a farm beside the River Earn (SRO RHP 34103). Holland's scheme produced a principal front of 15 bays with two pediments and Ionic portico of 5 bays. It was carried out in a curtailed form by the architect William Stirling. Lord Melville in 1787, purchased the farm of Meobie, Woodend of Meobie, Dunira and Garrichera (Matheson, op. cit., p.119), and in 1801 he bought the adjoining Comrie estate, giving him a total of 20,000 acres (ibid., p.312).

and laid out according to the ideas of 'Mr. Price's Essay on the Picturesque', certainly did.[72] Seeds and plants for the garden were sent from Dicksons of Perth between 1802 and 1810, and it was shortly afterwards extended to include a shrubbery around the expanding house.[73] Here, the lone Duchess played out her rôle as a highland Marie Antoinette, with hothouse plants from London, a velvet and mahogany game larder for the venison, and with the lakeside setting of L'Hameau replaced by one overlooking the Spey.

Dunira, near Comrie, was much more grandly conceived than Kinrara. Its builder, Lord Melville, posed as a farmer rather than a shepherd, and he had bought the estate about 1784 as an alternative to its suburban counterpart at Melville Castle, just beyond Edinburgh.[74] He was quite certain what he was about at Dunira and scornfully wrote in 1802 that 'it is inconsistent with the habits and advocations of a gentleman's life so to economise in the management of his farm as to produce nearly what a judicious farmer by profession will do'.[75] This attitude he felt justified a certain style, and at Dunira he established 'a comfortable residence without wanting anything that a country life can require'.[76] In the architectural sense this 'certain style' was supplied in 1798 by Capability Brown's son-in-law, Henry Holland, who more or less doubled the building, making the grandeur and prestige of the house match a similar growth in the size and value of the estate between 1787 and 1801.[77] When Holland's building was finished in

Plate 82. View of Kinrara, Banffshire, from Sir John Stoddart *Remarks on the Local Scenery and Manners in Scotland*, 1801

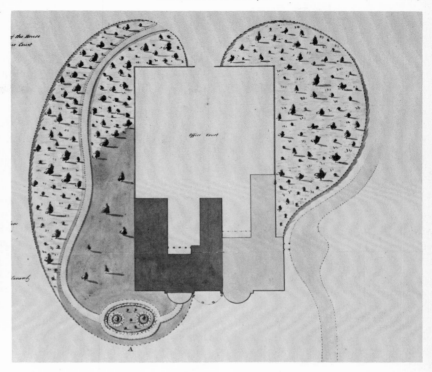

78. The reconstruction carried out between 1803 and 1809 cost some £11,802 (Dundas Mss. Comrie House, 'Plans and Estimates for Dunira 1803–1809'). After the sale of the estate by Lord Melville's son in 1824, the western lodge and gateway were built in 1827, and the year before the walled garden and hothouses by the Perth architect W.M. Mackenzie (ibid., Accounts 1826). Both of these survive more or less intact. Its site on low ground beside the mountain stream Allt Eas an Aoin caused constant flooding which persuaded Sir David Dundas to pull it down and build again close to, but on a higher and rocky plateau (for this information I am indebted to Sir Robert Dundas). The new house was designed by William Burn in 1851/2, see *Catalogue, Drawings Collection RIBA B*, p.127.

79. Stoddart, op. cit., vol.II, p.299.

1809, Dunira was revealed as a bleak, classical house, starkly contrasting with and much inferior to its setting of woods and steep mountains, and placed – fatally as it turned out – on the edge of flat pastureland beside the river Earn.[78] Close by the house was the fine waterfall on the Allt Eas an Aoin with its 'trembling Alpine bridges' that were illustrated in Nattes's drawing if 1799 in *Scotia Depicta* (Plate 83). Almost vertically above, rose the rocky and steep hills, where at 'points of attractive prospect, rude sheds, moss houses, or other appropriate seats have been placed'.[79]

In the formation of this landscape, Melville was probably his own master. While Holland, knowledgeable about plants, concerned himself sufficiently with the immediate landscape around the expanded house to recommend 'A light iron fence almost invisible inclosing a private garden', the more important landscaping of the hillsides was undoubtedly Melville's contribution (Plate 84).[80] In the various buildings he erected on the estate, Lord Melville seems to have fulfilled his

Plate 83. Waterfall at Dunira, Perthshire, from Fittler and Nattes *Scotia Depicta*, 1804
Plate 84. Dunira, plan of the gardens by Henry Holland, 1798

80. See note of his 1798 layout plan of Dunira (Dundas Mss. Comrie House, 'Plans and Estimates for Dunira 1803–1809'). How much Holland interested himself in landscape is hard to say, although in his work at Carlton House and at the Brighton Pavilion for the Prince Regent he concerned himself with the garden, see Dorothy Stroud *Henry Holland* (London 1966) pls.44 and 65.

81. These are shown in a series of unsigned and undated plans: SRO RHP 6763–6773. The draughtsman is the same in all, and several sheets bear the watermarks of 1806–1807.

82. Loudon *Encyclopaeda of Gardening* (1822) p.1252. Around 1810, it seems to have served as a residence for the Duke's brother, Lord Montagu, and was then destroyed in the floods of 1816 (*Gardener's Magazine* VII (1831) p.554). It shared this fate with Dunira.

83. SRO GD 224/655/2: Playfair's designs are in the Soane Museum and noted 'Begun to be built in 1787' (Soane Museum, Playfair drawings II S/19): see also NLS Adv. 33.5.25 f.48: Drawings by Holland for Langholm are at Selkirk, Bowhill Muniments Plans. Playfair was recommended to the Duke by Mr Douglas, his client at Bothwell House (SRO GD 151/11/32).

84. See Anthony Brett-Jones *General Graham* (London 1959) pp.233–9; see also E. Maxton-Graham *The Beautiful Miss Graham* (London 1927). Before this, Graham seems to have interested himself in estate improvement, building houses at Pitcairn Green in 1788 (NLS Acc. 2540/(1)). Tatham's designs were exhibited at the Royal Academy in 1807, and referred to as 'now commenced' in his Prospectus of 1808 or 1809. William Playfair made designs for a Dining Room and the Dalcrue Bridge, see Edinburgh University Library, Playfair drawings f.36. James Playfair was continuously at Lynedoch (Lednock) and Balnagowan from 1787 until 1790 at least. In 1789, he

adopted rôle as a gentleman farmer and evenly mixed purpose with propriety. Several of his projected farm buildings were in the true picturesque taste, with latticed windows, thatched roofs and wooden columned porticoes as 'shade to sit under', which would have admirably suited the Duchess of Gordon's style at Kinrara.[81] Unfortunately, they made Dunira's own lack of charm and informality all the more obvious.

Closer to the ideal cottage *orné* were those of Lynedoch or Langholm, as conventional as they were picturesque. Langholm Cottage has now disappeared, but according to the well-informed Loudon it was 'a picturesque heath covered cottage, built as a temporary residence by the late Duke, in a romantic situation, with beautiful pleasure-grounds'.[82] It was, as Loudon implied, a makeshift home while Playfair's new Langholm Lodge was building in 1787, and it may have become, like many temporary things, both loved and permanent.[83] It may also have been designed by Playfair. Certainly his Lynedoch Cottage was cast in the same and rather heavy handed form of the picturesque. Begun by General Graham, the future Lord Lynedoch, in 1786, it was completed before 1791 and until its radical alteration by Tatham in 1807 was no doubt typical of Playfair's cottage style and paralleled by at least one other, at Ogle, of 1789.[84] But it never lost the Regency charm of its Austrian roses and honeysuckle, despite alteration, and as it grew older, more dilapidated and less habitable, it became all the more the cynosure of the cottage *orné*. An evocative photograph taken just before it toppled into its grave in 1870, showed an irregular building, deliberately haphazard, which precociously displayed the full vocabulary of picturesque architecture (Plate 85). It equalled in rusticity and irregularity Clerk of Eldin's Hut or Adam's cottage at Dalquharran, although it reflected little that was intrinsically Scottish. The same may have been true of Langholm.

Adam's almost exclusive concern with the castellated building and the cottage *orné* was fully in line with the tenets of the picturesque. The successful combination of the gothic silhouette and asymmetry with the informal landscape was essential to the picturesque. The second plate of Knight's didactic poem *The Landscape* of 1794 relied on this mixture as did in more scholarly fashion Sir James Hall's *Essay on*

designed a Gardener's Cottage and the garden façade of the Farm, presumably Cottage (NLS Adv. 33.5.25 ff.29 verso, 30 verso, 47 verso). For Ogle, see ibid., f.50. Playfair's connection with Lynedoch was strengthened by the patronage of Robert

Graham of Fintry who acted as General Graham's agent at Lynedoch after 1787. It is possible that the gardens there were by the elder Thomas White, who had been consulted at Fintry (Linlathen) in 1782 (SRO GD 151/11/4).

the *Origin, History and Principles of Gothic Architecture*. The core of Hall's
book was first published in the *Transactions of the Royal Society of
Edinburgh*, in 1797, and was significantly expanded for its appearance
in book form sixteen years later.[85] The most crucial of Hall's additions
was his last chapter, which dealt with the merits of the classical and
gothic styles in a landscape setting. The distant view of a gothic
building was, he claimed, the best: 'The beauty and variety of the
Grecian style', he wrote, 'which reside in the details of execution, are
lost in the distant view; and the edifice then exhibits the dull and
abrupt appearance of its timber original, in its rude and unornamented
state'.[86] Hall found the sight of a gothic building at close range un-
appealing: 'A distant view is most favourable to the Gothic style; for its
form being boldly varied and strongly characterized in the general
plan, produces its full effect, as far as the eye can reach'.[87] He summed
up this balancing of stylistic merits with the statement that 'it results
from this comparison, that the Grecian style excels in all those qualities
of elegance and grace, which depend upon nice adjustment and masterly execution of details. Whereas the Gothic style, which, with great
truth, has been compared to the genius of Shakespeare, is lively,
picturesque, and sublime, qualities which are derived from the bold
variety, and often from the wild irregularity of its forms'.[88]

Hall, like few other theorists of the picturesque, was prepared to

85. See Sir James Hall *Essay on the Origin, History and Principles of Gothic Architecture* (Edinburgh 1813) and *Transactions of the Royal Society of Edinburgh* IV, (1797) pp.3–27. Hall noted that his paper was 'by no means in a state for publication. To bring them to such a state must be a work of much labour and time'. (ibid., p.5). The drawings for the 1813 edition are in the RIBA, see *Catalogue, Drawings Collection RIBA. G–K*, pp.83–4.

86. Hall, op. cit., p.146. His particular example of this deficiency was the ruins at Agrigentum in Italy, whose timber origins made them seem as 'large barns' (ibid., p.147). Hall was in Italy 1785 and used the services of James Byres as *cicerone*; for his references to Byres see ibid., pp.7 and 10.

87. ibid., p.147.

88. ibid., p.18.

Plate 85. Late nineteenth-century photograph of Lynedoch Cottage, Perthshire

89. See Wolfgang Herrmann *Laugier and 18th Century French Theory* (London 1962) p.196, and Pennant, op. cit., vol.I, p.83.

90. Loudon *A Treatise on Country Residences*, II, p.408. The frontispiece to the *Essay on Gothic Architecture* was like the other illustrations 'chiefly executed by Mr Blore a young artist of great merit' (ibid., p.20). The cathedral served as a guinea pig for Hall's theory of architectural evolution, see ibid., p.18. The plates that illustrated his paper for the Royal Society were largely his own work and initialled 'S.I.H. del'. According to Mitchell this 'sylvan cathedral had fallen into neglect and disrepair', between 1820 and 1842 (Joseph Mitchell *Reminiscences of my Life in the Highlands*, London, 1883, p.312).

91. Pococke described Dunglass in 1760 as 'the sea appears at the end of the lawn, which is before the house, on each side of which is a wood, and a rivulet runs towards the end of the lawn under a small arch over which the ground is raised . . . on the east side of the avenue hid by trees is the Collegiate Church founded in 1450. . . . To the back of the house is a beautifull Glyn covered with Wood of 40 years growth, it is about 120 feet deep to the north and 90 to the south, in which the perpendicular cliffs of freestone add to the Picture. . . . There is a little hill to the west of the house which was fortified with bastions of earth, as 'tis said, by the Queen Regent during Queen Mary's minority: The late owner built a Summer house on it, and made a bowling green within the fortress' (Pococke, op. cit., pp.325–6).

92. See SRO GD 206/2/315/10. Payments for work on the roof and for plastering occur in the garden accounts in 1795 and 1796 (SRO GD 206/5/106).

93. SRO GD 206/2/160.

stand by his theories in practice. To prove his notion that the construction of the Gothic arch and its decoration was derived from the branching of a forest tree, an idea with which he had been experimenting since October 1792, he had a miniature cathedral constructed out of willow by the local carpenter and set up in the garden of his home at Dunglass in 1795. His source for this might as easily have been Laugier's seminal *Essai sur l'Architecture* of 1753, as Pennant's remark in his *Tour in Scotland* that the trees of the river terraces at Taymouth 'formed a fine *gothic* arch; and probably that species of architecture owed its origin to such vaulted shades'.[89] The model, which served as the frontispiece of his *Essay on Gothic Architecture*, was still there in 1813. It was described by Loudon as 'a hut constructed of branches of trees, not affectedly, but simply, and covered with heath or thatch, [that] forms a proper shelter in a woody dell', and seen by the engineer Joseph Mitchell as an avenue of trees trained 'in the form of the nave and transept of a cathedral'.[90] The rest of Dunglass was conceived from an equally picturesque viewpoint during the evolutionary period between Hall's delivery of his paper to the Edinburgh Royal Society and the publication of the *Essay on Gothic Architecture*. His estate at Dunglass was, of course, an improver's paradise, with a rocky coast nearby, a late medieval chapel 'founded in 1450', 'a beautifull Glyn covered with Wood' planted in 1720, and a small fort of the time of Mary Queen of Scots (Plate IV).[91] It was this glen that was later chosen by Sir James and Alexander Nasmyth as the best possible site for the new Dunglass, taking advantage of a setting that Bishop Pococke had astutely defined in 1760 as having a composition like a picture.

Sir James Hall had inherited a house about which Pococke said little, and like any old building it was in need of constant repair. It had been altered in 1748, again in 1787, and six years later, in 1793, the architect Alexander Stevens gave a detailed report on the structure and what might be done to keep it habitable and watertight.[92] Despite Hall's favourable opinion of Stevens and his report, nothing radical came of it until 1807, when Richard Crichton produced his estimate for replacing it with a new house.[93] At the same time Alexander Nasmyth, as a family friend of the Halls and a fellow radical, executed two small pencil sketches showing classical and gothic designs for a new Dunglass (Plate 86).[94] Although neither of these drawings seems to have been developed further, they were appealing and influenced the ultimate form taken by Crichton's house. This casual, almost back-of-an-envelope way of presenting his ideas seems to have been typical of Nasmyth. He did much the same at Taymouth around 1806, where he

94. NGS Prints and Drawings, D.3727/9 and 10. D.3727/9 is initialled 'AN' and annotated in pencil 'design for Dunglass'. .3727/10 is inscribed 'My Father's design for Sir James Hall's new house at Dunglass'. For the association between the Halls and Nasmyth families, see GD 206/2/315/15 and James Nasmyth *An Autobiography*, ed. Samuel Smiles (London 1883) p.64.

95. For his designs for Taymouth see NGS, Prints and Drawings, D.3727/12; D.3727/13; D.3727/14. The last is dated 1806. His sketch plan for Dean House was marked 'Laying out a plott of Dean Land for Sir J. Nisbet, 1817'. There is a design for a castellated house on the verso of this sheet (NLS Ms.3241 f.5).

gave two castellated drawings, one for the partially rebuilt castle and the other for the bridge across the Tay, which matched the impressionistic style of his small unexecuted scheme of 1817 for landscaping the garden and rebuilding Dean House, in Edinburgh (Plate 87).[95] Such drawings probably showed Nasmyth at his best, suggesting rather than performing and capturing in this Adamitic way the germ of the picturesque. When taken a stage further, they invariably lost much

Plate 86. Dunglass, East Lothian, alternative schemes by Alexander Nasmyth, *c*.1800

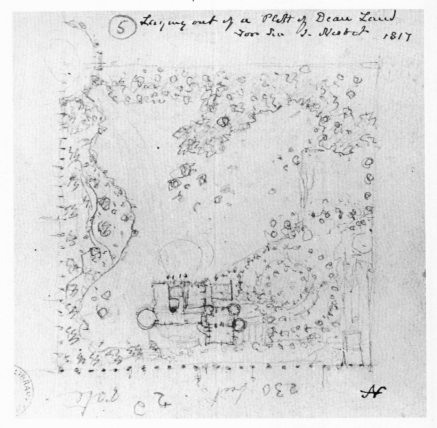

96. For his unexecuted lodge design for Culzean, see Ailsa Collection, Plan 47; for his lighthouse and castle ruin at Inveraray see Muniment Room, Inveraray Castle, and also Lindsay & Cosh, op. cit., p.291. All these drawings are watercolours, precise in style and rather run of the mill in subject. More impressive were the views he made of Culzean from the sea, presumably contemporary with his architectural design, see NGS Prints and Drawings, D.3727/25.

97. According to Loudon, the grounds at Loudoun Castle in Ayrshire were 'lately planted from suggestion by Nasmyth' and at Dreghorn Castle the mountainous parts were planted 'from designs by the celebrated landscape painter, Nasmyth'. (*Encyclopaedia of Gardening* pp.108 and 1087). Similarly, at Tullibody in Clackmannanshire, the Ochil hills there were 'finely planted from the designs of Nasmyth' (ibid., p.1091). In the *Edinburgh Encyclopaedia*, Loudon wrote that 'we recollect to have seen, in 1802, sketches by this artist for planting part of the range of Pentland Hills behind Dreghorn, and part of the Ochil Hills near Airthrie, and Alva' (ibid., XII, p.543). He may also have had a hand in the gardens at Rosneath, Dunbartonshire, where about 1803, 'The Steeple' of the Home Farm, was constructed as a tower '90 feet in height, designed by Nasmyth of Edinburgh, but which after the fire, was curtailed of its lofty proportions' (W.C. Maugham *Rosneath Past and Present*, Paisley 1893, p.75). For his reference to Nasmyth's work at Colington House, Edinburgh, as the 'Edinburgh drawing-master', see *Country Residences*, II, p.411. Drawings for the house, and two hothouse schemes attributed to William Forsyth, of c.1802, are in NLS Acc.4796/222 and 227.

of their spontaneity and originality, as his timid designs for estate buildings at Culzean and Inveraray made sadly plain.[96] Nasmyth's success undoubtedly lay in his painter's eye, and it was this gift he exploited in landscaping the grounds at Loudoun and Dreghorn Castles, Alva, and very likely at Colinton and Dunglass.[97] What he had realised in sketch was vividly but differently shown in his paintings, where beneath a Claudian glaze it is just possible to find his landscape proposals. His view of Dreghorn was no exception, and there the continuous belts of trees that circle the lawn and loop into the hills above the castle were presumably Nasmyth's work (Plate 88).

The two thumbnail sketches Nasmyth gave to Sir James Hall show an asymmetrical castle with inner keep and enceinte walls, and a similar building, more domestic than baronial in style, with terrace

Plate 87. Dean House, Edinburgh, improvement plan by Alexander Nasmyth, 1817

gardens stepping down the cliff-side that Pococke had so ardently admired. Both must have been the spontaneous early stages of a design whose shadow was dramatically retained in the massing and silhouette of Crichton's building, with its strongly eclectic form of classical detailing. Crichton was no doubt at the mercy of the persuasive and combined talents of Nasmyth and Hall, who settled for a classical and gothic hybrid as a brilliant variation on 'the modern style' coined by Richard Payne Knight. As such Dunglass was a further development of Adam's castellated picturesque, and much less a personal statement by Crichton (Plate 89).[98] Its design was an attempt by Hall to obtain the best of both worlds and was, unlike many such essays, highly successful. He was fully aware of the pitfalls. The chief failing of the gothic style, he had maintained in his *Essay on Gothic Architecture*, was paradoxically and disappointingly the strength of the classical. Any gothic building close to was 'heavy and awkward' in its detailing, and while the Grecian excelled 'in all these qualities of *elegance* and *grace* which depend upon the nice adjustment and masterly execution of details', it lacked the grand effect of the distant view, only 'favourable to the Gothic style'.[99] At Dunglass, Hall attempted to reconcile these defects and use them to advantage in a picturesque landscape. Although alive to the disasters of mixing styles without 'a regular system' he still suggested that 'we might take advantage of every style according as it suited our purpose, and adapt it to our use

98. For a discussion of this aspect of picturesque architecture, see S. Lang 'Richard Payne Knight and the Idea of Modernity' in *Concerning Architecture*, ed. John Summerson (London 1968) pp.85–97; and for its particular application to Dunglass, see Christopher Hussey *The Picturesque* (London 1927) pp.222–3, and David Watkin *Thomas Hope and the Neo-classical Ideal* (London 1968) p.130.

99. Hall, op. cit., p.147.

Plate 88. Dreghorn Castle, view from the park by Nasmyth (detail), *c*.1800

without destroying its effect'.[100] In this way, the house might follow rather than set the scene and, at Dunglass, the mansion built by Crichton was fitted into a landscape that had already been improved. A gothic bridge of two bays with battlements and quatrefoil had been designed for the Bilsdean burn in 1797, by George Burn, and this probably matched the style of the Gothic Temple that Pococke had seen in 1760.[101] In 1795, garden seats were positioned to take advantage of the views over the Tower and Chapel Hills, and the woods around the old house were opened up to allow vistas from the windows. It was into this landscape, partially man-made by Sir James's energetic and capable gardener, Robert Girvan, that the new building was introduced as an equal, possibly minor, partner, and so accomplished a revolution undreamed of by the formal gardeners. So much so, that when the turmoil of building was over and the area around the new house turfed, all that was outstanding was the landscaping of two new approaches to the house. These completed, it was only a question, as Lady Hall noted in 1821, of 'the removal of the Balustrades on the top, from one part to another. The vases on the Ramps, with posts & chains leading to it . . . Fruit trees for the garden – & making and fencing *outside the border*'.[102]

This notion of partnership, where house and garden were to all

100. ibid., p.148.

101. SRO RHP 5504. George Burn of Haddington appears in the accounts for Dunglass in 1779 as quarrying stone for work on the new bridge on the estate (Reading University Library, EAS 1/2/56). Burn also worked in north-east Scotland until his bankruptcy in 1803. He was the brother of James Burn of Haddington, also a bridge builder and one who worked largely in East Lothian and Aberdeenshire from c.1784. He was known fondly as 'Auld Timmer'.

102. SRO GD 206/2/160.

Plate 89. Dunglass from the ravine

intents and purposes balanced, was typical of the late phase of the picturesque. Its swansong, for Scotland anyhow, was probably made by Thomas Meason, in his *Italian Landscape Architecture*, of 1827, which virtually concluded with the assumption that 'we meditate on the castle in ruins; we delight in the restoration of an ancient edifice made again habitable; but the best imitation of an old castle or monastery, calls up no recollection of days of yore. There is, however, in this irregular architecture only one object in view, picturesque buildings to embellish the landscapes of our country'.[103] But the Gothic Revival was to prove Meason wrong and the revival of the formal garden where architecture was dominant destroyed his notion of balance. Sir James Hall's dislike at Blenheim in 1793 of the 'appearance of art which chills the imagination and the idea of aristocratic insolence which takes the place of Ducal splendours', was an attitude typical of both Hall, Meason and the informal taste. To them and others the incidental architectural elements of the landscape, such as the bridge or temple, often better and more sympathetically accorded with their setting than the mansion house itself. In this way, the houses and parks of Duddingston and Taymouth had to be appreciated on their own and distinct terms. Perhaps the *ferme ornée*, despite all its artificiality and preciousness, was alone in accomplishing some kind of intimate harmony between house and garden. At North Merchiston, Blair Adam, and more grandly at Dunira, the landscapes that evolved were both practical and ornamental, striking a functional and aesthetic balance between house and grounds. This sort of approach to the picturesque can be seen in the intellectual attitudes of James and Robert Adam, where the former delighted in 'an easy quiet, and a safe retreat', and the latter in a barren and untamed gothic landscape. While Robert Adam shared in his watercolours and drawings a vision similar to that of John Clerk of Eldin, it was nonetheless a distinct one, unique in its acceptance that architecture took its place naturally as one of several elements that constituted the picturesque.

103. Thomas Meason *Italian Landscape Architecture* (London 1827) p.117. For a note on him see Hussey, op. cit., p.227.

THE LANDSCAPE

While Robinson was the most notable landscape gardener in Scotland during the second half of the eighteenth century, his discreditable bankruptcy permitted the Thomas Whites to add Scotland to their English practice. In stylistic terms, this was tantamount to a replacement of the ideas of Kent with those of Brown – more a changing of the guard than anything as dramatic as a revolution. Within the framework sketched out by Capability, the Whites, father and son, worked with success and ingenuity. In the later gardens of White junior, the Brownian tradition was adapted to incorporate some of the less radical ideas of the Picturesque. Both men pursued their careers in Scotland with an almost relentless zeal, and White senior, at least, practised as a 'new ground workman' what he preached on his linen and watercolour improvement plans. Between them, they changed the face of much of the lowlands and eastern Scotland between 1780 and 1820, and despite their obvious limitations established the landscape garden in Scotland for good and all. Yet they made remarkably few concessions to the genius of the place and their landscapes remained at best a hybrid or at worst an importation. They astutely avoided improving a highland landscape, with the possible exception of Rossdhu, and were more at home in the undulating pastures of the beech than the wild, rocky scenery of the Scots Pine. This was their strength. The later career of White junior was built upon a not undeserved reputation to reproduce the beautiful, rather than the picturesque of Nasmyth and Loudon. In the end, of course, Loudon and his like won the day. The Whites and their contemporaries, such as the surveyor turned gardener James Abercrombie junior and the gardeners turned designers like John Hay and Walter Nicol, passed with their gardens into neglect and disrepute.

James Abercrombie was a modernised version of Thomas Winter. He was a surveyor turned improver, capable, busy, and reasonably modest. But there the similarity ended, for Abercrombie's plan for Glamis of 1768 set a new level and one which made those of Winter and the like old-fashioned overnight.[1] He had come to Glamis as a sur-

1. James Abercrombie junior, fl.1768–94, was a surveyor and landscape gardener. He may well have been related to John Abercrombie, 1726–1806, from Prestonpans near Edinburgh who was a horticultural writer, see *DNB* and Henrey, op. cit., II, pp.363–71. Charles Abercrombie the road surveyor, fl. 1800, may also have been a relation. For his work at Glamis, see Glamis Castle, Charter Room, Box 30. It was probably Abercrombie senior who made the survey plan of Careston in 1753, see SRO RHP 31,444.

III. Aerial view of Culzean Castle, Ayrshire, 1979

veyor, draining, planning and planting for Lord Strathmore from 1766 to 1771.[2] Like others of the period, such as Charles Ross of Paisley, he raised the trees he planted and, though their roles overlapped, he still managed to work in reasonable harmony with the Earl's gardener George Baillie. Such evident trust possibly encouraged Abercrombie to extend his commercial planting into the ornamental, and make a plan for remodelling the park and gardens immediately around the castle. For this he gave two designs, one dated 1768, and the other undated but surely of about the same time. In doing so he began an intermittent career as a landscape gardener, which lasted as late as his consultation at Ross Priory, Dunbartonshire, in 1793. While Abercrombie's shift from surveyor to improver was unremarkable, the quality and maturity of his two plans – possibly his first essays in this field – were totally unexpected. Both designs were in ink, without watercolour and in a precise, perhaps overneat hand that showed a full understanding of the informal landscape. Neither betrays the former surveyor – there are no angles or straight avenues – and the composition is an expansive one making a comparison with Winter's Glamis scheme as extraordinary as it is inexplicable. It is only the fortuitous survival of an incomplete plan by Robert Robinson that places Abercrombie's two drawings in their correct perspective.

Robinson had also been consulted by Lord Strathmore about draining Forfar Loch and had visited Glamis for that purpose in April 1764.[3] He had departed by July with little accomplished, and left behind a large, attractive but incomplete, improvement plan.[4] In this, he wished away all the existing avenues and any of the formal planting, and proposed instead three distinct areas that complemented each other (Plate 90). The first contained the approach to the castle from Glamis Village, which ran along the banks of the Glamis Burn with, on the other side, the park giving a view of the rebuilt stables amidst a scattering of specimen trees. The approach road then left this valley, entered a second area over a new bridge of two bays, and arrived at the castle, which Robinson had isolated in an island of lawn surrounded by the Dean and Glamis Burns. The existing New Bridge linked this island by a short wooded path to a sort of Elysian Fields, kidney-shaped and thickly planted around its edges; this was the third area. Such a composition, tight, neat, and geometrical, was typical of Robinson and appeared in his plan of the same year for Castle Grant. More than that, he continually returned to it throughout his professional career.

Abercrombie capitalised on this plan almost as much as Robinson's

2. ibid. Charter Room, Box 30. He was similarly consulted at Kinnaird Castle in 1769 about draining the Haughs of Careary (Southesk Mss. No. 3 bundle 4).

3. There is an account at Glamis from the 9th to the 13th April, for 'Mr. Robinson's Bill of Entertainment when taking the survey and level of the Loch of Forfar'. (Glamis Castle, Charter Room, Box 39). There was a further payment to him in July of five pounds, 'to account for work done to the Earl of Strathmore'. In the latter bill he is referred to as 'Robertson'.

4. This plan of Glamis is unsigned and without date. However it closely resembles that produced by Robinson for Castle Grant in July, 1764, see pl.42. Though a key is given on the plan with symbols running from A to G, there is no correspondence between them and the buildings and objects shown on the plan. It also lacks the usual title of place and owner. It is at present in the Charter Room.

5. Of the two plans, that dated 1768 is described as 'A plan for a new Disposition of the Ground and Plantations at Glamis Castle': the other is similarly titled and initialled by Abercrombie. While it closely follows that of 1768, a different site is proposed for the kitchen garden and a system of lakes is introduced, see SRO RHP 6497 and 6498. It is impossible to say in which order they were made, but it is likely that the more ambitious and undated scheme was first, followed by a more realistic scheme. Both drawings are at Glamis, one in the Charter Room, the other in the Estate Office. The SRO plans are photocopies.

unexplained and precipitate departure. His two plans set the castle in a very open park, with deep planting confined to the margins of a proposed pleasure ground of nearly 3,000 acres (Plate 91).[5] The

Plate 90. Glamis Castle, Angus, improvement plan by Robert Robinson, 1764

dated plan was the more interesting of the two, with greater variety and a more sophisticated use of water. It also carried a perhaps naive explanation of the scheme and a plea in the style of Winter for the preservation of at least part of the existing garden architecture. Abercrombie wrote that his proposed new lawn in front of the castle should be 'neatly seeded, turfed and planted with flowering shrub accompanying a gravel walk of 7 feet that winds along the top of the sunk fence which divides it from the rest of the lawn – The lawn is occasioned by the Great Gate, which I cannot advise to pull down, if the Gate be dispensed with the Lawn may extend to the water, and the roads be brought to land at the Entry of the House; and altho' this Lawn with the House and Offices seem to make a formal figure upon paper this would be effectually avoided upon the ground as it cannot come all under the Eye at once, and it is my humble Opinion that this Gate is in a great measure a necessary Ornament to the House for the extra ordinary height of the Building without something of this kind to accompany and soften it would not look well for which reason I have proposed a Groupe of spruce and silver firs on either side – The South Avenue while it stands, which will not be many years, may serve as the road to the House, after that I think what is here proposed is the more proper Approach'.[6]

Abercrombie was unlike Robinson in conceiving his design as a means rather than an end and in his anxiety to preserve some of the garden architecture of Glamis. Such professional self-effacement was not characteristic of Robinson. Equally distinctive but in a different way was the openness of Abercrombie's proposed landscape and the importance to it of water. In some ways, too, it was a more modern vision of Arcadia. If Robinson's ideas often distinctly echoed those of Kent's, Abercrombie's seemed to lean towards the early designs of Brown. The width of the park, with its great expanse of undulating lawn, the expansion of the Glamis and Dean Burns into two small connected lakes set in a hollow, with their bridges forming a real and visual connection between fore and middle ground, was Brown's Blenheim all over again. Even the attempt to save the old avenue and its architecture had a parallel with that park. Perhaps Abercrombie's eagerness to accommodate the past and placate conservative taste made it inevitable that his rather than Robinson's was the plan followed at Glamis. But whether he directed the transformation is another matter, for he was gone when the fir avenues around the castle were taken down in 1773 and 1774 and their roots grubbed up and turfed over.[7] At the same time, a new kitchen garden and shrubbery

6. SRO RHP 6497.

7. Glamis Castle, Charter Room, Box 30, Volume: 'Improvements on the Estate'. In July, 1773, payment was made for 'cutting and breaking the tops of the fir trees in Avenue above the Castle', and for 'taking up their roots'. In 1774, there was further payment for pulling up the roots of the firs (ibid.) Some of the timber was used in building the new offices beside the castle. According to Repton, naturalising a fir avenue was an impossible task: 'An avenue of firs is the most obstinate to break, because they leave no lateral branches'. (Humphry Repton *Sketches and Hints on Landscape Gardening* (London 1795) p.24.) Pennant's view of the castle, made by Moses Griffiths around 1769–72, showed the end of the fir avenue and the building unaltered. That of Sandby, published in 1782 though drawn in 1746, showed a classical forecourt with urns and balustrade, and the avenue planted with obviously deciduous trees. Pennant also referred to 'a drawing from an old print, which the Earl of *Strathmore* did me the honour to present to me'. (Pennant, op. cit., vol.II, p.171). This was published in 1779 as 'Malcolms Cross', and showed an extensive and probably hypothetical old castle.

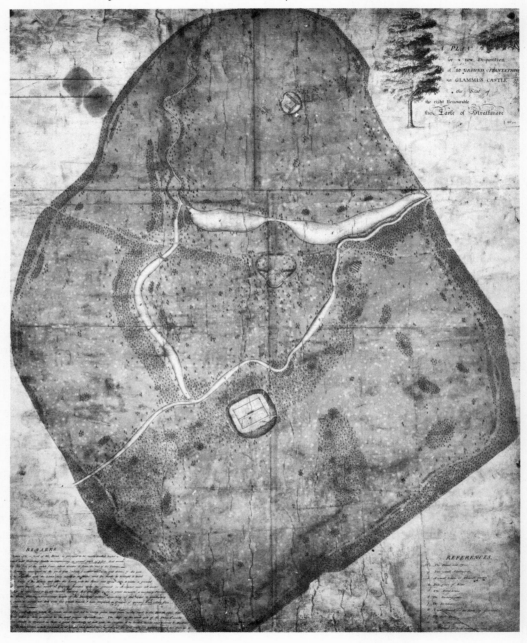

Plate 91. Glamis, improvement plan by James Abercrombie, 1768

8. The old gardens 'att fareside of Castle' were levelled in 1775, walls of the new kitchen garden adjoining the rebuilt offices were completed in October, 1774. (Glamis Castle, Charter Room, Box 30, vol.5: 'Improvements on the Estate'). The new shrubbery was projected in March, 1775, in a different site from that suggested on either of Abercrombie's plans. Work on the new approach was in hand in August, 1774. There survives at Glamis an anonymous and unfinished drawing of c.1750, which suggests the removal of the old avenue and its replanting. (Glamis Castle, Charter Room, Box 39). The offices at 'The Barns' are shown in Winter's plan, see pl.33, and in Robinson's they were to survive as the stables.

9. Glamis Castle, Charter Room, Box 30, vol.5.

10. *Miscellaneous Prose Works of Sir Walter Scott*, ed. 28 vols. (Edinburgh 1834–6) vol.21, p.47: see also John Starton *Glamis, a Parish History* (Forfar 1913), and the *New Statistical Account*, vol.xi (1845) p.345, which gives a confused and inaccurate summary of the improvements.

11. SRO RHP 2594. The estate of Guynd was fairly near Glamis and the Ochterlonys its owners were on social terms with Lord Strathmore in the later eighteenth century.

12. SRO RHP 2595. There is an early nineteenth-century album of unsigned drawings for Guynd, see SRO RHP 2617/1–7, and Thomas White's design made provision for a new mansion, see his plan preserved at Guynd.

13. For Abercrombie's plan for Ross, see SRO GD 47/1163; and for Arbuthnott, RHP 9277. Little seems to have been done at either house, both of which were later improved in the early nineteenth century; for Ross around 1821, see GD 47/575; and Arbuthnott about the same time, see J.P. Neale *Views of the Seats of*

Noblemen and Gentlemen (London 1826) vol. 3, 2nd series. The bridge in the park, shown on the extreme left on Neale's view, was built in 1821 to allow a new

approach to the house, see P.S-M. Arbuthnot *Memoirs of the Arbuthnots of Kincardineshire and Aberdeenshire* (London 1920) p.26.

were laid out near the castle, and an approach formed running from Glamis Village to where the offices – 'The Barns' – had been and then onwards along the line of the old avenue to the castle.[8] A lawn was made in front of it in 1774 with turf removed from the former bowling green (Plate 91).[9] The great gate, for which Abercrombie had pleaded in his note, was probably taken down at this time and removed to its present position at the entrance to the park. While nothing came of his suggested lakes and their bridges, enough had been done for Sir Walter Scott to bewail the loss of a historical landscape and its replacement with a 'parkish' setting devoid of character. He wrote that 'a disciple of Kent had the cruelty to render this splendid mansion more *parkish*, as he was pleased to call it; to raze these exterior defences, and bring his mean and paltry gravel-walk up to the very door'.[10] It was only in the later nineteenth century that some attempt was made to make amends (Plate v).

In none of his later schemes did Abercrombie approach again the sweep and grandeur of those two schemes for Glamis. It may have been beginner's luck, for compared with them his succeeding commissions were small and practical, and his solutions invariably pedestrian. His plan for Guynd in Angus of 1775 – probably earned on account of his Glamis work – was no exception, and while it offered some of the elements of his 1768 schemes, it was in a much circumscribed form (Plate 92).[11] The explanatory key given for this drawing goes from one to seven, and includes the usual run of offices, gardens, approach, lawn, gravel walk, and a ride which he explained 'may be carried (at pleasure) round the farm, among the planting, entered at "a"'. The last was a toy compared with the woodland ride that skirted the periphery of Lord Strathmore's 2,700 acre park. Little of this scheme was executed, and a plan of the Guynd estate in 1839 showed the early nineteenth-century house standing beside a lake in the more open and extensive landscape devised by Thomas White in 1799.[12] In the improvement plans Abercrombie gave for Ross Priory in 1793 and for Arbuthnott the year before, he showed little spirit, and seemed to have turned his back on the large park with its clump of trees for a more traditional and Scottish solution of fields. Here they were edged by narrow strips of planting closer to those Loudon devised at North Berwick shortly after 1800.[13] The explanation may have been that the

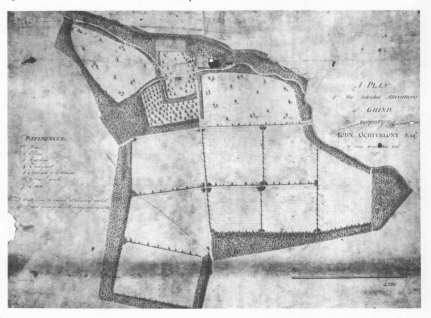

14. See SRO RHP 9277 for Arbuthnott; and GD 47/605 for Ross Priory.

15. At Ross Priory, Abercrombie seems to have superseded James Ferrier who wrote at least two rather condescending letters about improving Ross in 1792 (SRO GD 47/585). The situation seems to have been the reverse at Guynd where Ferrier appeared as surveyor in 1808, see RHP 2608. At Ross some tree planting and farm building was done in 1796/97, but work in the garden etc. followed the alteration and expansion of the house by Gillespie Graham in 1812 (GD 47/1243). Thomas White senior, wrote that after having Abercrombie recommended to him, 'upon application made to him he told me he did not chose to undertake the business' (SRO GD 151/11/41).

16. Charles Ross built in 1760 at Easter Greenlaw near Paisley 'a good house, with a portico after the Ionic Order . . . there he keeps a complete nursery of all kinds of fruit trees, forest trees, flowering shrubs and evergreens; and also a neat little green-house'. George Crawfurd *The History of the Town and Parish of Paisley* (Paisley 1782) pp.28–9. According to Crawfurd, he had been 'in the practice of surveying nearly forty years'. The Girning Gates at Garscadden, Drumchapel, now demolished, may well have been his work. There are several of his surveys in the SRO, but none for landscape gardening. George Brown worked at Gordon Castle as estate surveyor and nursery gardener between 1791 and 1798. He also claimed to have undertaken several government surveys at this time for which he had not been paid (SRO GD 44/51/374). He worked as well on the Castle Grant estate and those of the Earl of Seafield. For both Ross and Brown, see Adams, op. cit., vol.I p.xiii and ff.

brief he held for these two small estates was predominantly an agricultural one. At Arbuthnott his plan emphasised the line of the 'Principal Drain of Moss', and at Ross Priory, his suffix in correspondence was that of 'Land Surveyor'.[14] It may well have been that such practical activities left him little time to indulge his latent talents as a landscape gardener. Certainly at Ross, he was sufficiently engaged, and in strong enough a professional position in 1793 to tell his client Miss Buchanan that she would have to wait. He was 'too busy in other parts of the country', and proved it at Dudhope Castle where he refused to act as Thomas White's surveyor for the improvement scheme of 1782.[15]

In working on both sides of the fence as it were, Abercrombie was in no way exceptional. There is every reason to suppose that most surveyors were willing to turn their hand to landscape gardening, if the opportunity arose and time permitted. In Lewis Kennedy there was a reverse instance where a successful landscape gardener turned land steward in the 1820s. Many of them had some sort of working arrangement with a nursery garden, if they did not own one themselves. Charles Ross, the Paisley surveyor, raised his own trees and shrubs, and the same was true of the George Brown of Linkwood, who was active in both fields in the 1790s.[16] Lewis Sinclair, the gardener at

Plate 92. Guynd House, Angus, improvement plan by James Abercrombie, 1775

Grant Castle, not only designed and built an excellent kitchen garden there, in 1803, but also worked in a minor way as a surveyor on the estate.[17] Less clear was the demarcation between gardener, surveyor and landscape gardener: some men were all three, some like Robert Robinson preferred to be considered architects and above all such categories. William Boutcher, the gardener and one time partner of Robinson, listed amongst the subscribers to his *Treatise on Forest Trees* a typical mixture of the sort, amongst whom a figure like James Bayne, 'land surveyor and designer of ground', was probably unremarkable.[18] The division between gardener and designer was even more vague, and as late as 1830 Loudon stated that 'both in England and Scotland, it is customary for nurserymen to give plans for laying out grounds, building garden structures etc', and this was made clear in Neill's appendix to his *On Scottish Gardens and Orchards* of 1813.[19] Thomas Hitt, the Scottish gardener and author of *A Treatise on Fruit Trees* of 1755, described himself boldly as a 'designer of gardens'.[20] John Home, a surveyor from Banff, was similarly prepared to 'lay out or survey such nobleman's and gentleman's grounds as will honour him with their employment, at most reasonable rates', and proved it by working as both at Haddo Miln in 1776.[21] William and Thomas Reid had their own nursery at Banff and acted as landscape gardeners, as did the 'late Mr. Kyle', Loudon's master John Mawer, and the 'late Mr. Meikle'.[22] Of the numerous gardeners who aspired to better things, Walter Nicol and John Hay, both hothouse experts, were probably the most successful and typical. They were the other new and bright side of the coin from the proverbial curmudgeons caricatured as Scott's Adam Fairservice and the despicable old Robert, of Stevenson's essay 'An Old Scotch Gardener'.

Walter Nicol reinforced his claim to be considered as more than a gardener by his authorship of so practical and straightforward a vade-mecum as *The Gardener's Kalendar*, of 1810.[23] In his advertisement he wrote of himself as an author who 'gives Designs for Gardens and

17. Sinclair's designs included a gardener's house at Milltown, Castle Grant (GD 248/702/2). For his work at Castle Grant, see p.80 n.98.

18. See Boutcher, op. cit. List of Subscribers.

19. For Loudon's remarks see *Gardener's Magazine* XV (1839) p.215. In Neill's account of walled gardens, hothouses etc. the majority were the work of their own gardener, like John Henderson at Brechin Castle in 1799, or by professional gardeners such as John Hay or Walter and John Nicol. Neill, invaluably, gives the following dates for several gardens: Buchanan Castle, 1792–1802, Wemyss Castle, *c*.1790, Raith, *c*.1785, Lundie House, 1807, Archerfield, 1778, Bothwell Castle 1759–82, Moncrieff House, 1796, Woodhall, Hamilton *c*.1786, Preston Hall, 1793, Amisfield, 1785, Fasque, 1792, Scone, 1806, Smeaton, 1782, Coilsfield (Montgomery House) 1808, Hope Temple, Paisley, 1797. (Neill, op. cit., pp.163–78).

20. Thomas Hitt *Treatise on Fruit Trees* (London 1755). Though he lived in Lincolnshire, according to Loudon he had come from Aberdeenshire, (*Encyclopaedia of Gardening*, 1824, p.1105; and Henrey, op. cit., vol.II, pp.357–8.)

21. See *Caledonian Mercury*, March 7th, 1763. There are several of his surveys surviving in the SRO for the period 1766–1800, with his Survey of Assynt, 1774–5, as his most ambitious work. (RHP 1672/1–16). His design, 'Plan for the Policies at Haddo Miln', showed him suggesting an enclosure system for arable land and proposing a small shrubbery and lawn area with a kitchen garden beside the house (SRO RHP 11775).

22. For the Reids' work at Gordon Castle see p.157 n.75. The nursery at Banff was 'adjoining the farm of Colleonard begun about 30 years ago, and has of late been greatly enlarged and improved. It occupied between 15 and 20 acres'. (*Statistical Account* (1797) vol.XX, pp.331–2). Meikle was dead in 1824. He had practised largely as a landscape gardener in the north of England, particularly at Corby Castle, Carlisle, Thirkleby Park, Yorkshire but also at Gordon Castle in 1782, see *Encyclopaedia of Gardening* (1824) pp.1079, 1081. Kyle was head gardener at Moredun, Edinburgh, in the 1770s, but also 'gave plans for *policies*' and was a designer of kitchen gardens and hot houses etc. (*Edinburgh Encyclopaedia*, XII, 1830, p.543). He wrote a *Treatise on Forcing Vines & Peaches* in 1778.

23. Nicol, who died in 1811, was presumably the father of John Nicol, the gardener, who died in 1824. He was a prolific if repetitive author, writing: *The Scotch Forcing Gardener* (Edinburgh 1797), *The Practical Planter* (Edinburgh 1799), *The Villa and Garden Dictionary* (Edinburgh 1809), *The Gardener's Kalendar* (Edinburgh 1810) and posthumously *The Planter's Kalendar* (Edinburgh 1812). For an account of his career see Henrey, op. cit., vol.II, pp.406–7. He was the son of John Nicol who laid out the walled garden at Wemyss Castle, see Neill, op. cit., p.167.

24. *The Gardener's Kalendar* p. advertisement. In this, he gave his address as Leith Walk, Edinburgh. Some insight into his ideas on design were given in his notes on the 'Formation of Shrubberies', ibid., pp.453–6.

25. See George Johnson *A History of English Gardening* (London 1829) p.275. For the plan for Balgay, see SRO RHP 3271. Balgay is now the Victoria Hospital of Dundee, and such parts of the landscape that remain are divided between a cemetery and public park.

26. According to Loudon the 'kitchen garden laid out by Nicol, and the pleasure grounds by White of Durham' (*Encyclopaedia of Gardening*, 1824, p.1041). His work here and his 'regular journal' were used as the source of the *Kitchen Gardener* of 1802 (ibid., p.487). For his work at Dalhousie c.1806, see *Gardener's Magazine* I (1826) p.251; for his kitchen garden at Gartmore and Ochtertyre, see *Encyclopaedia of Gardening* (1824) p.1092. His work at the former was probably around 1806 when the garden walls were built and when the landscape around the new building was planted see NLS Acc. 6026/36 Accounts 1804/6; and 6026/38 and 39. At Raith, Nicol must have come in contact with Thomas White who was working there in 1784, see Scone Palace Muniments, bundle 1233; for a contemporary description see Robert Forsyth *The Beauties of Scotland*, 5 vols (London 1805) vol.IV, p.78, and a view

Hot Houses, the laying out of Villa Grounds, Parks, Lawns, Approaches, etc., in the newest style'.[24] Nicol was perhaps the archetypal Scottish gardener, dour and hard working who had begun life as a plumber, made his career in England, and spent his fame in Scotland. He had worked over the Border for Lord Townshend at Raynham Hall in Norfolk, but was back in Scotland by 1801, when he made an improvement plan for Balgay, then just outside Dundee.[25] He was afterwards established at Wemyss Castle in Fife, where he extended his father's gardens of 1790 to complement Thomas White's landscape, and it was from his experience there that he wrote his books concerned largely with the humdrum aspects of gardening. He did, however, work as a landscape gardener at Dalhousie Castle about 1806, and according to Loudon was employed at Ochtertyre and Gartmore, both in Perthshire, as well as at Raith, near Kirkcaldy, where he was again in contact with the elder White.[26] But in so many of these enterprises, his energy was exclusively directed to laying out the complicated but utilitarian kitchen garden and the proliferating but expensive hot- and cold-houses. His reputation was founded on this to such an extent that Loudon unfairly and probably jealously dismissed him in 1817 as 'of the old school', and as one for whom 'No crime (was) so great as daring to excell'.[27] However, he did on occasion attempt greater things, especially after his return to Scotland, and at Invermay, in Perthshire, he appeared in the triple rôle of gardener, landscape gardener, and architect.

At Invermay, Nicol designed and built the peach- and grape-houses, laid out in 1802 the western approach to a small classical mansion through the vaguely gothic gate lodges, designed by B. D. Hodge, and landscaped the small park, dramatically and romantically exaggerated in Swan's early nineteenth-century view (Plate 93).[28] More ambitiously, he proposed an extraordinary, Gothic, domed and battlemented temple for a point on the Humble Bumble (part of the River May behind the house) and, perhaps emboldened by this, an impressive two-storied, classical tea-house, with a conservatory below. Neither was built but as a consolation the landscape remains as Nicol left it (Plates 94 and 95).[29] At Balgay, Dundee, he again under-

of the park from the lake in John Leighton *History of the County of Fife*, 3 vols. (Glasgow 1840) vol.III p.151. According to Loudon, 'Nicol, while practising as head gardener at Raith, Wemyss Castle, and other places, kept a regular journal of this sort; he published it as his *Kitchen-Gardener* in 1802' (*Encyclopaedia of Gardening* (1835) p.748). It is unlikely that the *Edinburgh Encyclopaedia* is correct when it stated that he 'planned and executed the extensive pleasure-grounds at Raith' (XI, p.180). This was an aspect only of his later career. Surprisingly, though there was a good gardening library at Raith it contained only Nicol's *The Planter's Kalendar*, of 1812, see *Catalogue of Books in the Library of Robert Ferguson of Raith* (Edinburgh, *c*.1820) p.40. He was associated with Dicksons in Edinburgh in 1797, until setting up in partnership as Nicol and Forrest, of Middlefield, Leith Walk, see Anderson, II, p.124.

27. For Loudon's dislike of Nicol see J.C. Loudon *Remarks on the Construction of Hothouses* (Edinburgh 1817) pp.61, 64.

28. For his design see NLS Acc. Ms.4796, Box 226: in May, 1802, the factor at Invermay, reported masons at work on the peach house (Invermay Factor's Letter Book, 1800–1806). For Hodge's various designs for these gates see NLS Acc. 4796, Box 226. These lodges and gates were completed in 1804, see Invermay, Factor's Letter Book, 1800–1806: in May 1802, the factor wrote that 'The new approach is fixed through the lawn as far as the planting went and ready for graveling' (ibid.).

29. NLS Acc. Ms.4796, Box 226. At Invermay, however, the extant dairy was built and thatched in 1803, and the now ruined gazebo in Kidhill park probably also dated from this time. Planting etc. continued at Invermay from *c*.1800 to 1808 at least, with seeds from Harrisons of Brompton Road, London and trees and shrubs supplied from Dicksons of Perth and Colville and Son, London (NLS Acc. Ms.4796, Box 188). A no doubt one-sided version of Nicol's work at Invermay is given in an account by the factor of his quarrel with Colonel Belshes over payment. 'Colonel Belshes employed Mr. Nicoll once when he saw him at Lord Rollo's is readily admitted: Mr. Nicoll staked out an Approach to the New Lodges, a sunk fence, and some walks through the woods, which business did not take up above 4 or 5 days at most. Mr. Nicoll was not employed or did he do anything else, besides making a plan which is here produced and for which he made a

took the design of everything on this small estate except the house. His surviving improvement plan, itself a competent piece of work, showed him suggesting new stables as well as laying out a small park divided into lawn and field by a sunk fence (Plate 96). He proposed to plant this area of about thirty acres with specimen trees, leaving the two approach roads, bowing out from the mansion, to form its lateral boundaries. Close behind the house, and at the base of Balgay Hill, he set his gardens, with the hill itself thickly planted. Most of this relatively humble scheme was carried out, but the stables remained where they were and made nonsense of the new park and approach.[30]

distinct item in his charge higher than the Colonel thinks it deserves. Mr. Nicol was several times more at Invermay but not by the Colonel's desire or appointment, and without doing any business . . . the works he here marked required no further superintendence by men of skill; they were simple and easy to execute by the Colonel's workmen'. (Factor's Letter Book, 1804) Nicol's demand was for £30.9. He had worked, presumably before 1802, at Duncrub, an estate of Lord Rollo close to Invermay. There, the house was remodelled and

given wings by Robert Burn in 1799, and at the same time Lord Rollo improved 'the ground and policy about the house by planting and draining' (SRO GD 56/163/9). It was rebuilt in the nineteenth century.

30. This is shown in the Ordnance Survey of 1862. At this date the grounds behind the house had become a cemetery and park. The layout of Balgay before Nicol's work is shown in RHP 3272, a survey of 1759. See too *Farmer's Magazine* VI, 1805, p.239.

Plate 93. View of Invermay, Perthshire, from Swan *Perthshire Illustrated* 1843/4

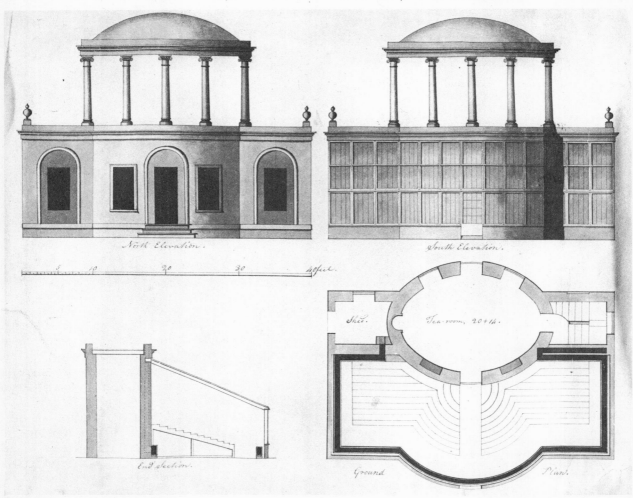

North Elevation.

South Elevation.

End Section.

Shed.

Tea-room, 20+14.

Ground   *Plan.*

31. At Dalhousie Castle, 'The principal approach from the west was laid out, about twenty years ago, by the late Mr. Walter Nicol . . . the garden and hot houses, which were designed by John Hay, garden architect, Edinburgh, in 1806', *Gardener's Magazine* I (1826) p.251. For the building of Dalhousie Castle at this time see SRO GD 45/19/123–4, 143; for a plan and description of Hay's garden see, M'Intosh, op. cit., I, p.50.

At Balgay and at Invermay, Nicol seems to have been given considerable responsibility. Both, of course, were small affairs – Balgay ran to only 130 acres – and where he worked on a grander scale, as at Dalhousie Castle, his freedom was limited and shared with others. The long river approach at Dalhousie was his, but the alterations to the castle were not, nor, more surprisingly, were the kitchen gardens and range of hothouses. These were by his rival John Hay in 1806.[31] Although often in competition, both he and Hay, and possibly William

Plate 94. Design for a tea-house at Invermay, by Walter Nicol, *c*.1802

Plate 95. Aerial view of Invermay, from the Humble Bumble burn, 1979

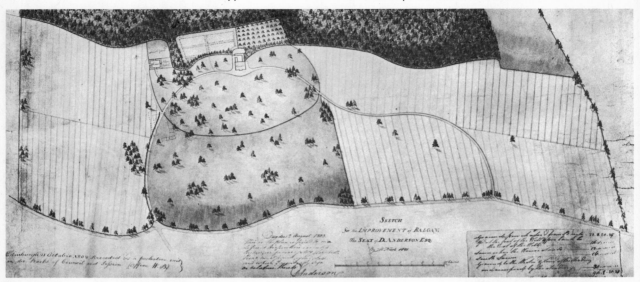

Plate 96. Balgay, Dundee, improvement plan by Walter Nicol, 1801

32. See *Gardener's Magazine* VIII (1832)
p.330; and *Encyclopaedia of Gardening*
(1824) p.463. He was the 'Mr. John Hay,
planner, Edinburgh', who was referred
to by Patrick Neill in his *Journal of a
Horticultural Tour . . . in the Autumn of
1817* (Edinburgh 1823) p.vi. In this tour
of France and Belgium, Neill was also
accompanied by James Macdonald, the
chief gardener at Dalkeith, and by Hay.
Added to the *Tour* were 'Extracts from
Mr. Hay's Journal in Hampshire' (ibid.
pp.557–61). He published an account of
the design of his hothouses in the
*Memoirs of the Caledonian Horticultural
Society* (1829) vol.IV, pp.582–90, which
listed his major works starting with
Prestonhall, Midlothian, 1794, and
finished with Craigielands,
Dumfriesshire, *c.*1825 (ibid., pp.583,
590).

33. His design for Lochnaw is dated
1815, SRO RHP 3983; for Cunnoquhie
before 1829 see, *Gardener's Magazine* VII
(1831) p.22; for Lundie House
(Camperdown) of 1801, see *Encyclopaedia
of Gardening* (1824) p.463, and Neill, op.

cit., p.168; for Saltoun Hall, see NLS Acc.
Ms.2933, map 2; and for Kilkerran, see
SRO RHP 14268.

Forsyth, were respected and trusted in certain circumstances, but only
to a point. Perhaps it was as well, for their solutions as landscape
gardeners were nearly as mechanical as their hothouses.

John Hay fitted neatly into this pattern. Although referred to by
the epithet 'planner', he rarely strayed into the wider pastures of
landscape gardening and remained essentially a sophisticated
designer of kitchen gardens and hothouses, sufficiently regarded to be
included in Patrick Neill's horticultural tour of northern France and
Belgium in 1817. While gardener to the Nisbets at Dirleton, he established his reputation by building a remarkable pineapple house at
Alnwick, in 1804, which was followed by others at Castle Semple and
Bargany, around 1818, and a 'magnificent suite of glazed houses' in
White junior's park at Dalmeny, near Edinburgh.[32] While these and
similar work at Lochnaw in Wigtownshire, Cunnoquhie, Fife, and
Camperdown House, Dundee, were eminently practical designs, his
plan for Saltoun Hall in 1818 (Plate 97), including a flower and winter
garden, and his design for the new garden at Kilkerran, in Ayrshire, of
1814, showed him equally alive to the more imaginative aspects of
garden design.[33] In the explanatory key for the last, he noted a 'small

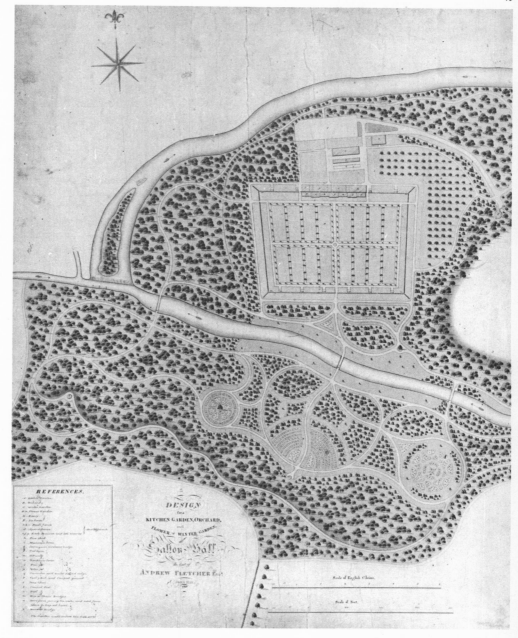

Plate 97. Plan for the flower garden at Saltoun Hall, East Lothian, by John Hay, 1818

34. SRO RHP 14268. His hothouses have now been destroyed but his walled garden remains. Kilkerran was seen by Loudon in 1832 who admired the 'romantic wooded dingle', and the 'magnificent silver firs' (*Gardener's Magazine* IX (1833) p.9). The garden was part of extensive improvements made at Kilkerran at this time. The formal gardens shown in Boutcher's plan of 1721 and extant in 1744 were eliminated, and a park laid out with a garden of five acres half a mile away. The former garden was grassed over. (Kilkerran, plans no. 31 and 32, and Sir James Fergusson, *Lowland Lairds* (London 1949) p.106). Hay's ideas for Saltoun were similar. There the plan was indexed A–X and included a moss house and wooden bridge as well as peach and apricot houses. In this design he moved the kitchen garden, and made his winter garden and rosiary on the other side of the Saltoun river, see Bell's survey of Saltoun in 1805 (NLS Acc. Ms.2933, map 1).

35. See SRO RHP 74; for an account of the buildings and family, but not garden, see RCAHM, *Peeblesshire*, vol.2, pp.281–3.

36. See *Encyclopaedia of Gardening* (1835) p.344. In his *Edinburgh Encyclopaedia* article he repeated verbatim much of his entry on the Whites, see vol.XII (1830) p.543.

37. He referred to White as follows: 'Mr. White, senior, we believe, was a pupil of Brown, of much information on country matters, and generally respected in Scotland. Of his profession we have said enough, when we mention their source'. Loudon also referred to the 'annual journeys have been made into Scotland'. However, on p.539 under the marginal heading 'Decline of Brown's School', he attacked this 'false taste' dominant in Scotland between 1795 and 1805, and particularly the 'English professor' (ibid.)

38. ibid., p.539.

orangery with an alcove seat which will serve as a Retreat in walking from the house to the top of the Lady Glen', and he recommended the fencing of walk 'HK' in 'peeled Oak or Larch, painted, covered with Honeysuckle, Ayrshire Roses etc.'[34] Such and smaller schemes of an acre or so were probably the backbone of his trade, and although he did occasionally take on bigger commissions, they were as a surveyor rather than designer. He never quite rivalled Nicol's range of practice, though he may have tried. In 1805 he made a plan of the small estate of Barns, in Peeblesshire, which he ambitiously called a Plan of Improvements, 'surveyed designed and drawn' by himself, although it was little more than a survey.[35] If this pleasant watercolour gives any insight into his ideas in landscape, they were remarkably like those of Walter Nicol and dogged by the same excessive sensibility.

It is easy to lay similar charges of lack of imagination and reluctance to depart from the familiar at the door of the two Thomas Whites. After all, it was largely from them that the Nicols, Hays and the rest, took their ideas in landscaping and so helped to bring both men into disrepute. Certainly the Whites, and the style they practised, were under attack even before White senior's death in 1811, and the career of his son was a continual swim against the tide of romanticism and the gardenesque. While Loudon, in his *Encyclopaedia of Gardening*, which first appeared in 1822, gave the elder White a favourable notice as a capable exponent of the 'principles of artificiality', by 1830 he had changed his mind and had written disingenuously of him in an unsigned article on 'Landscape Gardening' in the *Edinburgh Encyclopaedia*.[36] Privately he showed the utmost contempt for White, both as a gardener and designer, as his manuscript 'Treatise on Scone' of 1804 showed all too plainly. Although he noted in the *Encyclopaedia* that White senior had been generally 'respected in Scotland', a few pages earlier he had scorned, without naming, both White and his gardens as the work of an itinerant 'English professor'.[37] This much travelled academic was easily identifiable as White, who, as Loudon himself wrote, 'was in the habit of making annual journies in the North, taking orders for plans, which he got drawn on his return home, not one of which differed from the rest in anything but magnitude'.[38] Of White's son he was equally dismissive though more accurate. He acknowledged that 'in what respects the talents of Mr. White, junior, differ from those of his father, or whether they differ at all, we are not aware'; for he had as a contemporary put it 'great knowledge in the management of Plantations and woods', and was regarded as a 'sensible well informed man' who took 'great pleasure in his profession by which I am told he has made a fortune'.[39]

But apart from professional jealousy and envy of such worldly success, Loudon detested the Whites for their woeful lack of imagination and, in the elder White's case, arrogant insensitivity to the past. As a pioneer of the return to formality, he ridiculed the immense 'sums spent in destroying old avenues and woods', and their replacement by a modern style that had only three forms: 'a clump, a belt, and a simple tree'.[40] He was, of course, extreme but just. The elder White in his less successful schemes did appear to work to a set of rules, diligently and unimaginatively applied, and did seem to have turned against any accommodation of an older style. Equally, he was also an unabashed follower of Brown, and steadfastly turned his face against the principles of the picturesque, to the extent that at least two of his gardens were later remodelled by Loudon and one by Repton when he was barely in his grave.[41] White probably saw the natural landscape as a sort of friendly savage in need of education and discipline. He was certainly blind to the elemental scenery of Scotland and deaf to the imaginative appeal of Ossian.

As Loudon's 'English Professor', White's Scottish practice was a peripatetic one, conducted at first from East Retford in Nottinghamshire and later from the small estate of Woodlands in County Durham.[42] His first documented commission in Scotland was Douglas Castle in 1770. There was then an apparent gap until Scone Palace in 1781, Dudhope and Fintry (Linlathen) in 1782, Nisbet in 1784, and after that a constant flow of work until about 1802, by which time he had been joined by his son.[43] After his unexecuted scheme for Blairquhan in 1803, White seems to have retired from the rigours of planting and constant travel, and allowed his son to take over. Despite the number and chronological range of these improvement plans, there was as Loudon maintained, little to choose between them and no obvious stylistic development. Nor, apart from size, was there any variation in technique. According to the *Edinburgh Encyclopaedia* White

39. ibid., p.543. This again paraphrased his entry in the *Encyclopaedia of Gardening* (1834) p.344. The contemporary opinion of White junior was that of Lord Bute's factor in 1814. White had visited Mount Stuart, where his father had been invited in 1794, and was shown the whole estate and asked to dinner. However, nothing came of it and the factor concluded 'we do not want any of his assistance, but I wished to know what stress might be laid on his opinions respecting the pruning of wood, which he gave me very fully'. (Mount Stuart Muniments, Letter-book of A. Brown, ff.402, 439).

40. *Edinburgh Encyclopaedia* XII, p.539. However it should be remembered that Price himself admitted to the destruction of a formal garden solely because it 'obstructed the prevailing *system*'. (*Sir Uvedale Price On the Picturesque*, ed. Dick Lauder, p.302).

41. At Armley Hall near Leeds, Repton reworked White's landscape and was in turn followed by W.S. Gilpin. For mention of White's employment there, see Repton's Red Book, Mellon Collection, Upperville, Virginia, and Dorothy Stroud *Humphry Repton* (London 1962) p.165; for Gilpin see NRA Report Gott Mss.16435. In Scotland, White was replaced by Loudon after 1798 but before 1806 at Mountquhanie, see his *Country Residences* I, p.248. The *Statistical Account* of 1792 referred to considerable plantations 'lately made' there which were further admired in the *New Statistical Account* of 1845, see ibid. IX, p.538. At Scone, White was once again eclipsed by Loudon, see pp.194–5.

42. This estate was purchased by White senior in 1770, and the house and grounds laid out 'five and twenty years or more' according to *The Planter's Guide* in 1828 (ibid., p.425). *The Beauties of England* stated the house was built before 1803, see John Britton and Edward Brayley *The Beauties of England and Wales*, 18 vols. (London 1801–15) vol.V, p.213.

43. How independent White junior was before his father's death in 1811 is difficult to determine. It is likely he collaborated with his father in some early schemes and later his own were signed White 'jun.' a suffix he obviously dropped after his father's death. In terms of style or draughtsmanship, it is virtually impossible to divide senior from junior until later in the son's career. For a list of their known works in Scotland, see Appendix III. It would seem that Mr Douglas, later Lord Douglas, was a sustaining patron of White's. After Douglas Castle, he recommended White in 1782 to Robert Graham of Fintry as well as employing him again at Dudhope Castle, Dundee, and possibly at Bothwell House after James Playfair's reconstruction (SRO GD 151/11/41).

44. *Edinburgh Encyclopaedia* XII, p.539.

45. For White's work at Burton Constable, see *Catalogue: William Constable as Patron, 1721–1791* (Hull 1970) p.41: for Douglas see RHP 21983.

46. SRO RHP 9170. In his edition of Price's *On the Picturesque*, Dick Lauder extends in a note Price's remarks on how quarries and gravel pits can be changed from deformities into picturesque objects: 'I notice a quarry at the Earl of Dunmore's seat of Dunmore Park, in Stirlingshire . . . by the judicious planting of trees, shrubs and creeping plants, it has been converted into a delightfully retired wilderness of sweets' (p.151). The landscape work at Dunmore may have been the work of W.S. Gilpin, see his *Practical Hints upon Landscape Gardening*, p.208.

47. Scone Palace Muniments, bundle 1233.

48. According to R.C. Nesbitt *Nisbet of that Ilk* (London 1941) p.113, 'Grazing sheep wander by the burn side where centuries ago there was a moat and later a lake . . . The lake has been filled in'. For White's improvement plan of 1784, see NLS Ms.5460; for garden work at Nisbet see Ms.5414 f.15. At Abercairney, 'About the beginning of the century, the grandfather of the present laird employed Mr. White, the landscape gardener, to lay out the grounds with the evident intention of building the present mansion. The lake in front of the house, consisting of several acres, was part of the plan, which appears to have been rather artistic'. (Hunter, op. cit., p.229). It probably disappeared when the gardens were formalised in the 1830s, see SRO GD 24/5/175.

bought the linen for these plans 'in pieces of some hundred of yards at a time from a celebrated bleach field adjoining Perth'.[44] On these he painted and drew with watercolour and ink, giving the title as a small inset vignette and an alphabetical key to the reforms he intended to carry out. Certainly the tonal range of these drawings altered remarkably little: a yellow tan denoted the parkland, and the woods were coloured blue-green in a sort of pointillist technique. The size of the plans varied, of course, according to the estate but for the most part their width remained at about three feet, while the length ranged from the small at Blairquhan to the large at Douglas. The rules for their composition were more complex than Loudon's dismissive combination of clump, belt, and specimen tree suggested. Water and the approach road were further important elements, as were the perspectives of the various views and the integration of plantation and lawn. As Loudon well knew, such a limited range of materials made all the greater demands upon the imagination and technical skill of the designer. While all the schemes had much in common, beneath their surface there were particular patterns that varied from one garden to the other.

There was in most of White's work a gradual movement towards a looser and freer style, particularly in planting. This is perhaps best seen in the size and shape of his clumps. In his design for Burton Constable, Yorkshire, in 1769, and at Douglas a year later, the interior of the park was spasmodically dotted with close little groups of trees, each independent of the other and forming no particular pattern.[45] In the 1780s they became less awkward and more fluid, often making an undulating woodland that disguised the edge of the park. An exception may have been Champfleurie of 1789, where tight circular clumps were used to disguise the quarries that White preferred to hide rather than exploit, as the picturesque would have done (Plate 98).[46] More unusual perhaps was his attitude to water, which, for all his devotion to the Brownian landscape, he preferred to do without if he could. At Touch in Stirlingshire (Plate 144), where he worked before 1801, his angular lakes were no more than a widening to river proportions of the two existing burns, and at Arniston and Blairquhan he advised leaving the rivers as they were. At Scone he did much the same, allowing the River Tay to form a long boundary to the park with little embellishment beyond suggesting that 'the water also must receive its greatest animation from the single trees, and clumps of wood, that are planted upon its banks' (Plate 99).[47] His lake at Abercairney was short lived and the small one he executed at Nisbet was not a success.[48] Placed in a hollow

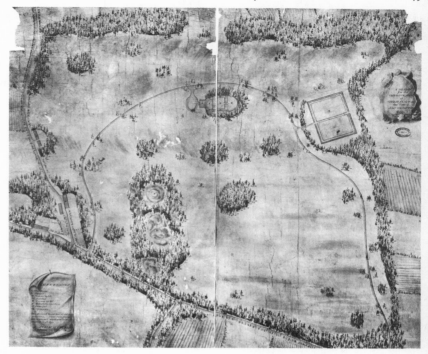

immediately in front of the house, it was too close to have any visual role in linking fore and backgrounds in the proper Claudian tradition, and it reverted to a rather reedy river shortly afterwards. If anything, White seems to have preferred the small scale of the river or pond to the larger and testing expanse of the lake. His use of a concatination of diminutive ponds in his own garden at Woodlands showed his fondness for water proportioned to the lawn, rather than the park. These pools formed a sort of aquatic ha-ha between the shrubs of the garden and the beech trees edging the park, similar in purpose to his water-fence at Scone.

In the planting of his parks and woods, White was preoccupied with a vision of a classical and permanent landscape. The hardwoods of his clumps and avenues were intended to have a full life span of two hundred or so years, and it was only on the more distant hills that the economics of forestry obtruded and the conifer predominated. In Scotland, he used both larch and Scots Pine for a variety of reasons and in most situations, but rarely because of their local character. He was

Plate 98. Champfleurie, West Lothian, improvement plan by Thomas White, 1792

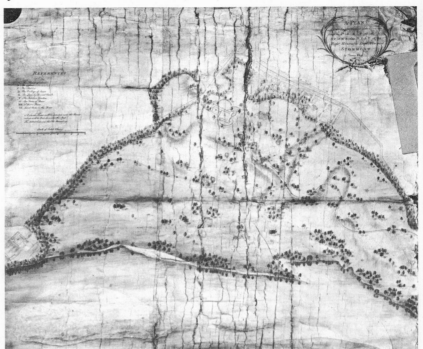

49. Scone Palace Muniments, bundle 1233.

50. SRO GD 151/11/41. White had visited Fintry, later Linlathem, in November 1782, and presumably carried out work there the following summer. He wrote that he would be 'very happy to give you any assistance in designing the improvements that may be made at Fintry when I am in Scotland next year in August' (ibid.). Robert Graham sold Linlathen in 1787, see Sir Francis Mudie and David Walker *Mains Castle and the Grahams of Fintry* (Dundee 1964) p.17.

51. *The Planter's Guide*, 2nd ed. p.425. In developing his estate in this way, White had an undoubted eye on publicity. It is likely that his probable commission for Donibristle in Fife, for the planting Earl of Moray, came from this enterprise. In 1781, Moray's letter to White mentioning 'The works here are going briskly on: they will, I hope, meet with your approbation', was reported in the *Transactions of the Society of Arts* II (1784) p.17. An improvement plan, unsigned, was produced for Donibristle in 1772 but not by White, see SRO RHP 14331. Planting was in hand at Donibristle from 1772 to 1782, see Darnaway Castle Mss. vol.VI/1. The fourth Earl of Bute referred in 1794 to White, 'who laid out Lord Moray's place' (Mount Stuart Muniments, letterbook of the fourth Earl). For the use of larch for White's coffin, see *Gentleman's Magazine* (1811) pt.II, p.194.

52. White received gold medals from the Society of Arts in 1778 for his larch, Scotch fir, Plane tree, Spruce tree, Silver fir: in 1779 for his Ash and Norfolk willow, and in 1786 for his English Elm, see *Transactions of the Society of Arts*, vol.II, pp.2, 3, 4; and vol.IV, p.4. There is a very complete account of Woodlands, or Butsfield as it was called before the house was built, in vol.V pp.5–37. See also Joseph Granger *General View of the Agriculture of the County of Durham* (London 1794) pp.48–9.

just as ready to plant beech or wych-elm as the acacia or the gean. The contrast he sought in his plans between deciduous and coniferous trees was invariably a paper one, designed to catch his client's eye and in no way a serious planting proposal. He was, of course, occasionally accurate: his scheme for Douglas deliberately showed the dominance of the fir, and at Scone, in 1781, he singled out a weeping willow for the riverside, whilst at Nisbet the woods were exclusively deciduous with only a scattering of conifers and the odd specimen tree.

Yet, for all the necessary emphasis White placed on the decorative value of his plans, he fully understood the tools of his trade. In explaining his plans to Lord Stormont at Scone, he defended his system of clumps as necessary, for 'the climate of the north of England and Scotland, will not allow single trees to get up as I have found by Experience, or otherwise I should have planted single trees in many places, wherein I have now disposed clumps'.[49] He was particularly knowledgeable, too, about the larch, and in 1782 described himself to a new client Robert Graham of Fintry as 'a great planter and am very

Plate 99. Scone Palace, Perthshire, improvement plan by Thomas White, 1781

partial to the larch'.[50] It was this tree that he used initially and almost exclusively in the afforestation of some 527 acres of wasteland on his estate at Woodlands. Later, he felled most of them, leaving only enough to shelter 'an excellent kitchen garden' with beyond 'shrubberies, a Piece of Water, and a handsome little park as an effective monument to his enterprise', and to make his coffin in 1811.[51] His skill and endeavour were sufficiently appreciated for White to be given both the Royal Society of Art's gold medal, and to have his work reported in their *Transactions* in 1786, and a few years later in the *Agricultural Survey of the County of Durham*.[52] As an advertisement for his abilities as an improver and indirectly as a landscape gardener, this could not have been bettered.

Thomas White had four large commissions in Scotland during the 1780s, of which at least three were executed under his supervision. All were beyond Perth in the north east, and White rotated between them. He worked unhappily and peripatetically at Scone Palace from 1781 to 1786, then moved to Gordon Castle, as his correspondence with Lord Stormont showed, and made his improvement plan there in 1786, although it was executed later between 1790 and 1792. From Gordon he passed to Cullen House, where he furnished three overlapping designs for the park about 1790, just after Adam's but contemporary with Playfair's appearance there.[53] He was consulted at Cairness in Aberdeenshire at this time, and he may also have worked in the same area for the Earl Fife at Duff House beside Banff.[54] In addition to these commissions there were, of course, several smaller ones that were fitted into an itinerary planned around grander and more lucrative employment. He was evidently consulted at Raith while at Scone, and he visited Cairness and Drimmie House (later Rossie Priory) on his way to and from Gordon Castle.[55] But his enemy in all these instances must have been time and the fatigue of travel, particularly when working in northern Scotland. It took him a good three days to make the journey from Scone to Gordon Castle – that is from Perth to Fochabers – and, not surprisingly, he charged by the day while on the road.[56] To this expense, he generally added a set fee for preparing the improvement plan. Where he was asked or was willing to execute it, his daily rate was about two guineas to compensate for his pains in such dull tasks as pegging the ground and marking the plantations. His final bill was never inconsiderable.[57]

White's system seems to have generally worked well in Scotland, with perhaps the notable exception of Scone. In 1781, he gave Viscount Stormont a scheme for improving its rather small, triangular shaped

53. His bill for the work at Gordon in 1790, notes that he was 'waiting upon his Grace from Cullen House' (SRO GD 44/374). His two plans for Cullen, for the park and for the western approach, are both at Cullen Estate Office.

54. White wrote to Charles Gordon of Cairness in July 1793 that 'I have the pleasure to acquaint you that your plan is completed and sent'. (Aberdeen University Library, Gordon of Cairness Ms.1160/3). According to Loudon, the park at Duff was 'chiefly laid out by the late Mr. White' (*Encyclopaedia of Gardening* (1824) p.1092). Work upon planting in the park was started in 1765, the bridge in the park built in 1772, and the mausoleum in 1792; see Tayler, op. cit., pp.20 and 72.

55. For Raith, see Scone Palace Muniments, bundle 1233: he left Gordon Castle for Drimmie House in 1786 and came to Gordon from Buthlaw (Cairness) in 1792, see SRO GD 44/374.

56. According to Loudon, a guinea a day was normal, though Nasmyth charged two. Repton charged 80 guineas for a visit of 160 miles in 1804, and in 1808 charged 50 guineas for a visit 100 miles away. (Dorothy Stroud *Humphry Repton* (London 1962) pp.134, 146.) W.S. Gilpin's rates in the 1830s were 'five guineas a day and his travelling expenses paid' (*Gentleman's Magazine* (1843) p.209.

57. The total bill for a twelve day visit in September to Gordon Castle in 1786 was £99.15: made up as £22.1 travel: £25.4 making observations, and £52.10 for his improvement plan. A charge for executing the work was over and above this (SRO GD 44/51/374).

park, closely shut in by the Perth road, Scone Village and the River Tay (Plate 99).[58] Planting was begun under his direction in the spring of 1784, and by April things were sufficiently far advanced for him to write that 'I am happy that your Lordship approve of the work at Scone for the little way we have gone, which I hope is in Ernest of your future approbation to obtain the pleasure of which no attention shall be wanting on my part'.[59] This was not to be the case. The reason for disagreement was obvious: the absence of both White and Lord Stormont from Scone, and their readiness to blame each other's men for the corresponding neglect and delay. White maintained that his system never allowed him to fix a definite time for a visit, and to have done so would have meant drawing 'the line of my peregrinations at the Tweed'.[60] Moreover, he felt that the foreman he had left at Scone during the winter of 1785 had directed the work to everyone's satisfaction, and such 'deficiencies' as there undoubtedly were came from 'the utter neglect of his Lordship's people'. Even more strongly he wrote that 'the place became a wilderness of weeds, and in a worse situation than when we left it. I have also to complain that my advice, and experience of twenty years, has been totally disregarded'.[61] In the end, Stormont's brother-in-law and near neighbour, the future Lord Lynedoch, was called in to arbitrate, and in September 1786 White washed his hands of the business with the dignified parting shot of: 'I have however reason to thank your Lordship that a business that has given me more pain than pleasure is to have *an end*'.[62]

Looking at White's improvement plan it is extraordinary that such a run of the mill design could have created so much unpleasantness, and especially when dealing with a sophisticated former ambassador like Stormont. It showed a conventional use of belting with the interior of the park planted in rather loose clumps. Yet adverse criticism followed as soon as it was put in hand in 1784.[63] To justify his work, White gave an invaluable summary of his 'principals in the Improvement of Scone'. First was conducting 'the approach in a more pleasing mode', and 'next to raise up such plantations as well shut out its deformitys, heighten its beautys, and by breaking the distant scenery as you pass along, introduce the same objects in different lights, and points of view and thereby give you an agreeable change of Scene'.[64] There was little that was new in any of this, and White's solution was a thoroughly typical one. He led a superlatively serpenting approach road from the southern entrance of the park, past the Friar's Den and then up the hill to the house, passing on the way the maximum number of his newly formed clumps. It was much the same route as later advised by

58. There was a constant attempt to divert to the east the Isla-Perth road as is shown in Andrew Cock's surveys of the period. (Scone Palace Muniments, plans 5 and 6). At the same time most of the village and church at Old Scone was moved to New Scone. The park was also to be extended to the north beyond the farm of Rome and this area may have been under consideration in White's letter of 1784 which referred to an estimate of 'Expenses of compleating the additional part of my plan' (ibid., bundle 1233). All of this was apparent in the schemes for Scone produced by Loudon in 1803 and 1804, see pp.193–8.

59. See White's letter to Lord Stormont of 1786 (ibid. bundle 1233).

60. ibid.

61. ibid.

62. ibid. This quarrel was exceptional, for White's obituary notice in the *Gentleman's Magazine*, emphasised his 'taste and skill in his profession and convivial manners' (*Gentleman's Magazine* (1811) pt.II, p.194).

63. Scone Palace Muniments, plan 4: 'A plan for the improvement of the Grounds about the Palace of Scone . . . T. White 1781'.

64. ibid., bundle 1233.

a shews the bad effect of formal detatched thickets

b shews the superior effect of open plantation or grove on knolls &c.

Loudon. For variety, he planted around the house and park some 136 varieties of trees and shrubs, and five different types of evergreen.[65] It was the clumps that particularly attracted Lord Stormont's dislike as too many and too random. But White was not perturbed 'that your Lordship should think that I had *dotted* too many of them, about the lawn, but you will please to consider, that the greatest part of them, are intended after a few years, to be singled out into dispersed trees, in a park-like order'.[66] Their appearance in Andrew Cock's surveys of the park, made in 1795 and 1801, showed compact little groups that seemed tighter and even more formal than those given in the improvement plan of 1781 and thinning them would have required both skill and eye (Plate 133).

Equally typical of White was his lack of interest in the river and, despite his note that 'water also must receive its greatest animation from the single trees, and groups of wood', little was made of it.[67] His failure to capitalise on the advantages of the wooded Friar's Den in the park, just below the site of his new kitchen garden, was characteristic too. Loudon, who followed hard on White's heels in 1803, judged with bias that 'the more recent but equally absurd plantations (dead or alive) here and there throughout the grounds disfigure and distort the whole place; while the insipid scenes of the shrubbery and other deformitys of art and ignorance, too many to be here enumerated have almost annihilated those ideas of grandeur and magnificence which nature first designed should reign here'.[68] This he cruelly

65. See Scone Palace Muniments, bundle 1401. There is there a 'List of Forest Trees and Flowering Shrubs sent by Mr. White to Scone, 22nd April, 1784'. This included 1,000 Weymouth pine and other trees in varying numbers down to two 'White berried spindle Trees'. The evergreens were sent later in May and comprised 200 laurels, 100 red cedar, 100 Pyracantha, 40 silver fir and 'candle berryd Myrtles' (ibid.). Larch and Scots' pines were conspicuously absent, though they were later used at Scone in Loudon's plantations.

66. ibid., bundle 1233.

67. ibid., bundle 1233.

68. ibid., vol. 117, f. 12.

Plate 100. Plantations, from Loudon's *Treatise on Scone*, 1804

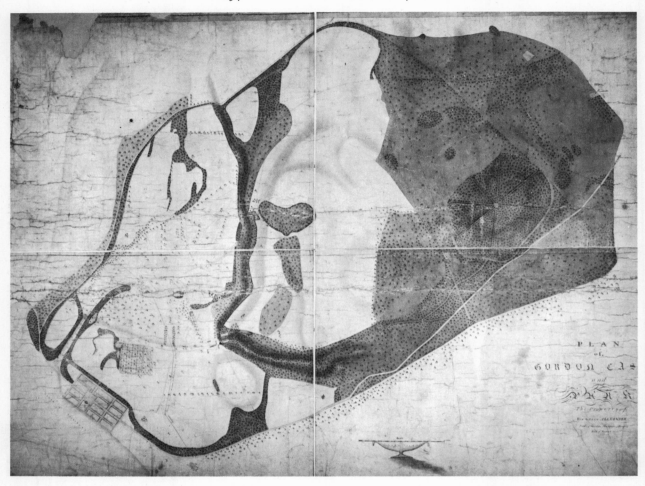

demonstrated with two comparative sketches, one showing 'the bad effect of formal detach'd thickets', the other 'the superior effect of open plantations' (Plate 100). This culpable blandness that Loudon felt he detected here was even more pronounced and on a much larger scale at Gordon Castle.

    Gordon Castle was the grandest of all four commissions. No doubt, too, the easy-going liberality of the Duke of Gordon was a pleasant contrast with White's unpleasant relations with Viscount Stormont at Scone. The Duke started off landscaping the grounds

Plate 101. Gordon Castle, Morayshire, incomplete plan of the improvements by Roy, 1808, after Thomas White

Plate 102. Aerial view of Gordon Castle, showing avenue from gate-lodge at Fochabers, 1979

around his new castle – finished by John Baxter in 1781 – with advice from both his head-gardener and Thomas Reid, the nursery gardener from Banff.[69] To them, and possibly to Robert Robinson, must go the dubious credit for razing the formal gardens. They filled in the long canal in 1779, turfed it over, cut down the avenues (apart from the Fochabers end of the Broad Walk), and planted the shrubbery.[70] This landscaping was sufficiently successful for Jacob Pattison to describe the park in his diary of 1780 as 'not indeed very large, wide shading trees, and pleasing walks in an extensive pleasure ground – here and there the top of a grot or bower was seen, and numerous small cascades'.[71] While White did not appear until a few years later, there was little that the Duke and Reid had done with which he could have disagreed. No friend of formality, he would undoubtedly have swept away the old planting in much the same way as he had proposed at Arniston in 1791. The plan he produced for the park in 1786, and for which he charged £52 10s, has not survived. An unfinished one, probably by the surveyor William Mackay, who worked with White for nine days in 1786, fortunately and predictably shows what was intended.[72] It corresponds fairly closely with the vast landscape set out in John Roy's survey of the new park in 1808 (Plate 101). They managed between them to emphasise the dreariness of the immense lawn in which the castle was more or less lost. The endless but unvaried forms of the shelter belts, and the scattered rather than clumped trees overwhelmed the approach road from Fochabers that led to the castle doors in the sweeping curve so disliked by the picturesque (Plate 102). A small elongated lake, which had almost evaporated by 1870, appeared rather like a puddle at one end of 'The Lawn', and apart from this little else disturbed the overwhelming greenery of grass and tree. This emptiness is still apparent in the mutilated landscape around the partially demolished castle, where White's lake remains as a triangle of rushes and scrub. The Quarry Gardens, with its temple and other pavilions, and the larger and islanded lake that replaced the kitchen garden at 'Willowtree Shade', were all later additions to White's landscape, although set within the framework of his woods.[73] Although plants like the Alpen rose and Dorset Heath were bought in London for a shrubbery in 1790, the park remained a huge woodland which, despite its larches, pines and rowans can have been little other than

69. For the period 1774–81, Reid was employed in estate and garden work, planting, making the sunk fence in the park, removing earth around the castle, and levelling, see GD/44/51/371. Alexander Allan was Master Gardener at Gordon Castle at this time and had been since at least 1769. (GD 44/51/370). He had been succeeded by John Mitchell as Principal Gardener by 1789. For the building history of the castle at this time, see A. and J. Simpson 'John Baxter, Architect, and the Patronage of the Fourth Duke of Gordon' *Bulletin of the Scottish Georgian Society* (1972) pp.47–57.

70. £117 was spent in 'Filling up the Canal and levelling the Green', work undertaken by Thomas Reid (GD 44/51/376). Plants for the new shrubbery came from Reid's nursery and cost in February, 1779, £5.5 (ibid.). The canal was clearly shown in Roy's survey of c.1747, running at right angles to the garden front of the castle, approximately where the 'Broad walk' existed. Much of this layout was repeated in a plan of 1768 which claimed to be 'the same scale and square of Mr. Robesons new plan . . . in English yards'. SRO RHP 2382. This is possibly a reference to Robert Robinson.

71. NLS Ms.6322 f.55.

72. Mackay charged £34.13.0 for making a survey of Gordon Castle in 1786. He also seems to have acted as surveyor to Thomas White and charged the Duke of Gordon £2.5.0 for 'attending the working with Mr. Whyte for 9 days'. (SRO GD 44/51/374: 1785–92). The plan is SRO RHP 2385.

73. The marshy remains of White's lake still exist. It replaced something similar in the 'Hare Warren' area of the 1768 survey. White's original kitchen garden was hidden by the plantations that now shelter the lake and adjoins the new gardens, see SRO RHP 2358. Both this lake and White's are shown in Thomson *Maps of Scotland Morayshire* (1826), and the former in the 1870 Ordnance Survey sheet. The buildings and garden at the Quarry were probably of c.1800, and the architectural work was by T. Browne of London, see RHP 2413 and 2414.

IV. Aerial view of Dunglass, East Lothian, 1979

74. SRO GD 44/51/374. These shrubs were purchased from Gordon, Dermer and Thompson, nursery and seedsmen at Mile End. They were dispatched by sea to Aberdeen and then overland to Gordon. The bill came to £2.13.3. The Duke also dealt with the London firm of Hewitt, Smith, Harrison and Cook of Brompton Road, from 1786 till about 1790 (ibid.). For these nursery firms see Henrey, op. cit., vol. II, pp. 325, 352–3.

75. After 1782, Thomas Reid dropped out of the picture. But in 1792 William Reid was still supplying larch, rowan etc. in their thousands to the castle (GD 44/51/374). Brown sold trees and carried out their planting in 1793–8 (ibid.).

76. SRO GD 44/51/374. This approach was no doubt White's drive from Fochabers, laid out after his seven day visit in 1790, and running through Baxter's gates and lodges, finished in 1793.

77. NLS Ms. 8026 ff.41, recto and verso, and 43, by J. Brown, and Ms.5203, vol.1, f.36 by J.C. Nattes. There is also a view of the Castle which shows a fair amount of the park in 1776 in Cordiner's *Antiquities and Scenery of the North of Scotland* (London 1780) p.56, pl.VII: see also James Hall *Travels in Scotland*, 2 vols (London 1807) II, p.354, visited in 1803.

78. Henry Skrine *Three Successive Tours in the North of England and Greater Part of Scotland* (London 1795) p.126. He visited the castle in 1793 during his third Tour, see op. cit., p.3.

79. However most of the major improvements at Gordon were over by c.1818, and the yearly garden costs of about £800 were largely incurred by maintenance, see SRO GD 44/51/165. Later work was principally on estate roads, bridges etc: see RHP 2008/1–10, and Loudon *Encyclopaedia of Gardening* (1824) p.1092.

monotonous on such an immense scale.[74] In its formation, White was aided by both Reid and the surveyor and nurseryman George Brown. Each of them supplied plants and seedlings from their nurseries, and Brown seems to have been trusted with the forming of the absent White's plantations between 1792 and 1798.[75] He was probably acting for him as early as June 1791, when he 'marked out an approach to the House, with sundry other lines, marking the same upon the plan'.[76] What was collectively achieved by this time is shown in several pen and wash views made by another Brown for his 'Sketches in Scotland' of 1791, and by Nattes a few years later in 1799.[77] A drawing by the former, taken from the park looking towards the castle and River Spey, clearly shows the tameness of White's composition and its critical lack of variety (Plate 103). Gordon had its admirers – even one who equated it with Cullen and Duff Houses as amongst 'the prettiest and most extensive in Scotland'; but to a true devotee of the picturesque, like the tourist Henry Skrine, it was little more than 'a flat and ill-kept lawn, surrounded by its thick plantations and not even commanding a view of the Spey, though perpetually subject to its inundations'.[78] Although in the nineteenth century, the castle was praised by Loudon for its 'fine woods, extensive gardens, and romantic walks', this was an appreciation rather than an assessment of White's contribution.[79]

A less direct criticism of both Gordon Castle and White was given

Plate 103. The park at Gordon Castle by J. Brown, 1789

in Dick Lauder's *Forest Scenery* in 1834, thirteen years after White's death. This account, for all its anecdotal good humour, barely disguised the contempt in which the eighteenth-century improver was then universally held. It appeared as 'an anecdote told us by the late Duke of Gordon', and though not identified, there can be little doubt that White was the 'certain landscape gardener from England – one whom we shall forbear to name, though he is long since dead'. According to Dick Lauder:

> The gentleman was delicate and indolent – the weather was gloomy and unfavourable for some eight days or so, and he preferred the comforts of a book and an easy chair in the draw-

Plate 104. Cullen House, Banffshire, improvement plan by Thomas White, 1789

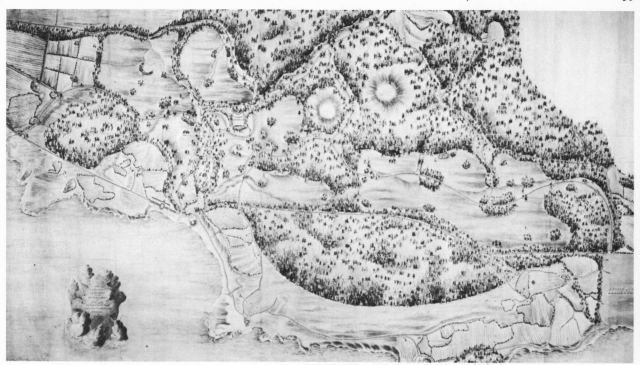

ing room to exposing himself to the raw damps which prevailed abroad. But, as he thus lacked exercise of limb out of doors, he made up for the want of it by exercise of jaws within; and the Duke's venison, and hock, and claret, suffered seriously from his daily attacks. But ten days' enjoyment of this Castle of Indolence had not gone over his head, when certain alarming twinges in his toe taught him, one evening, that an old monitor was about to revisit him, to remind him of the infinite nothing-ness and vanity of all human happiness, and next day he was laid up in bed with a swingeing fit of the gout. Some weeks of great suffering and of gradual convalescence brought him again to his easy chair, and by degrees he became so far well as to be able to return to his venison and claret, and finally, one clear sunshiny day, he ventured forth on crutches into the lawn before the castle. There, levelling his opera-glass silently around him for some time, he at last begged to know in what

Plate 105. Cullen House, improvement plan by Thomas White, 1790

direction lay the course of the river Spey; and, on this being explained to him – 'Ha!' said he gravely, 'I thought so'; and then pointing to a grove of magnificent old forest trees which stood at some distance in the park, – 'we must open a view in that direction. Your Grace will please to order those trees to be cut before next season, when I shall have the honour of revisiting Gordon Castle, to judge of the effect of their removal before going further'. Next morning this tastemonger took his departure. The noble trees which he had condemned bowed their mighty heads before the axe, as many noble heads have bowed before it, under the sentence of judges no less unworthy and merciless. The seasons revolved, and so did the wheels of the tastemonger's carriage, which brought him back to Gordon Castle, where the same scene of sloth, easy chair, eating, venison, hock, claret, gout-admonitory and gout-mordant, recovery, and revisitation of the ground, took place. Now, it happens that the Spey opposite to Gordon Castle cuts against lofty friable banks, of a bright red coloured mortar, which are perpetually crumbling down; and although these were, even at the time we speak of, for the most part hidden by the younger and more distant woods towards the boundary of the park, yet it so happened, that whereas no part of the water of the Spey was visible, the tastemonger had no occasion even to use his opera-glass to discover a broad stretch of blood-red bank, which, being higher than the rest, was seen towering most offensively over the delicate greens of the offscape, like a troop of heavy dragoons looking over a hedge. 'We must throw a clump up in that direction', said the tastmonger, waving his hand towards the place with a very important air; 'we must have a clump on that gentle swell, to shut out yonder hideous brickfield'. 'A clump!' exclaimed the Duke, with horror in his eyes. 'Why, my good Sir, on that very gentle swell grew those goodly trees which you ordered to be cut last year, and if you choose to satisfy yourself of the fact, you may go yonder to look at the roots which are yet remaining!' The gentleman was silent; the Duke left him to his own meditations; and the result was, that he had shame enough left to desire his carriage to be got ready, and to order it to transport him whence he came, an order which his Grace took no measures to thwart or retard.[80]

80. *Forest Scenery*, vol. II, pp. 237–9.

By such ridicule, libellous or not, Dick Lauder and indeed Loudon helped to clear the way for the return of the formal garden. For if the

81. The two surviving plans at the Cullen Estate office are billed 'An extension to a Design for the improvement of Cullen' of 1790; and 'A Design for the Continuation of the West Approach at Cullen House' 1789. It can be presumed there was a third improvement plan of which these two survivors are extensions. White left Cullen in 1790 for Gordon Castle and he was perhaps first at Cullen sometime in 1788. In a letter of 1788 in the Seafield Papers, a visiting gardener to Cullen wrote 'I have never saw Mr. Whyte and perhaps never may, but if his ideas are all as good, they must be approved'. (SRO GD 248/589/2). Little of White's ambitious schemes seem to have come to anything, and the same was true of Adam's set of impressive designs for a Porter's Lodge, Solitude, Banqueting House etc. of 1783 (SRO RHP 2544). However, planting was carried out on quite a large scale at Carnach wood in 1788. In 1790 clumps of beech, oak and larch were formed in the Hills of Boyndie, see GD 248/589/2 and 591/2. A description of the garden and park subsequent to White is given in David Souter *Agriculture of the County of Banff* (Edinburgh 1812) pp.85–7.

eighteenth-century landscape was arrived at in so casual and so careless a manner, there should be no hesitation, respect or sympathy, so it was implied, before sweeping it away.

White's plans for Cullen were larger, more sylvan, but only partially executed as the setting for James Playfair's vision of a classical and aristocratic demesne. Two drawings survive, dated 1789 and 1790: one titled 'Design for the Continuation of the West approach', the other, 'An Extension to a Design for the Improvement of Cullen' (Plates 104 and 105). There was obviously a third, made before 1789, which supplied the missing part of the western approach, and which was summarised in the expanded design of 1790.[81] This absent first scheme must have caught Lord Findlater's eye, for the new kitchen garden was sited at White's suggestion to the south of Cullen House at the junction of the Cullen and Glen Burns. Possibly encouraged by success, White produced two supplementary schemes which together devised an enormously long approach drive to Cullen from the west. This he proposed should branch off the public road at what is now Carnach wood, and then continue in serpentine fashion to the house some three miles away. Apart from turning this area into parkland, his most striking suggestion was to block out, by a vast semi-circular clump, the sea and the whole of the exposed but magnificent headland at Portknockie and beyond, whose particular character had been

Plate 106. View of coast at Cullen, from Cordiner Remarkable Ruins and Romantic Prospects of North Britain, *1786–95*

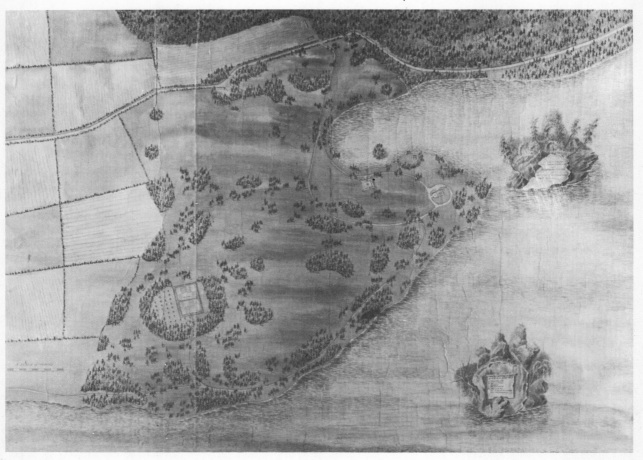

described in Cordiner's *Remarkable Ruins and Romantic Prospects* (Plate 106).[82] In this he was not so much proposing to set Cullen in an impressively wooded park as in a forest kingdom. But apart from the sheer size of this scheme, there was little that was new and, as Repton pointed out in his *Theory and Practice of Landscape Gardening*, 'One great error, in Mr. Brown's followers, has been the unnecessary extent of parks. It is my opinion that, provided the boundary can be disguised, the largest parks need not exceed two or three hundred acres, else they are apt to become farms within a park, or they are forests rather than parks'.

No doubt White would have destroyed May's wilderness garden,

Plate 107. Rossdhu, Dunbartonshire, improvement plan by Thomas White, 1797

82. See Cordiner, op. cit., vol.1, introduction.

83. For the earlier garden of May and Robinson see p.84. This area had by 1782 become more informal and was then described as 'the sides of the den are covered with all kinds of trees and flowering shrubs, through which serpentine gravel-walks have been made. The semi-circular hollow under the windows is laid out in a grass plot . . . was lately made a *fine ride* round the whole policy' (Douglas, op. cit., p.304).

84. SRO GD 248/589/2.

85. White's plan for Rossdhu remains at the house. It is inscribed 'A description for the improvement of Rosedoe the Seat for Sir James Colquhoun Bart. by T. White, 1797'. The house was built by John Baxter in 1772 as a classical villa after designs by Sir James Clerk(?) (Rossdhu Muniments, Box 32). It replaced the 'good mansion house' adjoining the old castle which Pococke had seen in 1760 (Pococke, op. cit., p.62). The existing landscape before White's improvements is shown in the 1776 survey of the estate (Glasgow University Library, Ms. Gen. 1006).

and his shutting the landscape off from the sea, while practical and necessary for the welfare of his new park, was not especially happy.[83] Of all his schemes, only the first and most modest – the siting and arrangement of the kitchen garden – appears to have been taken up by Lord Findlater and his gardener Machattie, perhaps through the rare instance of praise from a visiting professional. Lord Glasgow's itinerant gardener enthusiastically wrote in 1788, 'I heartily congratulate you on the new situation of your garden as the old one was vastly awkward (indeed) for so great a domain. Mr. Whyte has certainly Great Merit in leading your Lordship to so approve a situation.'[84] The walls were built for it in 1789, fruit trees sent up from Kew in the same year and planted in the following, but by that time White was hard at work executing the more remunerative commission of Gordon Castle.

Much the same traits were to be found in a smaller scheme he produced in 1797 for Rossdhu beside Loch Lomond (Plate 107). A small classical mansion by Sir James Clerk stood there, remarkably at odds with its romantic setting on an isthmus jutting out into the loch, with the slopes of Ben Lomond rising steeply on the other side (Plate 108).[85] Regrettably, there was little in White's improvement plan that could have reconciled the villa house to its superlatively evocative setting. He proposed a wooded approach road which, after it had

Plate 108. View of Rossdhu, from an engraving by William Green, *c*.1800

Plate 109. Cameron House, Dunbartonshire, improvement plan by
Thomas White jun., 1819

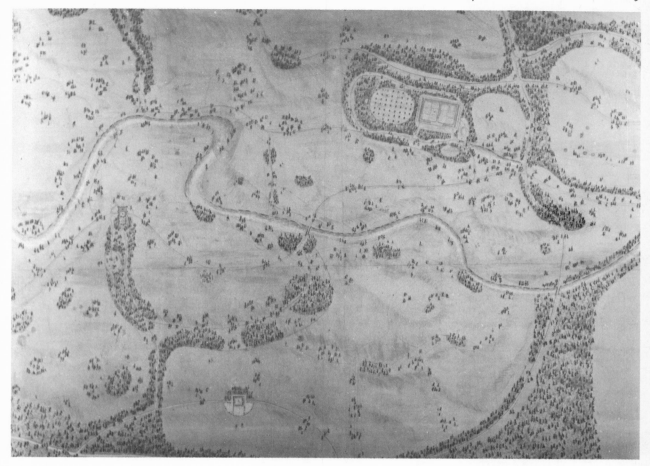

crossed the neck of the isthmus, diverged to run north and south, and meet again in a circle of lawn in front of the house. The longer southern route, which passed by the new kitchen garden, imitated the traditional peripheral bridle path and wound through the plantations at this end of the park. Although neither of those approaches presented anything more subtle than a more or less constant view of the house and loch, White's disposition of his trees along the water's edge was more imaginative than the suggested arrangement at Cullen. Instead of a virtually continuous shelter belt, which hid the interior of the park in most of his schemes, he developed at Rossdhu a series of rather

Plate 110. Bargany, Ayrshire, part of improvement plan by Thomas White jun., 1802

86. Work was in hand on Lodges and bridge in 1798 (Rossdhu, Box 32), and in 1801 the gardener John Dudgeon was at work on the new garden and causeway bridge (ibid.). According to Loudon, 1,000 acres were planted at Luss before 1794 (*Encyclopaedia of Agriculture* (1825) p.1143) and a view of the tower and house in the 1790s is given in Thomas Garnett's *Observations on a Tour through the Highlands . . . Scotland*, 2 vols. (London 1800) vol.I, pl.4.

87. SRO RHP 20113.

loose clumps that formed an inner circle with oblique and ragged views through their depth over the loch. He also made a more tangible concession to the picturesque by giving his new stables round corner towers and a gothic air. But it went no further, and so emotive objects such as the old tower and the fifteenth-century church of St Mary were planted out of sight, the former turned into a wash house, the latter a mausoleum. In this way, the two island vignettes that illustrated his plan were closer to the spirit of the place than anything he proposed. Although White never visited Rossdhu again, parts of his scheme, particularly the approaches, were realised by the capable head gardener John Dudgeon about 1801.[86] His local reputation, however remained sufficiently high for White junior to be consulted virtually next door at Cameron House, in 1810.[87]

Cameron House was an even smaller estate, further down the loch from Rossdhu, with the principal disadvantage of being bisected by the public road from Dumbarton to Luss (Plate 109). White junior's plan was to use this road as a sort of *cordon sanitaire* between the dressed grounds of the house and the parkland adjoining the home farm. He planted thickly around the landward edges of the park, with a spur of trees pointing inwards that almost surrounded the house, gardens and offices in a thick bower. The approach road ran through the lower parkland, straighter than most of his father's, and gave a constant vista of both house and loch.

Plate 111. The park and classical bridge at Bargany

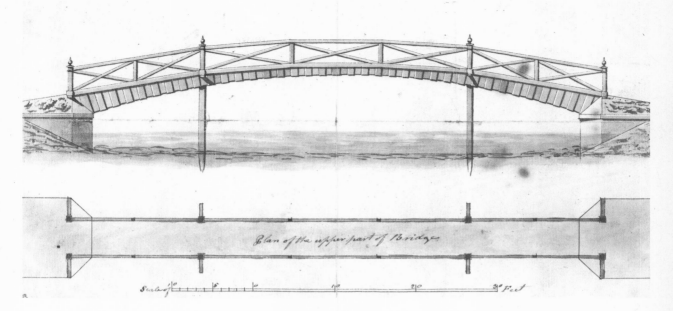

Plan of the upper part of Bridge

Scale of Feet

Neither of these two highland plans was impressive, and that for Cameron singularly out of step with the romanticism of the early nineteenth century. Ironically, such a conservative and unimaginative attitude to landscape made it possible for White to step without effort into his father's practice about 1803.

White junior practised in Scotland for almost twenty years. Although he did not die until 1836, few Scottish schemes appeared after about 1820. It may well be that by then he had outlived his useful career. Bargany was perhaps his first independent commission in Scotland and here he was part of a chain of gardeners associated with the house, from George Robertson in 1774 to W. S. Gilpin in the 1820s. His scheme, however, outshone them all, for it was larger, grander, bolder and more mechanical and less sensitive than any of the others. While Robertson's plan showed a willingness to work with the formal elements of the existing setting and Gilpin's scheme a sympathy with the romanticism of the house and its old-fashioned setting, White's was inflexibly modern (Plate 110). His enormous design of 1802, physically cast in his father's mould, not only wished away the public road from Dailly to Girvan, as well as the system of small lakes fed by the Weaver's burn, but also demanded the destruction of the classical

Plate 112. Wooden bridge proposed for Bargany by C.R., after 1794

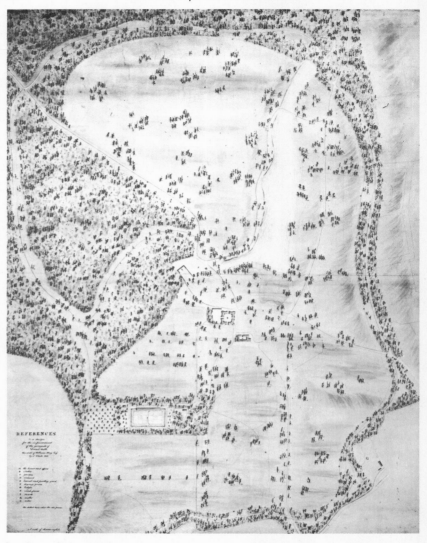

REFERENCES

88. The road was moved to the line suggested by White early in the nineteenth century, probably when Hay's glasshouses were built in 1818. The Gothic 'intended' new house never materialised though its site was marked on White's plan.

bridge of about 1753 and its replacement by three others, the razing of the existing U-shaped house, and the tripling of the park so that it extended across the River Girvan and upstream as far as the village of Dailly (Plate 111).[88] Any trace of the formal gardens that had been sensitively naturalised in Robertson's scheme was removed. Only the bowling green was allowed to remain, and it and the surrounding

Plate 113. Duns Castle, Berwickshire, improvement plan by Thomas White jun., 1812

89. Quoted from a poem, the result of unrequited love, which continued 'Let Resignation to my mind be given /Here worship God and pave the way to Heaven/ . . . My Books, the Bible and the Common Prayer /Add Ganganelli, Addison and Blair' (SRO Bargany Letters, vol.II, f.7). The drawing for the wooden bridge, initialled CR and watermarked 1794, is in the National Monuments Record, Edinburgh. It was probably for Robertson's lakes.

beech woods were thrown into the new kitchen garden and the adjoining gardener's cottage. Presumably the Hermit's Hut of about 1778, set deep in the Lady's Wood with its 'wattled roof of Straw', and the rustic bridge of 1794 were destined to follow the rest into oblivion (Plate 112).[89] What the ultimate effect of so radical a reform in so old a landscape would have been is hard to say, for little if anything of White's scheme was ever attempted. The abandonment of what he had marked on his map as the 'intended new castle' on the other bank of the Girvan from Dailly no doubt led to a similar shelving of the equally grandiose landscape park.

Plate 114. Aerial view of the park at Duns Castle, from the Hen Poo, 1979

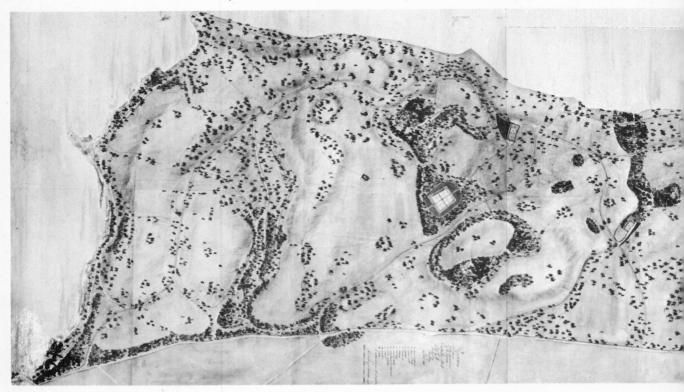

90. Improvement plan in the Blairquhan Estate office. Though White's plan met with little success, the planting notebook of Sir David Hunter Blair lists nearly half a million trees set out between 1803–14, with a vast preponderance of larch and Scots pine, and the layout of a summer and winter shrubbery in 1811. (Ms. notebook at Blairquhan). Sir David's interest in gardening is shown by his ownership of Monteath's *Forester's Guide*, of 1827, and more romantically in Gandy *Cottage Architecture*, of 1805. A house was built and landscaped by William Burn in 1821 with its predecessor and its formal gardens shown in Whiteford's map of 1787. Burn's house and its setting were admired by Dick Lauder in his edition of the *Essay on the Picturesque*, see op. cit., p.210.

91. SRO GD 109/3772/1. The character of *ad hoc* improvements which were carried out at Bargany at this time is confirmed in the *Gardener's Magazine*, which remarked in 1833 that 'for the last 25 years has been the scene of extensive improvements in the way of road making, draining, planting etc.'. It also mentioned the kitchen garden and pleasure grounds of 'about 13 acres' (IX, 1833, p.9).

92. *Gardener's Magazine* VIII (1832) p.330. These houses are still extant.

93. In a memorandum of the gardener James Dodd in 1827, 'Supposed calculation of Expenses for executing various improvements', Item 4 was for 'Completing the Pond including the

various improvements laid off by Mr. Gilpin between the pond and the west part of the house'. Item 9 was 'Plantations laid off by Mr. Gilpin' (SRO, Bargany Letters, vol.II, f.59) Most of this work had been executed by 1832. Calculations were made for planting in 1826 and spring of 1827, and probably by that time Gilpin had visited Bargany. For Gilpin's career in Scotland see App.III. Dodd had attended in 1826 courses in tree planting given at Allanton by Sir Henry Steuart. He wrote that 'Your Overseer *Dodds* came here, and staid several days . . . he learned much more of my principles and practice than all other pupils put together, *Smith of Jordanhill* alone excepted' (ibid., vol.II, f.38).

Plate 115. Dalmeny, West Lothian, improvement plan by Thomas White jun., 1815

Such an economic pattern was a familiar one in Ayrshire. It was repeated a year later, in 1803, at the next door estate of Blairquhan, where White senior's commission and the proposed new castle vanished simultaneously in a proprietorial change of heart.[90] Sadly for White at least, Bargany was instead patched up, and in 1813 a certain amount of levelling and turfing was carried out around the front of the house as a sop to landscaping.[91] A pineapple house was added by John Hay about 1818, when the gardens and greenhouses were set up in a position a little beyond that marked for them in White's plan.[92]

Sometime about 1826, the park was finally and decisively shaped by William Sawrey Gilpin, taking in the area on the other side of the Girvan as White had intended. It was then laid out in characteristic Gilpin fashion with the plantations tortuously grouped in his picturesqe style, while on the other side of the eighteenth-century bridge the open and clumped parkland contrasted with the dense woods that overhung the enlarged lake. Gilpin seems to have carried this out with a sensitive hand, sparing much of the formal planting around the bowling green, and forming Robertson's two lakes into a larger one with a small and thickly wooded island similar to that he intended fcr Bowhill a little later. Under his directions, the head gardener James Dodd formed the plantations, worked on the lake, and laid out the present east and west approaches to the house, where a gate lodge, remarkably like that of Blairquhan, was built.[93] The final effect fell radically short of White's total vision of a classical park. Instead, the fortuitously haphazard landscape with its bits and pieces of different styles made a better if less cerebral garden.

The schemes produced by the Whites for Bargany and Blairquhan were remarkably similar. The blind spots were much the same – the lack of interest in water, insensitivity to the past – and the conventions similar – the circular belts, the peripheral ride, the alignment of house and approach with a constant and clear view of each other. Later on, White junior's dependence upon his father's style lessened, but never dramatically. His schemes for Duns Castle in Berwickshire of 1812 (Plate 113), his vast and executed design for the park at Dalmeny of 1815 (Plate 115), and for Fordel in Fife, of 1818, all showed something of this loosening of the bonds.[94] He turned his back in such plans on the stock paternal devices where a contrast was forced between the

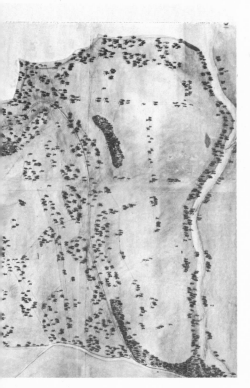

94. For White's plan for Duns, see SRO RHP 14531, the original is at Duns Castle; for Fordel, see RHP 3803. White's plan for Dalmeny was evolved before the present house was built by Wilkins. His plan followed hard on the heels of Wyattville's rejected schemes of 1814 and made provision for what seems to have been a classical house with adjoining offices. In this respect it was similar to his scheme for Bargany. The plan showed the destruction of Barnbougle Castle (which did not happen), the preservation of the two existing approaches and the creation of the present Chapel approach and lodge. It was to this that W.S. Gilpin referred when he wrote in 1832 that 'the shape and character of the ground at both entrances forbids any attempt to the

erection of a lodge corresponding with the architecture of the house; and, I think, good taste has substituted a simple building at each of them' (W.S. Gilpin, op. cit., p.213). A surviving map at Dalmeny shows several of White's clumps with notes that they were planted and fenced off around 1815–20.

95. The naturalism of White's plantation is even more obvious when compared with an earlier scheme for landscaping Duns of around 1789, see SRO RHP 14516 and 14517. These two plans, of which RHP 14517 is a rather formal and professional version of RHP 14516, both show very obvious periphery belts with tight clumps in the centre of the park, smaller than those formed by White. It also suggested a lake with three islands in front of the castle. Such improvements were probably meant to coincide with John Baxter's extension of the house between 1792 and 1794.

96. See William Cockburn's plan of Duns in 1744 at Duns Castle. For some account of the gardens at this time, see also Francis Hay *The Family of Hay of Duns Castle* (Edinburgh 1922) p.13. Neale in his *Views of Seats*, described this avenue as a 'second, but much longer avenue, . . . is to be the principal approach from the south and west, the gateway to which is not yet erected' (Neale, op. cit., 1823, vol.VI, up).

97. See Hay, op. cit., pp.33–5.

98. ibid., p.34. The present park follows White's plan sufficiently closely to confirm his working at Duns. According to William Hay a new garden was laid out between 1802 and 1807. After Hay's succession in 1807, more extensive work was put in hand and the expansion of the Hen Poo into White's lake was probably the general date for the execution of his scheme (ibid., p.35).

interior of the park, open and clumped, and its edges, and where deep plantations shut out the countryside to enclose a pastoral fable of houses and landscape (Plate 116). At Duns there were only periphery woods, whose inner edges expanded and contracted in an uneven pattern, but at Fordel there was a deliberate and almost imperceptible transition from the loose clumps near the house to the plantations of the exterior.[95] The main south approach he designed for Duns was straighter and more formal than any his father had ever executed, and he went so far as to preserve, as a subsidiary drive, the old lime avenue of the 1720s as well as the existing lake (Plate 114).[96]

In all of these designs, White was somewhat belatedly attempting to keep in step with the less extreme forms of the picturesque, those of Repton rather than Price or Knight, as he proved with the retention of the Cockle Burn dell at Dalmeny. But it was too little and too late. It was clear from the undated Memorandum of his Duns client, William Hay, that the early nineteenth century had left the Whites and their Arcadia far behind.[97] Hay undoubtedly regretted employing White and carrying out his design, and he felt that had he read Price's *Essay On the Picturesque* earlier 'I should have escaped many errors into which I have fallen, and saved both money and land, as better effects could have been produced by less sacrifice'.[98] His ideal for Duns was the creation of a forest that embowered the castle, 'giving the lawns and fields the appearance of having been cut out of the woodland, the luxuriant encroachments of which could hardly be restrained'. He sought the richly casual landscape of 'Gainsborough, Wynants, Ruysdal, and Hebbimar, rather than the followers of Brown, Repton and

Plate 116. Beech clumps in the park at Duns Castle

99. ibid., p.34.

(ungraciously) Whyte', whose name he misspelt.[99]

It is easy to see the physical impact of the Whites upon the Scottish landscape at the turn of the century. In his heyday the elder White was in constant demand. The fourth Earl of Bute was probably typical when he appealed to his Edinburgh lawyer in 1794 to 'find out whether *White* the English gardener, or Surveyor, who laid out Lord Moray's place and many others, means to be in Scotland this year'. Both father and son were popular, worked hard, travelled widely in the lowlands and the north east, and made a fortune. They displayed no originality and as consolidators and pillars of orthodoxy, they reaped the benefit of a harvest sown by Robert Robinson in the late 1760s. The landscape they offered was perhaps too deeply and exclusively that of Brown. They ignored to their cost the arrival of the picturesque and later romanticism, forces that together significantly changed the Scottish view of Scotland. It is not altogether surprising that when White junior departed from the Scottish scene, his style was more or less outdated and his legacy barren.

THE ROMANTIC

Loudon's career as a gardener in Scotland was youthful and brief. It ended with his final departure for London in about 1804. Although he returned for any length of time only in 1831, he was kept well informed of what was happening through the various correspondents of the *Gardener's Magazine*, of which he was the founder and editor. But from this early period stemmed his ideas on the history and style of the Scottish gardens, which found eventual expression in his *Encyclopaedia of Gardening* of 1822. There, he dealt with them in the novel fashion of a distinct and separate entry. In many ways he was their most distinguished apologist, able to list starkly their numerous shortcomings, while at the same time spelling out their individual character. It is likely that Loudon's own natural style of landscaping with its reliance upon certain formal elements was largely derived from so hopeful an analysis. He wrote prophetically in his *Treatise on Country Residences*, of 1806, that 'Scotland, for example, is at present an interesting country, as expressive of a peculiar character, *the wild, naked, and romantic*. If that character be partially changed, the effect will be displeasing . . . but, change it completely, and the expression will be superior to its present state, and much more rich and noble than England, and perhaps most countries'.[1]

In writing his influential *Observations on Several Parts of Great Britain, particularly the High-Lands*, William Gilpin had described Scottish taste, and by inference gardens, in 1776 as 'still at least half a century behind the English'.[2] This remark was specially aimed at the state of the Scottish landscape garden during the transitional period, for he courteously and truthfully added in 1789 that 'it must be understood however that I speak of things, as I found them a dozen years ago. Many improvements may by this time be introduced'. Even so, he still warned that 'it will be long however before this taste can become general'.[3] In writing in this way Gilpin was a little unfair, for almost the opposite view was held by Edward Topham at about the same time. In his *Letters from Edinburgh* of 1776, he stated that 'Amongst the number of improvements which have been encouraged in Great Britain within

1. Loudon *Country Residences*, ii, p.521.

2. Gilpin *Observations*, ii, p.143.

3. ibid.

a few years, there is one which seems to have made a great progress in this country as in England; I mean, the improvement of taste in Gardening, Parks, Plantations, and Pleasure Grounds'.[4] Although opposed in their opinions, neither Gilpin nor Topham saw the Scottish landscape garden as anything more than an imitation of the English and, like most imitations, probably inferior. Only with the appearance of Loudon's brand of historical journalism from 1804 onwards was there any sustained attempt to define the characteristics of the Scottish park and its gardens, which Dick Lauder was to appreciate so rapturously thirty years later. Much of the fascination of Loudon's *Observations on Planting* of 1804 for the reviewer in the *Farmer's Magazine* and others was that it was written by a Scotsman, and seriously considered as 'the first of the kind undertaken by a native of this country [Scotland]'.[5]

In the *Observations*, Loudon set out in conventional enough fashion the effects that could be achieved by trees in a landscape design. Much of it seems to have sprung from his work at Scone for the Earl of Mansfield, where his manuscript 'Treatise on the Improvements', written in 1804, set out ideas repeated in both the *Observations* and his *Country Residences*, of 1806. His categories were the familiar ones: the beautiful, the picturesque, and the sublime or grand. Less conventional were the actual ground plans he gave, which were supposed to correspond to the principal characteristics of plantations described in the three types.[6] To deepen the originality of his recommendations, he scorned and denigrated the forms used in the Brownian landscape garden and compared them unfavourably with his own. In writing in this way, he was of course little more than echoing the opinions of the Price-Knight school and their quarrel with both Brown and Repton. His own special advantage was that he was fortunately and fortuitously able to class all that he disapproved of as 'English gardening', and in doing so was taking up more or less where Sir John Dalrymple had left off in the 1750s.

He was quite clear about what he considered English gardening and what he felt were its principal defects. He dealt with them in his *Observations* under three broad categories: ground, water and wood. He disliked the almost 'uniform flow' of the Brown or White park. Its lake, he was convinced – and rightly in the case of White – was designed to come as close to 'the appearance of a made canal as possible', and its woods were a dull combination of belt and clump where 'on each side of the mansion, the pleasure ground would be made – the boundary a sunk fence – its contents, circular and oval

4. See Edward Topham *Letters from Edinburgh* (London 1776) p.226. Letter 28 'On their Gardening and Improvement in Planting etc.' was addressed to William M, presumably William Mason the poet and gardener, whose literary tastes probably appealed to those of Topham.

5. The *Farmer's Magazine* VI (1805) p.88. The review of Loudon's *Observations on Planting* was followed by a rather unfair attack which accused Loudon of being 'raw and ignorant where he introduced his own ideas', and among other things whose hothouses were an 'imitation so imperfect of those constructed by Mr. Hay' (ibid., p.239). For Loudon's reply see ibid. pp.354–62. In his *Country Residences*, Loudon particularly mentioned his Pineapple house at Prinknash, Gloucestershire, and his pits at Glenfuir, Stirling, see ibid., I, pp.295–7.

6. Loudon *Observations on Planting* p.30 and pl.11. Loudon also named certain types of tree and shrub as typical of those categories, ibid., p.32.

7. ibid., p.259.   8. ibid., p.246.

9. At the end of *Observations on Planting*, there was advertised a further work which 'Speedily will be Published, by the same Author, Illustrated by Engravings, Observations, Descriptive and Critical, on Most of the Gentleman's Places in the East, West and South of Scotland' and which was 'tending to illustrate the Arts of Rural Ornament and Improvement, and point out the Beauties of Gentlemen's Places in Scotland'. This never appeared in the form described but may well have been incorporated into Loudon's *Treatise on Country Residences*, which lent heavily on his Scottish experience. A similar sort of parentage was probably true of Loudon's *Observations on Planting*, which seems to have derived from an article 'On Plantations' published in the *Farmer's Magazine* of 1804 and initialled 'J.L.L. & J', see *Farmer's Magazine* v, pp.323–7.

10. The *Gardener's Magazine* VIII (1832) pp.3–4. This account of Scottish gardens was described in the General Index as a 'Gardening Tour, during July, August, and part of September, in the year 1832, from Dumfries by Kirkcudbright, Ayr and Greenock, to Paisley, By the Conductor'. The Conductor was obviously Loudon and the correct date 1831. This was confirmed by Jane Loudon's 'A Short Account of the Life and Writings of John Claudius Loudon', see John Gloag *Mr. Loudon's England* (Newcastle 1970) pp.206–7. According to Mrs Loudon, they stayed with Sir Charles Menteath at Closeburn Castle in Dumfriesshire and at Jardine Hall in the same county, as well as at Munches, near Castle Douglas and 'other seats' (ibid., p.206). These are further described in *Gardener's Magazine* IX (1833) pp.4–7. His generalisations based on the three counties of Dumfriesshire, Kirkcudbrightshire and Wigtownshire, gave a virtual cross-section of the landscape of Scotland, and as such were no different to his remarks on the Scottish garden in the *Encyclopaedia of Gardening*.

patches of all sorts of shrubs – and, through among these, a serpentine gravel walk would lead you to the riding in this belt'.[7] What particularly irritated him about such gardens was their lack-lustre uniformity, and the consequent destruction or neglect of any natural landscape. Instead he maintained that the only landscapes which 'require to be *changed*', were those which inspired actual disgust, such as 'scenes of *ugliness* and *deformity*'.[8] He remained reasonably true to such principles throughout his career, and sufficiently so to repeat elsewhere the attack developed in both his *Observations* and his *Country Residences*. Although he later shifted his ground to a less national standpoint in the *Encyclopaedia of Gardening*, and in his unsigned article in the *Edinburgh Encyclopaedia* of 1830, his contempt nevertheless remained.

While Loudon was quite positive about his dislike of what he termed English gardening, he was less sure about the landscape style desirable for the purged Scotland. It was not until his return to Scotland in 1831 that he was prepared to cut and cure the Scottish garden, although he may have held such operation as vital to its health for some time.[9] He wrote as the Conductor of the *Gardener's Magazine*, a critical account of a visit in that year to several of the more important gardens in south-west Scotland. Fairly and objectively he summarised his findings in the following paragraphs:

Nature has done more for the landscape scenery of Scotland than she has for that of England, by supplying the most striking or interesting features; but man has not been endowed with sufficient taste, or rather, perhaps, wealth, to make the most of them. We have heard it alleged, that the difference between Scotch and English parks, with regard to wood and lawn, is owing to the inferiority of the northern climate; but this is one of the greatest mistakes that can be made on the subject . . .

The park scenery of Scotland is inferior, as far as art is concerned, to that of England, chiefly from its confined extent, and the formality of all the lines and forms connected with it. This formality may be traced to the love, in Scotch landowners, of agricultural profits; straight lines, and surfaces uninterrupted by trees, being most favourable for aration. The English *beau idéal* of a park is that of a portion of natural forest scenery, with smooth glades of lawn in some places, and rough thickets of shrubs and ferns in others; but the Scotch idea of a park (judging from the parks as we found them) is that of a pasture field of considerable extent, varied by formal clumps of trees and strips of plantation . . .

11. *Gardener's Magazine* VIII (1832) p.5. Loudon considered that the garden front of the house, over which the drawing room should look, ought to contain 'the most highly polished scenery, and the finest display of flowers', and that the entrance front should be simple and without flowers, 'the plainer the entrance front is, the better it will contrast with the drawing-room front'. A similar, but less sophisticated account of the ideal flower garden, was given by Patrick Neill, in the *Edinburgh Encyclopaedia* of 1830. He wrote that it should 'have a separate situation, generally at some distance from the fruit and kitchen garden. It should indeed form an ornamental appendage to the mansion, and be easily accessible in all kinds of weather. There is no objection to the flower garden being seen from the windows of the house: on the contrary, this is sometimes considered desirable' (Patrick Neill, 'Horticulture', *Edinburgh Encyclopaedia* (1830) XI, p.286.

12. For a short account of the early eighteenth-century garden in Scotland, see Cox, op. cit., pp.54–66. Cox remarked upon the Scottish fondness for a series of walled gardens adjoining the parterre. According to Neill, the flower gardens at both Raith and Wemyss Castle were adjoining the hothouses (*Edinburgh Encyclopaedia*, XI, p.192).

13. *Gardener's Magazine* VIII (1832) p.5.

14. ibid., p.132. From this criticism he excepted Munches in Kirkcudbrightshire, which had recently been laid out probably by the Rev. Mr. Carruthers of Dalbeattie, Closeburn Castle, and parts of St Mary's Isle. These estates exhibited the 'greatest judgement' in park scenery (ibid.). Closeburn Castle was the home of Sir Charles Menteath, who was a knowledgeable amateur and correspondent of the *Gardener's Magazine*. The woods at St Mary's Isle were described by Loudon in his *Encyclopaedia of Gardening* in 1824, as

It is remarkable that, in a country abounding with so many fine situations for country residences, there should so often be houses placed in dull flat situations, with nothing to recommend them but the richness of the soil. This we can only account for on the principal that fine situations, being so common, are not duly valued; and that wealth which can procure a large well-built house anywhere obtains among a poor people more applause than the taste which would place that house in a beautiful situation.[10]

While innate conservatism and parsimony may have helped to spoil the Scottish park, the pleasure garden – the area of lawn and shrubbery that lay between it and the house – suffered from further and different defects. Loudon wrote that in Scotland and particularly the south west, he frequently met with 'a degree of coarseness of surface, rough grass, and a total absence of flowers and fine shrubs all round the house; while there was a flower-garden, and a portion of highly kept lawn at some distance from it, in a shrubbery, or near the kitchen-garden. This we consider both as a want of taste, and a great waste of expense, because no adequate effect is produced'.[11] For Loudon, it was tradition rather than botanic or economic reasons that separated the Scottish from the English garden. The survival and development of the walled garden, the isolated patch of trim lawn descending from the old bowling green, and the formality still apparent in the planting of the park, endowed gardens like Bargany with a distinct character apparent even in the cases of the newer ones such as White's Raith or Wemyss Castle.[12] While for Walter Scott and the romantics this was visual history, for Loudon it was timid conservatism of the worst sort. Faint-heartedness, Loudon felt, was the radical source of their failure to achieve distinction. He maintained that they collectively lacked 'what the painters call effect, or what some would call display, which with us is every thing'.[13]

Loudon also objected strenuously to the tools that gave such poor results. He disliked the use of the stone dyke or thorn hedge to make an enclosure for young trees, maintaining that they gave 'all the opposite qualities to those which are desirable in a temporary fence'.[14] He felt that the money laid out on them could have been much better spent 'in trenching the ground previously to its being planted, and in

'grounds much diversified by woods . . . in imitation of a natural forest by a former possessor' (ibid., p.1088). Later he found 'impardonable' fault with its deficiency in exotics, 'without which, when laid out in the natural style, there can be no gardenesque' (*Gardener's Magazine* IX (1833) p.7).

15. *Gardener's Magazine* VIII p.133.

16. ibid., p.519. Loudon anticipated that the introduction of the 'recently invented mowing machine' would lead to lawns which 'will be kept as we could wish them' (ibid.). This volume of the *Gardener's Magazine* contained a description of 'Budding's Machine for cropping or shearing the vegetable surface of Lawns, Grass-plots etc.' (ibid., pp.34–6).

17. ibid., p.519.

18. Neill, op. cit., pp.163–79. Abercairney was landscaped by 'Mr White' – probably Thomas White junior – around 1800. (Hunter, op. cit., p.229). The area around the house was substantially altered in a formal style during the 1830s, see SRO GD 24/5/175. Kennedy described his work there, realised and in hand, in December 1813 (GD 24/5/128). He was the son of John Kennedy (grandson of Lewis) partner with Lee in Vineyard Nursery at Hammersmith, see E.J. Willson, *James Lee and the Vineyard Nursery* (London 1961) p.52. The Vineyard Nursery was not only the leading place for exotics but it also appears to have supplied designs with its plants as was the case with the rosaries at Donington in 1809 (Mount Stuart Muniments, Box 35, bundle 14). Kennedy had a considerable Scottish practice being consulted by the Duke of Atholl at Dunkeld and Blair Atholl, and starting the formal revival garden at Drummond Castle around 1822. Shortly afterwards he became exclusively a land steward for Lord Gwydyr at Drummond and elsewhere, see pp.234–5. According to Charles M'Intosh, he was around 1815 'the leading landscape gardener in England' (M'Intosh, op. cit., I, p.620). For his English career, see John Harris *A Catalogue of British Drawings for Architecture, Decoration, Sculpture and Landscape Gardening, 1550–1900, in American Collections* (New Jersey 1971) pp.127–9.

thinning out the trees in due time'.[15] He criticised similar waste in the design of hot houses, where too much time and money was spent on the woodwork and glazing and too little on employing an improved system of hot water heating. He disliked the gravel paths of the average Scottish garden as 'rough, loose, and very unpleasant to walk on', and found few of the adjoining lawns 'mown often enough to produce a very fine velvet turf'.[16] Kitchen gardens alone seemed to satisfy Loudon, and these he praised as 'generally formed at greater expense, and afterwards kept with more care and neatness, than they are in England. The reason may be, that the climate requires a greater variety of fruits to be cultivated against walls; and that the kitchen-garden, being usually well sheltered, and also ornamented with flowers, is, contrary to the English practice, as much used as a place to walk in, by the female part of the family, as the pleasure-ground'.[17] The truth of his statement was clear from the appendix to Neill's *Scottish Gardens*, where there was a good descriptive list of such gardens, which ranged from the grand and famous, like Archerfield and Eglinton, to the smaller and less significant. Lewis Kennedy's Abercairney of 1813 was perhaps typical of the latter sort. It contained an arbour, trellis work and bridge à la Suisse, set amongst flowers and fruit trees, the whole skilfully put together by a botanist of Loudon's persuasion and former partner in the nursery firm of Kennedy and Lee, of London.[18]

To an expatriate like Loudon, whose early career had been passed largely in the Lothians but who was knowledgeable and reasonably fair, the Scottish garden in 1831 fell short of its English neighbour. It lagged behind in most technical developments, whether it was the proper use of the lawnmower or hot water pipes. Its owners were comparatively poor, and what money they had was more often squandered than spent. As like as not, they showed little taste and 'very little feeling for any kind of beauty connected with park scenery'.[19] In his description, published in 1832, of Burn's Blairquhan in Ayrshire, he generalised that 'there is evidently, among the Scottish gentlemen, either a great want of taste, or a great want of means; perhaps both'.[20] But above all, Loudon laid much of the blame for this lamentable state of affairs on the financial circumstances of their owners. In the West of Scotland, which was more or less typical, the majority of the country houses were empty when Loudon visited them in 1831. He explained that 'very few of the proprietors reside at them, chiefly, as we are informed, from not having the means (owing to the diminution of their rents, and other causes) of keeping up the requisite establishments,

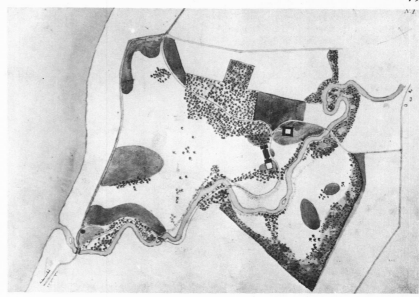

and paying the interest of the mortgages or other encumbrances on their estates'.[21] But 'the prevailing cause, however, of the sufferings of the Scotch landed proprietors we believe to be the great extent of their mortgages', a situation exacerbated by their inability to sell entailed property and 'it has been shown in a late number of the *Edinburgh Review* that more than half the landed property in Scotland is very strictly entailed'.[22] This had been especially true with Loudon's former clients the Agnews of Barnbarroch, who appeared in print on the subject.[23] Its practical effects were set out in the 'Remarks on the depressed State of the Nursery and Gardening Professions, more especially in Scotland', by J. G. in the *Gardener's Magazine*, who foretold that 'If we look upon the increasing mortgages on land in Scotland, weighing so heavily upon the spirit of improvement, the future becomes gloomy'.[24]

Such ideas had been developed over the years. Probably Loudon's earliest attempt to define something more than the natural characteristics of Scotland appeared in his *Country Residences* of 1806. Although there he was principally concerned with offering an alternative and, he thought, better style to those of Brown and Repton, it contained, almost as a corollary, an attack on the wholesale application of English solutions to Scottish problems. This obliged Loudon in turn to describe

19. *Gardener's Magazine* VIII (1832) p.133.

20. ibid., IX (1833) p.8.

21. ibid., VIII (1832) p.3.

22. ibid.

23. John Vans Agnew of Barnbarroch was in severe financial straits in the 1820s, see his *Resolutions . . . the expected re-enactment of the Statute imposing the Property Tax* (Edinburgh 1816); see also, *Some Important Questions in Scots Entail Law* (Edinburgh 1826).

24. *Gardener's Magazine* VIII (1832) p.135.

25. *Country Residences*, II, pp.650–3.

Plate 117. Valleyfield, Fife, improvement plan by Repton, 1801

26. See *The Landscape Gardening and Landscape Architecture of the late Humphry Repton*, ed. J.C. Loudon (London 1840) pp.214–15. In this Repton paraphrased his addition of December 1801 to the Red Book for Valleyfield; 'Although I have never seen Valley Field myself, yet it flatters me to learn that, under the direction of my two sons, by taking advantage of the deep romantic glen and wooded banks of the river which flows through the grounds, and then falls into the Firth of Forth at a short distance from the house an approach has been made, which, for variety, interest and picturesque scenery, may vie with any thing of the kind in England' (ibid., p.214). The Red Book remains at Ardchattan Priory in Argyllshire: see Appendix I. Loudon dated the improvements there as begun in *c.*1799, and finished in 1804, see *Country Residences*, II, p.438.

27. ibid., pp.436–7. Loudon wrote 'The occasion of this barbarous treatment was, that the approach to the house should be conducted through it . . . but, in place of a natural and irregularly margined road, the most formal, high-finished narrow gravel walk that can be imagined was carried stiffly along its banks, while all the wood was thinned – all the undergrowth, creepers, ferns etc. were cut down, and every broken or abrupt part of the surface taken away. Even some perpendicular rocks, overhung with large trees, with their edges varied by roots, bushes, and other intricate concealments were totally bared' (ibid., p.436). The character of this drive is shown in Nasmyth's view of Valleyfield from the sea, as well as in the illustrations to the Red Book. The latter were presumably worked up from sketches made by his sons on the spot. Gilpin in his *Forest Scenery* had defined and described the glen as a valley which had been 'contracted to a *chasm*, it becomes a *glen*' (William Gilpin *Remarks on Forest Scenery*, 2 vols (London 1808) vol.I, p.205). He also warned that 'great care should be taken not to load it with ornament' (ibid., p.207).

the ideas he thought appropriate to such a landscape, and how his 'natural' style had been developed with such circumstances in mind, paying attention to the ten 'leading distinctions' – woods, buildings, water, parks, pleasure grounds, kitchen gardens, and so on – which separated him from 'the affectedly graceful system of Brown and Repton'.[25] Attack was defence, and the instrument for his xenophobia was Repton's landscape at Valleyfield, which had been executed by two of his sons, John Adey and George Stanley Repton. It was finished before 1804 and still survives though in a mutilated state. Loudon had disparaged both it and Repton anonymously in his *Observations on Planting* of 1804, and two years later pressed home his attack in volume two of *Country Residences* (Plate 117).[26] He felt that Repton's insensitivity and his careless indifference to the Scottish landscape were damningly obvious in the sacrifice of the 'most exquisite' dell in Scotland simply to form a showy and wholly inappropriate carriage drive.[27] While much of this was probably true, Repton's carriage drive was not a minor or capricious incident in his scheme, but an essential one which drew dramatically house and water together and offered the traveller a surprising range of picturesque views. His own watercolour of this driveway from his surviving Red Book showed what he termed 'the deep romantic glen' as an unexceptional and blameless woodland ride, similar to those he had made at Stanage and elsewhere in Eng-

Plate 118. Watercolour of the dell at Valleyfield, from Repton's Red Book of 1801

land. It was designed, he maintained, 'to avoid destroying the privacy and seclusion of the whole valley by a gravel road' (Plate 118). Closer perhaps to the truth, and certainly more contrived, were the two rusticated bridges Repton built to carry his driveway over the Bluther Burn, one of which is shown in a pencil sketch by Nasmyth (Plate 119). This was soundly constructed with an applied surface of rugged rock-work, which matched the grotesquely shaped stones that lined the approach road and the boulders that formed a cascade in the burn. Although artificial, it sought naturalism. This was more than could be said of the particularly fancy and formal flower-garden that Repton designed near the house, more or less as an afterthought, as the Red Book makes clear. At the bottom of this garden and parallel to the Bluther Burn, he devised a canal with its long vista closed by 'a covered seat between two aviaries' (Plate 120).[28] The contrast between this and the rocky Fife landscape could not have been more extreme, and its bizarre stylistic and botanical mixture was virtually guaranteed to offend Loudon's naturalism. He considered the effect as 'equally unnatural, misplaced, or out of character', and he felt that its owner Sir Robert Preston had 'thrown away an immense sum of money in

28. Repton claimed that his flower garden with its canal added contrast and variety to an otherwise natural landscape. He wrote that an 'attempt to make the scene natural would be affected'. (Humphry Repton *Observations on the Theory and Practice of Landscape Gardening* (London 1803) p.144).

Plate 119. View of Bluther Burn at Valleyfield by Alexander Nasmyth (detail), *c*.1805

29. *Country Residences*, II, p.438.

30. Humphry Repton, *Sketches and Hints on Landscape Gardening* (London 1795) p.75.

31. *Country Residences*, II, p.440. Loudon was here quoting from James Grahame *The Birds of Scotland*, 3 parts (Edinburgh 1806) pt.1, p.22. Grahame acknowledged in both his preface and notes, see pp.182–8, that many of his ideas came from Price's *Essay On the Picturesque*. He also repeated all the defamatory anecdotes about Brown.

counteracting nature, and deforming his grounds'.[29] By making both the driveway and the flower-garden in the way he did, Repton was accused by Loudon of neglecting the vital principle of consulting the genius of the place, the more culpable for he had never visited Scotland let alone Valleyfield. Loudon indignantly maintained that the natural scenery of Scotland had not only been neglected but destroyed through arrogant ignorance. He might well have referred Repton to his own quotation of 1790: 'Despotic Fashion, in fantastic garb,/Oft, by the vot'ries, for the magic robe/Of *taste* mistaken, with ill guiding step/Directs our paths'.[30] It was, he must have felt, the Friar's Den at Scone all over again. As an indication of what had been lost, he quoted effectively from the rural poet James Grahame's *The Birds of Scotland*.

> . . . But should the tasteful power
> Pragmatic, which presides, with pencilling hand,
> And striding compasses, o'er all this change,
> Get in his thrall some hapless stream that lurks
> Wimpling through hazelly shaw and broomy glen,
> Instant the axe resounds through all the dale,
> And many a pair unhoused hovering lament
> The barbarous devastation: all is smoothed,
> Save here and there a tree; the hawthorn, briar,

Plate 120. Watercolour of the flower-garden at Valleyfield, from Repton's Red Book

The hazel bush, the bramble, and the broom,
The sloethorn, scotias, myrtle, all are gone;
And on the well-sloped bank arise trim clumps,
Some round and some oblong, of shrubs exotic.[31]

32. Repton was consulted by Lord Mansfield about Kenwood in 1793, and Loudon may have felt that he might be called in too at Scone. (Scone Palace Muniments, bundle 578). This feeling was expressed more strongly in a footnote to *Country Residences*: 'I hope the proprietors of that lovely county will never again admit such a formidable foe. If they do, I conjure all my countrymen to unite in declaiming against their taste: and if they will not then refrain, let the poets enrol their names among the enemies of nature' (ibid., II, p.439). Loudon continued his attack on Repton in the Appendix, and in the *Gardener's Magazine* of the 1820s. Yet for all this, Loudon clearly learnt from Repton, not only in a general way but also in the imitation of the Red Books, see his description of that made for Sir Hew Hamilton Dalrymple before 1805, see p.192.

No doubt Loudon's attack on Valleyfield was not entirely disinterested. The possibility of the extension of the Repton practice into Scotland was certainly a threat to his livelihood and he may well have thought he saw its shadow at Scone in 1803.[32] This probably explained his sustained attack on Repton throughout the *Country Residences*, and the much mellower and respectful later tone of his edition of Repton's *Landscape Gardening* in 1840, where criticism was limited to the odd footnote, when Repton was dead and Loudon's reputation secure. In the latter, he repeated Repton's condescending remarks on the garden at Valleyfield without comment or demur. But if the pair of landscapes painted of the house and park by Nasmyth were reasonably accurate, then Loudon was perfectly justified in his criticism of the smoothness and blandness of Repton's conception (Plate 121). Perhaps deliberately, both show a distinct division between the open parkland around the house and the natural areas of the glen, or dell, and the seashore, and it is upon these last features that Nasmyth lovingly dwelt. Repton could claim little credit for them, however, for the woodland stick-

Plate 121. View of Valleyfield by Alexander Nasmyth (detail), *c.*1805

gatherers beneath the ivy-festooned trees were outside his improved landscape as was the rocky shoreline. While there may be many reasons why Valleyfield was Repton's only Scottish garden, its failure to find favour in Scottish eyes was a strong one.

In the course of his *Country Residences*, Loudon gave several, often elaborate descriptions of ideal landscape gardens in his natural style. Of these, the one belonging to an imaginary absentee owner, now returned from abroad and ready to settle at home, came closest to an obviously Scottish scene.[33] In this he was perhaps harkening to Sir John Dalrymple, whose essay recommended a highland landscape as suitable for 'A man who is fond of great projects, or great exploits; or who has a high regard for the splendour of his ancestors' and especially for 'the ancient nobility and gentry of *Wales* and *Scotland* are observed to be fond beyond the rest of mankind, of their Seats'.[34] There, he anticipated that the returned expatriate who would take up improvement, like Ossian's Macpherson at Belville, so that the 'barren mountains became clothed with wood; and on their bleak sides, which formerly produced only heath or moss, now cattle and sheep crop'.[35] Similarly, Loudon's mansion house was to be rebuilt as 'an ancient castle' and set 'in a mountain recess', with close by 'a rapid stream,

33. Loudon's ideal improver was 'the representative of an ancient and noble family arriving in his native country after a long absence' (*Country Residences*, II p.693). For his description of a typical estate in his natural style, see pl.xxvi, no.4. By and large, this lacked 'Mr Brown's style – generally prevalent at the present day', in the interpretation of 'natural character', see ibid., pp.644–7.

34. Dalrymple, op. cit., p.7.

35. ibid., p.695.

Plate 122. View of Scone from Loudon's *Designs for Laying out Farms*, 1811

which has its source amid the distant mountains. From them it flows in a romantic glen, beneath canopies of wood and impending rocks, until, washing the adamantine base of the castle, it bursts into liberty'.[36] However idealised this description may have been, it was barely less romantic than the highly fanciful scheme Loudon had conjured up from the unexecuted parts of his 'Treatise on Improvement' for Scone, and which he illustrated in his *Designs for Laying Out Farms* of 1811 (Plate 122). There, a strange house, half castle, half Milan cathedral, topped with the octagon from Ely, and unlike either old Scone or Atkinson's new building stood on the edge of a cliff looking down and over a swampy lake isolated in a naturally wooded park of some five thousand acres.[37] Not surprisingly, this Vathek-like fantasy remained a day dream.

Yet neither it nor his emotional landscape of castle, mountain and water came anywhere near the depressing reality of the gardens he found in Southern Scotland in 1831. Even the best of them lacked imagination, were conservative, and still incorporated many of the less favourable aspects of the English landscape garden. Amongst them, Barnbarroch was outstanding in that many of its failings had been turned to advantage by the natural style of Loudon's improvements made there around 1805. Both Barnbarroch and the abortive scheme for Mabie, near Dumfries, made a good contrast with the more

36. ibid.

37. Loudon illustrated his design for Scone in his *Designs for Laying Out Farms and Farm-Building in the Scotch Style Adapted to England* (London 1811). This scheme was titled 'Ideal Sketch of Lord Mansfield's Estate at Scone to contain 5000 Acres'. This was not executed though some plantations were made there in accordance with his ideas, see *Country Residences,* II, p.548 and pp.195–6.

Plate 123. View of Mabie, Kirkcudbrightshire, from Loudon's *Country Residences,* 1806

39. Loudon remarked that 'Unfortunately for the execution of my ideas, the proprietor now proposes to sell the place' (ibid.). He probably worked at Mabie before 1800 for he noted in *c.* 1806 that the etched view was 'done from an almost obliterated sketch taken a considerable time ago' (ibid.). The cottage-mansion was rebuilt in the nineteenth century, though a small octagonal gatelodge has survived from Loudon's period. Ironically the estate is now a forest, controlled by the Forestry Commission.

cosmopolitan, picturesque form Loudon had used at Farnley Hall in Yorkshire, a seeming inconsistency that was itself natural, or so he claimed. He wrote broadly and disingenuously that 'sometimes a residence will assume one character, as that of Farnley Hall, sometimes another of a different kind, as does Maybo. This is exactly what we find in natural scenery'.[38] Certainly Loudon's plan for Mabie relied for its success on an almost exclusive development of the natural landscape. The raw materials of his commission were a steep hillside overlooking the estuary of the River Nith, with at its foot a series of flat rather marshy fields (Plate 123). This he rearranged as a sort of vertical and terraced composition with the ruined castle of Mabie at the top, the long cottage house of its owner Richard Howat just below, and then a stream zig-zagging its way through the rocks and woods to make a small lake on the flatland at the bottom.[39] Loudon's naturalism was such, that so seemingly artless an element as the smoke rising upwards from the cottage adjoining the lake, was a vital and considered part of his composition. Regrettably, none of it was ever realised.

Barnbarroch was probably Loudon's most notable garden in south-west Scotland, nearly as early and natural as his posthumous design for Castle Kennedy was late and formal. But it was not an easy commission. Its setting in a flat and bleak landscape had little charac-

Plate 124. Barnbarroch, Wigtownshire, before Loudon's alterations, from *Country Residences*

Plate 125. Loudon's ruined additions at Barnbarroch

ter, and the house itself was unassuming and classical, built for the Agnew family between 1778 and 1780 (Plate 124).[40] Loudon concerned himself with both, and in 1806 produced some twenty-three drawings, now in the Mellon Collection, for altering and extending this building, making a new range of offices, an icehouse and some gateways. A certain amount of this was executed during 1806 and 1807, though not under his direction, and on a simpler and more limited scale.[41] The missing landscape drawings must have been part of this set and were probably made before 1805 while he was still writing *Country Residences*. About 1820, Loudon's suggestions appear to have been taken up again when his garden portico was added, perversely, to the entrance façade and a new gateway built at the main approach.[42] He had intended these half-hearted Jacobean alterations to give the house and the surrounding buildings a picturesque air, in keeping with his proposed landscape. The before and after views that appeared in *Country Residences* underline the romantic mood of an old house, deep in its woods, which he sought to revive and enrich at Barnbarroch. In many ways the present derelict and ruined house, presiding over a

40. SRO GD 99 Box 52. These accounts refer to the builder James McMillan rather than to any architect. His account for masonry work ended in May 1780. See also P. H. McKerlie *History of the Lands and their Owners in Galloway*, 5 vols. (Edinburgh 1870–9) vol.I, p.383, who said 'it was built in 1780, it is understood, on or near the old site, and has been considerably added to'.

41. What was built at this time was principally the extension to the south referred to as the 'new part of the house' in the accounts of 1811 (SRO GD 99 Box 47). This was executed in a picturesque classical style and it is to this that McKerlie undoubtedly referred when he wrote of the house being 'considerably added to'. Some of the building accounts for this work and other internal alterations in 1806/7 are in GD 99 Box 71.

42. SRO GD 99 Box 57.

silted and reeded lake, and almost engulfed in wild undergrowth, gives a general picture with which Loudon would have been sympathetic (Plate 125).

The most essential part of his new landscape was the formation of two streams – the Sheep and Maltkiln burns – into a small lake and waterfall. This was to lie directly in front of the garden façade of the house, with the bank on which it sat cut away to make a rocky and precipitous slope thickly planted on either side. These improvements had still to be completed when *Country Residences* was published, and the present devastated landscape about Barnbarroch destroyed by fire in 1940 and subsequently despoiled, make it difficult to know how much was executed. Loudon himself recounted how he had (in his usual fashion) persuaded his client Robert Agnew to reject 'a plan given in by a modern improver, for making another piece of water', and accept instead his own scheme for this and more.[43] An essential part of his design and one that added enormously to its charms, was a waterfall that served both as a causeway and a screen to the artificial water-head created to maintain its supply, much in the style of Repton's earlier work at Stoneaston in Somerset (Plate 126). This waterfall was intended to be as appealing to the ear as the eye, and Loudon anticipated that its sounds 'will resound through the woods, and even the apartments of the house, and give an air of enchantment to that fine old place'.[44] To continue and enhance the illusion of naturalism, he created a stepped retaining wall at its western edge and

43. *Country Residences*, II, p.402. According to Loudon, Agnew immediately saw the superiority of his design 'over the mode of clumping and surrounding every place with a belt' (ibid., I, p.248).

44. ibid., II, p.396. The style of waterfall that Loudon devised for Barnbarroch, Mabie and Machany Castle in Perthshire, was of 'a variety which may occasionally be seen in nature, and is well worthy of imitation: though, so far as I know, it has never been attempted. It is where a small rivulet or rill, at its junction with a river or brook, falls over a rock in one small sheet' (ibid.,). Loudon particularly admired the sound it made – 'graceful harmony'. He also gave practical advice for forming 'Heads for Pieces of Water', see ibid., II, pp.623–4.

Plate 126. The lake and bridge at Barnbarroch, from *Country Residences*

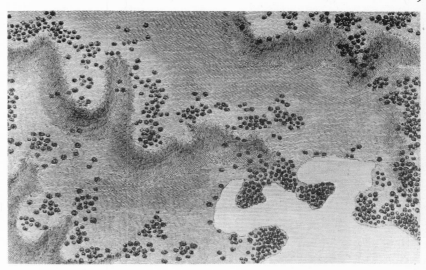

planted ivy between the joints of the stones. On the other bank, Loudon formed his lawn and flower garden on to which his proposed portico would have opened. The view outward from this swade was perhaps the best on the estate, for the eye was directed over the deep pool of the lake and waterfall, above the smaller trees that edged its banks to the open sea in the distance at Luce Bay. Loudon's plan for these lakeside woods, illustrated in *Country Residences*, shows a plantation picturesque in outline, with details of the trees chosen to create this effect – oaks predominant on the higher ground, birch, willow, and berberis at the water's edge (Plate 127). He also claimed to have used several varieties of poplar – the Hoary, Canadian and Carolina – 'in rather singular circumstances about the estate', where their quick growth gave an almost immediate woody effect.[45]

To the west of the house he formed a rather empty-looking park with a curved sunk fence finished in 1811, which separated it from the entrance and approach road. Across and slightly to one side of this park were the stables and offices, which looked with a Gothic face towards the house with little or no planting between.[46] Carrying the south carriageway to the mansion was a small bridge with gothic wrought-iron railings, which spanned the 'new river' and fed the lake. Like the sunk fence, this was completed in 1811.[47] Little of it has survived. The river and its lake have silted up and filled with reeds, the bridge has fallen down, and the plantations that ran downstream to

Plate 127. Plan of the planting at Barnbarroch, from *Country Residences*

45. *Country Residences*, ii, pp.483, 649.

46. The rather exposed nature of his building was justified by Loudon in *Country Residences*: 'To bring them (offices, farm buildings etc) into view so as to form subordinate masses to the mansion, care must be taken, 1st, not to place them upon a lower level than the mansion, but if possible on rather more elevated ground . . . 2ndly, in designing the offices, the present poverty and formal simplicity should be avoided'. He summed up that he hoped that 'by bringing all the parts into view, a more splendid effect will be produced for a given sum' (*Country Residences*, i, pp.172–5).

47. SRO GD 99 Box 47.

Barnbarroch have been felled. These woods, mostly larch and pine, were probably the first Loudon planted, with trees taken from a nursery that had been established on the estate in 1807.[48] Yet for all this thought and energy the youthful landscape seemed to have had little appeal and, ironically, impressed at least one visitor as being too much part of the local scenery. Coming to the house in 1825, he found that 'the gate at Barnbarrow is like that at a turnpike and the avenue fully much resembles the high road . . . fields around the house . . . some trees growing as if by accident for they interrupt the view, a judicious person however might make them very useful in ornamenting the fields before the windows of the house'.[49] It is unlikely that even Loudon would have taken this as praise.

Whether such remarks meant that Loudon had overplayed his naturalism and Scotticism can hardly be resolved now. Certainly his proposals for changing an unpretentious house on a sloping bank beside a small stream into a picturesque object set on a rocky bluff, below which a fast moving burn tumbled over a waterfall into a tree-edged lake, were all impressive and tempered with sound practical sense. Through them he heightened rather than destroyed or even recast a disappointing natural setting. Certainly the views from the garden front of the house over the lake and woods to the south, and northwards across the park to the moorland hills beyond, were intended as foils to one another, making what Loudon termed 'the opposite expression of richness, and bleak sterility'.[50] In working in this way, he was adapting an uncompromisingly Scottish landscape to express his ideal of a natural garden and a naturally Scottish landscape – one that Loudon patriotically and optimistically felt might be 'much more rich and noble than England, and perhaps most countries'.[51]

Loudon's designs for Barnbarroch were made in considerable detail, as much from anticipation that they would be carried out by the local gardener, more or less unskilled and possibly in a piece-meal fashion, as from his own passion for precision and professionalism. Such circumstances prevailed in both Scotland and England, and they were matters on which Loudon held strong opinions, which he expressed with customary vigour in the *Gardener's Magazine*.[52] He was vitally concerned about professional standards. He was certain that some sort of code of conduct should prevent the inevitable dispute over fees, undercutting, and the like, and could result in a higher standard of gardening and of gardens. He sought to rationalise the existing chaos by forming a system more or less modelled on his own. He acknowledged, but did not recommend, the practice where a

48. SRO GD 99 Box 71.

49. See SRO GD 99 Box 58. The diarist was Archibald Arbuthnot.

50. *Country Residences*, II, p.522.

51. ibid.

52. See 'Remarks on the Charges made by Landscape-Gardeners and Garden Architects' *Gardener's Magazine* XV (1839) p.213–16.

53. Loudon wrote that 'it is customary for nurserymen, to give plans for laying out grounds, building garden etc; and as, in such cases, they generally get the work to execute, the plans are not charged for' (ibid., p.215). Belonging to this category was Loudon's master John Mawer of Dalry, Edinburgh, whom Loudon had served as 'draughtsman and general superintendent' from roughly 1797 to 1800. Mawer had a system of yearly visits to gardens he had laid out 'with great advantage to several proprietors' (*Country Residences*, I, p.290. and II, p.637).

nursery gardener, like Hay or Nicol, turned designer and executed work either with an inclusive charge or by asking 'two or three guineas a day: and the party for whom the plan is made is at liberty to have it executed by whom he chooses.'[53] Loudon also noted the frequent practice of designers, like the Thomas Whites, who, after charging for their plans, 'undertake to see the work executed under the direction of a foreman, either for so much for the entire work, for so much a year while it lasts, or for their usual charge per day for the time occupied in making professional visits, while the work is going on, corresponding with the foreman, examining his accounts etc'.[54] But he preferred his own way of charging for everything according to time: for time spent in travelling, time in making his plans, his assistant in copying them, time used in staking and pegging out the plantations and approaches. He emphasised the importance of the plan or descriptive report and the 'sound principle' of always charging for them separately. They were, he maintained, the key to the design, especially when the designer might well be absent, and they had to be clear, explicit and detailed. The large decorative plans produced by Robinson or the Whites were far too vague for *in absentia* gardening, those of Repton too slapdash, and all of them conspicuously lacked the accuracy and detail of a Loudon scheme.

The break with the customary eighteenth-century improvement plan was marked by the publication in 1813 of Horner's *Description of an Improved Method of Delineating Estates*, a work which Loudon naturally enough admired.[55] This 'improved mode of delineating estates', was essentially designed to provide the landowner with a general survey, clear and detailed, which allowed him to 'judge of the best means of opening roads, cutting canals, erecting buildings for either use or ornament; enclosing, planting, laying out of water, and in short, of making any improvement belonging to either agriculture or to rural embellishment'.[56] Loudon carried this system even further, and demanded that the landscape gardener not only explained himself visually but also in writing. He must give *'reasons in writing* for all that he proposes', and that *'In all these discussions* proper references will be made to maps and sketches. Simple language will of course be employed in describing future effects; but, above all, simple sketches, which shall owe little of their effect to shading, and none to colouring, or finishing, are essentially necessary'.[57] This was a further and lightly veiled attack on Repton's Red Books with their pretty watercolour views – described in that for Valleyfield as '*Sketches* to explain the general effect' – vague notes, lack of plans, and their system of hinged

54. ibid. Apart from the categories of nursery men and gardeners like the Whites, Loudon also described those who were called new ground workmen. They chiefly carried 'plans into execution, more especially in cases where there is much ground to remove, as in forming pieces of water, new kitchen gardens etc. The persons who undertake this department frequently make plans, and charge for them on the same principle as nursery-men do, deducting the whole or part of the charge, as they may execute the whole or part of the work'. Capability Brown he felt fell into this category while Repton did not (ibid.).

55. See Thomas Horner *Description of an Improved Method of Delineating Estates* (London 1813). Little is known of Horner, who practised as a land surveyor from Church Court in the Inner Temple, London. According to his own statement, he made 'surveys of various estates (in the neighbourhood of London, and in several parts of Scotland') (ibid., p.20). A further printing of this book appeared in 1814, and his Prospectus, *View of London and the surrounding County, taken with mathematical accuracy* (London 1823) was on the same theme.

56. Horner, op. cit., pp.16–17.

57. Loudon *Encyclopaedia of Gardening*, p.1038. This section of the *Encyclopaedia* gave a succinct analysis and history of such an aspect of landscape gardening, see pp.1037–9.

58. Loudon thought that there was an inevitable bias in favour of the altered view, 'since the view in which the cut paper forms a part can never look so well as the other, even from the mere circumstance of the bounding line of the paper' (ibid., p.1038). In this he was continuing the argument he had started in *Country Residences*, see vol.II, pp.705–8. His final thoughts on the matter were given as a footnote in his *Landscape Gardening* of 1840 (ibid., pp.31–8). In his Red Book for Valleyfield, Repton wrote that 'no map or plan upon paper can be so accurate and satisfactory as to preclude the necessity of marking the lines of roads, walks and plantations on the spot; and I trust the drawings which accompany this small volume (and particularly those in the course of the Approach thro' the valley) will rather be considered as *Sketches* to explain the general effect of improvements suggested, than as *pictures* of Scenery' (Appendix I).

59. Loudon *Encyclopaedia of Gardening* (1822) p.1198.

60. *Observations on Planting*, p.286.

61. See *Farmer's Magazine* VI (1805) pp.126–7: Loudon published extracts from this account in his *Country Residences*, II, pp.614–15.

62. *Farmer's Magazine* VI, p.127. According to the account of this Magazine, Loudon also gave a separate design for the house, see p.127. In his *Encyclopaedia of Gardening*, Loudon described North Berwick as 'A good house, surrounded by an extensive suite

flaps which Loudon thought, not unreasonably, to be 'not perfectly fair'.[58] Instead he recommended his own detailed but thoroughly impractical system of '*Notitia* or *Book of Improvements*' invented specifically to enable the local gardener to follow the scheme 'with nearly as much certainty as an architect directs a builder to raise an elevation of masonry'.[59] In his *Observations* of 1803, he frankly owned that this system was closely derived from Repton's Red Books and that he had 'styled my red books *Reports* or *Treatises*'.[60]

It was from some such scheme of *Notitia* that Loudon doubtless reproduced the drawings for Barnbarroch that he illustrated in *Country Residences*. While only fragments have survived, the prototype was fully described in the *Farmer's Magazine* for 1805. This was made for Sir Hew Dalrymple Hamilton's estate at Leuchie House, North Berwick, and, as well as the usual system of maps, comprised a clay model that showed 'all the trees, hedges, roads, rivers, buildings etc . . . by which any gentleman may try, upon the model, the effect of any proposed alteration or improvement'.[61] Its companion was 'an elegant manuscript volume, illustrated by drawings and sketches containing Mr. Loudon's ideas of the situation . . . accompanied with *working plans*, a large *vertical profile* shewing the effect of the whole, and a general estimate of expense'.[62]

Apart from the clay model, this was much the same system he employed fifteen years later, in 1818, for an English client at Woodley Lodge or Bulmershe Court, in Buckinghamshire (Plate 128). There, he was commissioned to refine and extend an early Repton landscape of the 1790s, and proposed an ambitious layout of two interconnected

of enclosures, subdivided by straight lines and strips, or double rows of trees in the ancient style; the object being to combine the general effect of a park as to wood and pasture, with the utility and convenience of enclosures (ibid., p.1087). Loudon worked there some time between 1800 and 1804.

63. Loudon's notes and drawings for his 'Report on Certain Plans for Improvement proposed for The Park and Demesne Lands of Bullmarsh Court', are now in the Mellon Collection at Upperville, Virginia. In his *Encyclopaedia of Gardening* he described the estate under its old name, Woodley Lodge, as

Plate 128. Watercolour by Loudon for improvements at Woodley Lodge, Buckinghamshire, 1818

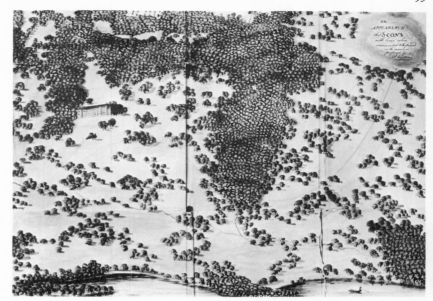

follows: 'The mansion is a neat modern edifice, built by the present proprietor's father, in the time of George II. The grounds were tastefully laid out by Repton, who mentions this Seat in his work. The Park having, in 1817, been greatly enlarged by an extensive enclosure; the author of the present work was employed to give designs, which have since been executing under the eye of the proprietor, who has great taste and considerable skill in rural improvements' (ibid., (1822) p.1237). For Repton's reference to the house see *Observations on the Theory and Practice of Landscape Gardening* ed. John Nolen (London 1907) p.187. Apart from the large improvements, Loudon also suggested the making of a 'cypress garden, labyrinth or star of clipt hedges, in the ancient style' the removal of the hamlet of Little Hungerford, and the gothicising of several of the estate cottages, see Report, ff.86, 110, 97.

64. 'Report . . . Bullmarsh Court', plan volume.

65. ibid., octavo volume, f.47. Loudon's client evidently settled the bill with a certain lack of grace for Loudon replied to him in February, 1819 saying that 'If I may be allowed to offer a remark arising from yours on the subject of the expense of Landscape Gardeners, I should say, surely they are not better paid than other artists'. He added for good measure that 'Brown alone made an independency by his profession', and that he himself, 'during the last fifteen years . . . have in the average scarcely been able to keep myself within the verge of decent existence'. Loudon was here charging 5 guineas per day. In 1804, he had advertised himself as having terms of 2 guineas per day, plus travelling expenses and with 'Plans, Reports etc., charged according to *their value*' (*Observations on Planting*, p. advertisement). In this he was true to what he later wrote in the *Gardener's Magazine* xv (1839).

lakes with a new approach road coming from the east.[63] His written description was given in an octavo volume of 161 pages, which cross-referred to twelve drawings, mounted and bound at the end of an additional folio. As a preface to the latter, he explained that 'As the eye can only comprehend one object at a time, the views are in part veiled, so as each may be examined separately, and so have its full effect. By lifting one or more of the veils, the view as it actually exists, and the improved view, may be compared together.'[64] From the outset it was clear that such detailed drawings and notes were very necessary, for the scheme was to be carried out by the client and his gardener. Yet, for all Loudon's professionalism, there was the usual dispute over the bill – £182.13.6 in this case – and the customary dignified but hurt letter of explanation: 'For an artist to attempt', Loudon wrote, 'an accurate estimate where he is not to contract for the work and finish it out of hand . . . is to lay himself open to charges of wilful deception, or professional ignorance'.[65] He should have known better, for this very situation at Scone had led to the discrediting of the elder Thomas White and to his own employment there.

Loudon followed Repton's methods fairly closely at Scone. His 'Treatise on the Improvement proposed for Scone . . . illustrated with

Plate 129. Scone Palace, Perthshire, improvement plan by Loudon, 1803

A Rivulet at Scone as deformed by Mr White the improver

section

Plan

The same in its natural state; or as I propose it to be made

Section

Plan

sketches and detached plans of the estate', made by him in Edinburgh, during September and October of 1804, was modelled upon the Red Books. His surviving plan, coyly titled 'The Appearance', showed only too well Repton's brand of studied vagueness (Plate 129).[66] As a manuscript, it was almost contemporary with his garden designs for Barnbarroch, but shortly before his more unusual *Notitia* for Leuchie House. While he avoided a too obvious copying of Repton's system of flaps, and contented himself with a less dramatic form of before and after plans, laid alongside one another, the style of the watercolours and the tone of the text – flattering and didactic at the same time – was similar to, but neither as good nor as subtle as that of the Red Books. Apart from the actual improvements he suggested for the estate, his Scone manuscript was outstanding for the bitter and highly unprofes-

66. Scone Palace Muniments, vol.117. Loudon added a manuscript note of October 13, apologising for 'grammatical errors in it . . . since 10th of September last when I left Scone, I have been incessantly engaged in it: and that the written part is almost wholly extempore and without a scrawl copy' (ibid.).

Plate 130. 'Rivulets', from Loudon's *Treatise on Scone*, 1804

sional attack it contained on the elder White. Here he referred to White by name, and mounted the usual rear attack. White's plantations were 'absurd', 'made upon a medium above *Thirty* times the necessary expence per acre', his levelling in front of the palace ruined the natural contours, his water fence was 'deformed', his disposition of clumps effected 'nothing but a distracting incongruity', and his pleasure garden was 'void of meaning'.[67] With Repton's work on the dell at Valleyfield closely in mind, he rigorously attacked White's work at the Friar's Den: 'His path there', he wrote, 'neither does it descend to the murmering brook at the bottom nor wind along the top of its banks; but forces itself and its appendages stiffly along the steep sides of each, assuming neither the character of a recluse path in a dell among undergrowths and shady trees; nor the gay elegant walk among groups of shrubs, and flowers, varied with lawn; but a kind of insipid medium, neither beautiful, varied nor interesting'.[68] He proved his point with a typical and heavily prejudiced drawing (Plate 130). Instead, he suggested a fully romantic walk 'through a dark wood upon an irregular dark path, encompassed on each side with evergreen undergrowths as Holly, Bay, Laurel, Box etc.', which led to an 'old cathedral-like door or gateway . . . into a dark passage' that received 'but very little light, through some coloured glass', and which opened into a conservatory full of flowers and light.[69]

While much of this criticism was a question of taste – the beautiful held deficient by the sublime – on the less subjective grounds of practical gardening Loudon was undoubtedly correct. White's plantations did contain too many trees of too many sorts. From his 'List of Trees' sent up to Scone in 1784, it was obvious that some would be out of place and others too tender for Perthshire. Several were already dead by 1803, and Loudon selected three plantations in the demesne to demonstrate how unnecessary and expensive such planting had been. At the two falls near the river by the Old Approach, White had formed a clump out of sixteen varieties of tree and undergrowth, at the cost, Loudon computed, of £118.3.4 per acre, all of which he suggested could have been done more successfully and attractively with oak and berberis for as little as £6.12 per acre.[70] The only good he had to say of White's improvements was that the kitchen garden, as at Cullen, was in the best place.[71] It was perhaps a pity that White's discontented and critical Lord Stormont was dead and that Loudon worked for his more pliable successor, the third Earl.

Loudon prepared three schemes for Scone: the impractical day dream published in his *Designs for Laying out Farms*, the Treatise of

67. ibid., f.13, f.40, f.135, f.37, f.86.

68. ibid., f.87.

69. ibid., f.89.

70. ibid., f.57, 88.

71. ibid., f.24. The site was that given in White's plan though both it and the orchard were completely restocked and planted in 1804, see Scone Palace Muniments, vol.115.

72. The sheet of plans and sections is signed by Loudon and dated 1803, see Scone Palace Muniments, plan 8.

73. See ibid., f.165 and *Country Residences*, II, p.548.

74. Loudon was quite categorical that the only approach to the house was through 'a village' (ibid., f.110). He noted on f.20 of his manuscript that the removal of the village from Old to New Scone was nearly accomplished and that the present approach was 'unnatural and unconnected with the ground' (ibid., f.112). This was confirmed by the pamphlet *Sconiana*, where it was stated that Lord Mansfield 'has laid out a very great sum already, and appears determined to spare no expense to render *Scone* as much an object to admiration and has bought up the old village and erected a new one', see *Sconiana* (London 1807) p.13. Loudon gave a drawing of his rather fortress-like lodges and their position in the village street, see f.110. Loudon's ideas for this long approach were carried out to some extent but with the significant alteration that the source for the road was at Old rather than New Scone. For the lodge designs for here by N.A. Mar, see Scone Palace Muniments, Bundle 786, and vol.117, f.118. In 1789, James Playfair designed and built a lodge at Scone, possibly at White's entrance to the park (NLS Adv.33.5.25 f.34 verso).

75. See Scone Palace Muniments, vol.114 'Minutes of Planting at Scone'. This lists the number of trees and variety planted from 1804 until 1833. Rarely was the yearly total below 100,000.

76. Vol.117, f.154. At Barnbarroch, he encouraged the use of poplars, hoary, Carolina, and Canadian see *Country Residences*, II, p.538. He also admired the Populus alba in the gardens around Edinburgh, see *Encyclopaedia of Gardening*, p.993.

1804, and a series of plans in 1803. All were complementary. The last consisted of at least three plans, all more or less concerned with crossing and laying out the park as far as New Scone and the bridging and tunnelling of the Bridge of Isla road (Plate 131).[72] Loudon's scheme was to set his pair of gothic entrance lodges at New Scone and to bring the main approach to Atkinson's Palace, 'presently building', through what is now Scone Wood, crossing the Perth-Bridge of Isla road by a tree planted arch. Only part of this ambitious scheme was ever realised. The plantations in this area and to the west at the farms of Rome and Sherífftoun were the improvements that Loudon referred to as 'to be executed immediately', in both his Treatise and in *Country Residences*, and they were carried out at this time.[73] But his grand approach was never fully undertaken. No doubt much to his regret, a gate was made instead on the Isla road and a drive led from it through the park, crossing the Friar's Den by means of a small stone causeway, and was there linked with White's much despised carriage-way (Plate 132). All this is shown much more clearly in the additions to Cock's survey of 1801 (Plate 133) than in Loudon's own incomprehensible drawing 'The Appearance that Scone will have when ornamented & improved'. For all the trouble it involved, it had a short life and was replaced in about 1842 by the present Queen's Drive. The lodges at New Scone were never built nor the arch for the Isla road, and instead the old north approach from the village was kept, with a small thatched lodge, designed in 1813, erected at its gates.[74]

A great deal of this scheme, in which he stressed the desirability of hiding by tunnel or cutting the Bridge of Isla road, was repeated a year later in his manuscript Treatise. In it he listed the trees – principally beech, oak, ash and some elm – that were to form the new woods at Scone and Sherífftoun, where planting had begun in November 1804, with 137,000 trees set out.[75] In the natural woods beyond the park at Cambusmichael, Loudon advocated their thinning and replanting with his favourite hoary poplar rather than the more conventional birch, larch, or oak.[76] Along the banks of the river, he proposed a continuous belt of willows and alders, and, more interestingly, aquatic flowers selected from Lightfoot's *Flora Scotica*.[77] He intended to set out these clumps and plantations according to the categories given in his *Observations* for the sublime and grand, and explained in his manuscript that 'Here the continuation and uniformity of the shapes produce sublimity', which could hardly be said of the 'distracting incongruity' of White's scheme.[78] Loudon was undoubtedly at his best in such matters, and his practical experience, combined with an eye

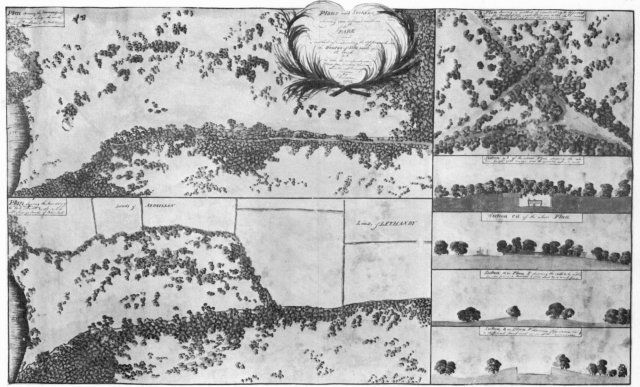

77. See John Lightfoot *Flora Scotica*, 2 vols. (London 1777). A typical entry of this sort of plant is that for the Marsh Hawkweed, ibid., vol.I, p.438: see also Loudon's remarks on this genus in *Country Residences*, II, p.378.

78. ibid., f.37. For his declensions of plantation according to such types see p.175.

79. For his Prospect Tower see Treatise f.95; for his decorated building f.96, for the Ionic temple f.99.

80. ibid., f.93.

81. ibid.

and taste for the natural, made him superior to White. But where White had been contented with a combination of tree, shrub and grass, and the variety and contrast that could be wrung from them, Loudon's taste for the sublime often drove him well beyond the boundaries of the natural – so much so, that he described and illustrated in his Treatise a prospect tower, a 'Decorated Building' of nine bays, an Ionic temple, and an alcove seat, all in a small area of the park (Plate 134).[79] He also proposed a bath house, fed with natural spring water, and decorated as gaudily as the temples at Dunkeld with 'varitys of Derbyshire, Devonshire, Cornwall etc. spars', and concave and convex mirrors.[80] He had, too, the inspired idea of 'an invisible self playing musical syphon', modelled after 'an ancient invention' to delight or distract the ear.[81] The theatrical variety of these unexecuted projects shown in the Treatise took up a theme apparent but never dominant in *Country Residences* that Scone might well become 'the first place in the

Plate 131. Plan by Loudon for area around the Bridge of Isla road at Scone, 1803

British Empire'.[82]

His taste in plants was as rich and as catholic as his architectural appetite. But here his interest tended to the humble and wild rather than the exotic, and he wrote that 'In nature, every collection of water, as well as earth, has its peculiar plants, from the *algae* in the sea, to the *caltriche* on the surface of the least pools'. He singled out for praise, in a footnote to *Country Residences*, the 'ziziana', presumably *Zizania aquatica*: '. . . in the lakes and stagnated waters at Braham Castle [it] passes description for singularity and beauty'.[83] It is unlikely, however, that the rest of Brahan Castle appealed to him or pandered to his special concern for the wild and natural. The then Lord Seaforth's attempt to replace the old castle with a villa designed by John Plaw, plant the grounds with American trees and shrubs, and fill the garden with 'Exotic plants', was not exactly Loudon's view of things 'proper for wild scenery', especially in Ross and Cromarty.[84] Of course, he modified his views as he grew older, and it is possible that he might

82. ibid., f.171. Apart from a sort of appendix, this was Loudon's final statement. Its imperial rôle was to be achieved by '"improvement" not mere whimsical alterations (as has been, and commonly are made), but founded in nature, taste, and utility' (ibid.).

83. *Country Residences*, II, p.378.

Plate 132. Aerial view of Scone Palace, from the Perth end of the park, 1979

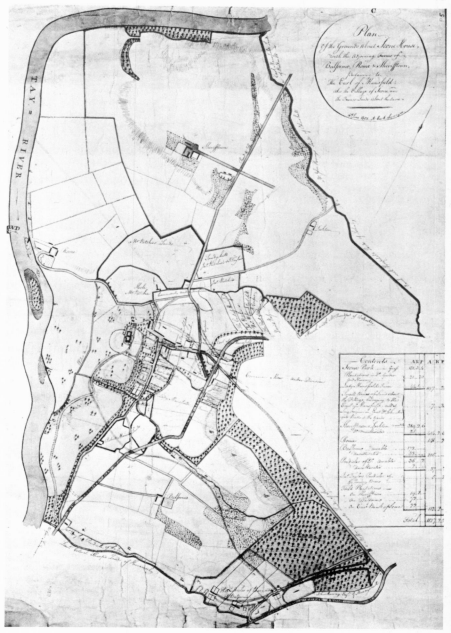

Plate 133. Plan, by Cock, of the grounds at Scone, 1801

later have approved of some of Lord Seaforth's botanical plants, at least from the stance of the gardenesque.

Such ambivalence was apparent, too, in his attitude to the gentleman-gardener George Parkyns, a disciple and brother officer of Francis Grose, the antiquarian, and to his only known Scottish garden at Millburn Tower, on the edge of Edinburgh. While Loudon wrote favourably about him in the *Encyclopaedia of Gardening* and bracketed him with Nasmyth (whom he had disparaged as 'a drawing-master in Edinburgh' in *Country Residences*), the garden at Millburn showed surprisingly little that was either Scottish or natural.[85] Parkyns's client there was the Americanphile diplomat Robert Liston, whom he had met in Washington. Parkyns came to stay in the autumn of 1804, to work both as a landscape gardener and find Scottish material for expanding his *Monastic and Baronial Remains*, which appeared as two volumes in 1816.[86] At Millburn, the garden that surrounded Atkinson's gothic house was Parkyns's work, although much of it was apparently modified after his departure by Lady Liston, an enthusiastic gardener like her husband.[87] Liston himself was possibly more concerned with making the adjoining village of Ratho into a model one, and Parkyns's position between two such enthusiasts must have been unenviable. He probably suggested the east and west approaches to the house, recommended the widening of the original Mill burn in front of it to form a river wide enough for an island, and the building at its eastern end of a bridge to carry the approach road.[88] The planting, and especially the formation of the American winter garden, was possibly a co-operative venture between Lady Liston, who acquired the plants, and Parkyns whose expertise arranged them.[89] This international character was Millburn's claim to fame, at least for the *Encyclopaedia of Gardening*. It was increased by the unique survival of a circular gate lodge, derived from a 'round house' designed in Washington by Latrobe in 1800.[90]

84. In 1786, John Plaw gave five drawings for a 'Design for a Villa and Offices', for F.H. Mackenzie who later succeeded as Lord Seaforth (SRO GD 46/1/413). It was unexecuted. A List of 'Amer. Shrubs & plants Most Beautiful and Very hardy', which included forms of Rhododendron, Azalea, the Tulip Tree, *Kalmia latifolia*, and so on, was sent from the nursery of John Cowie in London, in 1787 (GD 46/1/416). In 1811, there was a list of the eighteen 'exotic plants that have lived the winter' at Brahan Castle (GD 46/17/37). This mentioned shrubs such as the *Arbutus unedo* (Strawberry tree) *Rosa indica* and *Veronica decumata*.

85. He described Parkyns as 'an excellent gardener' *Encyclopaedia of Gardening* (1834) p.344. In his *Suburban Gardener* of 1838, he referred to Parkyns as looking 'on gardens entirely with the eye of a painter and a poet', ibid., p.558. He also referred to Parkyns in his *Gardener's Magazine* as 'about the year 1800' producing 'a folio contained designs for villas including the details of the house as well as of the grounds'. In this, he mentioned Sir Robert Liston, 'at Milburn Tower, near Edinburgh, who was intimate with Mr. Parkyns', as having a copy of this work in 1804, see *Gardener's Magazine* XVII, (1841) p.654.

86. George Parkyns *Monastic and Baronial Remains*, 2 vols. (London 1816): the first edition appeared in 1793, see ibid., vol.I, p.vii. Most of the notes about the Scottish monuments are dated between 1804 and 1807 and are contained in volume II. Liston had been the British minister in Washington from 1796–1802. Parkyns was in the United States, and especially Washington, between 1795 and 1800, see Eleanor McPeak 'George Isham Parkyns' *Quarterly Journal of the Library of Congress* XXX, no.3 (1973). According to the preface of *Monastic Remains*, there was 'a sudden call to North America, where he was some years detained, endeavouring to settle the titles of considerable tracts of land he had unfortunately been persuaded to

purchase in Europe' (ibid., vol.I, p.viii). During this time he issued his 'American landscape Proposals . . . Twenty Four Views', of which only four were executed, one according to Loudon, a plan of General Washington's grounds at 'Vermont' (Mount Vernon), see *Encyclopaedia of Gardening* (1824) p.1113. Parkyns wrote to Liston after he had arrived in Edinburgh in August 1804, that 'Tomorrow I hope to present myself

at Milburn where I shall be truly happy to devote the slender abilities I possess, wholly, and for as long a time as you judge necessary, to your service' (NLS Ms. 5608 f.112).

87. For Atkinson's associations with the house in c.1805, see *Farmer's Magazine* VI (1805) p.361. The house was altered again between 1810 and 1815 in the castellated style (NLS, Ms.5715–17). After

Parkyns's departure in January 1805, the Listons used a nephew A.L. Ramage as both factor and amateur architect. He and Lady Liston were responsible for the conservatory of about 1811 (NLS Ms.5620 f.36). In 1822, Mrs Grant described Liston as having 'made a road through the village, built a pretty school-house and some neat cottages, and laid out a lawn, with many other matters, useful and ornamental' (Anne Grant *Memoir and Correspondence of Mrs Grant of Laggan*, ed. J.P. Grant, 3 vols. (London 1844) vol.III, p.223).

88. In 1805, Lady Liston reported 'slow progress of the Tower – Except deepening & almost forming the piece of water in the front . . . the island we propose to fit up for the accommodation of the Ducks. My American Garden has received a great accession of Plants, some for *love*, some for *money*. The ground is all trenched & the gravel walks partly made ready for the complete *forming* in Spring' (NLS Ms.5609 f.132). These improvements, doubtless followed

Parkyns's scheme of the autumn of 1804. According to Sir Walter Scott in 1828 'the artifical piece of water is a failure like most things of the kind' (Scott *Journal*, p.493). This lake is now mostly silted up and overgrown.

89. Neill wrote of Millburn that according to Loudon, Lady Liston 'while in America, during Mr. Liston's embassy to the United States, she made a collection of transatlantic plants, which now form an American garden at Milburn Tower' (Neill, op. cit., p.173). In this, Parkyns's practical experience in gardening in the United States, where the gardens at Woodlands, Philadelphia and Montecello are attributed to him, would have been of great advantage.

90. Maryland Historical Society, Latrobe Papers, VI–3.

91. Parkyns's ideas were fairly well set out in his *Six Designs for Improving Grounds* in 1792. This book shows the type of garden appropriate to the

following, Fairfield Cottage, Chalk Lodge, Laurel Hill, Rose Cottage, Belmont, The Grange. They illustrate a conventional landscape little removed from the style of The Leasowes, though with fewer garden buildings. There is no hint in them of singling out particular plants or planting according to a botanical arrangement: in this Millburn was presumably exceptional. The draughtsmanship of these plates is different from that found in *Monastic Remains* and points to the influence of James Moore, 'an amateur draughtsman', to whom he was introduced after 1782 by Grose (*Monastic Remains*, I, p.vi). Little is known of Parkyns's further work in Scotland, except that he departed for Glasgow in January in 1805, and was at the Earl of Buchan's Dryburgh Abbey later that year. (Glasgow University Library, Murray Mss.502/56/7). The majority of his Scottish views in *Monastic Remains* are of places around either Edinburgh or Glasgow.

Plate 134. Design for an apsidal building, from Loudon's *Treatise on Scone*

Such a garden with its rare plants and shrubs was obviously the ideal prototype for Loudon's gardenesque but, this said, it belonged more truly to the same anti-natural category as did Scone or Brahan Castle. Parkyns's ideas were in reality very little different from those of either Robinson or the Whites.[91] To Loudon's self-conscious stand at this time as the exponent of the Scottish landscape, its Americanism ought to have been just as damning as the English taste that Repton had displayed at Valleyfield. For both Parkyns and Repton had singularly failed in their different ways to consult the genius of the place, as Loudon demanded, as he had shown at Barnbarroch and Scone, and as he had set out in his *Country Residences*. His ideas, like those of any prophet, were for the future, and in Scotland were taken up and exploited by the arch-romantic and patriot Sir Walter Scott. The naturalism he preached was likewise converted into instant history by Sir Henry Steuart's practical theories on the transportation of trees.

THE REVIVAL

In the final phase of the landscape garden in Scotland, there were three figures of considerable importance, all more or less devotees of the ultimate form of the picturesque. Sir Henry Steuart of Allanton in Lanarkshire was one, who through his authorship of *The Planter's Guide*, of 1828, significantly shaped practical as well as aesthetic attitudes towards planting.[1] Another was its reviewer, Sir Walter Scott, writing anonymously and favourably in the *Quarterly Review*.[2] Scott had been a gardener since his days at Ashiestiel and had at one time intended a publication along similar lines to *The Planter's Guide*. The third figure, again intimately connected with the critical standing of *The Planter's Guide*, was William Sawrey Gilpin, nephew of the Reverend William Gilpin and author of *Practical Hints upon Landscape Gardening* of 1832. In his book, Gilpin was a careful and fair critic of *The Planter's Guide*, less so perhaps of its over enthusiastic notice in the *Quarterly Review*. Between the three of them, they charted the decline of the picturesque and marked at the same time the rise of a formal style that took its motifs and associations from the Scottish gardens of the sixteenth century and its trees from Loudon's *Arboretum et Fruticetum Britannicum* and Hooker's *Flora Scotica* of 1821. Despite their fears for the future, all three, Scott, Gilpin and Steuart, contributed to the destruction of the eighteenth-century garden and the aristocratic concept of landscape. They cleared the way for almost its reverse – a garden, popular, urban, formal and strongly botanical.

Scott's introduction to the world of landscape gardening had probably come about through his family's professional connection with the Abercorns, of Duddingston. Both his father and his brother had acted as their Scottish agents, and Scott kept up a fairly constant correspondence with the family.[3] It was to Lady Abercorn that he wrote, after the purchase of the future Abbotsford in 1813, that 'I have been studying Price with my eyes and [am] not without hopes of converting an old gravel pit into a bower and an exhausted quarry into a bathing house . . . [see] how deeply I am bit with the madness of the picturesque'.[4] The same, rather flippant attitude to the picturesque

1. There were in all four printings of *The Planter's Guide*: the 1st and 2nd editions of 1828, a New York edition of 1832 which was based upon the 2nd edition, and a third edition of 1848, which contained a memoir of the author and in addition three further sections: 'accompanied with notes, on the nature and cultivation of British forest trees, which had been drawn up by Sir Henry Steuart previous to his death, with a view to a third edition'. These were sections 12, 13 and 14, with notes. It also reproduced the Raeburn portrait of Sir Henry, with a specimen of his signature below.

2. *The Planter's Guide* gained immediate attention through its favourable notice by Sir Walter Scott in the *Quarterly Review* of 1828, and by that of James Main in Loudon's *Gardener's Magazine* IV (1828) pp.115–26. In a more professional account than Scott's, Main described the book as 'illustrated by the resources of the scholar, the sagacity of the philosopher, and the experience of the practical phytologist'. Further notices of the book appeared in vol.VI, pp.45 and 413. *Blackwood's Magazine* also enthusiastically reviewed it in 1828 and noted, like Scott, that now 'any gentleman anxious to create sylvan scenery suddenly, may do so at the thirteen part of the expense necessarily accompanying any other method' (*Blackwood's Magazine* XXIII (1828) p.430). Originating from these reviews were Wither's *Letters to Sir Walter Scott* (London 1828) and William Pontey's *A Letter to Sir Henry Steuart*, Bart. (Huddersfield 1829).

was true of his feelings about its apologist Repton, whom the Abercorns may have employed along with Sir John Soane at their English home, Bentley Priory. Scott's before and after descriptions of the improvements he had undertaken at Abbotsford were, he pretended, in imitation of Repton's flaps, 'what is & what was which Mr. Repton exhibits by means of that ancient contrivance a raree show omitting only the magnifying glass & substituting his red book for the box and strings'.[5] In public he was more conventional and circumspect. For the readers of the *Quarterly Review*, Repton was paraded as 'a man of very considerable talents'.[6]

Scott shared with Repton an almost evangelical enthusiasm for landscape, and after his acquisition of Abbotsford he was continuously involved in gardening and planting for others: in the siting and laying out of Milton Lockhart, Lanarkshire, in 1829; in the sublime fashion at Craighall Rattray, near Blairgowrie, in the late 1820s (Plate 135); and on a ducal scale at Drumlanrig Castle and Bowhill.[7] At the last two houses, particularly over the years 1812 to 1819, he was in constant attendance as adviser to successive Dukes of Buccleuch. The late seventeenth-century castle and grounds at Drumlanrig had been seen and unenthusiastically commented upon by William Gilpin in 1776, but few changes had been made before William Crawford's survey of 1812.[8] The gardens had been neglected and the woods around the castle had been sufficiently devastated by the last Duke of Queensberry, the notorious old Q, to give Scott and Duke Charles carte blanche in this direction. Just before Duke Charles's premature death in 1819, Scott reported that he 'had already planted double the quantity of wood and the young plantations already begin to look *beautiful*'.[9] But the longer term and more radical reforms did not begin until about 1831, when Loudon reported the 'extensive improvements now carrying on in the grounds', possibly after a scheme of W. S. Gilpin's, which was to

3. For Scott's correspondence with the Abercorn family, see *The Letters of Sir Walter Scott*, ed. H.J.C. Grierson, 12 vols. (London 1932–7) vols.I–IV especially.

4. ibid., vol.III, p.240. For Scott's holding of books, on this subject see, 'Catalogue of the Library at Abbotsford', *Maitland Club* (1838) pp.299–300. For Scott's opinion of Sir Uvedale Price, see his essays in the *Quarterly Review* of 1828, and in *Miscellaneous Prose Works of Sir Walter Scott*, vol.21 pp.102–5. See also, Marcia Allentuck, 'Scott and the Picturesque' *Scott Bicentenary Essays*, ed. Alan Bell (Edinburgh 1973) pp.188–98.

5. *The Letters of Sir Walter Scott*, vol.IV, p.292.

6. See *Miscellaneous Prose Works of Sir Walter Scott*, vol.21, p.102.

7. A succinct account of Abbotsford is given in John Fleming *Scottish Houses and Gardens open to the Public* (London 1954) pp.98–101. A more subjective account of it in 1825 has been given in J.G. Lockhart *Memoirs of Sir Walter Scott*, ed. A.W. Pollard, 5 vols. (London 1900) vol.IV, pp.267–76, and p.269 for the garden. Craighall Rattray was remodelled around 1830, see *New Statistical Account*, vol.x (1845) p.242. According to Lockhart, Scott first visited Craighall in 1793, and it later served as his model for Tully-Veolan, the seat of the Bradwardines in Waverley, op. cit., vol.I, pp.208–9.

8. For Gilpin's remarks see *Observations*, vol.II, pp.83–5. William Crawford, of Meadow Bank, Edinburgh, who was in partnership with David Crawford, produced a large and impressive survey of the Buccleuch estates which was finally completed in 1827 (SRO GD 224/665/6). The bound volume of the plans is at Bowhill, Selkirk and that for Drumlanrig is dated October, 1810. For Crawford's plan of the garden and lawns see NRA Report, Drumlanrig Castle, plans f.36.

9. The *Letters of Sir Walter Scott*, vol.v, p.187.

10. *Gardener's Magazine* IX (1833) pp.1–2. However Loudon continued that 'there is little for a landscape gardener to do except forming two new approaches to the house, a new kitchen-garden; and modifying by planting and by some changes on the surface, of the path and pleasure ground'. Typically Loudon also suggested a restoration of the terrace gardens which had been laid out by David Low in 1738 (SRO RHP 1918). These gardens had partially disappeared when Pococke visited the house in 1760, see Pococke, op. cit., p.9. However, a plan by W. and D. Crawford of 1817 showed the eighteenth-century cascade as still extant, and suggested the restoration of two of the compartments of the old gardens, see SRO RHP 9458. These were incorporated in the plan of the gardens in 1840 (RHP 9677/5).

Plate 135. View of Craighall Rattray, Perthshire, from Swan *Perthshire Illustrated*

culminate in Barry's restoration of the formal gardens in 1840.[10]

At the sister Buccleuch house of Bowhill the pattern and Scott's rôle were much the same. While he and the Duke discussed planting and exchanged seeds and plants with one another, it was only with the appearance of Gilpin there after 1832 that gardening rather than planting was given an impetus and undertaken on any scale.[11] The situation was naturally enough different at Scott's own Abbotsford, where he planned as well as planted, and mixed a practical with an incorrigibly romantic attitude to his tasks. Although he claimed that he began with 'Kames's gentleman farmer so soon as he gets home and when he is master of that goes on with Tulls husbandry', he was no farmer and valued his land more as an emotional than economic anchor.[12] However happy he may have been to discuss husbandry with his grieve Tom Purdie, he was keener to walk and contemplate his land, typically christening a wooded valley, 'the Rhymers Glen,' and from time to time, 'sticking in sprigs which are to become trees when I shall have no eyes to look at them.'[13] This natural desire not only to make but to see the results of improvement was apparent in his work at Abbotsford from the very start. In 1812, he instructed Purdie to plant on a grand scale: 'Get out of your ideas about expense . . . we are too apt to consider plantations as a subject of the closest economy, whereas beauty and taste have even a marketable value after the effects come to be visible'.[14] With this in mind, Scott continually and ruinously expanded the estate by purchase and earmarked much of the new ground for planting. His invoice from the nurserymen Eagle and Henderson in February, 1818, was typical of the scale of his operations, listing as it did weeping birch, poplar, silver fir and Filbirds by the thousand, and laburnum, Scotch elm, and horse-chestnut by the three thousand.[15] But to realise some part of his dream, he had to turn to Sir Henry Steuart and his system of transplantation.

Scott had little personal liking for the 'knight of Allanton', who had achieved a certain notoriety through his intemperate behaviour

11. However, by that date Atkinson's work on the house and stables had been completed, and some plantations made, see RCAHMS, *Selkirkshire*, p.65. The Duke's death in 1819 and the succession of a minor brought such improvements to an end. On hearing of his death in Lisbon, Scott wrote, 'If it is thought proper to suspend the works at Bowhill perhaps the measure may be delayd till the decision of this matter' (op. cit., vol.v p.377–8). For Gilpin's work at the house, see pp.232–3.

12. ibid., vol.v, p.179.

13. ibid., vol.III p.308. For an account of Purdie's career see Florence MacCunn *Sir Walter Scott's Friends* (Edinburgh 1909) pp.350–5.

14. *Letters of Sir Walter Scott*, vol.III, p.161. Scott wrote that 'If I were to buy a picture worth £500, nobody would wonder much. Now, if I choose to layout £100 or £200 to make a landscape of my estate here after, and so much more to its value, I certainly don't do a more foolish thing' (ibid.).

15. ibid., vol.v, p.79.

16. ibid., vol.IV, p.488.

17. *Letters of Sir Walter Scott*, vol.VIII, p.91. Scott paid a later visit to Allanton in 1829, and was no further impressed by its owner, 'a sad coxcomb, and lifted beyond the solid earth by the effect of his book's success' (*Sir Walter Scott's Journal*, p.577). Nonetheless, after the visit of 1823, he wrote to Steuart a friendly though careful letter which concluded 'I cannot flatter myself that anything I have said can be very interesting to you. Most of my neighbours go to work in the barbarous old way of lopping, and topping, and planting many deformed and maimed pollards by way of beauty, on which subject, I cry like Wisdom in the highways, and am not regarded. I would rather have a decayed tree, than a deficient one: as some beau said he would choose rather to have a hole in his stocking than a darn: the one might be negligence, the other inferred premeditated and confessed poverty. I am happy to think that your discoveries may prevent both extremities, and am, dear Sir Henry, your obliged humble servant'. (*The Planter's Guide*, ed. Elizabeth Seton Steuart (Edinburgh 1848) p.xxi). Scott's opinion of Steuart was a fair one. In 1803, the lady author Mrs Grant described him as 'literate and well-bred man, quite of the old Court, with much dignity, and considered stately' (*Memoir and Correspondence of Mrs. Grant of Laggan*, vol.I, p.36). In 1815, she was more cryptic and direct, Steuart was 'as kind as his nature could afford' (ibid., vol.II, p.107).

18. *Miscellaneous Prose Works of Sir Walter Scott*, vol.XXI, p.51.

during a genealogical squabble over the *Vindication of the Memorie of the Somervilles*, which he had written anonymously in 1817. Scott found the quarrel ridiculous and remarked that 'it was indeed impossible to doubt that the article was of his writing & the solemn manner in which he referd to his own opinions & sentiments & authority is ridiculous enough'.[16] Nor did Scott's visit to Steuart at Allanton increase his regard 'I went to Sir Henry Stewart's', he wrote in 1823, 'to examine his process of transplanting trees. He exercises wonderful power, certainly over the vegetable world, and has made his trees dance about as merrily as ever did Orpheus; but he had put me out of conceat with any profession of a landscape gardener, now I see so few brains are necessary for a stock in trade'.[17] But whatever misgivings he may have had of Steuart as a person, he praised the book as offering both an inexpensive and virtually infallible system for moving and replanting trees up to forty feet tall. It was this knowledge that Scott drew upon at Abbotsford, where on parts of the estate he was able in Shakespearian fashion to 'countermarch the whole advance of Birnam Wood to Dunsinane'.[18] In a building designed to capture the air of 'old-fashioned English halls which your gentleman of £500 a year lived comfortably in in former years', it was vital to have some plantation of maturity which would foster the illusion of the antiquity at Abbotsford and other baronial *nouveaux riches*.[19] But like all planters, past and present, Scott basically wished to be able to see his efforts fulfilled. He wished to be able to stand, rather than lie, in the shade of his new oaks, and he was discontent that 'all my trees are in their infancy and it is a future age that will enjoy them otherwise than in the minds eye'.[20]

Scott wrote two reviews for the *Quarterly* both concerned with landscape: the 1828 article on Steuart's *The Planter's Guide* and, a year earlier, a rather belated notice of Monteath's *The Forester's Guide*, of 1824.[21] In both, Scott admirably displayed his enthusiasm and knowledge as a plantsman – showing his grasp of theory with Steuart and practical skill with Monteath. Although these reviews were complementary, it was in his essay on *The Planter's Guide* that Scott more obviously revealed his deep love for the Scottish landscape and the history it evoked.[22] In this he was supported by his fellow champion of Scottish rusticity, Sir Thomas Dick Lauder, who viewed with horror the destruction of the few formal gardens still surviving in the 1840s. At Elphinstone (Carberry Tower), some 'Vandal mercilessly destroyed so beautiful a specimen of the ancient style' and, earlier at Saltoun Hall, John Hay's garden of 1818 replaced the 'beautiful old bowling-green, surrounded by a yew hedge of immense height and

19. *The Letters of Sir Walter Scott*, vol.IV, p.302, see also Allantuck *Scott Bicentenary Essays*, p.197. Nevertheless he abhorred the speedy growth of the pine and the like, and their lack of grandeur. The Scotch pine, or as he termed it, 'Highland fir', was a case where he attempted to distinguish between the real and the imitation. He contended that the 'species of fir, which in an evil hour was called *Scotch*', were no more than an ordinary fir brought from Canada 'not more than half a century ago', and were 'inferior in every respect to the real Highland fir'. The proper Highland fir was 'when planted in its appropriate situation amongst rock and crags, dignified and even magnificent', and he recommended getting seed from them regardless of trouble and expense.

20. ibid., vol.V, p.280: see also *The Planter's Guide* (New York 1832) pp.279–80.

21. 'On Planting Wastelands' *Miscellaneous Prose Works of Sir Walter Scott*, vol.XXI, pp.1–76.

22. This is apparent in both his reviews. In that of Monteath, where he is dealing particularly with trees and their relationship to the landscape, he made a difference between commercial and ornamental planting. He felt that the results of the former were often disappointing in their use of larch and Scotch fir, especially where plantations were made in strips or squares. Scotland he maintained, offered an unrivalled opportunity to plant wastelands on a heroic scale. Where that happened, the larch particularly, gave 'a variety of outline which they do not possess when arranged in clumps and patches, and furnish that species of the sublime which all men must recognise in the prevalence of one bit of colouring in a great landscape' (ibid., p.31). In the review of *The Planter's Guide*, he gave a succinct account of landscape in Britain, with special reference to its examples in Scotland—his own cottage garden at Rosebank, near Kelso, Barncluith, Glamis and Duddingston.

thickness'.[23] But for all Dick Lauder's rhetoric his interest in such gardens was historical rather than horticultural. There was little between his attitude and that of Robert Burns' lament in 1787 on the destruction wreaked by the Duke of Roxburghe at Roxburgh Castle, where 'a fine old garden planted by the religious, [was] rooted out and destroyed by an English hottentot, a Maître d'hotel of the Duke's, a Mr. Cole'.[24]

But Scott's taste for the picturesque and romantic did not, however, blind him to change, and in both reviews he clearly appreciated the new spirit that demanded of the nineteenth century not so much a garden as the gardenesque. Although he viewed landscape gardening as a private world almost exclusively concerned with a personal choice of trees and shrubs, he was aware of the growing interest in botany and the particular demands of popular gardening clearly seen in Smith's *Parks and Pleasure Grounds*, with its chapters on Public Parks, the Villa, and the Arboretum.[25] He appreciated that the age of Brown, Repton and the Whites was over, and that the majority of improving proprietors would not necessarily turn to landscape gardeners like Loudon or Gilpin for help.[26] They might and did turn, as happened at Mount Stuart and Ross Priory in 1821, to their own gardener, if he were well informed in the Samuel Smiles tradition, for advice on both the suitability of plants and their composition. Or they might try their own hands as did Lord Adam Gordon at Prestonhall and The Burn, and Charles Craigie Halkett at Cramond, each with sufficient success to earn a reputation as a landscape gardener.[27] Scott wrote discerningly that 'there are thousands of proprietors who have neither scenes capable of exhibiting the perfection of the art, nor revenues necessary to reimburse the most perfect of the artists, but who may catch the principal on which improvers ought to proceed, and render a place pretty though it cannot be grand'. He was echoed less disinterestedly by a magazine like the *Scots Gardener*, which in 1822 emphatically stated that the gardener and his employer could do better than 'three-fourths of the landscape gardeners who keep cantering and capering over the ground for a few hours, heaping suggestion upon suggestion, and are then off to some other quarter, leaving no point decided'. In such a self-educating process *The Planter's Guide* had a pioneering role as 'one of the most powerful and speedy means of effecting a general and interesting change in the face of nature'.[28]

Scott's ideal garden of the 'new school' was not remarkable and probably rather conservative. He anticipated that it would 'reject the tame and pedantic rules of Kent and Browne, without affecting the

23. See Dick Lauder *Scottish Rivers*, pp.309, 324–5.

24. Robert Burns *Tour of the Borders*, ed. R.L. Brown (Ipswich 1972) p.17: see also Dick Lauder *Forest Scenery*, I, p.263.

25. See Charles Smith *Parks and Pleasure Grounds* (London 1852): Smith was the son of the gardener at Hopetoun and worked as a landscape gardener. He was a protégé of Loudon's *Gardener's Magazine*, see *Gardener's Magazine* x (1834) p.455 and xi, p.673, for his work at Thirlestane Castle, ibid., xviii (1842) p.581; and at Dalkeith, SRO RHP 9531. While his *Parks and Pleasure Grounds* paid attention to Gilpin and Price, it was just as much influenced by Scott's essay in the *Quarterly Review*, see ibid., pp.217, 221.

26. 'On Landscape Gardening' in Smith, op. cit., p.103. By and large, Scott felt that the failure of many of the late eighteenth-century gardens was through the employment of a professional and his 'an habitual disregard of the *genius loci*, and a proportional degree of confidence in a set of general rules'. The system whereby gardeners like the Whites, Loudon and Nasmyth charged on a daily basis meant that, 'the party consulting them is not unnaturally interested in getting as much out of the professor within as little time as can possibly be achieved' (*Quarterly Review*, p.106).

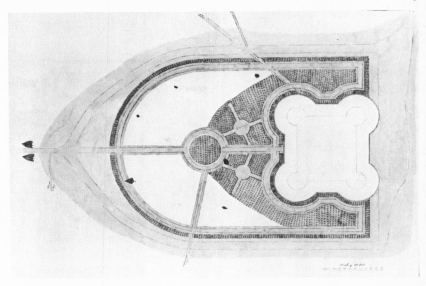

27. For Lady Bute's garden at Mount Stuart, see Mount Stuart Muniments and for Ross Priory, SRO GD 47/575. At Ross a note excused the drawings as 'a very clumsy attempt at a plan of flower plots. I fear it will not give you any clearer idea of their appearance then you had before' (ibid.). This design incorporated an old garden into one dominated by roses. For Lord Adam Gordon's work at Prestonhall, Midlothian, of *c.*1770, and at Burn, Kincardineshire, *c.*1780 see Dick Lauder op. cit., p.293 and George Robertson *A General View of the Agriculture of Kincardineshire* (London 1813) p.140. For Craigie Halkett, see Dick Lauder p.45; and for his most notable garden at St Martins, near Perth, of *c.*1855, see Hunter, op. cit., pp.523–4.

28. *Miscellaneous Prose Works*, vol.XXI, pp.107–8.

29. ibid., p.107.

30. Inveraray Castle Muniments, plans 66 and 67. Plan 67 was annotated as the design of the then Duchess of Argyll, though it is clearly in the hand of the local land surveyor John Brooks, see plan 66, initialled 'JB'. Brooks was connected with the Castle from around 1812, and worked from Inveraray over the western Highlands, see SRO RHP 189 and 3130.

31. *Quarterly Review*, p.104.

32. For Nesfield see pp.222–3; for Rous or Roos at the House of Falkland, see M'Intosh, op. cit., vol.I, p.618.

grotesque or fantastic – who shall bring back more ornament into the garden, and introduce a bolder, wider [?wilder] and more natural character into the park'.[29] Yet by 1828, there can have existed comparatively few Scottish gardens that did not subscribe in some way to this vague blend of formal informality, so much so that in the very heart of the archetypal, sublime landscape at Inveraray a parterre with avenues radiating from it was proposed in 1823 (Plate 136).[30] But Scott was determined that there should remain a balance between the two styles, and that the taste for terraces, urns and balustrades would not be carried too far and the equilibrium upset. While admiring Gilpin's work in this manner at Balcaskie he probably appreciated it more as an old garden restored than a new one made. He felt that landscaping had now shifted from the extreme position of 'the total absence of ornament', to the reverse, where ornament was 'once more verging to its excess'.[31] He was certainly out of step with the later and extreme formality of Gilpin at Windsor and would have shown little liking for Nesfield's gardens, or sympathy with those of Rous at the House of Falkland in Fife (Plate 137).[32] He liked the formal for being old and as a piece of history, and this spirit drove him to load his own courtyard garden at Abbotsford with bric a brac of architectural history (Plate 138). In many ways, this sort of evocation was closer to an imitative

Plate 136. Design by John Brooks for the formal garden at Inveraray, 1823

literary garden, like Sir John Clerk's Clermount, with a gothic mood taking the place of a classical one, and gargoyles substituted for Latin tags.

For Scott and others like him, *The Planter's Guide* undoubtedly marked a change in both the practice and purpose of gardening. It symbolised the passing of the landscape gardener as the eighteenth century had known him, and the arrival of a more practical, popular and scientific fellow. Something of this revolt can be felt in Paterson's

Plate 137. View of the gardens at The House of Falkland, Fife, from Charles M'Intosh *The Book of the Garden,* 1853

v. Aerial view of the park at Glamis Castle, Angus, 1979

33. Nathaniel Paterson *The Manse Garden* (Glasgow 1838): Thomas Cruickshank *The Practical Planter* (Edinburgh 1830) pp.337–68.

The Manse Garden or Thomas Cruickshank's *The Practical Planter*, which praised and followed Steuart in emphasising the usefulness of his book to the owner of a small or suburban property working without advice from any grand designer.[33] In common with most of the literature of the period, *The Planter's Guide* both saluted and encouraged the gardener of limited means, and in this way helped to edge the landscape gardener out of private and into public service.

The Planter's Guide appeared in two editions in 1828, with the second seventy pages longer, having one more plate and a different arrangement of notes. Both editions, however, finished with the laudatory report of a small committee of the Highland Society of Scotland, which had visited Allanton at Steuart's invitation in September 1823. The composition of Steuart's text was both historical and practical – the former giving an account of the past errors of transplanting, the latter, its success under Steuart's 'preservative principle'. Characteristically, Steuart had little good to say about current or past planting habits. He frowned alike on systems that required either the setting out of new trees more than a foot or two tall or, in an attempt to gain an immediate woodland effect, to transplant by mutilating existing and mature forest trees. He castigated the ordinary method which transferred 'Old Trees, in the same way as Nursery-plants, that is, by lopping off a third part, a half, and sometimes the whole of the Top,

Plate 138. The courtyard garden at Abbotsford, Selkirkshire

34. *The Planter's Guide*, p.59.

35. William Pontey of Kirkheaton, Huddersfield, was the author of numerous works on planting. He was assisted by a nephew, William Pontey, when 'by personal infirmities, disabled from taking his accustomed journies' (William Pontey *The Rural Improver*, p. advertisement). Steuart referred to him as 'one of the most extensive and successful planters now living, and also a landscape gardener of no small distinction' (*The Planter's Guide* pp.62 and 481). He particularly admired his *The Rural Improver* (ibid., p.402). However according to White junior, 'Pontey's Book in many cases both in England and Scotland has done harm' (Mount Stuart Muniments, letter-book of A. Brown f.402).

36. *The Planter's Guide*, 2nd ed., p.10.

37. ibid., p.11.

erroneously conceiving that both can be managed on the same principles'.[34]

In support of his view, he quoted the distinguished planter William Pontey, of whom, unlike the Whites, he more or less approved. Pontey had found the old method 'extremely tedious and hazardous also', and even 'in case of success, such trees, for several years grow so slowly, as to remind one of the "striken deer". It is indeed seldom that they harmonize with anything about them'.[35] It was to tackle this double failure that *The Planter's Guide* was written. Steuart reckoned that with an intelligent application of his scientific methods – in preparing the soil, selecting the correct type and size of tree, and in the proper use of his improved planting machine – 'an *entire Park*, could be thus *wooded at once*, and forty years of life anticipated'.[36] Indeed he was even bolder: 'By these means', he wrote, 'some of the most interesting objects, both agricultural and ornamental, have been accomplished, at *a very moderate expense*, and brought within the reach, not only of the great and opulent but of any person of limited fortune'.[37] In support of this he pointed to the home of the amateur architect James Smith at Jordanhill in Renfrewshire (Plate 139). Smith had enlarged the house there about 1824, when he replanted and laid out the surrounding park

Plate 139. View of Jordanhill House, Renfrewshire, from Ramsay *Views of Renfrewshire*, 1839

38. ibid., p.362. For some account of Jordanhill and Smith's career see J.G. Smith and J.O. Mitchell *The Old Country Houses of the Old Glasgow Gentry* (Glasgow 1878) p.142.

39. *The Planter's Guide*, 2nd ed., p.361.

40. *The Planter's Guide*, 3rd ed., p.xxxviii. For Steuart's concern at Quernmore see NRA handlist 16185 – MacLean. It is extremely likely that landscape work was in hand in all these houses around 1828. Keir may have been an exception, for Charles Stirling having laid out his own park and lake at Cawder (Cadder) *c.*1817, did much the same for his brother at Keir probably using Steuart's gardener (Sir William Fraser *The Stirlings at Keir* (Edinburgh 1858) p.78). In Ireland his men were alleged to have worked at 'the seats of Mr. Shaw, the Recorder of Dublin', and at Abbeyleix, Lord de Vesci; Bessborough House, Co. Kilkenny, Lord Duncannon; Oak Park, Co. Carlow for Colonel Brown; Clogher, Co. Tyrone for the Bishop of Clogher, and Westport Co. Mayo for the Marquess of Sligo (ibid.). Steuart's ideas are known to have been followed at Hartham Park where the gardener George Smith had read *The Planter's Guide*, see *Gardener's Magazine* IV (1828) p.340.

41. John Brown *The Forester* (Edinburgh 1851) p.472. Brown used at Arniston in the 1840s a version of the machine employed at Kingston (ibid. p.479). Brown was mistaken when he gave 'Blower' as the architect, and Derbyshire as the county, see Colvin, op. cit., p.118.

42. *The Planter's Guide*, 2nd ed., pp.244–8, pp.43–4.

on Steuart's advice and according to his principles.[38] The *Guide* maintained that such was the aptitude of this 'man of science' that in the space of a fortnight, 'he removed Trees of thirty and five-and-thirty feet high, and of great thickness, with the utmost success'.[39]

Steuart also seems to have undertaken some sort of training scheme for gardeners, as well as sending what were termed 'Sir Henry's people' to work for various interested owners. The domain at Wortley in Yorkshire was laid out by one of them in 1828, and in the third edition of *The Planter's Guide* it was explained that 'several of his workmen, and others who had been long trained in his service in transplanting at Allanton, were permitted by Sir Henry to visit various parks of England and Ireland, for the purpose of showing more efficiently the practical working of the system'. Steuart himself advised at Quernmore Park in Lancashire, and his men, or so it was claimed, worked at The Haining near Selkirk, Keir in Perthshire, Newbeith near Haddington, and at Urie in Kincardineshire.[40] At Kingston Hall in Nottinghamshire the 'bulk and general outline' of the new Elizabethan house by Blore was effectively disguised by a timely application of Steuart's principles and, more particularly, of his modified planting machine in 1843.[41]

Steuart's principles were relatively simple and ideally suited to a didactic role. There was little to misunderstand about digging up a suitable tree more than fifteen but under forty feet tall and removing it with the ball of soil around its roots by means of the transplanting

Plate 140. Steuart's planting machine, from *The Planter's Guide*, 1828

43. ibid., p.245. Steuart remarked that as his sole 'object being a Park-practice, to which dispatch and success are the chief recommendations, I prefer the simple Machine of Brown, with some improvements which I have made upon it' (ibid., p.246). There were several variants on Brown's Machine in use at this time. One had successfully been used by Lord Manners at Thoresby Park c.1814, and a further one introduced to Ireland from Scotland by 'Mr. Robertson, a Scottish Engineer', see Samuel Hayes, op. cit., p.72, and Steuart *The Planter's Guide*, p.46. A more primitive version of the machine must have been used at Thorndon in the 1730s, where Lord Petre transplanted elms of about 40 to 60 feet without mutilation, see Sir George Clutton and Colin Mackay, 'Old Thorndon Hall, Essex' *Garden History Society Occasional Paper No. 2*. (1970) p.35. There was a further development of Steuart's machine in that of J. Kidd, the gardener at Rossie Priory, Perthshire, where by 1840 he had a machine 'for the removal of large shrubs' (*Gardener's Magazine* XVI (1840) p.252–4). It was described as '5 pronged fork, mounted on a pair of wheels and axle, the latter serving as a fulcrum for lifting up a tree' (ibid.). According to M'Intosh, Steuart's machine was defective, and the inventions of Mr Saul and Mr McNab of Edinburgh superior. (M'Intosh, op. cit., II, pp.132, 137, 139). Further, and much more elaborate machines were invented in the 1840s by Mackay, the gardener at Kingston Hall, and McGlashan, who worked with M'Intosh at Dalkeith (ibid., pp.381–7).

44. *The Planter's Guide*, 2nd ed., p.255.

45. For an account of Steuart's career see the entry in the *DNB*. His antiquarian pursuits seem to have been characterised by trouble and bickering as his surviving correspondence with his researcher at Register House showed, see NLS Adv. 2629 f.57. The centre of the trouble was his anonymous publication of *The Genealogy of the Stewarts refuted* (Edinburgh 1799). There was a further

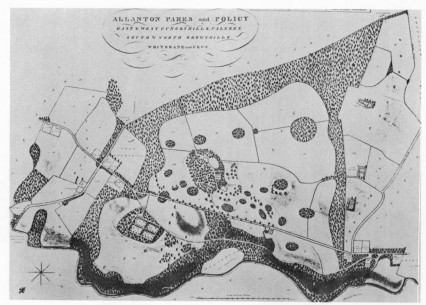

machine to a carefully prepared position in the new park. The machine for executing this manoeuvre was of great importance, and was fully described and illustrated by Steuart in *The Planter's Guide*. Plate III gave a general view of his modified machine at work, while Plate IV showed a detailed working drawing for its construction (Plate 140).[42] It was a development of that used throughout the eighteenth century, closest, as Steuart admitted, to that associated with Capability Brown.[43] However, he claimed that his machine was simpler, easier and less expensive in that it required fewer horses to draw it or men to guide it. It had been made to his instructions on the estate at Allanton and he advised any interested reader to apply there to his carpenter Thomas Nesbit.[44]

Sir Henry Steuart vigorously followed the maxim of practising what he preached. He had retired from the army, prematurely, in 1787 and had settled at Allanton as a dilettante historian with a penchant for antiquarian and genealogical studies.[45] In 1788, he rebuilt and extended the house he had inherited, and engaged the elder Thomas

and related quarrel in 1817 over an article 'Sitting below the salt, and the Steuarts of Allanton' *Blackwood's Magazine* I (1817) pp.349–52.

Plate 141. Allanton House, Lanarkshire, survey plan by John Leslie, 1808

White to lay out the park between that date and 1808.[46] Later, between 1816 and 1822, he replanted and extended the park, and largely from this experience wrote *The Planter's Guide*. The unremarkable scheme that White carried out at Allanton was very clearly shown in John Leslie's detailed survey of the whole estate in 1808 (Plate 141). This indicated a fairly conventional landscape for its time with clumps of trees and an almost continuous plantation around the periphery of the park: it is unlikely that Steuart had anything to do with it. In such a bleak and desolate countryside, as an estate survey of 1765 showed Allanton all too clearly to be, White's scheme was a notable triumph

Plate 142. Aerial view of the park at Allanton, 1979, showing the new lake and bridge

46. See Rev. Peter Brown *Historical Sketches of the Parish of Cambusnethan* (Wishaw 1859) p.56. Nonetheless, when Cobbett in the course of his rural rides visited Allanton in 1832, he described the house as 'old' while admiring the landscape as 'anything in greater perfection than this, as far at any rate as relates to trees, it is impossible to conceive. The trees are not only of the proper sorts, but in their proper places'. (*William Cobbett: Rural Rides*, ed. G.D. and Margaret Cole, 3 vols. (London 1930) vol.III, p.843. According to the 'Memoir of the Author', in the 1848 edition of *The Planter's Guide* 'Sir Henry, on his return to Scotland, resolved to remove the less secure parts of the building, with the exception of the tower, and erect a more modern mansion in its stead. Being unwilling, however, to remove the ancient tower or keep, he made arrangements to retain that portion of the fortress, and to connect it with the new buildings which he planned. On removing the other portions of the castle, this ancient tower was accidentally in some parts undermined, and was discovered in consequence, to be afterwards so insecure that it likewise was obliged to be removed, together with the greater part of the building. Between the first and later additions to the house at Allanton, a period of about thirty years intervened' (*The Planter's Guide*, 3rd edition, pp.x–xi). Allanton has now been demolished.

47. See SRO RHP 3665.

48. Sir Henry Steuart married the sister and eventual heiress of Archibald Seton of Touch, who died in 1818. Owing to the financial difficulties of Seton's father and his own permanent residence abroad, mostly in India, money matters were in the hands of Trustees. For a full history of the Seton family at this time see Sir Bruce Seton, *The House of Seton*, 2 vols. (Edinburgh 1941) vol.II, pp.483–6.

against adversity, and the value of his previous experience at Woodlands cannot be under-estimated.[47] Steuart later continued the development to the south, where a bridge or causeway in the style of that at Blenheim was made to carry a new driveway across an L-shaped lake. A new entrance was formed at this end of the park, shown as Plate V in *The Planter's Guide*, and the lodge and surrounding plantations completed in 1826 (Plate 143). The view from this end of the park was probably Steuart's most impressive creation. The new drive wound out of the dense plantations beside the gate-lodge, past the western edge of the lake with a distant and occasional glimpse of the house through the trees, and then to the bridge. It was only when this had been crossed that the house swung into full view, topping the rise of the park, with a thin line of trees closing the vista on its eastern flank. While the effect of this superlative landscape was Sir Henry Steuart's creation, it relied upon and to some extent harmonised with the earlier work of Thomas White. The professional relationship between these two men was a complicated one, perhaps more clearly seen in their work at Touch in Stirlingshire.

Touch was the estate belonging to Lady Steuart's absentee brother, and was managed for him and his Trustees by Sir Henry.[48] The advice he gave there closely followed the pattern of improvement that had already been established at Allanton. Accordingly, the

Plate 143. View of entrance to the park at Allanton, from *The Planter's Guide*, 1828

architect he recommended to his brother-in-law, Archibald Seton, was Gillespie Graham, who had early connections with Lanarkshire and possibly Allanton; John Leslie was chosen to follow his Allanton survey with one for Touch in 1810, and the landscape gardener was again Steuart's 'worthy friend' Thomas White, presumably the senior.[49] Not unexpectedly, the two houses were intended to share much the same character. Although both were originally Scottish tower houses, the ancient homes of two old families, Steuart quirkily proposed with Gillespie Graham's connivance to turn Touch, like Allanton, into an aggressively classical building. Presumably in Sir Henry's mind the picturesque was the evocation of an exclusively classical past, and this led the former antiquarian into going so far as to congratulate Seton on the removal of the tower, which 'having neither beauty nor convenience belonging to it' was all the more ripe for destruction.[50] Certainly, it was along such lines that he had proceeded at Allanton, where he had taken down the old tower to build instead an austerely classical house. At Touch he recommended 'the best style of Greek architecture,' so that its character would be dominated by 'chastness and Doric simplicity'.[51] White's improvement plan for the surrounding landscape seems to have been intended to complement such a classical mood, for White, rather like his patron, appeared more than able to resist the full blandishments of the picturesque, as his proposed scheme for Rossdhu had shown, and it seems likely that both men had their eyes fixed on some Arcadian landscape, pictorial rather than real, but at the same time rich and cultivated rather than wild or barren. At Touch, Sir Henry wanted an estate composed of fertile and productive farms, impossibly tenanted by a unique sort of 'scientific agriculturalist of superior education and abundant capital', who would make improvement financially worthwhile.[52]

Although the surviving correspondence between Seton and Steuart about the improvement of Touch started in 1809, there existed two earlier plans. The first was inscribed 'Designed plan of the House and Policy of Touch the Seat of Archd. Seaton, Esq., by Thomas White', but signed by the Edinburgh land surveyor John Bell and dated 1800; the second plan was a year later, signed I. D'Auvergne, and noted as 'reduced from one of Mr T. White' (Plate 144).[53] Neither of these plans, nor the White original from which they were derived, appears to have been executed to any extent. In a letter of 1812, Archibald Seton referred to the heavy planting of the western side of the estate – a conspicuous feature of all these schemes – as having yet to be undertaken and even decided upon. So much so, that a visitor to the

49. Gillespie Graham's career seems to have started off under the patronage of Lord Macdonald in Skye, see Macaulay, op. cit., p.229. He may have known Sir Henry's son-in-law, another Macdonald, and in this way have become connected with Allanton. He was sufficiently in Steuart's favour to be described by him in 1809 as 'an Architect, Mr. Gillespie (by far the best we have in this country)' (NLS Acc.4912, Box 2). John Leslie's survey of Touch has remained there. In a letter to Steuart in 1812, Seton wrote that 'my mind strongly leans towards the line of approaches recommended by you and Mr. White'. Unfortunately, nowhere in *The Planter's Guide* did Steuart distinguish between the two Thomas Whites, or give any date for the end of their partnership.

50. NLS Acc.4912, Box 2. Steuart's letter is dated April 1809.

51. ibid.

52. ibid.

53. Both plans are at Touch. D'Auvergne's design is titled 'A design for the improvement of Touch the seat of Archibald Seaton, Esq., reduced from one of Mr. T. White by I.D. 1801'.

house in 1808 found almost the reverse, with everything in a muddle and trees cut down rather than planted.[54] A little later, Seton was still writing vaguely that 'the *whole* of the hills, to the southward and south westward, should be covered with wood, or, in other words, that the plantations should be extended in these directions, as far as our boundary stretches', and that the 'low lands should be adorned with clumps and dropped trees'.[55] Nor had any other far-reaching proposals been firmly decided, let alone executed. White had suggested in his plan that two new approaches should be made to the house, and that the offices and the kitchen garden should be removed to a more distant spot. These points were raised again in 1812, with Seton deferring, unequally, to Steuart and White. He was sensible that 'the approach to a gentleman's seat is a part of the embellishment, that *requires* particular attention', and so he sought the advice of both Steuart and White in this matter.[56] But of the two aesthetic advisers Steuart was undoubtedly the more forceful and his was inevitably the last word. It was he who, in Seton's words, 'pitched upon the spot . . . best calculated for the new garden', even though a site had been provided and marked in White's plan of roughly twelve years earlier.[57] By this time, however, both the plan and its two copies had become the basis for discussion rather than action. All were of course freely interpreted by Seton's personal 'fountain of Taste', Sir Henry Steuart.

White's improvement plan for Touch suggested a fairly extensive remodelling of the surrounding landscape. He intended to divide the park and policies into three unequal areas separated from each other by plantations of varying depth. The largest unit was that which was to contain the house and the proposed lake. The Touch burn should have fed this lake and formed a river-loch similar to that made at Allanton in the 1820s. But like so much at Touch the lake remained a Will-o'-the-wisp, and for all Sir Henry's pains very little seems to have been accomplished on the estate. Only the planting of the hillsides at Garnselloch belonged to this phase of improvement, and it was to this that Steuart probably referred when he wrote in 1818 of 'large tract of ground which I planted within the last twenty years', at the same time as 'rebuilding 2 cottages at Craigninen (for which I gave the plan)' on the estate.[58] But the lake was never dug, neither was the avenue cut through 'the fields of Woodend and Whirlbog', nor the kitchen garden moved from beside the house to the spot selected by Steuart. The Ordnance Survey sheets of 1860 showed all too plainly how little the landscape was changed aesthetically. The old system of fields and fences that were shown dotted in White's plans remained virtually

54. According to Ramsay 'In some of the belts, the oaks 30 years old are cut down, and the beeches left, *because* the bark of the latter would not sell' (*Letters of John Ramsay*, Scottish History Society, ed. Barbara L.H. Horn (Edinburgh 1967) p.233). However, in the 3rd edition of *The Planter's Guide*, Steuart gave an account of an ash tree planted at Touch in the middle of the fifteenth century close to the 'old house and tower' p.473).

55. NLS Acc.4912, Box 2.

56. ibid. Seton described at length his intended improvements and in the minute detail of someone far from home. His letter was a reply to one of Steuart's of April 1810, in which Steuart suggested a new approach for Touch, described according to Seton 'in your own picturesque language (or rather as sweetly *painted* by your own charming pencil, in your own lovely colours)' (ibid.).

57. ibid.

58. SRO GD 47/758.

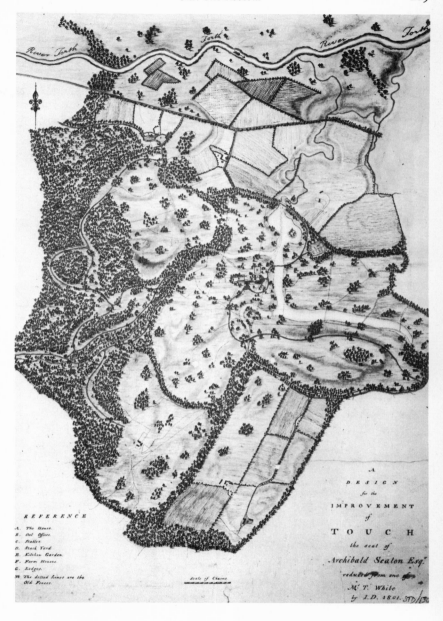

Plate 144. Touch House, Stirlingshire, improvement plan after Thomas White, 1801

intact, as did the skeleton of the formal avenue to the rear of the old tower.

White's original plan for Allanton appears to have disappeared as completely as that for Touch. No copies seem to have been made, and only Leslie's detailed survey of the estate in 1808 revealed the pattern that White had established for the park (Plate 141). True to himself, he planted an almost continuous belt around its boundaries, set the kitchen garden at a considerable distance from the rebuilt house, and separated the offices from the house by a thick shrubbery planted as a circle, similar to those proposed for Champfleurie and Gordon Castle (Plates 98 and 101). The disruptive element in this Elysium was the public road to Hamilton, which ran southwards through the lower portion of the parkland. The removal of this road to a line outside the park – an idea mooted in Leslie's survey as 'the new intended road' – was the catalyst for Steuart's ambitious landscaping schemes of 1816 and 1821. The new lake and causeway, the lodge and entrance drive from the south, all lay on its site (Plate 142). With the addition of this area, the park was swelled to 120 acres, not large by eighteenth-century standards but just enough to accommodate about 700 of Steuart's transplanted trees. This man-made and instant landscape was rightly a source of great pride to its creator. It appeared at its most tranquil as a frontispiece in Scott's *Miscellaneous Prose Works* of 1849, where Steuart's daughters draw and read 'The English Garden' beneath the umbrageous trees, with the planting machine discreetly parked in the distance (Plate 145). No wonder he demanded its proper appreciation and was annoyed by its absence. So much so, that he wrote a rather hectoring letter to Sir Robert Liston, explaining that a short and unaccompanied visit to Allanton was inadequate: 'you have unluckily been induced to spend only a few minutes on the Examination of an Art (I mean the Transplanting of grown trees) which it would have taken *some hours* or days fully to apprehend'.[59] Liston, as a dedicated gardener and pioneer of the American garden at Millburn, no doubt adequately appreciated Steuart's achievement and little needed or appreciated his condescension. But Steuart, like any evangelist, was unwilling to let an opportunity to proselytise slip by unexploited. He instructed Liston that 'my Lake, which is richly wooded at present, and *wholly* done by the Transplanting Machine; – and perhaps you will be surprised to learn, that 6 or 7 years ago, *there was not one tree near it*'.[60] A glance at Leslie's survey shows this to have been an exaggeration, though one which did not seriously detract from the landscape that Steuart had made almost at a stroke. The opportun-

59. NLS Ms. 5674 f.186. Steuart suggested that Liston should 'honour me with your company tomorrow to breakfast, in your way to Edin . . . to explain to you, as far as I can, the principles of science, which I have endeavoured to apply to an Art well worthy of the attention of the public' (ibid.).

60. ibid.

61. SRO, Bargany Letters, vol.II, f.38. Steuart was interested in Sir Hew's knowledge of French gardening, presumably for incorporation in the relevant section of *The Planter's Guide*. He was on this evidence very little interested in the French style of formal gardening.

62. *The Planter's Guide*, 2nd ed., p.17. According to the 'Memoir of the Author', during the 'winter of 1819–20, Sir Henry employed nearly two hundred of the unemployed weavers in forming an extensive piece of water', *The Planter's Guide*, 3rd ed., p.xxxii. Steuart dated the second phase of his work at Allanton as between 1816 and 1822, which would mean that the causeway was made after the lake in 1820 but before the close of operations in 1822, see ibid., pp.17–19.

63. According to *The Planter's Guide*, the reader was directed to 'the Frontispiece, Plate 1, where he will find a View of the lake here, taken in 1827, from the western side of the Lake' (ibid., 2nd ed., p.18). According to Martin Hardie, William Turner of Oxford made his first Scottish trip around 1838, that is ten years after the Allanton view was made, see Hardie *Water-colour Painting in Britain: Romantic Period*, vol.II, p.237.

64. See J.B. Papworth *Hints on Ornamental Gardening* (London 1823) particularly pl.x.

ity to create was a deep force within him, for without a son and dogged by ill health, Steuart had little faith in a long future for himself or his garden. Rapid and effective maturity was the cornerstone of *The Planter's Guide* and its system, as he wrote to Sir Hew Dalrymple Hamilton of Bargany. It provided 'an opportunity of producing landscape at once'.[61]

According to *The Planter's Guide*, the surviving lake at Allanton was made in 1820, with the causeway that traversed its northern end presumably built between that date and 1822.[62] Enough of it has fortunately survived to prove the accuracy of William Turner's drawing of 1827, which appeared as the frontispiece to both the 1828 editions of *The Planter's Guide* (Plate 146).[63] This showed a classical bridge of three bays with rather shallow niches set between each of the quoined arches, similar in style to those illustrated in J.B. Papworth's *Hints on Ornamental Gardening*.[64] Sited as it was, it linked the artificially raised causeway on either side of the lake and permitted the approach drive to the house to climb smoothly from the edge of the water through the open planted park to the mansion on the crest of the slope. Only the ghost of this landscape precariously survives. This bridge and the western lodge were probably designed by Steuart, advised on technical matters by Gillespie Graham. Together they formed the entrance to the park from the small village of Bonkle, developed by Steuart about 1817 to house workers on the estate. A view of this was

Plate 145. View of Allanton from Scott's *Miscellaneous Prose Works*, 1849

65. *The Planter's Guide*, 1st ed., p.503. Neither Hunt's *Half a Dozen Hints on Picturesque Domestic Architecture* (London 1825), nor his *Architettura Campestre* (London 1827) provided any close parallels with the lodges at Allanton.

66. Steuart wrote that 'A good Lodge should present the idea of an "Ornamental Cottage" always *harmonizing with the style of the Mansion house*' (ibid., 2nd. ed., p.500). In this he was adapting Repton's generalisations at Blaise Castle. There Repton wrote that the entrance gate 'should correspond with the house, in style, if not in order; that is the Grecian and Gothic should be kept separate, although the design may not be copied from the house', see *The Landscape Gardener*, p.252. Hunt in *Architettura Campestre* argued the opposite see ibid., p.xviii.

given in the second edition of *The Planter's Guide*, which showed the lodge as a classical building with an apsidal Tuscan portico terminating the vista from the tiny village street. Steuart was probably the leading spirit here, deriving his design from pattern books like those of T. F. Hunt, whose 'various sketches for buildings of this description,' he admired as 'a very tasteful selection'.[65] The choice of an obviously classical rather than picturesque form arose from Steuart's notion that house and lodge must harmonise in terms of style – classical with classical, gothic matching gothic. His preference was for the former.[66]

Following the appearance of *The Planter's Guide*, Allanton naturally attracted considerable attention and was probably rightly seen as the proof of Steuart's literary pudding. Its evaluation by the coming Victorian gardener W. A. Nesfield, who passed Allanton during a Scottish tour, was published in the *Gardener's Magazine*, of 1838. Nesfield's critical remarks were of course made from the point of view of a later and formal designer, who was largely out of sympathy with White's and to a certain extent Steuart's work at Allanton. The water troubled him particularly. He disliked the river-lake form that Steuart had taken over from White's design for Touch. Nesfield noted that, 'above the bridge, the water narrows, and indicates the character of a river, which has not been quite satisfactorily accomplished; because,

Plate 146. Causeway and bridge at Allanton, from *The Planter's Guide*

VI. Aerial view of the gardens at Drummond Castle, Perthshire, 1979

although the channel makes a long bend in reality to the left, it does not *appear* to do so from the bridge, but seems to terminate not only too abruptly, but at too short a distance above the bridge itself'.[67] He sensibly felt that the bridge was unnecessary, if a few yards later the river could be walked around. He also thought that its banks were too smooth and too monotonous, and would like to have found here and there, 'shingle, or a few large scattered stones'.[68] While this line of criticism might have been expected from any advanced devotee of the picturesque, a more obviously nineteenth-century note appeared in his criticism that some of the best views in 'a composition so accidently complete' had to be sought out and could only be found by the curious and imaginative.[69] He felt such vistas should be clearly if not blatantly spelt out by an approach or private drive, rather than be hidden from all but the amateur of the picturesque. Yet with all this said, he conceded that 'he who is inclined to be sceptical as to the result of the practical, as well as the theoretical knowledge of the late Sir Henry Steuart, should, before he ventures to pass an opinion, go and witness the living proofs of his success; and it is impossible that he can return otherwise than full of admiration and enthusiasm'.[70]

A further account of Allanton appeared in Loudon's 'Recollections of a Gardening Tour', printed again in the *Gardener's Magazine* of 1841.[71] He agreed with Nesfield's criticism but also drew attention to 'the manner in which the single trees were scattered along the two approach roads, both of considerable length, so as to form foregrounds to the distant scenery, without destroying breadth of effect'.[72] Its effectiveness, he thought, ought 'to be studied by the gardener'. However, and perhaps perversely, Loudon felt that Steuart's preservation system was expensive and in many cases, tedious and unnecessary. He preferred the Continental system of decapitation for all trees except those in the most prominent situations: on such 'extraordinary occasions' *The Planter's Guide* was still the best.[73] But probably the most influential reaction to *The Planter's Guide* came four years later in W. S. Gilpin's *Practical Hints upon Landscape Gardening*, which appeared in 1832 and again, with an additional essay on the Scots Pine, in 1835. Gilpin devoted some thirty-five pages to a sustained criticism of Steuart and particularly of his fondness for a too regular grouping in his plantations. This, he felt, could have been more strongly commented upon by Scott in the *Quarterly Review*, and he suspected that Sir Walter was too much in sympathy with Steuart's rather old-fashioned tastes. Certainly he described and illustrated his own style of planting as invariably of an 'irregular and varied form', and this was

67. 'A slight sketch of a visit to Allanton', *Gardener's Magazine* XIV (1838) p.16. In Gilpin's obituary in *The Gentleman's Magazine* in 1843, the following conversation was reported: 'Mr. Gilpin, that *his* profession at least was not numerous, he quietly replied, 'No, there is but *one*'. He afterwards admitted that there was one Pontet, 'a gardener' in Derbyshire, Mr. Nesfield, of Eton, may be regarded as his successor in his art' (ibid., p.209).

68. ibid., p.17.

69. ibid.

70. ibid., p.15.

71. Though they are unsigned, they are undoubtedly Loudon's journalism: see *Gardener's Magazine* XVIII (1841) pp.387–8.

72. ibid., p.388.

73. ibid., p.387.

no understatement (Plate 147). Although in a sense all of this was the nineteenth-century questioning the eighteenth, his remarks, unlike those of several of the professional planters, were objective and he readily acknowledged the obvious influence of any book that had circulated as widely as *The Planter's Guide*.[74] He was fair, and wrote that 'Sir Henry Steuart's very ingenious treatise upon the transplanting of trees will be found highly useful in forming these foregounds, as it

74. *Hints upon Landscape Gardening*, p.106.

Plate 147. Picturesque plantations, from Gilpin's *Hints upon Landscape Gardening*, 1832

Plate 148. Aerial view of Whittingehame and tower, 1979

75. ibid., p.51–2.

76. According to Gilpin 'Scenery, therefore, may be divided into the *Grand*, the *Romantic*, the *Beautiful*, the *Picturesque* and the *Rural*'. He added that 'the Romantic will, perhaps often include the Picturesque' (ibid., pp.5–6). His example of the Grand was Brockenhurst in the New Forest: Bolton Abbey, the Romantic: Addington Park near Croydon, the Picturesque: Longleat, Bowood and Marston, the Beautiful; and numerous buildings in Surrey for the Rural.

77. ibid., p.x.

78. For an account of the earlier part of Gilpin's career, see I.A. Williams 'The Artists of the Gilpin Family' *Old Water-colour Society's Club* (1951) pp.16–24. Gilpin's Scottish practice included work at Bowhill, Dalkeith, Whittingehame, Balcaskie, Bargany, Kinfauns and Strichen House, Aberdeenshire. It is possible also that he was associated with Ardgowan, Renfrewshire, Dunmore Park, Stirlingshire and Drumlanrig Castle, Dumfriesshire.

79. See White's plan for Balbirnie, SRO RHP 24,334; for a history of the Balfour family at Whittingehame, see M.B. Lang *Seven Ages of an East Lothian Parish . . . Whittingehame* (Edinburgh 1929) pp.130–60. Lang also wrote that until 1817, 'the policies, hitherto largely left to themselves except round the old castle, were planted and laid out with all the taste that the expert gardener and forester of the day could put forth, Mr. Gilpin, the celebrated English arborist, being employed . . . the house is approached by three great avenues, from east, south and west' (ibid., p.152). No drawings by Gilpin appear to have survived the dispersal sale of Whittingehame in 1927. It is possible that Gilpin had some professional connection with Smirke. The families were related and Smirke's father had been taught

directs the choice of tree, as well as the mode of removal, so as to produce at once the desired effect'.[75] Gilpin may have been out of sympathy with Steuart's taste, but he still respected his system.

Gilpin demanded more from the landscape than Steuart offered. In his *Hints upon Landscape Gardening* he returned – not very imaginatively – to a series of categories reminiscent of Dalrymple's but in fact closely modelled upon Price's *Essay On the Picturesque*. Apart from the Beautiful, the Picturesque, and so on, he added the Grand – a situation with panoramic views over the hills and sea – and the Rural, scenery associated with the cottage *orné*.[76] These, he felt, contained all the necessary elements of 'richness, intricacy and variety, [which] have entered the lists against insipidity, distinctness, and dull uniformity' typical of so many early nineteenth-century gardens.[77] He was a devotee of the picturesque as became the nephew of William Gilpin. He had helped his uncle with the *Wye Tour* in 1781, and his own drawings and watercolours, made before his transition to landscape gardener about 1806, were a more extreme but less competent variation of the avuncular style.[78] Yet as a gardener he was successful with a sizeable English and Irish practice and a smaller Scottish one, offering, after Repton's death in 1818 and before his own in 1843, a conservative alternative to Loudon's gardenesque. Like Sir Henry Steuart, he was more or less prepared to practise what he preached, and his justification of the borrowings and extensive quotations from Price was his determination to 'concentrate' the book and render it 'practically useful'. His zeal to show the ease with which these clarified principles might be applied was apparent in his written explanation of the improvements he suggested for Bowhill after 1832. There he referred to statements already made in *Hints upon Landscape Gardening*, which were themselves derived from work he had carried out at Whittingehame in about 1819. At that house he created a landscape setting for Smirke's Grecian mansion of two years earlier, built for a younger son, James, of the same Balfour family who had employed the younger White in 1815 (Plate 148).[79]

His most striking contribution to Whittingehame was in his Picturesque style, where the scene was 'marked by smaller and more abrupt folds of grounds, with but little flat surface, and clothed in a rougher mantle'.[80] One of the two long riverside approaches ran from a

drawing by Capt. J.B. Gilpin. Apart from Whittingehame, Kinfauns was another Smirke house, and Gilpin also worked with him at Nuneham Courtenay,

Oxford, see Mavis Batey *Nuneham Courtenay, Guide* (1970).

80. *Hints upon Landscape Gardening*, p.7.

81. This approach, like that from Papple, is now disused. The wooden bridge over the Whittingehame Water was washed away in 1947, but the stone arch over the public road has survived. This and the other approaches were probably laid out around 1819, when payment was made for building a road to Whittingehame by James Balfour (SRO GD 1/1/222/204). See also an estate plan of this period, which showed Smirke's house without roads, SRO RHP 8762.

82. See SRO GD 1/1/222/191.

83. *Hints upon Landscape Gardening*, p.13: for his bridge, see p.217. Gilpin disliked 'what is termed *a rustic bridge*', and wrote that where 'a bridge is required merely to cross a rivulet or brook, which interrupts the approach; and under such circumstances, whatever be the extent and magnificence of the domain and the mansion, picturesque effect should prescribe the character of the bridge . . . I prefer a plain wooden bridge for the crossing of a shallow stream' (ibid., p.216–17).

84. Gilpin suggested improvements for Bargany before 1827, and probably in 1826. In the manuscript letter, 'Supposed Calculation of Expenses for executing various improvements' references were made to 'Completing the Pond including the various improvements laid off by Mr. Gilpin between the pond and the west front of the house', and to 'Plantations laid off by Mr. Gilpin' (SRO RH 4/57, Bargany Letters, vol.II, f.59). For Gilpin's work at Balcaskie see *Gardener's Magazine* X (1834) pp.529–30, and for the earlier work at Bargany see pp.167–71. According to Loudon 'Mr. Gilpin and various other landscape-gardeners, have been consulted respecting the laying out of the grounds' (*Gardener's Magazine* XIII (1837) p.60.) There are several landscape drawings for Kinfauns Castle during the period of its building in the early 1820s. It is possible that an undated but watermarked plan of 1818 for the shrubberies may have been by Gilpin, see NMR Edinburgh PTD 64/34. Gilpin

also referred to Kinfauns in *Hints upon Landscape Gardening*, p.11.

85. *Forest Scenery*, ed. Dick Lauder, II p.239.

lodge at Ruchlaw Mill, followed the course of the Whittingehame Water for half a mile, then crossed it, and later went over the public road in a rough stone arch to emerge in the flat parkland in front of the house.[81] On the other bank of the river and a little further downstream, Gilpin exploited to the full the old tower as an ornament amongst the plantations seen from the drawing room windows of the new house (Plate 149).[82] It was an almost text-book application of a range of ideas he later expressed in the *Hints upon Landscape Gardening*. The river approach showed, as he stipulated, scenery that was not visible from the house, the simple wooden bridge he used on the Ruchlaw approach was similar to those illustrated in *Landscape Gardening*, and the house as Grecian in style was 'best suited to preside over the scenery designed by the term *Beautiful*' (Plate 150).[83]

At Bargany, in the shrubberies surrounding Smirke's Perthshire castle of Kinfauns, and especially at Balcaskie, Gilpin achieved intricacy and richness by playing formality against the picturesque.[84] More than that, this unhistorical blend was popular and earned him a Scottish reputation in the 1830s as having 'the sound judgement and good taste of Mr Gilpin, a near relation of our author (William Gilpin), whose advice regarding the operations of landscape gardening, given to various individuals of our acquaintance, have always appeared to us to be rational and judicious, as to do him the greatest possible credit'.[85]

Plate 149. The terrace at Whittingehame, East Lothian, towards the tower

86. *Sir Walter Scott's Journal*, p.316,
Scott's comments at Balcaskie were made
in 1827, and it is likely that Gilpin was at
Bascaskie about the same time he was at
Bargany. *The Gardener's Magazine*
described the gardens as having a 'lawn
in front in the form of a parallelogram,
divided in three parts by broad holly
hedges neatly squared up. In the eastern
division is a well laid out modern flower
garden . . . On each side of the carriage
drive to the house are some of the
plantations formed by Mr. Gilpin, the
outlines of which are most laboriously
twisted and turned about' (ibid. x (1834)
pp.529–30). The old gardens at Balcaskie
were those of the late seventeenth

Sir Walter Scott, was probably one of these acquaintances, and in 1827
he praised his work at Balcaskie as having restored the gardens 'in the
good old style with its terraces and yew hedges. The beastly fashion of
bringing a bare ill sheared park up to your very door seems going
down'.[86] In this Scott was not altogether accurate, for although Gilpin
recommended keeping the three southern terraces at Balcaskie, it was
largely at the prompting of the youthful owner, Sir Robert Anstruther
(Plate 151).[87] While preserving the late-seventeenth-century terrace
gardens and contributing a flower garden to the top terrace, he followed his client's wishes further and planted the park beyond them to
the south with individual trees, not so much in the manner of Brown as

century, see Maxwell op. cit., p.147.
They were altered again in 1857.

Plate 150. Wooden bridges, from *Hints upon Landscape Gardening*

87. There survives in a portfolio of plans of Balcaskie, a 'Memorandum for Mr. Gilpin' undated but watermarked 1827. Item 13 asked for Gilpin's opinion on the 'possibility of retaining the old garden'. Gilpin executed a flower garden here, but a more formal exercise was carried out by W.A. Nesfield in 1848.

88. *Gardener's Magazine* x (1834) pp.529–30 and for reply ibid. xi (1835) p.51. The criticism came from Charles Smith, the gardener and landscape gardener, and author of *Parks and Pleasure Grounds*. His plantations, 'the outlines of which are most laboriously twisted and turned about', were particularly criticised: Gilpin was consulted about this approach in the 'Memorandum for Mr Gilpin' Items 3 and 4. The lodge at the entrance to this road was built by William Burn around 1833 on the site chosen by Gilpin. Possibly the relationship was similar to that involved at Bowhill.

89. See SRO RHP 9715/12 and 13. These two designs are undated and unsigned,

of Kent. The contrast was absurd. Much the same ambiguity was obvious in his new western approach, where the hedges that bordered it outside the park proper made a startling contrast with the scale and formality of the surviving eastern avenue (Plate 152). Both this and the style of his plantations anticipated the opinions of *Hints upon Landscape Gardening* and even the criticism of the *Gardener's Magazine*. [88]

These ideas were apparent again in his design for a large and elaborate parterre at Dalkeith Palace, possibly of about 1832 (Plate 153). [89] He offered his Scottish patron, the Duke of Buccleuch, a pair of interlocking and almost circular gardens, one with a fountain in the centre and the other pivoting on a conservatory designed by William Burn in 1827. [90] He felt that these were the ideal shapes, 'as curved forms in a Garden are always more agreeable to the eye than *squares* &

but they are clearly in Gilpin's hand and were, presumably commissioned at the time of his consultation at Bowhill. Gilpin was replacing with these designs the existing Flower Garden shown in Crawford's survey of Dalkeith of *c*.1810, see Bowhill, Buccleuch Estate Plans. The survey plan showed the Greenhouse marked in Gilpin's plan as 'to be taken away' (RHP 9715/12). Neither scheme seems to have been executed and RHP 9715 was marked 'Dalkeith Flower Garden near stables not executed'. Most of the work carried out at Dalkeith between 1830 and 1840 was concerned with the kitchen garden and the various greenhouses – fig, orchid, camellia – see SRO GD 224/524/6.

Plate 151. The south terraces at Balcaskie, Fife

Plate 152. Aerial view of Balcaskie showing the western approach, 1976

90. This conservatory was designed by William Burn and was illustrated in Charles M'Intosh, op. cit., vol.I, pl.xv. It had been commissioned before 1834, when it was illustrated in the *Gardener's Magazine* x (1834) p.185, and shown in an unfinished plan for the gardens of 1831 (SRO RHP 9540). According to M'Intosh, who was the gardener at Dalkeith, it was 'a detached building placed in a small flower-garden, intended to have been very much enlarged. Other arrangements, however, having since been made, this intention is not likely, at least for the present, to be carried into effect' (M'Intosh, op. cit., vol.I, p.364).

91. SRO RHP 9715/13.

92. Gilpin noted on his design that the banks were to be grassed with a walk along them leading to the 'American garden' (SRO RHP 9715/12). A similar style was used at the other Buccleuch house of Drumlanrig, where succeeding the flower garden 'upon a noble grassy lawn, the gardenesque form begins and beyond that, the refined picturesque is introduced, which unites the whole with the surrounding scenery' (M'Intosh, op. cit., vol.I, p.619). It is these developments that Loudon referred to in 1831, when he described 'exclusive improvements now carrying on in the grounds'. This formal garden, consciously repeating the patterns of an earlier one, was completed by 1840 and covered 45 acres, see SRO RHP 9677/5. Work was possibly begun in 1838 when the Duke was given an estimate for one of the ponds in this garden (SRO GD 224/667/16; and *Gardener's Magazine* IX (1833) pp.1–3). Gilpin also worked for the Buccleuch family at Montagu House in London, see SRO RHP 9715/34. His designs for flower baskets, an essential part of Loudon's gardenesque, were carried out as part of the new terrace in 1833 (SRO RHP 9715/33 and GD 224/413/3). For Gilpin's ideas on baskets and picturesque stands, see *Practical Hints upon Landscape Gardening*, p.63.

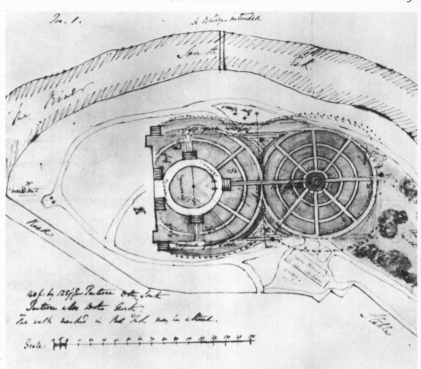

angles & they will not do in this case'.[91] In noting his drawing in this way, Gilpin was obviously still concerned with softening the geometric effect of the formal garden where it collided with elements of the picturesque. He allowed the general shape of his garden at Dalkeith to be formed by its site on a loop of the river South Esk beside the Laundry Bridge, but was careful at the same time to suggest the alignment of the banks beneath so that they repeated the garden's outline.[92] The conservatory was more rigid. Set on a plinth and approached by a series of stone steps, with a path leading to the fountain parterre enclosed by a screen of laurels and fir trees, it was treated as an outstandingly formal piece of sculpture (Plate 154). While there was little indication of horticultural character in Gilpin's sketches, he showed his parterre beds raised with a stone coping higher than the walks, and probably intended as a sort of winter evergreen garden. This was continued on the adjoining grass slopes, which were to be laid out with yews and an American garden with

Plate 153. Design for the parterre gardens at Dalkeith Palace, Midlothian, by Gilpin, *c*.1832

'rock intermixed' formed to the north east. Around these slopes was intended a series of winding paths in the more obviously picturesque style. It was this weak transition from the formal to the informal that was criticised some twenty years later by the then head gardener at Dalkeith, the formidable formalist Charles M'Intosh. He particularly disliked Gilpin's grassy bank that ran from the edge of the parterre to the river as 'not sufficiently grand', and thought that it 'should have been an architectural garden, and, descending from that level, another in the same style of greater diameter, also enclosed by a parapet, the descent from it leading to the natural ground-level'.[93] It was the very swing of the pendulum that Scott had so much feared.

The *Hints upon Landscape Gardening* was arranged with particular sections on the approach, the lake, and the various other features typical of any large garden at this time. The advisory notes Gilpin made on Bowhill followed a similar sort of pattern. Those on the lake started and startled with a frank statement on their origin: 'The Opinion I have expressed on the Practical Hints upon Landscape Gardening is well illustrated on the water at Bowhill' – that is between pages 151 and 175 in his book. His greatest problem with the Bowhill lake was its small size and the few ways in which this could be effectively disguised (Plate 155). Largely for this reason Gilpin strongly objected to a path closely following its banks, pointing to his theoretical statement that 'under no circumstances, should you be permitted to walk all around a piece of water, as, its limits being thus betrayed, its extent is easily ascertained'.[94] This was paraphrased in his notes for the young Duke of Buccleuch as 'The size, and character of the Lake is materially

93. M'Intosh, op. cit., vol.I, p.364.

94. *Practical Hints upon Landscape Gardening*, p.156. Gilpin continued 'whereas, when the walk is so conducted as occasionally to come upon the water, and that at the best point of view, and to be constrained by the intervention of planting etc., again to leave it, not only is the apparent extent, as well as the variety greatly increased, but the wish to explore what is thus hidden creates an interest beyond any that complete disclosure can afford' (ibid.).

Plate 154. Circular conservatory at Dalkeith Palace by Burn, from M'Intosh
The Book of the Garden, 1853

injured by the walk around it. No piece of water should be that surrounded not only as it diminishes the apparent size of it, but also as it deprives it of all foreground so essential to composition'.[95] Instead, Gilpin proposed to the Duke that the walk on the opposite bank from the house 'should be obliterated and the trees be also plunged as it were into the water'.[96]

In this way the age-old Claudian formula for distance could be applied, with the lake serving as the middle ground and the trees on the far bank forming the back ground. He proved this with a small sketchy view showing the lake and its islands as they might be glimpsed from the library window (Plate 157). The two islands presented further difficulties, for Gilpin wished to see that nearest the shore cleared of its trees so as to open a view of the house through the adjoining beech trees (Plate 156). The other island, he suggested, 'should be planted with alder, weeping and other willows so as to hide its shape', and at the same time give the desirable 'unequal height' that he recommended in *Hints upon Landscape Gardening* and had derived from Price's *Essay on the Picturesque*. His other proposed improvements concerned the Selkirk approach to the house and the renovation of the half moon terrace garden that faced the library windows in the style of his work at Heanton in Devonshire. Once again, his ideas were little more than those of the *Hints upon Landscape Gardening*, and showed a similar fusion of the formal with the picturesque. 'A double row of Limes on each side of the Approach' was to be matched by 'a picturesque sort of Gate House among the willows' in a typically mixed composition.[97] Gilpin exhibited, too, a strongly practical streak, which bolstered both his picturesque and formal ideas. At Bowhill, he gave instructions for fencing the new plantations that he had staked out, and for protecting the new trees by pales and wire-netting from sheep. These animals were to be used in their turn to keep the grass down between the plantations and so give life and 'cheerfulness' to the sylvan lawn on which they grazed. But in all of this his taste was that of the late picturesque, Price modernised and simplified, which may well have seemed to his Buccleuch patrons a little old-fashioned. For, of all his proposals only the lake had been carried out by 1840, when the rigorously architectural gardener, Charles Barry, hopefully offered 'any assistance in the changes which are in progress at Bowhill'. The likely dropping of Gilpin for Barry effectively signalled the end of the picturesque as a fashionable style in Scotland.[98]

While its expiration may have been sudden, the true picturesque had been dying for some time. A return to formality had been hinted at

95. This manuscript in the Buccleuch Collection at Bowhill is undated but must be placed between 1832, the publication date of *Practical Hints upon Landscape Gardening*, and Gilpin's death in 1843. It is titled 'Bowhill' and divided into three parts, 'Terraces etc. under the House', 'The Lake', 'The Approach' with a separate and short Memorandum at the end concerned with the practicalities of planting: see Appendix II.

96. 'Bowhill' f.3.

97. ibid. Gilpin included with his manuscript three plans and two views of his proposed improvements. They were meant to be used in conjunction with the text, 'The Plan explains these remarks'. They were much inferior to those of both Repton and Loudon in presentation and technique.

98. Drumlanrig Castle Muniments, Bundle 1162.

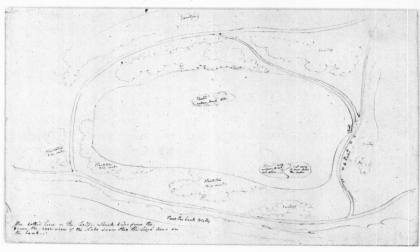

Plate 155. Bowhill, Selkirkshire, plan of the improved lake by Gilpin, after 1832

99. Dennis, op. cit., p.86.

100. ibid.

101. For Lewis Kennedy's career as a landscape gardener see App.3. By the 1820s, he seems to have become the land steward for Lord Willoughby d'Eresby, running the estates of Drummond, Grimsthorpe and Gwydyr Castles. For his connection with the landscape at Drummond, see Loudon *Encyclopaedia of Gardening* (1824) p.1090. George Kennedy's design for the formal garden at Drummond is noted 'additions and improvements since 1838 by George P. Kennedy, Arch'. The watercolour is at Drummond Castle. The gardens at Drummond had been landscaped probably in the 1780s and are shown in Knox's estate survey of 1810.

in Repton, cautiously advocated in Price's *Essay on the Picturesque*, and was seen as a *fait accompli* when Jonas Dennis wrote his *Landscape Gardener* in 1835. Dennis went so far as to bewail the destruction of the landscape parks for parterres, terraces and flower gardens, that were the essentials of the new form of gardening. He wrote that the 'modern devastator of a good grass-plot, for the idle purpose of cutting out roundos or ovalos, triangles or quadrangles, double hearts or single diamonds, true-lover's knots or hateful labyrinths, should consider whether in adoption of such taste, he excel by very many degrees, his grandfather's metamorphosis'.[99] In writing in this extreme fashion, Dennis was describing but not understanding the movement. The revivalist did not wish to excel but merely equal his grandfather's garden and saw little shame in once again cutting 'yew trees into a dumbwaiter, a prince's coronet, or a fantail peacock'. Equally mistaken was his identification of the formal garden with the alien influence of France: 'in consequence of renewed intercourse with France, through the termination of the revolutionary war, English principles have been injured, and English taste impaired, by adaptation to French style'.[100] In this Dennis was wrong, although he would have been nearer the mark had he pointed to a growing taste for prints by Perelle and Marot of French baroque gardens.

Such Francophile leanings were apparent at Drummond Castle, where a vast formal garden was revived around a sixteenth-century obelisk sundial by Lewis Kennedy and his son the architect George

102. See George P. Johnston *Catalogue of Rare and Most Interesting Books . . . Drummond Castle* (Edinburgh 1910) pp.24, 45. The library contained other eighteenth- and nineteenth-century gardening books with the bookplate of Lord Gwydyr.

Kennedy, in the 1820s and 30s (Plate v i).[101] The details of the compartments of the parterres there may well have been derived from Ducerceau, *Desseins du Jardin*, or John James, *The Theory and Practice of Gardening*, both of which books were owned by the then master of Drummond, Lord Gwydyr and were in the library at the Castle.[102] The immense new garden was close to the baroque spirit, not only in the scale of the parterre but in the dramatic series of viewing terraces and the double staircase that magnificently linked castle and garden. This grandeur was captured in the fanciful view Kennedy painted of Queen Victoria and her entourage picnicking at the edge of the garden during

Plate 156. Aerial view of Bowhill, 1979, showing the two lakes

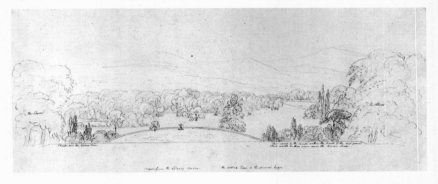

103. SRO RHP 14447/2.

104. Drumlanrig Castle Muniments, Bundle 1162. In full, the books Barry recommended to the Duchess were: 'Les Jardins francais de Louis Quatorze 1670'; 'The Gardens of England, France, Belgium, Holland & Germany'; 'The French Gardens of the Luxembourg, Versailles, – Boyceau' (J. Boyceau, *Traité du jardinage* (1638)); 'Practice of Gardening' by le Blond (*La théorie et la pratique du jardinage* of D'Argentville (1722?)); 'Dieterlin's Architecture' (Dietterlein, *Architectura* (1598)); 'Papworth's Hints' (J.P. Papworth, *Hints on Ornamental Gardening* (1823)); 'Percier & Fontaines Maxims de plaisance' (C. Percier and P. Fontaine, *De plus célèbres Maisons de Plaisance de Rome*' (1809)); 'Villa Pia by Bouchet' (J.F. Bouchet, *La Villa Pia des Jardins du Vatican* (1837)); 'Landscape Gardening and Landscape Architecture' (J.C. Loudon, *Illustrations of Landscape Gardening and Garden Architecture* (1830)); 'Perelle, Plus Belle vues des Maisons Royale de France'; 'Le Laurentin ou Maison de campagne de Pline le Consul by L.P. Haudebourt' (L.P. Haudebourt, *Le Laurentin, maison de campagne de Pline le Jeune* (1838)).

the royal visit of 1842 (Plate 158). This and the exhibition of the picture in the 1851 Royal Academy marked the popularity and prestige of Drummond, although as early as 1836 it had been reported as a remarkable restoration. An illustrated account of the new gardens was given in that year to the Duchess of Buccleuch who was contemplating a full blooded revival of the gardens at Drumlanrig, probably under Barry's direction.[103] So seriously was the matter treated that Barry was asked in 1840 to furnish the Duchess with a reading list on the formal garden. The bibliography he produced was dominated by France, and he advised the Duchess to get hold of 'Les Jardins Francais de Louis Quatorze, The French Gardens of the Luxembourg, Versailles etc., Perelle, Plus Belles vues des Maisons Royale de France, La théorie et la pratique au jardinage of D'Argentville', and a curious miscellany 'The Gardens of England, France, Belgium, Holland and Germany', of which the only copy he knew belonged to the Marquess of Tweeddale at Yester.[104] Curiously, although he mentioned Loudon's edition of Repton as useful, he did not list Loudon's *Encyclopaedia of Gardening*, which had given since 1822, a unique historical account of the various national gardening styles. Presumably he by-passed Loudon for the same reason he included Marot and Perelle – for their wealth of clear and copyable illustrations. For both Barry and his contemporaries, like W. A. Nesfield and William Burn, were more interested in learning visually than either historically or botanically about the formal garden. Such an attitude to the past permitted the utmost freedom and made the best illustrated work the most influential. For whatever yearnings romanticism may have encouraged, the formal gardener ultimately borrowed readily, frequently and easily from the late seventeenth-century garden.

All three figures – Scott, Steuart and Gilpin – were in their differ-

Plate 157. View from the library at Bowhill, drawing by Gilpin, after 1832

ent ways conscious of the ending of the eighteenth-century system of gardening, which even Repton had seen in 1817 as 'artes perditae'. Gilpin was perhaps the most successful in adapting to new attitudes and adopting a taste for formality, although even he remained essentially a gardener to the private landowners. Scott and Steuart were both outstandingly gifted amateurs whose taste for publicity decisively shaped the history of nineteenth-century gardening. Yet for all this, they were at heart designers in the late-eighteenth-century manner and as such were sceptical, if not fearful, of the return to formality. All three were nonetheless united in their vision of landscape gardening as the cynosure of art. But it cannot be doubted that Gilpin's *Hints upon Landscape Gardening*, though a popular book, marked the decline of the picturesque as a meaningful style. His conception, which he shared

Plate 158. View of the restored gardens at Drummond Castle, by Kennedy, 1842

with Scott and Steuart, of landscape gardening as 'the united study of nature and the works of the best landscape painters' no longer sufficed. As Loudon wrote in his review of Gilpin in the *Gardener's Magazine* of 1832: 'mere picturesque improvement is not enough in these enlightened times: it is necessary to understand that there is such a character of art as the gardenesque as well as the picturesque'. It was on this practical rock that the picturesque and the landscape garden foundered. 'A landscape-gardener', Loudon declaimed, '. . . knows but a part of his profession, who is not conversant with the numerous families of American and other trees'. As Gilpin readily admitted, he was 'very little conversant with flowers as to their varieties, cultures etc.'. He and others like him may have perceived but discounted the growing influence on design of practical gardeners like Nicol, Lewis Kennedy, and more typically Neill in the *Edinburgh Encyclopaedia*. But it is unlikely that they contemplated even in their heart of hearts a future where the city rather than the countryside called the tune, and where the gardeners like Loudon and Kemp found reputation and remuneration in public rather than private service.

ENVOI

The movement towards an informal style in gardening arose during the career of William Adam. It ended with the Scottish gardens of W. S. Gilpin, whose *Practical Hints upon Landscape Gardening* of 1832 marked an about turn in fashion and a revival of the formal style. It could be argued that for Scotland, at least, the landscape garden was an aberration, forced upon the country through its close association with England after the Union of the Parliaments in 1707, and that temperamentally, historically, and in practical terms the formal garden of the seventeenth century, seen from Aberdour to Balcaskie, was the ideal national form. The talents of its gardeners were always those of practical men, schooled in the kitchen garden – ever a bastion of geometry – more interested in botany, more at home with geometric patterns and used to schooling their plants. Perhaps this style of gardening merely retired to the wings during the hundred years or so after 1730, ready and impatient to make a return, and that a gardener like the elder Boutcher had a faithful pupil in Charles M'Intosh, the distinguished nineteenth-century head-gardener at Dalkeith. Yet while this tradition was tenacious it was not exclusive, and in Scotland, much more so than in England and elsewhere, there was always a dramatic contrast between such formal gardens and the vast acreage of wild and natural scenery. Chatelherault showed the styles could exist side by side, with one as a virtual foil to the other. The revolution in taste was for Scottish gardening a switch: the small shrubs, the flowers and fruits vanished behind a wall, just as Boutcher complained in his *Forest Trees*; and the woodland tree, like the wych-elm and sycamore, advanced to fill the space vacated. In similar fashion the old gardeners, the nurserymen and seedsmen retired and were succeeded by those who worked in 'the natural way', like William Adam and the Bowies.

For the landscape gardener in Scotland to consult Pope's genius of the place was not so much sensitivity as necessity. The history and traditions of a conservative country were everywhere visible, as over-powering and dramatic as the natural landscape itself. The painterly and picturesque appeal of such historical landscapes enriched the work of both Robert Adam and John Clerk as well as Loudon. The quarrel between the elder White and Loudon at Scone was as much about this as about the old-fashionedness of White's design. Along with Repton at Valleyfield he was pilloried for allowing English ideas to blind him to the native genius of the place. Yet such animosity, as much nationalistic as professional, did not limit the Whites's practice in Scotland, which was both prolific and presumably successful. Their popularity lay without doubt in their despised professionalism. The elder White was a noted arboriculturalist, and for the run of the mill commissions he and his son were capable and accomplished. But they were also resolute in their opposition to or suspicion of the picturesque and, paradoxically, they encouraged it as an essential attribute of the Scottish landscape. The faltering and failure of their practice after 1810 was directly due to their inability to move with the times. As they fell, the triumph of the Scottishism of landscape gardening became inevitable.

Although the picturesque was exploited by both Loudon and Walter Scott for their own ends, both men united in an almost religious veneration for the Scottish countryside, a taste fully shared in a more literary fashion by Sir Thomas Dick Lauder. For all of them the true landscape was that of humble plants and native trees, in a setting formed by a working system of fields and woods where any view might hold a particular historical appeal. The last attitude they shared with Adam and Clerk, and Sir Henry Steuart's purpose as a transplanter was to assuage their thirst for instant antiquity. What removed them and their spirit from similar feelings voiced by both Richard Payne Knight and Uvedale Price was an evocative historical sense. While the eighteenth century had dreamed like the youthful Lord Buchan of a primeval Caledonia, its successor thought of a medieval and domestic past, with gardens derived from the cottage style and planted with the flowers that Scott and the young Loudon had ardently admired. Neither he nor a gardener like W. S. Gilpin bargained for a return to a formality that extolled so wholeheartedly the precision and bombast of the baroque garden.

But this is perhaps to view history through too narrow a glass. If the formal was the ascendant style in the late seventeenth century and again early in the nineteenth, the informal or landscape garden was itself revived in Scotland under the influence of Robinson, Jekyll and the Surrey School in the 1880s. Yet its resuscitated form was as different from the parental English style as from its eighteenth-century precursors. The gulf between Osgood Mackenzie at Inverewe and

Thomas White was almost as wide as that between them and William Adam. It could be argued, too, that the Edinburgh notes that Frances Hope contributed to the *Gardener's Chronicle* in the 1860s, and especially her article 'A Plea for Wild Flowers' of 1867, anticipated the idea of the cottage gardens of Gertrude Jekyll. Her smallish garden at Wardie Lodge, beside Edinburgh, with its beds of kale, and those of Inverewe and Brodick Castle, all made their appeal by the subtlety and virtuosity of their planting and its successful integration with a sublimely wild landscape. In so many ways they matched the ideal garden lyrically sketched out by Loudon during his Scottish phase, where plants like the brier, the sloethorn, the fern, and the bramble, 'independent of many more which are less generally known, or abound only in rare parts of natural scenery, would, if introduced into the picturesque grounds of a residence, have a most enchanting effect'. In this way, Loudon felt the landscape could match 'the effect of the *alchemetta alpina*, *thymus saxifranga oppositifolia*, and others upon many hills in the highlands of Scotland'. His moving setting for the gardening proprietor's death in *Country Residences* was thus a timeless and national one: 'on a seat in the Saxon alcove at the end of the western terrace, where in an evening of September he sat down with his family to admire the splendour of the sky, the gloom of the distant mountains, the reflections of the evening sun, and the lengthened shadow of the islands upon the still expanse of the lake. A few days afterwards, about the same hour in the evening, his remains were conveyed over these waters, and interred in the family vault of the burying-ground'.

THE TEXT FROM HUMPHRY REPTON'S
RED BOOK FOR VALLEYFIELD, *c*.1801

INTRODUCTION

Sir,

In delivering a plan for the improvement of a place so considerable as Valleyfield in its character and effect on the surrounding country, I shall endeavour to shew that the general outline of its improvement is founded on and regulated by simple and well known principles, on the adaptation of which the several instances of detail will also depend.

It is evident that no map or plan upon paper can be so accurate and satisfactory as to preclude the necessity of marking the lines of roads, walks and plantations on the spot; and I trust the drawings which accompany this small volume (and particularly those in the course of the Approach thro' the valley) will rather be considered as *Sketches* to explain the general effect of improvements suggested, than as *pictures* of Scenery, of which the Art of Painting can give no adequate idea.

I have the Honor to be Sir,

Your Obedient & Humble Servant.

H. Repton.

SITUATION

Valleyfield possesses great advantages in point of Situation, and will perhaps be more striking from the force of contrast, than from any other circumstance. Where the general face of a country is open, naked, and ill cultivated with respect to Beauty, a Stranger must be particularly struck on bursting at once upon a place, where the extent of lawn is ample, and the lines of wood bold; and great, still further contrasted by a romantic Valley which seems to have been formed by Nature in her happiest mood: besides various other advantages, such as a proper aspect, good soil; fine home scenery; the views it commands of the Firth; and its opposite shore bounded by the Pentland hills, and the fine outline of Acle (Oakley) Mountains to the north, make it a subject of no common beauty.

The first circumstance of attention with regard to Valleyfield, is one on which all rational improvement of every place must be founded – The Character of the place – for it is evident that a Mansion, a Villa, and a Sporting Seat will require appropriate consideration, and very different treatment. From a due attention to the Character of Valleyfield, it appears that the situation of it may be materially improved.

CHARACTER

The Character of Valleyfield will be found to differ materially from that of Woodford,[1] in as much as the one will be the residence of an ancient and affluent Family in Scotland; the other the Villa of a merchant in the neighbourhood of London: in the latter, privacy and seclusion are more requisite than extent; in the former not only an appearance of extent, but of undivided property is indispensible.

Compared with the general face of the country, Valleyfield is at present undoubtedly well wooded; and with regard to its Aspect and its views the house well placed: but there appears to be in every direction a chasm between the house and the wood and a want of comfort in the ground near the house. The great objects of improvements should be, to make every part of the place in character with the magnificence of a Family mansion, and with the comfort of a Gentleman's residence, and still farther to increase the contrast between the rich cloathing of Valleyfield and the nakedness of the surrounding country.

In the neighbourhood of a large house, a certain extent of ground appropriated to the place appears necessary, which I call park whether it be fed by deer or not, and tho' a Gentleman may amuse himself by occasionally occupying a part of his park in arable land, yet I have no hesitation in asserting that a decidedly permanent farm near the drawing room windows of a large house is out of Character and ill placed. But in treating of the view to the west a stronger reason may be given against the farm, by shewing that such a view in that direction will militate against the comfort of the house. It appears also very material both to the Character and comfort of Valleyfield, to distinguish a Gentleman's residence from a grazing farm, and to prevent cattle lying under the windows by surrounding the house with mowed lawn, or pleasure ground: for the effect of which the following sketch No. 11 may serve to give some idea.

APPROACH FROM EDINBURGH

The various and uncommon circumstances of beauty that attend this Approach, will make it the most interesting part of Valleyfield, and its first source of pleasure will depend on its *variety* or the force of *contrast*.

1. The Woodford Repton refers to is probably Woodford Hall, Essex, where he worked about 1800; see Stroud, op. cit., p.174.

After skirting along the magnificent open road from Queensferry, commanding the finest views of the Firth; winding with every curve of the shore; and taking advantage at every step of new Bays, Promontories and bends of the river, we are at once immersed in a deep, romantic, and richly wooded Glen: on leaving which the place will open by degrees, shewing Valleyfield in all its grandeur, its masses of wood, and extent of lawn terminated by mountains of the finest outline; and where all the surrounding country seems to lead to the house, as to its common centre. After considering the general character of this valley it is obvious that a road thro' it in any direction *must* be beautiful; the first object was therefore not to choose the most *beautiful* but the most practicable line of road; and as a variety of difficulties would occur in any part of the valley, to prefer that direction in which there appeared the fewest, and those most easily surmounted.

This approach was therefore guided by the following principles, first to make it the most simple, the easiest and most natural road to the house; secondly to take advantage of the most beautiful points of view, to pass near the finest trees and particularly third – to avoid destroying the privacy and seclusion of the whole valley by a gravel road. Indeed this valley may be fancied one of Nature's favourite children; and except where it is necessary to carry a road of approach (which is evidently a work of Art) it should appear to be left to the management of Nature only –

>..................... where if Art
>E'er dar'd to tread 'twas with unsandal'd foot;
>Printless, as if the place were holy ground.

Having described the general effect and character of this approach, I shall endeavour to convey an idea of several parts of its scenery and of their most striking improvments, by the help of the following sketches.

The sketch No. iii is a view of the Entrance to the park from the end of the street with the effect of removing the Keeper's house and of covering this part of the park with plantation. This should continue the whole way to the dam, to do away the naked, field-like appearance of the hill to the left, and to confine the attention to the valley.

Sketch No. iv represents the dam across which it will be necessary to build a bridge of the most simple form, taking advantage of the dam as a foundation: – from hence the road should pass thro' this romantic Den on Sir William Erskine' side, if possible as commanding the most magnificent scenery and as the most practicable line of road till it enters a part of very different character where the valley begins to open and the size of the trees to increase (Sketch No. v). On leaving the valley it crosses a simple bridge No. v i, and by taking off a part of the top of the hill and filling up the flat, boggy bottom the ascent to the house will be natural and easy.

Sketch No. v i i is a view from the brow shewing the opposite straight formal boundary of firs, and the manner of breaking them by masses of round headed trees (particularly Oaks and Sycamores) sweeping down the hill.

Sketch No. v i i i is the point in which the house presents itself, from the Approach with great advantage.

VIEW FROM THE HOUSE, SOUTH

The great effect of improvement in this view, as shewn in the sketch No. i x & x both in point of comfort and character will depend, 1ˢᵗ on converting the ground immediately under the windows into mowed and dressed pleasure ground, instead of letting the place appear a grass farm: Secondly, on removing the fences and bank by which the grove to the S. West is impounded, to give an air of freedom and extent to that part of the lawn: Thirdly, in destroying the bald, naked, ugly lodge in the middle of the valley; and when the approach in that direction is done away there can be no reason for its remaining, as a building on the hill to the West would command a much finer view, and might be made a circumstance of great beauty, instead of a disgrace to the Scenery.

Fourthly, in boldly planting the hills opposite the house; and lastly, in cutting down several bad stunted oaks to the south-east, that keep up a decided line, which is evidently a defect; and prevent the eye from looking into the wooded Glen, terminated by a green hill, which may be considered as the finest part of this View.

VIEWS NORTH AND WEST

Every attention to the character and comfort of Valleyfield seems to call loudly for a material alteration of the view towards the North West.

A farm so near the windows appears certainly out of character with the size of the house, and the importance of the place; but there is another and a stronger reason for altering the character of this view.

A drawing room lighted to the West *only*, would be very unpleasant and scarcely habitable by reason of the setting Sun, and with the addition of the window to the South (which the good taste and judgement of Lord Meadowbank led him to suggest) the room would be apprised by too much light. Yet this may be obviated; the objection to the farm done away, and the glare of the setting Sun broken by continuing the wood as described on the map; making the view to the west consist of open grove; and leaving only such a space of ground immediately under the windows, as may be sufficient for dressed pleasure ground.

This will farther be of great use in sheltering the house from the western winds; will take off the present bald appearance of the house; and improve its situation from every direction.

Pleasure ground

But the great beauty of the pleasure ground, will arise from a circumstance that I shall beg leave to consider.

In the neighbourhood of so magnificent an arm of the sea, it may at first sight appear inconsistent to recommend, what may be termed an artificial piece of water. But I trust it will be considered that in a hilly country such lakes appear to be formed by the most simple process of Nature. A river meets with an obstruction in its course, and if this obstruction happens to occur in a plain surrounded by hills, it naturally spreads over the low ground; & according to the width of the plain or the height of the obstruction; such a river expands and becomes an immense lake or a small pool: and therefore altho' the interference of Art would be necessary to form such a piece of water, it would seem to be unartificial because both the place and the means are pointed out by Nature; and it is only by assisting her that such a pool is produced. With respect to its vicinity to the Firth of Forth it should evidently rather be measured by the size of the valley and of the river, than by the Forth – Indeed Valleyfield seems to consist of two parts, totally different in character; the house, the lawn, the woods, the distant view will constitute its grandeur and its magnificence; the valley with its several accompaniments (amongst which I hope this Loch will be reckoned) may be considered as an Episode, in which Variety will be found no less necessary than Beauty. –

Of kitchen gardens

When the taste for Geometrical gardening began to be exploded in this country, the desire of giving freedom and extent to their places was one of the first principles by which the votaries of the new stile of Gardening were directed; yet by abusing this principle they frequently converted it into a weapon still more distructive of comfort than the straight lines and square courts, which they had destroyed. This observation might be confirmed by many examples, but I shall confine myself to the disposition of their kitchen gardens, as more immediately applicable to Valleyfield.

Because they found the kitchen garden immediately under the windows of a house, they thought it necessary to banish it to as great a distance as possible, and in almost every place which I have been called to improve, the first object has been to remove the kitchen garden nearer the house (very often to its original situation) or else to make a fenced walk, and by that means to extend the dressed ground over an uninteresting part of the grounds, solely for the purpose of connecting the garden with the house.

If we suppose for a moment that the kitchen garden at Woodford were removed to a distance from the house, the place would undoubtedly lose one of its greatest advantages; and altho' at Valleyfield it will be found necessary to have a garden for early fruits and vegetables near the Firth; yet I consider it as an essential circumstance of comfort to have a small succession fruit garden, *nearer* to the house: a part of this may be appropriated to useful purposes and will of course be concealed; but the beautiful recess by the gardener's house may be considered as a variety in the course of the pleasure ground, and being planted with ornamental fruit trees and flowering shrubs and disposed in irregular knots and groupes, may form a scene

> . . . . . qui plâit sans régle & sans art,
> Sans airs, sans apprêts, sans grimaces,
> Sans gêne et comme par hasard;
> . . . . .l'ouvrage charmant des graces!

CONCLUSION

I have already observed that the great effect of Valleyfield will depend on its contrast with the surrounding country; and that its comfort will depend on its being sheltered from the west Winds – these two objects are only to be attained by planting largely.

The opinion of a great and justly celebrated Author who excelled in the several Arts of painting, poetry and gardening, seems so applicable to Valleyfield, as to direct the very lines of wood as well as the position of the different kinds of trees, where he

> forbids
> All poverty of cloathing – Rich the robe
> And ample let it flow that Nature wears
> On her thron'd eminence: where'er she takes
> Her horizontal march, pursue her step
> With sweeping train of Forest; hill to hill
> Unite with prodigality of shade –
> There plant thy elm thy chesnut: nourish there
> Those sapling Oaks, that at Brittannia's call,
> May heave their trunks mature into the main,
> And flout, the bulwarks of her Liberty.

But if the fir, give it its station meet,
Place it an outguard to th'assailing north,
To shield the infant scions, till possest,
Of native strength, they learn alike to scorn
The blast, and their Protectors. –

December 14, 1801   Addition
Concerning the Flower Garden at Valleyfield

Although I have never seen the place myself and I am flattered to learn that under the direction of my two sons by taking advantage of the romantic glen & wooded banks on the river, an approach has been made which for variety interest & picturesque scenery may vie with any thing of the kind in England while it remains a specimen of the powers of Landscape Gardening in that part of Scotland, where the Art had only been introduced by the imitators of Mr. Browns manner since Mr. Brown himself had never travelled out of England. To common observers, the most obvious difference between his stile and that of the Ancient Gardens, was the change from straight to waving or serpentine lines. Hence many of his followers have supposed good taste in gardening to consist in avoiding all that is straight or parallel, & in adopting forms which they deem more consonant to Nature, without considering what objects were natural & what were artificial. This explanation is necessary to justify the place which, I recommend for the canal in the Flower garden: For while I should condemn a long straight line of Water, in an open park where every thing else is natural; I should equally object to a meandering canal or walk where every thing else is artificial. A Flower garden should be an object detached & distinct from the general scenery of the place; & whether large or small, whether formal or varied, it ought to be inclosed by an inner fence to keep out hares: within this inclosure rare plants of every description should be encouraged & a provision made of soil & aspect for every different clays. Beds of bog earth should be formed for the American tribe. The aquatick plants, some of which are peculiarly beautiful should grow on the surface, or near the sides of the water, and the numerous class of rock plants, should have banks of rugged stones provided for their reception, without the affectation of their appearing to be the natural production of the soil. But above all there should be poles & hoops for those beautiful creeping plants which form themselves into natural festoons when supported by Art & attention. Yet with all these circumstances of beauty, the flower garden should not be visible from the roads or general walks about the place. It may therefore be of a character quite different from the rest of the scenery & its decorations should be as much those of Art as of Nature. Thus at Nuneham a seat of Earl Harcourt, the flower garden without being formal, is highly enriched, but not too much crouded with seats & temples, & statues, & vases & other ornaments, which being works of Art, beautifully harmonize with that profusion of flowers & curious plants which distinguishes the flower garden from natural Landscape, altho' the walks are not in straight lines. But at Valleyfield where the flower garden is in front of a wall 300 feet in length, the attempt to make the scene natural would be affectation. As the two great sources of interest in a place are Variety, & Contrast, the only means by which these can with propriety be introduced are in this flower garden, which becomes as a separate object, a kind of episode to the general scenery of Valleyfield.

The water being every where else a lively stream rattling over a shallow bed of rock or stones, the smooth expanse of a fish pond, will be the greatest possible contrast. To produce this must be a work of Art, & therefore instead of introducing an open channel from the river to supply it, or making it a branch of that river; I recommend the water should pass under ground by means of Culverts, with regulating sluices or shuttles, to keep the water always at the same height; & thus this Canal will be totally detached from the river, & become a distinct object forming the leading feature of the scene to which it belongs; a scene purely artificial, where a serpentine Canal would be as absurd as a serpentine garden wall, or a serpentine Bridge, which I mention because I have seen such absurdities introduced, from an abhorrence of straight lines.

This canal or fish pond may be enriched with borders of curious flowers; & a light fence of green laths will serve to train such as require support. While it gives me an air of neatness & artificial attention. But as the ends of this water should also be marked by some building or covered seat, I have supposed the entrance to be under a covered passage of hoops, on which may be trained all kinds of creeping plants: & the farther end may be decorated by an Architectural building, which I suppose to consist of a covered seat between two aviaries.

It will perhaps be objected that a long straight walk can have little Variety; but the greatest source of Variety in a Flower garden is derived from the selection & diversity of its shrubs & flowers.

THE TEXT OF W. S. GILPIN'S
IMPROVEMENTS FOR BOWHILL, *c.*1832

Terraces under the house

The ground immediately connected with the Mansion is of a very different shape from what might be wished. The levels are so sudden that it is not possible with any good effect to make the Terraces on so large a scale as otherwise might be desirable; tho I confess, for my own part, that I think there is sufficient space to give character to the general scenes, indeed that character will depend more upon removal than upon creation.

The long and uninteresting line of plantation and the hedge accompanying it ought to be broken, so as to admit the eye into the interior of the plantation, which is now only conducted along the outside boundary. The sketch made from the Library window would, if realized, do more to improve the scene than will be imagined by a common observer. To effect this purpose, it will be necessary that all the ground below the Terrace boundaries should be treated as Park in order to unite it with the openings made into the plantation. The hedge will be totally removed, and the ditch filled in. The masses planted in the ground below the Terraces will be adjusted from the windows so as to favour the Park character. As some attention must be paid to the appearance of the ground below the terraces when seen from the plantations walks, such material will be used in the planting of it as will not rise too high for the effect from the house; thorn, holly and other undergrowth of Park character will serve well such purpose.

As I think the Lake may be brought into view by a judicious removal of a few trees, I have so represented it in the sketch; of course the subject would be well studied in the winter when the trees were bare of leaf. The smaller pond will be well caught by the removal of three or four spruce firs; as also shown in the sketch.

I would recommend a gravel walk close to the south slope of the Library extending from the old wall west of the house to the east end of it as shown in the plan. If trees do not interfere this walk should be eighteen or twenty feet wide.

There being considerable difficulty in procuring stone that will stand well in contact with the ground, it will be more advisable to finish the Terraces in grass; but, if without great inconvenience, a mere cubic foot of stone could surround the semi circular form it would add much to the finish and effect of it, a dial, or other ornament would look well so accompanied.

If the drive that now goes below the dress ground can easily be removed it will have a better effect than the Park lawn shd. be divided by a road: if it be inconvenient to change the drive it might be passed over by spreading a little earth on the road, and sowing it down. the cutting line of the road would thus be removed, and yet the drive be firm for the wheels. I should prefer seeing the sheep on their lawn of Park, but as they must not go into the wood a wire fence might be run anywhere without interruption to other effect as recommended and explained in Practical Hints on Landscape Gardening.

The present Gateway into the Stable Yard might I apprehend be necessary to bring the Carriage up to the end of the house terrace but the building may be planted out, as expressed in the sketch. The present Approach road from the Cottage to the house will be done away, and the road turned into a walk leading to the Kitchen Garden. As the road is too wide for a walk eight feet of Gravel might be left in the middle, and evergreens planted on the two sides: box and other shrubs will flourish there, and a considerable number may be obtained from what will now become the entrance side of the house, and where no shrubs ought to be found.

As this walk would merely lead to the garden I should plant it up after the turn to the Garden, as it had a bad effect to keep open what is connected with nothing; besides which the lower part shews the trees standing on hillocks which is far from beautiful.

Memorandum

Put the hedge back by the Gravel pit as I have staked it out the present line interfering with the opening to the Lake. Wherever the young trees in the hollow on this side of that hedge grow so as to show their heads in the Lake opening they must have them cut off.

The forms marked for planting would be protected by a wire fence, as being so near the eye any coarse fence would not do. The wire fence as described in the Practical Hints is not an expensive one.

The sheep feeding there adds much chearfulness to the scene. Wherever the openings are made into this wood they will require this fence; but the absence of the scenery requires these openings as nothing can be more uninteresting than the present line.

The approach

With regard to the Approach from Selkirk I think there can be no comparison between the existing one, and any others that can be made. It is hardly possible to come upon a worse form than the present line of plantation presents at the ruins of the bridge, to repair which as a line of approach I think would be far worse than money thrown away as no planting could make it tolerable for half a century to come and many difficulties arise in the prosecution of that line after you have entered the wood. The whole is in my opinion so destitute of character as not to be worth an hours study. As the entrance to any place is of considerable consequence, stamping as it frequently does the general character of the domain; nothing surely must improve upon the present Entrance to Bowhill from the Main road. A little decoration of the present bridge, and a picturesque sort of Gatehouse among the willows would give an Entrance which, the nature of the ground would justify being carried on its present line till you come to the wide space above; here the character should improve in order to which I would not pursue the present line, but breaking thro somewhere about the shrubbery door, I should take the line amongst the old trees, and past the Gardeners house to the north west of the Mansion in something like the line marked on the plan. I would plant up the present line from the open ground and place a handsome Lodge at that entrance, as the different farm roads would, or might without objection, be retained. I should plant a Double row of Limes on each side the Approach from the bridge to the inner Lodge; and I think the approach so conducted would not only be incomparably better than any other that could be obtained but would be altogether very appropriate to the general scenery of Bowhill.

The lake

The Opinion I have expressed in the Practical Hints upon Landscape Gardening is well illustrated on the Water at Bowhill. The size, and character of the Lake is materially influenced by the walk round it. No piece of water should be that surrounded not only as it diminishes the apparent size of it, but also as it deprives it of all foreground so essential to composition. I should turn the walk going southward from the boathouse up the bank among the trees and unite it with the drive. The catches of water thus obtained thro the trees would give a varying picture from the different points of the walks, and a foreground be every where obtained. Where the walk turns up the bank the trees should be planted down to the water side, so as to prevent the possibility of keeping the shore. On the opposite side of the lake the walk should be obliterated and the trees be also plunged as it were into the water. The Drive becomes the walk, as nothing can be worse than a drive and a walk running alongside of each other. In short the waters should be seen by accidental openings as it were which defy the attempt to ascertain size and limits.

The opening to the water would be between the row of Beeches, and the large Scotch fir; to be made with caution. The corner Island may, and I think would interfere with that opening; in which case it might be cut away to the spruce fir in the middle of it, something like the line in the plan. The other Island should be planted with alder, weeping, and other willows, so as to hide its shape, in planting it part of it should remain visible else it would be equally uninteresting as it is at present. In planting to the edges of the Lake, alder and willow should be introduced so as to hand over and exclude in places the cutting line of the shore. The Plan explains these remarks. In thinning out the plantation opposite the House let the Larch be removed as generally as may be convenient, as nothing is so offensive to Park character. A more extensive view of the Lake may be obtained from the Duchess's apartment, and the effect would be very striking if made with judgment. This second opening as I will call it, would be between the two Scotch firs and the high beech in the plantation. The bridge above the fir plantation on the far side excludes from the drive the best view of the lake, and should be taken away, leaving here and there a good thorn. It is expressed in the plan.
W. Gilpin.

LIST OF LANDSCAPE GARDENERS
AND THEIR WORK IN SCOTLAND

The following are persons who carried on the practice of landscape
gardener or 'planner' in Scotland, between 1730 and 1840. Gardens
designed by them outside Scotland are not listed here. Where a
gardener had an essentially practical career, he is not given unless
it can be established that he was a landscape gardener.

JAMES ABERCROMBIE jun. fl.1768–1794

Arbuthnott, Kincardineshire	1792	RHP 9277
Glamis Castle, Angus	1768	RHP 6497/8
Guynd, Angus	1775	RHP 2594
Ross Priory, Dunbartonshire	1793	GD 47/1163

WILLIAM ADAM 1689–1748

Arniston, Midlothian	c.1726	*Burlington Magazine* (1969) p.132
Blair Adam, Kinross	c.1738	Adam *Blair Adam* I, p.72
Brunstane House, Edinburgh	1743	NLS Saltoun Papers SC 55
Buchanan, Stirlingshire	1745	RHP 6150
Cally, Kirkcudbrightshire	1742	GD 10/1421/vol.IV f.212
Castle Kennedy, Wigtownshire	c.1730	GD 135/144 f.19
Craigston Castle, Aberdeenshire	1733	Craigston Castle: Album of Plans, f.44
Culhorn, Wigtownshire	c.1730	GD 135/144 f.19
Duff House, Banffshire	c.1735	*State of Process*, p.9
Makerston, Roxburghshire	c.1730	RHP 14094
Mavisbank, Midlothian	c.1723	RHP 3863
Mellerstain, Berwickshire	c.1727	Charter Room, Mellerstain
Newliston, West Lothian	c.1731	Blenheim Palace, Muniments plan
Taymouth, Perthshire	1720	RHP 721

JOHN ADAM 1721–1792

Balnagowan, Ross and Cromarty	c.1762	SRO GD 129/7/7
Blair Adam, Kinross-shire	1748–1785	Adam *Blair Adam* I, p.94
North Merchison, Edinburgh	c.1760	ibid., p.95
Yester, East Lothian	1751	NLS Acc.4862/Box 49/F2

WILLIAM AND JAMES BOWIE fl.1752–c.1768

Alderston, East Lothian	c.1750	NLS Acc.6862/Box 98/F2
Bothwell House, Lanarkshire	1768	RHP 7
Duff House, Banffshire	c.1765	RHP 31,394
Redhall, Edinburgh	1758	Inglis, op. cit., p.93
Yester, East Lothian	1752	NLS Acc.6862/Box 98/F2

REV. MR CARRUTHERS
Munches,
  Kirkcudbrightshire   before 1832   *Gardener's Magazine* VIII (1832) p.133
St Peter's Dalbeattie,
  Kirkcudbrightshire   before 1832   *Gardener's Magazine* IX (1833) pp.6 and 7
Woodhall,
  Kirkcudbrightshire (attr.)   c.1795   Heron *Observations* II, p.135

WILLIAM SAWREY GILPIN 1762–1843
Ardgowan,
  Renfrewshire (attr.)   before 1832   Gilpin *Observations* p.10
Balcaskie, Fife   before 1834   *Gardener's Magazine* X (1834) p.530
Bargany, Ayrshire   before 1827   RH 4/57/vol.II
Bowhill, Selkirkshire   c.1832   Bowhill Ms. Notes & Drawings
Dalkeith Palace, Midlothian   c.1832   RHP 9715/12 & 13
Drumlanrig Castle,
  Dumfriesshire   c.1831   Gilpin, op. cit., pp.10,11,208
Dunmore, Stirlingshire   before 1832   ibid., p.208
Kinfauns Castle, Perthshire   c.1820   *Gardener's Magazine* XIII (1837) p.60
Newliston, West Lothian   1835   *Edinburgh–Glasgow Railway Bill* (1838)
                                             p.59
Strichen House, Aberdeenshire   c.1826
Whittingehame, East Lothian   c.1820   Lang *Seven Ages*, p.152

LORD ADAM GORDON d.1801
Prestonhall, Midlothian   c.1767   Dick Lauder *Scottish Rivers*, p.293
The Burn & Arnhall,
  Kincardineshire   c.1781   ibid.

JOHN HAY 1758–1836 (in the following, he is almost exclusively concerned
with flower and kitchen gardens, and hothouses)
Archerfield, Dirleton,
  East Lothian   before 1805   *Gardener's Magazine* I (1826) p.252
Bargany, Ayrshire   c.1818   *Gardener's Magazine* VIII (1832) p.330
Barns, Peeblesshire   1805   RHP 74
Castle Semple, Renfrewshire   1818   *Caledonian Horticultural Society* IV (1829)
                                             p.584
Craigielands,   *Caledonian Horticultural Society* IV (1829)
  Dumfriesshire   c. 1825   p.590
Cunnoquhie, Fife   before 1829   ibid., p.589
Dalhousie, Midlothian   before 1806   *Gardener's Magazine* I (1826) p.251
Dalmeny, West Lothian   before 1822   *Encyclopaedia of Gardening* (1824) p.463
Kilkerran, Ayrshire   1814   RHP 14268
Lochnaw, Wigtownshire   RHP 3983
Lundie House (Camperdown) Dundee   *Encyclopaedia of Gardening* (1824) p.463
Prestonhall, Midlothian   1794   *Caledonian Horticultural Society* IV (1829)
                                             p.583
Saltoun Hall, East Lothian   1818   NLS Acc. 2933 Map 2

JOHN HOME fl.1766–1800
Haddo Miln, Aberdeenshire   c.1766   RHP 11775

J. [G?] JOHNSTONE 1773–1835

Craigston Castle, Aberdeenshire	1799	Craigston Plan 61
Dalgety Castle, Banffshire	1810/14	Mountcoffer Mss.
Haddo House, Aberdeenshire	c.1805	*Gardener's Magazine* XI (1835) p.552

LEWIS KENNEDY 1789–c.1840

Abercairney, Perthshire	1813	GD 24/5/128
Drummond Castle, Perthshire	c.1822	*Encyclopaedia of Gardening* (1822) p.1090

WILLIAM KYLE fl.1780

Moredun, Edinburgh		*Archaeologia Scotica* I, p.321–2

JOHN CLAUDIUS LOUDON 1783–1843

Barnbarroch, Wigtownshire	1804	*Country Residences* II, p.538
Castle Kennedy, Wigtownshire	1842	*Gardener's Magazine* XIX (1843) p.253
Castlewigg, Wigtownshire	c.1804	*Country Residences* II, p.371
Drummond Castle, Perthshire	before 1804	*Country Residences* II, p.563
Glenfuir, Stirlingshire (hothouses)	before 1804	*Country Residences* I, p.297
Gosford House, East Lothian	before 1805	*Farmer's Magazine* VI, p.361
Leuchie House, East Lothian	before 1804	*Country Residences* II, p.615
Machany, Perthshire	before 1804	*Country Residences* II, p.396
Mabie, Kirkcudbrightshire	c.1802	*Country Residences* II, p.647
Mountquhanie, Fife	before 1804	*Country Residences* I, p.247–8
St Mary's Isle, Kirkcudbrightshire	before 1803	*Country Residences* I, p.218
Schaw Park, Clackmannanshire	before 1803	*Country Residences* II, p.571
Scone Palace, Perthshire	1803	Scone Palace, Plan 8

JAMES McDERMENT

Rozelle, Ayrshire	1834	Parks Department, Ayr

ALEXANDER NASMYTH 1758–1840

Airthrey Castle, Stirlingshire	c.1802	*Edinburgh Encyclopaedia* XI, p.543
Alva, Clackmannanshire	c.1802	ibid.
Colinton House, Edinburgh	before 1805	*Country Residences* II, p.411
Culzean Castle lodge, Ayrshire		Ailsa Mss. Plan 47
Dean Bridge (St Bernard's Well) Edinburgh		Nasmyth *Autobiography* pp.43–4
Dean House, Edinburgh	1817	NLS Ms.3241, f.5
Dunglass, East Lothian	c.1807	NGS D3727/9 and 10
Dunkeld, Perthshire		Nasmyth, op. cit., p.38
Dreghorn Castle, Midlothian	1802	*Encyclopaedia of Gardening* (1822) p.1250
Inveraray, Argyllshire	1802	Lindsay & Cosh *Inveraray* p.252
Loudoun Castle, Ayrshire		*Encyclopaedia of Gardening* (1822) p.1252
Rosneath stables, Dunbartonshire	1802	Lindsay & Cosh, op. cit., p.291
Taymouth Castle and bridge, Perthshire	1806	NGS D3727/12 and 13
Tullibody, Clackmannanshire	before 1822	*Encyclopaedia of Gardening* (1822) p.1252

JOHN NICOL d.1824
Mount Melville, Fife   before 1820   *Gardener's Magazine* VII (1831) p.681

WALTER NICOL d.1811
(in the following, he is largely
concerned with flower and kitchen
gardens and hothouses)

Balgay, Dundee	1801	RHP 3271
Dalhousie Castle, Midlothian	*c*.1806	*Gardener's Magazine* I (1826) p.251
Duncrub, Perthshire	*c*.1800	Invermay, Factor's Notebook
Gartmore, Perthshire	before 1811	*Encyclopaedia of Gardening* (1822) p.1256
Invermay, Perthshire	*c*.1802	NLS 4796 Box 226
Ochtertyre, Perthshire	*c*.1805	*Encyclopaedia of Gardening* (1822) p.1255
Raith, Fife	*c*.1800	Johnson *Dictionary of Gardening* p.274
Wemyss Castle, Fife	*c*.1800	*Encyclopaedia of Gardening* (1822) p.1255

CAPTAIN GEORGE ISHAM PARKYNS 1749–1820

Dryburgh Abbey, Berwickshire (attr.)	*c*.1804	Glasgow University Library, Erskine Ms.201/56/7
Millburn Tower, Edinburgh	1804	NLS Ms.5608

JAMES RAMSAY ?–1800

Cally, Kirkcudbrightshire (garden and Gothic tower)	*c*.1788	*Encyclopaedia of Gardening* (1822) p.1252
Gosford, East Lothian	before 1808	*Encyclopaedia of Gardening* (1822) p.1251
Hermand House, Midlothian	1798	NLS Ms.5177
Leith Head, Edinburgh	*c*.1780	*Encyclopaedia of Gardening* (1822) p.79
Rednock, Perthshire (garden and stables	1797	RHP 24993

HUMPHRY REPTON

Valleyfield, Fife (exc. George & John Repton)	*c*.1801	Ardchattan Priory, Red Book

GEORGE ROBERTSON, fl.1774

Bargany, Ayrshire	1774	RHP 1724

JAMES ROBERTSON fl.1750–1780

Dalhousie, Midlothian		*Encyclopaedia of Gardening* (1822) p.79
Dalkeith, Midlothian		ibid.
Duddingston House, Edinburgh	*c*.1768	ibid.
Hopetoun House, West Lothian		ibid.
Livingston, Midlothian		ibid.
Moredun, Edinburgh		ibid.
Niddry, Midlothian		ibid.
Whim, Peeblesshire		ibid.

ROBERT ROBINSON 1734–after 1782

Achoinany (?)	before 1762	GD 248/178/2
Archerfield (Dirleton) East Lothian	1778	GD 6/1625
Balbirnie, Fife	1779	RHP 24334
Balmain (Fasque) Kincardineshire	before 1762	GD 248/178/2
Banff Castle, Banffshire	1764	GD 248/346/5

Capefield (?)	before 1762	GD 248/178/2
Careston, Angus	1761	RHP 31,443
Castle Grant, Morayshire	1764	RHP 13947
Crathes Castle, Kincardineshire	c.1762	GD 248/178/2
Cullen, Banffshire	1766	GD 248/539/1
Glamis Castle, Angus	1764	RHP 6497
Gordon Castle, Morayshire (attr.)	before 1768	RHP 2382
Kings Inch, Paisley	1777	Houston Plans
Monymusk, Aberdeenshire	1762	GD 248/178/2
Paxton, Berwickshire	c.1767	Plan at Paxton House
Pittencrieff, Dunfermline	before 1762	GD 248/178/2

JOSEPH SPENCE 1699–1768

Prestonfield House, Edinburgh (with William Walker)	1764	Yale University Library, Spence Mss., Box IX

C.H. SMITH

Canonmills Cottage, Edinburgh	before 1835	*Gardener's Magazine* XII (1836) p.333
Hopetoun House, West Lothian (attr.)	c.1820	
Thirlestane Castle, Berwickshire	before 1841	*Gardener's Magazine* XVIII (1842) p.581

RICHARD STEPHENS

Balnoon (Balnamoon) Angus	1812	NRA Report 0033 p.3
Kimmerghame, Berwickshire	1821	RHP 12870 (copy of plan by Thomas Bonar)
Lees, Berwickshire	1816	Copy NMR Edinburgh

WILLIAM TAYLOR fl.1756–1779

Kilravock Castle, Nairn	1756	RHP 3077

JOHN WALLACE fl.1828

Murthly Castle, Perthshire	before 1828	*Garden.. s Magazine* III (1828) p.227

THOMAS WHITE c. 1736–1811

Abercairney, Perthshire	c.1799	Hunter, op. cit., p.229
Airthrey Castle, Stirlingshire	c.1798	*Encyclopaedia of Gardening* (1822) p.80
Allanbank, Berwickshire (attr.)	1782	*Portrait of Sir John Soane*, ed. A.T. Bolton (1927) p.46
Allanton, Lanarkshire	before 1800	*Planter's Guide* (1828) p.202
Arniston, Midlothian	1791	Arniston Charter Room Plan
Blairquhan, Ayrshire	1803	Blairquhan Estate Office
Cairness, Aberdeenshire	1793	Aberdeen University Library
Castle Fraser, Aberdeenshire	1794	Plan at Castle Fraser
Champfleurie, West Lothian	1792	RHP 9170
Cullen House, Banffshire	1789/90	Cullen Estate Office: copy NMR
Donibristle, Fife	c.1781	*Transactions of the Society of Arts* II (1784) p.15
Douglas, Lanarkshire	1770	RHP 21983
Drimmie House (Rossie Priory) Perthshire	1786	GD 44/51/374
Dudhope Castle, Dundee	1782	GD 151/11/41

Duff House, Banffshire	c.1786?	*Encyclopaedia of Gardening* (1822) p.1256
Dunninald, Angus	1789	Plan at Dunninald
Fintry House (Linlathen) Angus	1782	GD 151/11/41
Glencorse, Midlothian	1793	RHP 13482
Gordon Castle, Morayshire	1786	GD 44/51/374
Guynd, Angus	1799	Plan at The Guynd
Mountquhanie, Fife	1798	RHP 10206
Mount Stuart, Bute (consulted)	c.1795	Mount Stuart Muniments
Mylnefield, Perthshire	before 1797	GD 44/51/374
Nisbet, Berwickshire	1784	NLS Ms.5460
Pitfirrane, Fife	1801	NLS Ms.6510
Polton, Midlothian	1791	Arniston Charter Room Plan
Raith, Fife	1786	Scone Palace Muniments
Rossdhu, Dunbartonshire	1797	Rossdhu Muniments Room
Scone Palace, Perthshire	1781	Scone Palace Muniments, Plan 4
Touch, Stirlingshire	before 1800	Copy Plan at Touch

THOMAS WHITE jun. c.1764–1836

Balbirnie, Fife	1815	RHP 24,334
Bargany, Ayrshire	1802	RHP 1725
Brodick Castle, Arran	before 1814	Mount Stuart Muniments
Cameron House, Dunbartonshire	1819	RHP 20113
Dalmeny, West Lothian	1815	Plan at Dalmeny
Duns Castle, Berwickshire	1812	Plan at Duns Castle
Fordel, Fife	1818	RHP 3803
Harburn, Midlothian	1815	Plan at Harburn
Herdmanston, East Lothian	1807	NLS Ms.5460
Kames Castle, Bute	1814	Mount Stuart Muniments
Lee, Lanarkshire	1805	NLS Acc.4322
Mount Stuart, Bute (consulted)	1814	Mount Stuart Muniments
Old Melrose, Roxburghshire	1809	RHP 3656
Wemyss Castle, Fife	c.1800	*Encyclopaedia of Gardening* (1822) p.1255

THOMAS WINTER fl.1726–1753

Castle Grant, Morayshire	1748	RHP 8946 GD 248/173/2
Easter Moy, Aberdeenshire	1747	RHP 9018
Glamis Castle, Angus	1746	RHP 6493
Taymouth Castle, Perthshire (?)	1754	RHP 961/3

LOCATION OF SITES

(† *denotes ruined or destroyed*)

ABBOTSFORD, Roxburghshire,
3 km w of Melrose
ABERCAIRNEY, Perthshire,
7 km E of Crieff
AIRTHREY, Stirlingshire,
2.5 km ESE of Bridge of Allan
ALDERSTON House, East Lothian,
2.5 km NW of Haddington
ALLANTON, Lanarkshire,
6.5 km ENE of Wishaw†
ALLOA, Clackmannanshire,
0.8 km E of Alloa,
10.5 km E of Stirling†
ALVA House, Clackmannanshire,
2.5 km ENE of Alva,
13 km ENE of Stirling
ARBUTHNOTT House, Kincardineshire,
4 km WNW of Bervie,
25 km NNE of Montrose
ARCHERFIELD House, East Lothian,
1 km NE of Dirleton
ARDKINGLAS, Argyllshire,
16 km NE of Inveraray
ARNISTON, Midlothian,
2.5 km SW of Gorebridge
ASHIESTIEL, Selkirkshire,
8.5 km WSW of Galashiels
BALBIRNIE, Fife,
0.8 km NW of Markinch
BALCASKIE, Fife,
3 km NW of Pittenweem
BALGAY, Angus, Dundee†
BALNAGOWAN, Ross-shire,
8.5 km s by w of Tain
BANFF Castle, Banffshire, Banff
BARGANY, Ayrshire,
7 km NE of Girvan
BARNBARROCH, Wigtownshire,
6.5 km SW of Wigtown†
BARNS, Peeblesshire,
6.5 km WSW of Peebles

BLAIR ADAM House, Kinross-shire,
17 km NNE of Dunfermline
BLAIR Castle, Perthshire,
1 km NNW of Blair Atholl
BLAIRQUHAN, Ayrshire,
1.5 km WNW of Straiton
BOTHWELL House, Lanarkshire,
2 km WNW of Bothwell†
BOWHILL, Selkirkshire,
6 km w by s of Selkirk
BRAHAN Castle, Ross-shire,
6.5 km SSW of Dingwall†
BRODICK Castle, Arran,
7 km N of Lamlash,
22 km WSW of Ardrossan
BUCHANAN Castle, Stirlingshire,
2 km w of Drymen†
BURN, The, Kincardineshire,
2.5 km N of Edzell
CALLY, Kirkcudbrightshire,
1.5 km s of Gatehouse-of-Fleet
CAMERON House, Dunbartonshire,
2.5 km WNW of Balloch
CAMMO, Edinburgh†
CAMPERDOWN House, Angus,
5.5 km NW of Dundee
CARESTON Castle, Angus,
6.5 km w of Brechin
CASTLE GRANT, Morayshire,
4 km NNE of Grantown-on-Spey
CASTLE KENNEDY, Wigtownshire,
4.5 km E by s of Stranraer
CASTLE SEMPLE, Renfrewshire,
12 km SW of Paisley†
CHAMPFLEURIE, West Lothian,
3.5 km ESE of Linlithgow
CHATELHERAULT, Lanarkshire,
3 km SE of Hamilton
CLERMOUNT, Penicuik, Midlothian
COLINTON House, Edinburgh†
CRAIGHALL RATTRAY, Perthshire,
4.5 km N of Blairgowrie

KINFAUNS Castle, Perthshire,
4.5 km E by S of Perth
KINNAIRD Castle, Angus,
5.5 km SE of Brechin
KINRARA, Inverness-shire,
5 km SW of Aviemore
KINROSS House, Kinross-shire,
1.5 km W of Kinross
KIPPENDAVIE, Perthshire,
1 km SSE of Dunblane
LANGHOLM Cottage, Dumfriesshire,
1.5 km NNW of Langholm†
LEUCHIE House, East Lothian,
2 km S of North Berwick
LIVINGSTON, West Lothian,
1 km N of Livingston†
LOCHNAW Castle, Wigtownshire,
9 km WNW of Stranraer
LOUDOUN Castle, Ayrshire,
8 km E of Kilmarnock†
LYNEDOCH Cottage, Perthshire,
11 km WNW of Perth†
MABIE, Kirkcudbrightshire,
7 km SSW of Dumfries†
MAKERSTON House, Roxburghshire,
8 km S by W of Kelso
MARCHMONT House, Berwickshire,
7 km SW of Duns
MAR Lodge, Aberdeenshire,
5 km WSW of Castleton,
32 km WSW of Ballater†
MARLEE, Aberdeenshire,
Invercauld estate,
6.5 km ENE of Castleton
MAVISBANK, Midlothian, Loanhead,
8 km S by E of Edinburgh†
MELVILLE Castle, Midlothian,
2 km WSW of Dalkeith
MILLBURN Tower, Midlothian,
4 km ENE of Ratho
MILTON LOCKHART, Lanarkshire,
5 km WSW of Carluke†
MONYMUSK House, Aberdeenshire,
0.5 km NE of Monymusk,
32 km WNW of Aberdeen
MOREDUN, Gilmerton, Edinburgh†
MOUNT MELVILLE, Fife,
4 km SW of St Andrews
MOUNT STUART, Bute,
8 km SSE of Rothesay
NEWBYTH (Newbeith) House,
East Lothian,
2 km SW of Whitekirk,
5 km NNW of East Linton

NEWLISTON, West Lothian,
2 km WSW of Kirkliston
NIDDRIE MARSHALL, Edinburgh
NIDDRY Castle, West Lothian,
1 km SE of Winchburgh†
NISBET, Berwickshire,
3.5 km SSE of Duns†
NORTH BERWICK, *see* Leuchie House
NORTH MERCHISTON, Edinburgh†
OCHTERTYRE, Perthshire,
5 km NW of Crieff
OXENFOORD Castle, Midlothian,
5 km ESE of Dalkeith
PAXTON House, Berwickshire,
8 km W by S of Berwick
PENICUIK House, Midlothian,
1.5 km SW of Penicuik
PITTENCRIEFF, Fife, Dunfermline†
PRESTONFIELD, Edinburgh
PRESTONHALL, Midlothian,
6 km ESE of Dalkeith
RAITH, Fife, 4 km W of Kirkcaldy
REDHALL, Edinburgh
REDNOCK, Perthshire,
7 km N of Port of Monteith,
9.5 km SSW of Callander
RETREAT, The, Berwickshire,
Abbey St Bathans, 8 km N of Duns
ROSSDHU, Dunbartonshire,
5 km S of Luss
ROSS Priory, Dunbartonshire,
7 km NNE of Balloch
ROSSIE Priory (Drimmie House),
Perthshire,
12.5 km WSW of Dundee
ROTHIEMAY House, Banffshire,
11.5 km N of Huntly
SALTOUN Hall, East Lothian,
2 km NW of East Saltoun
SCONE Palace, Perthshire,
4 km NE of Perth
SETON House, East Lothian,
3 km NE of Tranent
SMEATON, *see* East Park
TAYMOUTH Castle, Perthshire,
8 km WSW of Aberfeldy
TOUCH House, Stirlingshire,
5 km W by S of Stirling
URIE, Kincardineshire,
3 km NNW of Stonehaven
VALLEYFIELD House, Fife,
2.5 km ENE of Culross†

WEMYSS Castle, Fife,
3 km NE of Dysart
WHIM House, Peeblesshire,
8 km s by w of Penicuik†

WHITTINGEHAME House,
East Lothian, 9.5 km E of
Haddington
YESTER House, East Lothian,
Gifford, 7 km SSE of Haddington

INDEX

(italic page numbers indicate plates)

ACKNOWLEDGEMENTS

The publisher is grateful to the following for permission
to reproduce illustrations in this volume

Sir Charles Fergusson 1; Mrs J. S. Finlay 3; Sir John Clerk
of Penicuik Bt 6, 70; Duke of Atholl 9; Trustees of the
National Galleries of Scotland 16, 66, 68, 76, 78, 86; (Pri-
vate owners 10, 77, 121); Mrs Dundas-Bekker 13; Mr
Christopher Scott 18; Marquess of Graham 19; Duke of
Argyll 26, 136; Mr T. Finlayson, Aberfeldy 29; National
Library of Scotland 31, 58, 81, 87, 94, 97, 103; Earl of
Strathmore 33, 90, 91; Earl of Seafield 34; Mrs Turner 38;
Paul Harris 40; John C. Balfour 44; John Home Robertson
46; Capt. N. Dalrymple Hamilton 51, 110; Major J. D. M.
Crichton Maitland 52; Major F. G. S. Graham 54; Keith
Adam 64; Pierpont Morgan Library 65; Trustees of Sir
John Soane 69; Mrs Elizabeth Noble 74; Perth Museum
and Art Galleries 85; Oscar & Peter Johnson Ltd 88; Mrs
Margaret Scott-Duff of Kertess 96; Earl of Mansfield 99,
100, 129, 130, 131, 133, 134; Controller, H.M.S.O. 101; Sir
Ivar Colquhoun of Luss 107; Major P. T. Telfer-Smollett
109; Mrs G. H. Hay 113; Earl of Rosebery 115; Col. R.
Campbell-Preston 117, 118; National Trust for Scotland
119; Paul Mellon Collection 128; Mr P. B. Buchanan 144;
Duke of Buccleuch and Queensberry 15, 155. Acknow-
ledgement is also made to the Scottish Record Office for
permission to reproduce several plans (some on loan to
them): they include 2, 17, 19, 34, 38, 42, 51, 92, 96, 98, 141.
Photographs for the following, supplied by the Royal
Commission on Ancient Monuments, Scotland, are
Crown copyright: 1, 3, 4, 5, 9, 18, 20, 27, 29, 32, 36, 39, 43,
44, 50, 57, 69, 74, 75, 101, 104, 105, 112, 113, 115, 117, 118,
136, 138, 144, 151, 152, 155, 157. The 1979 aerial views were
taken by John Dewar.